# DATE DUE

| APR 2 6 1970 | | |
|---|---|---|
| APR 2    978 | | |
| MAR 22 '78 | | |
| | | |

CROSSCURRENTS *Modern Critiques*
Harry T. Moore, *General Editor*

 CROSSCURRENTS *Modern Critiques*

*John Henry Raleigh*

# THE PLAYS OF
# Eugene O'Neill

WITH A PREFACE BY

*Harry T. Moore*

Carbondale and Edwardsville

SOUTHERN ILLINOIS UNIVERSITY PRESS

*To the Memory of
my Mother and my Father*

FIRST PUBLISHED, MARCH 1965
SECOND PRINTING, JULY 1965

# PREFACE

JOHN HENRY RALEIGH's The Plays of Eugene O'Neill
considerably exceeds the length set for volumes in this
series. But it is so fine a critical study, just as it stands,
with not a single word cut, that we decided to go ahead
with it and let it appear in Crosscurrents/Modern Critiques at the comparatively low price of these volumes.
The Director of the Press and I have firmly determined
not to run overspace in this way again but, as Mr.
Raleigh's book will show, the extension in this case was
justified—we are delighted and proud to have this volume
in the series. John Henry Raleigh, author of Matthew
Arnold and American Culture, is Professor of English at
the University of California, Berkeley.

Eugene O'Neill, greatest of American dramatists, was a
dramatic figure, somber and brooding; and what he wrote
has made a dramatic impact upon the lives of many of us.
I can remember, as a highschool boy in Los Angeles in
the 1920s, seeing my first O'Neill play, All God's Chillun
Got Wings. A white actor, the late Irving Pitchell, played
the Negro with sympathy and power. The experience was
a shattering one—stirring and, despite the necessary dramatic ugliness (such as Ella's calling Jim "You dirty
nigger"), exalting. As a boy I learned much from the play
about race relations, although O'Neill didn't have a didac-
tic purpose; Mr. Raleigh in one of his notes refers to
O'Neill's statement to the effect that "The play itself, as
anyone who has read it with intelligence knows, is never
a 'race-problem' play. Its intention is confined to portraying the special lives of individual human beings. It is
primarily a study of the two principal characters, and their
tragic struggle for happiness."

Of course; and O'Neill went on, in a passage not quoted by Mr. Raleigh, to say that he had no wish "to stir up race feeling. I hate it." Yet: "It is because I am certain God's Chillun does not do this but, on the contrary, will help toward a more sympathetic understanding between the races, through the sense of mutual tragedy involved, that I will stand by it to the end." The play certainly helped me, at the time, "toward a more sympathetic understanding," and I also felt that the pathetic situation of Jim and Ella had a wide application. To see this play at that particular time was for me an enrichment of the experience of living. And this is what most of us get from the O'Neill plays, even from the crudest failures. As it keeps reappearing on television, Anna Christie, in the Greta Garbo film that followed the play rather faithfully, still seems effective; and it is by far Garbo's best film.

Those of us who lived in Chicago in the late 1920s and early 30s will never forget the impact of O'Neill's Strange Interlude and Mourning Becomes Electra. In those days, major Broadway productions had what was known as a Chicago company (the first time George Jean Nathan saw Vincent Price, he called him "a Chicago-company Brian Aherne"); the Theater Guild, O'Neill's producer, often sent out its original cast. Lynn Fontanne, who played Nina Leeds in New York, didn't come to Chicago; from the Gelbs' biography of O'Neill, the reader may assume that Miss Fontanne didn't think too highly of the play, though it ran in New York for seventeen months. Judith Anderson was the Chicago company's Nina, with Glenn Anders and Tom Powers from the New York cast. No one who heard Judith Anderson's throaty "My three men!" speech will ever forget it.

A few years later, Mourning Becomes Electra was sent to Chicago, but without Alice Brady and Alla Nazimova of the New York cast. We didn't care: Judith Anderson played Lavinia and Florence Reed was Christine. (Florence Reed was one of my own favorite actresses, and I was among the minority that considered Nazimova a ham.) It was very exciting in those days to go out for dinner in the middle of the plays; they were staged at the Blackstone, and we would generally eat (I went to several performances of each play) nearby at the Blackstone Hotel, now the Sheraton-Blackstone, or the Stevens, now the Conrad Hilton.

These were, or seemed to be, great days—and great nights—for the American theater. Today, Strange Interlude and Mourning Becomes Electra still stand up pretty well as experimental plays, though spoiled here and there by mawkishness. The device of the soliloquies isn't theatrically necessary, though at the time they seemed as apt as they were startling. The rhetoric was often grandiose as well as meaningless: "Yes, our lives are strange dark interludes in the electrical display of God the father!" In a generally appreciative essay, Joseph Wood Krutch has noted the failure of O'Neill's language, citing the scene in Mourning Becomes Electra in which Orin stands by the coffin and addresses his dead father. "No one can deny that the speech is a good one, but what one desires with an almost agonizing desire is something not merely good but something incredibly magnificent, something like 'Tomorrow and tomorrow and tomorrow . . .' or 'I could a tale unfold whose lightest word . . .' " But the language O'Neill provides lacks the eloquence the situation deserves. Krutch in another essay quotes a parody by Lee Simonson, who designed the sets of some of O'Neill's plays for the Guild: Simonson imagined O'Neill writing one of Hamlet's soliloquies:

God! If I could only kill myself—get away from it all. There's nothing to live for. I'm afraid! Afraid to do anything. Afraid of death. Spooks. What they told me when I was a kid. (Looking at the snowman) I'm just so much mush—mush like you. . . . If I could only thaw with you tomorrow—thaw, just dissolve, trickle into the earth—run off into the sewer.

Krutch says that whenever he read this parody aloud in his classroom, he drew a laugh. "But I never knew any student to dismiss O'Neill because of it."

In the present book, Mr. Raleigh says that O'Neill's two masterpieces are The Iceman Cometh and Long Day's Journey Into Night; and surely he is correct. Since performances of a dramatist's plays are very important, I can't refrain from mentioning that I was lucky enough to see the first productions of these two which Mr. Raleigh singles out as the best. That is, I saw the first production anywhere of Iceman and the first American performance of Journey (whose world première had taken place in Sweden). Much was wrong with that first production of

Iceman in New York in 1946, and through part of the run of the play James Barton suffered from laryngitis, which reduced the effectiveness of his delivery of Hickey's long speeches. The 1956 version, with Jason Robards, Jr., as Hickey, is supposed to have been far better; but that's hard to believe. Robards is an actor who seems to sleep through most of his performances, occasionally flaring out for an effective moment, but too often chewing his best lines. I'd prefer Barton, laryngitis and all. As to Long Day's Journey, that first American performance (in Boston in 1956) demonstrated the force of the play, but not so convincingly as it might have done if some cuts had been made. In reading the play, you can skip when O'Neill repeats, for Journey is repetitious in an encircling way and you can see the repetitions coming like the figures that keep passing on a merry-go-round. Apparently the play was cut down somewhat before its New York opening: O'Neill during his lifetime had usually opposed such reductions, but his widow could be more reasonable. Robards was in that production of Journey, once in a while coming wonderfully to life; the Frederic Marches, who are not actors of magnitude, were a little harder to take. But, for all its faults of redundancy of dialogue and ineptness of production, Long Day's Journey Into Night was a great theatrical experience.

Mr. Raleigh's book is, in its own way, a great reading experience. It provides the rare excitement of firstrate criticism; it deals with an author who is incontestably major, and it examines him thoroughly, brilliantly, and wisely. Mr. Raleigh doesn't take up the plays one at a time, in order of composition, but treats them in what might be called a simultaneous encompassment. He goes from one to the other as he considers their thematic, psychological, historical, moral, symbolic, and philosophical aspects. At the same time he manages to present the fullest possible picture of the consciousness creating the plays; the book is not in its principal aim biographical, but much of O'Neill himself emerges: the climate of the temperament of this playwright. No simple attempt to synopsize Mr. Raleigh's method can do justice to it, for the book itself has an organic quality that has to be experienced directly.

Certain incidental elements, however, may be noted. One that is particularly interesting is the constant "placing of O'Neill, not only as a twentieth-century writer but also as an extension of the great day of American writing in the nineteenth. In ranging across all modern literature, Mr. Raleigh consistently finds points of resemblance between O'Neill and writers as disparate as Proust and Melville; and he carries this off brilliantly. One of his fine touches is the demonstration of O'Neill's indebtedness to the play which his father, James O'Neill, starred in year after year as Edmond Dantes, sometimes with the future playwright as a minor member of the cast. In many of Eugene O'Neill's plays, as Mr. Raleigh notes, "one can see the ghost of Monte Cristo hovering in the wings." This has been suggested previously, but no one before Mr. Raleigh has developed the point at such great length, showing specific resemblances between the old melodrama and Eugene O'Neill's plays. Yet the day came at last, as Mr. Raleigh says, when this Edmond Dantes was able to escape, as his father never really had, from the dungeon of the Château d'If: "Days Without End [written 1932–33] exorcised for O'Neill many ghosts, including the ghost of Edmond Dantes"—and Mr. Raleigh proceeds to show us, by means of a fine discussion of the technique of O'Neill's subsequent plays, just how this was done. One of the author's important perceptions concerns the development of O'Neill's sense of the ironic.

But these are only a few examples of the excellence of of this truly important critical achievement. Mr. Raleigh is not only informative, he is consistently evaluative. A new and more titanic O'Neill, faults and all, comes up from these pages of tightly packed paragraphs which so fully and so discerningly explore the universe of the plays of Eugene O'Neill.

HARRY T. MOORE

Southern Illinois University
November 26, 1964

# CONTENTS

# INTRODUCTION

O'NEILL'S PLAYS are best approached in the manner that one of his dramatic mentors, Strindberg, enjoined his audience to consider his own *Miss Julie*. In his "Author's Foreword" to this complex and powerful play Strindberg said: "What will offend simple minds is that my plot is not simple, nor its point of view single. In real life an action—this, by the way, is a somewhat new discovery—is generally caused by a whole series of motives, more or less fundamental, but as a rule the spectator chooses just one of these—the one which his mind can most easily grasp or that does most credit to his intelligence." Strindberg then proceeds to list twelve, or really thirteen, motives for Miss Julie's actions and her tragedy. Four of them are long-term, that is, issuing from her life in the large sense: her mother's character; her father's mistaken upbringing of her; her own nature; and the influence of her fiancé on a weak, degenerative mind. The other eight or nine motivations are short-term and immediate: the festive mood of Midsummer Eve; her father's absence; her monthly indisposition; her preoccupation with animals; the excitement of the dancing; the magic of dusk; the strangely aphrodisiac influence of flowers; and the chance that drives the couple into a room alone—to which must be added the urgency of the excited man. Strindberg continues: "My treatment of the theme, moreover, is neither exclusively physiological nor psychological. I have not put the blame wholly on the inheritance from her mother, nor on her physical condition at the time, nor on immorality. I have not even preached a moral sermon; in the absence of a priest I leave this to the cook."

O'Neill himself, as his now numerous biographies document so exhaustively, was a Strindbergian conglomeration.[1] It should be said, first, that the main interest of the present study is neither biographic nor genetic, but is rather concerned with an analysis and evaluation of the completed, published plays. I do, however, deal in part with the autobiographical elements in the plays, especially in Chapter 4, and I also deal with their cultural genesis, that is, their relationship to American culture as a whole, in Chapter 5. When considering any play as autobiography, I am not attempting to reduce the play to an autobiographical document, pure and simple, but am merely pointing out the autobiographical strand in that particular play. Furthermore, I am convinced that it would take another book to do full justice to the complexity of the autobiographical strands. For example, there is the use of masks. In *The Tempering of Eugene O'Neill* Doris Alexander says that O'Neill's father, James, pointed out to him the functional resemblances between the burnt cork "masks" of the end-men in a minstrel show and the real masks of classical Greek tragedy. This observation, one might say, planted the seed. But when we come to examine the mature reasons for O'Neill's use of masks, we find another whole series of motivations: his dislike of subjectivity, his detestation of acting "tricks," his desire for an impersonal art, his craving for abstraction, and so on. Similarly, Chapter 5 does not attempt to reduce O'Neill's plays to an example of American culture (nor vice versa) but tries to demonstrate that the two, the particular plays and the general culture, throw a mutual and reciprocal light upon one another.

At the center of the stage then are the plays themselves considered not in chronological sequence but as one great organic whole, made up of a Strindbergian variety of themes, characters, preoccupations, issuing into the realms of psychology, morality, religion, history, sociology, and so on. They are also treated as if they constituted a natural universe as well, with a powerful and pervasive sense of place, on land and sea, on city and farm, and presided over by great cyclic phenomena, such as night and day or quiet and storm.

Each separate play is a kind of wedge driven into this 360-degree circle, or created world. Accordingly, each play is simultaneously a psychological document, a moral document, an historical document, a philosophical document, and so on. No one play can be reduced to one theme or preoccupation or genetic theory; rather each is a microcosm mirroring, in its own way, the macrocosm of the whole. Thus the nostalgic aspects of *The Iceman Cometh* are discussed in one section of the book, its comedy in another, its moral and philosophical ambiguities in another, its language in another, and its form in still another. *Long Day's Journey Into Night*, especially Act IV, is practically ubiquitous, as it turns up in almost every section of the book. And its ubiquity, along with that of *The Iceman Cometh*, *Hughie*, and some of the other late plays, is a reminder that O'Neill's dramatic career was evolutionary as well as monolithic. For the late plays do not owe their power and finality to O'Neill's having broken new ground or discovered new themes but to his having finally gained complete mastery over the same elements that appear in less felicitous ways in his earlier plays.

These differing analyses of the same artistic material are neither mutually exclusive nor contradictory. If there is a "logic" to the creative process, it resides in the fact that work of the first order is a series of happy coincidences, by which many motivations and elements, quite disparate in themselves, are orchestrated into a harmony.

What made O'Neill a great playwright in his late plays was precisely the ordering of this immense range of impulses, influences, and cross-purposes that went into their making. Only a kind of Strindbergian enumeration can account for the four Tyrones of *Long Day's Journey Into Night*, and what they do to themselves and to one another. These last plays then are peopled by "real" human beings, beholden to no thesis and no moral, practically detached, it would seem, from their creator himself. They are thus "free," as Strindberg's people are free, to cooperate with their destinies and will their own tragedies, which they do, so terribly. They are never reduced to a formula, a thesis, or an authorial aberration. In their complexity and in their tragic freedom, there is born, in Yeats's phrase, "a terrible beauty."

I wish to thank Prentice-Hall for permission to use "Eugene O'Neill and the Escape from the Chateau d'If" included in John Gassner, Editor, *O'Neill: A Collection of Critical Essays*, © 1964, by permission of Prentice-Hall, Inc., Englewood Cliffs, New Jersey; *Ramparts* for permission to use material from "Eugene O'Neill" published in that journal in Spring, 1964; Random House for permission to quote from *The Plays of Eugene O'Neill*. I also wish to thank Yale University Press for the following permissions: *Long Day's Journey Into Night*: Reprinted by permission of Carlotta Monterey O'Neill and Yale University Press from *Long Day's Journey Into Night* by Eugene O'Neill, Copyright © 1955 by Carlotta Monterey O'Neill. A *Touch of the Poet*: Reprinted by permission of Carlotta Monterey O'Neill and the Yale University Press from A *Touch of the Poet* by Eugene O'Neill, Copyright © 1957 by Carlotta Monterey O'Neill. *Hughie*: Reprinted by permission of Carlotta Monterey O'Neill and Yale University Press from *Hughie* by Eugene O'Neill, Copyright © 1959 by Carlotta Monterey O'Neill.

I wish also to thank my typist, Elizabeth Walser, whose scholarly accuracy, critical acumen, and general dedication to the job were such as to make parts of this book almost a collaborative effort. My thanks go as well to Charles Long and Henry Nash Smith who read the manuscript with care and made many valuable criticisms and suggestions.

My wife proferred even more than her usual amount of patience, strength, understanding, and intelligent criticism.

JOHN HENRY RALEIGH

University of California, Berkeley
December 3, 1964

The Plays of Eugene O'Neill

# 1  COSMOLOGY
AND GEOGRAPHY

O'NEILL WAS NOT a cosmologist in the proper sense of the word. Consciously and intellectually, he usually thought of the world, when he could bear to think of it, as a meaningless chaos; thus much of the time his cosmological mood was, in the Joycean phrase: "Doubt arises like Nieman from Niegards found the Nihil." There were periods in his life, however, when he was a God-seeker; also as a playwright he created dramatic universes in which there are cosmologies, sometimes theistic, sometimes scientific. This phase, his argument with the universe, is largely confined to his mid-career, the plays of the late 1920's and early 1930's, and culminated and came to an end in his two most explicitly religious plays, *Dynamo* (scientific) and *Days Without End* (theistic), in which there is invoked, unambiguously and for the only time, the orthodox, benign Christian God. Underneath the mood of doubt or the intermittent attempts at belief, however, there is in the plays a cosmological principle—and I think O'Neill himself was not fully aware of the ubiquity of his outlook in this respect—underlying everything he wrote, from first to last: the principle of polarity; the universe and human existence conceived of as an endless series of polarities, oppositions, antitheses, antinomies; the world as a kind of perpetual dialectic without synthesis, or the world as a perpetual alternation between opposites, which are both separate and inseparable. The scientific phenomenon that captured his imagination was electricity, and the attraction resided precisely in the fact that electricity was a polar force, a mysterious—for the layman—power that was both unified and dual. Morris Cohen, who insisted on "The

Principle of Polarity" as a philosophical standing-ground, invariably used the metaphor of electricity as an analogue to the principle itself: "The principle of polarity is suggested by the phenomena of magnetism where north and south pole are always distinct, opposed, yet inseparable." [1] Again in *Reason and Nature* Cohen spoke of "the principle of polarity. By this I mean that opposites such as immediacy and mediation, unity and plurality, the fixed and the flux, substance and function, ideal and real, actual and possible, etc., like the north (positive) and south (negative) poles of a magnet, all involve each other when applied to any significant entity." [2]

In an untutored way, philosophically speaking, O'Neill also felt that polarity was the essential design of the world and that electricity was its sign and emblem. Accordingly, when he came to construct his most ambitious and original cosmology in *Dynamo*, it is electricity itself that is seen as the possible modern equivalent to the old, exploded theisms. This attempt at a new faith was, of course, only speculative, but the play itself, *Dynamo*, is much more vital, powerful, and successful than *Days Without End*, his other attempt to confront the universe, this time in orthodox Catholic terms. This is to say that the split, apocalyptical, raging cosmos of *Dynamo* is presented by the dramatist in a much more convincing fashion than is the monist world of the orthodox God of *Days Without End*.

O'Neill's sense for the polar also affects the time-scheme of his plays as well as dictating their setting or locale. Unlike most modern playwrights, O'Neill tried to bring the physical universe into the theater by insisting, whether the play takes place indoors or outdoors, on the connection between the play and the greatest cosmic polarity of all, night and day. For in O'Neill's plays day and night are never simply time indications, but have distinct and respective meanings, moods, and effects upon human character. Most characteristically, many individual acts and scenes in O'Neill's plays are given a cosmic extension by being seen under a blend of night and day, either sunrises or sunsets.

Geographically, this same inherent sense of the polar conditions the choice of locale for most of the plays. Considering the plays simply as geography, we find two basic pairs of antithetical settings: sea and land, and city and farm. Once more each has its separate meanings and characteristic qualities and defects. Unlike J. Alfred Prufrock, and many modern writers, O'Neill, consciously or unconsciously, assumed the universe.

## 1 The Universe

O'Neill's universe is a disorderly place, sometimes teleological, more often blind and purposeless, and is never a static conception from play to play. As in most other respects, there is a sharp distinction between his cosmological conceptions in his first career as a playwright and those of his second career. Up through *Days Without End*, the last play of the first period, some kind of cosmology, God-filled or God-less, purposeful or Hardyesque, is generally assumed to exist and to have some relationship to and bearing upon human life. This cosmos can be, and is, apprehended in either theistic or scientific or intuitive terms. Yet whatever its multiple faces or however various are the ways of apprehending it, this universe does exist, and human life is part of some larger scheme of things, be it God or the evolutionary process. But in the world of the last masterpieces the curtain drops on the cosmos, and human life is seen as self-contained, except in the imaginations of women like Mary Tyrone in *Long Day's Journey Into Night* and Nora Melody in *A Touch of the Poet*, both of whom believe in God. For most of the other characters in these plays, however, "God is dead," in the Nietzschean phrase quoted by Edmund Tyrone in *Long Day's Journey*. The longing for a universal design to things that O'Neill dramatized over and over again from different perspectives in his first career disappears, and the ambiguities and perplexities of human existence which in the earlier plays were given at least a partial explanation by reason of the fact that they are tied to cosmological processes become in the late, dark masterpieces uniquely and solely human: "Of his pity for man hath God died," continues Edmund. Like Margaret Fuller, O'Neill finally came to accept the universe and, having accepted it, ceased to worry about it.

In the plays of the first career, however, the universe looms large, and explanations for, or guesses at, its ways and purposes occupy the minds of the characters and are woven into the fabric of the dialogue. At this stage O'Neill and God were like Tolstoi and God, who, according to Gorki, had a most uneasy relationship, like two bears in the same den. Like Tolstoi, O'Neill could neither take Him nor leave Him alone. O'Neill's own spiritual-intellectual peregrinations were best summed up by himself, mockingly, in the patently autobiographical *Days Without End* in which the protagonist, John Loving, is a *persona* for the playwright. In Act I Father Baird, a benign Catholic priest who wishes to bring the apostate Loving back to Catholicism, gives a good-natured but satirical account of the spiritual wanderings of John Loving (which were also the wanderings of O'Neill himself and many of his generation) after his aspostasy from Catholicism. Loving was a militant skeptic and constantly communicated with Father Baird as he discovered each new spiritual-intellectual panacea. He had begun with unadorned atheism, but this soon became wedded to socialism which, in its turn and because it was too "weak-kneed," gave way to anarchism, "with a curse by Nietzsche to bless the union." Then came 1917 and the Bolshevik dawn and a new love affair with Karl Marx. He was further exhilarated by the practices of the Russian State, especially by its attempt to banish marriage and by its official atheism. But the inevitable disillusionment set in, with a consequent general disgust for all sociological nostrums. After a long silence Father Baird finally heard again from Loving, who had by then found a new "hiding place" as far away from home as possible, namely, Oriental mysticism, beginning with China and Lao Tze but passing on to Buddha and the ecstasies of solitary contemplation—"I had a mental view of him regarding his navel frenziedly by the hour and making nothing of it!" But the lure of the East did not last and Loving soon turned Westward once more, to Greek philosophy, especially Pythagoras and numerology. Finally—the last Father Baird had heard—Loving came to rest in evolutionary scientific truth, a confirmed mechanist. It should be added that Father Baird's rather lengthy exposition is not only amused and satirical; it also has a point of view, namely, the Catholicism with which O'Neill himself was flirting at the time and to which he brings his hero back at the end of the play. Thus the Russians are described by Father Baird as erring schoolboys throwing spitballs at "Almighty God" and the Russian State is a slave-owning State, "the most grotesque god that ever came out of Asia."

O'Neill was as uncertain and changeable about these matters in his plays as he was in his life, and in the plays as a whole up to *Days Without End* there are several different kinds of cosmologies, sometimes purposive, sometimes not. In most of the early O'Neill plays, God does and does not exist and does and does not rule the cosmos. Moreover, there is not one God but a whole pantheon of Gods, each with a different set of attributes, which lurks in the wings and is praised, damned, exhorted, regretted by the various characters in the plays. In *Beyond the Horizon*, O'Neill's first, successful, full-length tragedy, there are in the minds of the characters at least three Gods. One is the traditional Calvinist God of nineteenth-century New England who is simultaneously and paradoxically the implacable Deity who visits mankind with punishment for his sins and the Eternal Referee who merely watches over his free subjects. This God, who is both an offensive and defensive weapon, is invoked by Mrs. Atkins, the peevish, chronically ill mother of the heroine. In Act I, Scene 2, she rebukes Mrs. Mayo for finding excuses for the ineptitude of her son Robert, as a farmer. Anyone, says Mrs. Atkins, can help anything if they have a mind to and as long as they are not, like herself, helpless, "through the will of God" (this as a pious afterthought).

But since *Beyond the Horizon* is a transition play between the nineteenth and twentieth centuries, the nonexistent Deity of the twentieth century is also invoked, appropriately, by the doomed protagonist, Robert Mayo: "I could curse God from the bottom of my soul—if there was a God!" (III, 1). But it seems, finally, in this play there is a God, only He is the limited deity of the Manichaean religion and of John Stuart Mill's *Theism*, the posthumous work in which Mill admitted the statistical probability that a deity may, in fact, exist. This God participates in part in the wrongdoings of mankind but He also allows some individuals to create freely their own particular Hells. Like the Calvinist God, He is paradoxical, both determining and undetermining. This God is invoked by Robert at the end of the play, just before his death.

*Beyond the Horizon* is a Hardyesque tragedy of mistakes

and unfulfilled aims. The wrong people marry one another, and everybody manages to thwart his or her inner
nature. At the end Robert Mayo and his wife are human
wrecks and the once prosperous farm is a ruin; Andy, the
brother who would have become a good farmer, has become instead an unsuccessful grain speculator in South
America. It is Robert, the most sensitive and intelligent
of the play's characters, who passes final judgment on all
of them. In Act III, Scene 1, on the brink of death he
can see before and after and separate the wheat from the
chaff and see the spiritual significance of what has happened to all of them. He and Ruth have failed, but they
have not been untrue to themselves and can justly lay
some of the blame "for our stumbling on God." But Andrew, who has changed during the eight or so years of
the play's action from a healthy young farmer into a tense,
hard, even ruthless—and unsuccessful—speculator, is the
greatest failure of all, for he has spent eight years running
away from himself and has been changed from creator to
parasite, dealing in scraps of paper. Thus God helped to
ruin Robert and Ruth, but He let Andrew ruin himself.

In subsequent plays this ambiguous God, in various
guises, appears and reappears. The most terrible God is He
who presides over the world of *All God's Chillun Got
Wings*. In Act II, Scene 3, Jim Harris, the protagonist
of the play, says sadly to his distraught wife: "Maybe He
can forgive what you've done to me; and maybe He can
forgive what I've done to you; but I don't see how He's
going to forgive—Himself." Other concepts of the Deity
are perhaps less harrowing but no less enigmatic. In *Desire
Under the Elms* He is "hard, not easy"; in *Marco Millions*,
"insane energy." In *The Great God Brown* He turns into
a Cosmic Joker, "that ancient humorist" (I, 3); Billy
Brown is "One of God's mud pies" (I, 1). Dion Anthony
inverts the Beatitudes (I, 1): "Blessed are the meek for
they shall inherit graves! Blessed are the poor in spirit
for they are blind!" And the Golden Rule (II, 3): "Hate
them! Fear thy neighbor as thyself!" Brown, in the dead
Dion's mask, proclaims (IV, 1): "This is Daddy's bedtime
secret for today: Man is born broken. He lives by mending. The grace of God is glue!" But perhaps He is not
joking; He is simply not there: according to Brown, God
has become "disgusted" and has gone away. In *Lazarus*

*Laughed* God is a dreamer; Miriam before she dies says that God must be a dreamer, or "how would we be on earth" (III, 2). In *Strange Interlude* the Deity is invoked several times, either as a sardonic humorist or as sheer Indifference. In the mind of Marsden He is merely contemptuous of man: "everything in life is so contemptuously accidental! ... God's sneer at our self-importance" (II). Nina's imagination gravitates between the concept of a Mother God, which will be discussed below, and a Father God, who is sometimes amused, sometimes omnipotent, sometimes judging: "yes, God the Father, I hear you laughing ... you see the joke ... I'm laughing too ... it's all so crazy, isn't it" (IX). Or, "Strange Interlude! Yes, our lives are merely strange dark interludes in the electrical display of God the Father" (IX). Or, now that she has stopped being Darrell's mistress, she thinks: "our account with God the Father is settled" (VIII). But Darrell himself thinks of God as merely indifferent: "Oh, God, so deaf and dumb and blind! ... teach me to be resigned to be an atom" (IX). In *Mourning Becomes Electra* God turns Calvinist once more, and in *Dynamo* He becomes electricity, and orthodox Christian in *Days Without End*. But in the plays of the last period He tends to disappear, except in the memory and imagination of Mary Tyrone and Nora Melody. What should be stressed about the earlier period is the variety of forms in which God appears in these plays and the fact that these various Deities are, by and large, dramatic devices which are used to reveal character and do not necessarily reveal the playwright's own point of view. Only at the end of *Days Without End* does He exist in a meaningful and complete sense for the total dramatic world created.

Side by side with these various metaphors for the Deity, there evolved in these same plays two other cosmological outlooks, the Pascalian nightmare and the polar universe. What I have called the Pascalian nightmare is a conception of human existence as made up of separate individuals existing in soundless solitude in infinite time and space in a boundless and meaningless universe. In Act II of *Strange Interlude* Nina says that she has tried hard to pray to the modern science God, has thought of spiral nebula, millions of light years, multiple universes, but it only served to make her, and all humans, appear trifling and meaningless. Michael Cape, the O'Neill *persona* of *Welded*, is similarly obsessed by all those light years and all those spiral nebulae, those terrible spaces and silences of Pascal, which frighten him. Dion Anthony has a cosmic vision of mankind as haunted, haunting ghosts who "dimly remember so much it will take . . . so many million years to forget" (II, 2).

There are, of course, other characters in these same plays who have the gift of common sense or who have learned wisdom from experience and who are the spokesmen, usually, for a kind of amused Stoicism which does not go whoring after cosmological solutions and absolutes. Significantly, the prostitutes often possess this kind of elementary wisdom. In Act III, Scene 2, of *Welded*, Michael Cape, having had a desperate argument with his wife, seeks out a prostitute. He cannot bring himself to go to bed with her, but they enter into a communication of sorts and she tells him some home truths, namely, that the whole "game" (life) is funny and that one has got to laugh and "loin to like it." Similarly, Cybel in *The Great God Brown* tells Dion Anthony, "Life's all right, if you let it alone" (II, 3). In other plays there are people who have learned from experience that life will not take too many questionings but must be lived moment by moment. Such a one is "Donk," the donkeyman of the *S.S. Glencairn* in *The Moon of the Caribbees*. Sitting placidly on the deck with Smitty, who, in the quiet of the beautiful Caribbean night, is painfully reminded of his English fiancée whom he lost because of his drinking, "Donk" tells him that one cannot live on memories, no matter how painful: "I puts 'em out o' me mind, like, an' fergets 'em." In Act III of *Strange Interlude* Mrs. Evans, the wife of a man who fell victim to hereditary insanity and the mother of a son, Sam, who could go the same way, explains to Nina the meaning of life. Mrs. Evans had once believed in God and worried about what was God's and what was the Devil's, but after having been punished so much for only having loved her poor, mad husband, she had to conclude that there was no "Him." The closest one can come to knowing what's good is, "Being happy, that's good! The rest is just talk!"

But for the majority of the more sentient characters in these plays, Stoicism is not enough and the Pascalian nightmare is insupportable. So for them there is the polar universe and a kind of religion of repetition, a refuge in the certainties of the basic "rhythms" of human existence, either repetitions or alternations or both. The classic O'Neill speech on the meaningfulness of repetitive rhythms is Cybel's benediction at the end of *The Great God Brown* (which I give in part): "Always spring comes again bearing life! Always again! Always, always forever again!—Spring again!—life again! summer and fall and death and peace again!—(*With agonized sorrow*)—but always, always, love and conception and birth and pain again—spring bearing the intolerable chalice of life again!" This vision of human existence as alternating between opposites and yet being circularly repetitive, abstract as it is, is about as close as, in his plays anyway, O'Neill came to seeing a consistent meaning and design to the universe. "Rhythm" was his name for these basic dialectical and repetitive movements and, side by side with the speculations on God and existential loneliness in the plays of his first career, there was also developing a kind of poetic mythology concerning the "religion of rhythm," particularly in *Welded, Lazarus Laughed, Strange Interlude,* and especially in *Dynamo,* in which the dance of polarities, in its manifestation in the physical phenomenon of electricity, is made explicitly into a religion. The characters in these plays are always talking about "light years," "splitting cells," "electrical displays," "positive and negative poles," and so on, in short in the language of the layman's version of the modern physical sciences, which are then propitiated in place of the lost God.

In Act I of *Welded* Michael Cape explains his passion for his wife, and hers for him, in cosmological terms, specifically in a modern scientific explanation of Plato's parable that mankind had once been androgynous, had been split into male and female by the Fall, and ever since had eternally desired to unite once more. Cape's version is that it, "life," had all begun with the splitting of a cell a hundred million years ago into a "you" and a "me," never to be completely happy or fulfilled until reunited. He then proceeds to an impassioned, but rather stalely, rhetorical apotheosis of "rhythm": "rhythm of our lives beating against each other, forming slowly the one rhythm —." In *Lazarus Laughed* similar speculations are heard although uttered in a more hortatory, apocalyptical manner; thus the exultant Lazarus exclaims: "Once as quivering flecks of rhythm we beat down from the sun. Now we re-enter the sun" (II, 2). The basic metaphysical assumption of *Lazarus Laughed* is that mankind lives, inescapably, in the middle of Manichaean antinomies. At the climax of the play, as Lazarus is being burned alive —i.e., man, the victim of his own cruelty, inevitably goes to his painful death—Lazarus laughs, i.e., the spirit of man rises above bodily pain and corporeal limitations. Throughout the play Lazarus' hyperbole, in addition to its admonitions to laugh, is a rhapsodic paean to life's inescapable repetitions and alternations: "Yes! Yes to the stupid as to the wise! To what is understood and to what cannot be understood! Known and unknown! Over and over! Forever and ever! Yes!" (III, 2).

In the imagination of Nina of *Strange Interlude* these obsessions with rhythm and polarity congeal into a kind of mythology about the existence of a Mother God. In Act II, her Gordon lost forever, her father dead, herself on the verge of a breakdown, she explains to the men that the religious mistake began when God was created in the male image. Instead, mankind should think of life as created in the birth-pain of God the Mother. Thus Her children would understand why they have inherited pain, and would know that "our life's rhythm beats from Her great heart," which is perpetually torn with the agony of love and birth. Death then would become a reunion with her, "a passing back into Her substance." But by the end of the play Nina must finally bow to God the Father, and resign herself to a life of passive acceptance.

Even if the principle of polarity was untenable as theology or was not sustainable on a religious plane, it still had the great advantage of possessing a kind of scientific validity, in that the mysterious modern force of electricity —and O'Neill had seen electric lighting come into use in his own lifetime—was polar in nature, with both positive and negative poles. Thus in Act IX of *Strange Interlude* when, all passion spent, the various characters of the play take their final leave of each other, Darrell the doctor turned scientist, tells Nina that perhaps in an afterlife the two of them will meet again by virtue of becoming part of the "cosmic positive and negative electric charges."

Directly following *Strange Interlude* in O'Neill's career came *Dynamo*, in which all this kind of thinking culminated in the creation of a religion of electricity. In this play Reuben Light, brought up on the harsh biblical Calvinism of his father, rebels and runs away from home in a lightning storm. He returns, having absorbed many scientific books and obsessed with the power and mystery of electricity which he announces as the new religion, and himself as its prophet. It is true that by the end of the play he is insane, but it is also true that the sane Earth-Mother, Mrs. Fyfe, the Cybel of the play, is also a worshipper of the new cult. The play is studded with Lazarus-like prophecies about electricity, its power and its mystifying polarity: electricity is the "Great Mother of Eternal Life" and power houses are "the new churches" (III, 1). Even the militant atheist of the play, Mr. Fyfe, uses supernatural metaphor when speaking of electricity, and refers mockingly to God's archenemy, Lucifer, as the "God of Electricity." In Act II, Scene 3, the dynamo itself is described as looking like a "massive female idol." The now insane Reuben proclaims: "even our blood and the sea are only electricity in the end" (III, 1), as is everything else in the universe, from the stars to the atoms.

The staging and sound effects of this strange play—one of O'Neill's strangest—are of great importance, more so perhaps than the actual words. O'Neill himself never saw the play staged to his own satisfaction, nor has it ever been staged properly. Perhaps it would be physically impossible to do it on an ordinary stage although movies or television might manage. At the opening of the play there is a thunder and lightning storm. What this is meant to suggest is that the first cosmic fear of the human imagination probably arose from the hearing and witnessing of a furious display of such sights and sounds. And this primitive fear often still hangs on in the most sophisticated modern minds. Joyce and O'Neill, for example, were made uneasy by and were superstitious about the electrical displays of "God the Father." This aboriginal terror is dealt out to Reuben's father and to Reuben himself in the first part of the play, while Mrs. Fyfe, naturally, revels in the storm. The chief sound effects of the last part of the play are the murmurings of the flow of water over a dam and the hum of the dynamo; in other words, nature's outburst of Act I is shown in Act III as the captive and servant of man but so mysterious and powerful as still to be fearful.

The most protracted and acute exposition of what O'Neill was after here has been given by the stage designer Lee Simonson in "A Memo from O'Neill on the Sound Effects for *Dynamo*." [3] In the memo to Simonson, O'Neill had written:

> I cannot stress too emphatically the importance of starting early in rehearsals to get these effects exactly right. It must be realized that these are not incidental noises but significant dramatic overtones that are an integral part of that composition in the theatre which is the whole play.

He continues:

> I may seem to be a bug on the subject of sound in the theatre—but I have reason. J—— once said that the difference between my plays and other contemporary work was that I always wrote primarily by ear for the ear, that most of my plays, even down to the rhythm of the dialogue, had the definite quality of a musical composition. This hits the nail on the head. It is not that I consciously strive after this but that, willy nilly, my stuff takes that form. (Whether this is a transgression or not is a matter of opinion. Certainly I believe it to be a great virtue, although it is the principal reason why I have been blamed for useless repetitions, which to me were significant recurrences of theme.)

O'Neill went on to spell out what he was after. It was a machine age, governed by "mechanical sound and rhythm." Furthermore, *none* of the sound effects of his plays, excluding the music, had ever been done properly.

> What is needed is lightning that will suddenly light up people's faces in different parts of the set, keep them in the general picture—not literal lightning, but a reproduction of the dramatic effect of lightning on people's faces. And thunder with a menacing, brooding quality as if some Electrical God were on the hills impelling all these people, affecting their thoughts and actions. The queer noise of a generator, which is unlike any other mechanical noise (it is described in the script), its merging with, and contrast with, the peaceful, soft Nature sound of the falls, also needs some doing. The startling, strained, unnatural effect of the human voice raised to try and dominate the generator's hum (in the scenes in the generator room), is also important and part of my conception.

O'Neill closed the memo by advising that whoever is to do the job of stage design should visit the General Electric plant at Stevenson, Connecticut, which had provided the sights and sounds of the play for O'Neill himself.

Simonson took on his impossible assignment with great and commendable enthusiasm. He did visit the plant and said that he had "never shared more directly the excitement, the adventure, and the power of the modern theatre than in following the trail of O'Neill's mind from a powerhouse on a Connecticut river to the play it inspired." Whereas, in the script, the singing, crooning, godlike dynamo seemed ridiculous or impossible, the actual dynamo was precisely like this, and Simonson, in addition to this aesthetic realization, was awed, like O'Neill, by the sheer power generated by the plant: "Here was water that became fire, energy that sang a monotonous tune, that did croon like a lullaby and then became incandescent light." When Simonson left the plant, he said that he had left many cathedrals less awed and humbled, for here was a transubstantiation no less miraculous than the Mass.

> Rereading O'Neill's script, I seemed to understand for the first time the myth of Prometheus the fire-bringer. I understood why primitive peoples had cringed in terror before thunderbolts and erected altars to invisible gods. I had experienced, through a poet's insight, the wonder, the humility and pride, the hunger for power, the ecstasy of calling it forth, in which religions are born.

Simonson ends his remarks by admitting that he did not capture these effects in the staging and that the play itself was faulty and failed at its climax. Nevertheless:

> For *Dynamo*, despite its failure in performance, was more nearly the kind of success that the theatre needs today [1932] than hundreds of its present successes. In setting *Dynamo*, in sharing a poet's intuition, in accepting his symbols, in attempting to make the commonplace mechanical shapes of our industrial environment significant of the forces for good and evil that they released, in building them into a rostrum on which the hope and despair of our effort today to dominate ourselves and the world about us could be voiced—I understood how the designing of a stage setting could be made a creative act, whether or not I myself could make it one.

As Simonson's splendid encomium would indicate, *Dynamo* is as yet "unperformed."

The "religion of rhythm" and the attempt to make science a religion reached an ambiguous climax and came to an end with *Dynamo*. But O'Neill's encounters with God were not yet terminated; these were to come to an end, a bad one, in *Days Without End*, his only Catholic play wherein for the last time he tried to get back to the simple, comprehensible, and benign God of his fathers. *Days Without End* is subtitled "Plot for a Novel" and is a Gide-like or *Pierre*-esque affair in which a writer, who is wavering between faith and skepticism, is writing an auto-biographical novel about a man's struggle to regain his lost faith. Book and life (or drama) thus coincide. But he cannot finish his novel until he concludes his own wrestlings, which is an interesting enough idea in itself. O'Neill agonized more over this play perhaps than over any other play he ever wrote. His protagonist, John Loving, is split between an idealistic, faithful man (John) and a cold skeptic (Loving), an actual alter ego, wearing John Loving's death mask, who appears on stage although he can be seen only by John. O'Neill struggled with and rewrote most of the ending, which takes place at dawn in a Catholic Church before an enormous wooden representation of the crucifixion. Here John "kills" Loving and regains his lost faith, with the happy (and impossible) Father Baird purring in the background. In another ending John killed himself or perhaps Loving killed John.[4] O'Neill later admitted that he had botched the ending, the priest, and the play; and it was to be his last religious play, his last play about modernity, and his final attempt in the plays to find a meaningful universe.

From now on in O'Neill's subsequent plays God is dead and the cosmos, whose mysteries once haunted his plays, dims and fades away, while man as man occupies the whole stage, absorbs all meanings, and embodies all mysteries and complexities; henceforth man is to be the measure of all. Considered in this light, *Dynamo* and *Days Without End*, whatever their failures as drama, were unqualifiedly salutary for O'Neill: first they exorcised his God-mongering and universe-mongering; second, they turned him permanently to the past and freed him from the yoke of contemporaneity and "modernity" which he bore with such lack of grace—and success—in *Dynamo*, *Days Without End*, and the other plays of the 1920's and the early 1930's when he attempted to find a general meaning to modern man, modern life, and the modern cosmos. From this time on his plays would be set in the past and would let the universe go its mystifying ways. He would begin the American history cycle-plays and, of course, would finally come to write *The Iceman Cometh, A Long Day's Journey, Hughie,* and *A Moon for the Misbegotten.* The only generalization that remained was the principle of polarity, for he could never see human experience except in terms of antinomies, alternations, and repetitions.

## II *Night and Day*

As in the Manichaean system proper, the great natural metaphor for the principle of polarity was the cosmological process itself, the diurnal turn from night to day and the nocturnal return; hence the high incidence of sunsets and sunrises in O'Neill's plays. In this area, as in so many others, there was to be a happy coincidence between O'Neill the melodramatist, who knows how effective, as theater, a spectacular sunrise or sunset can be, and O'Neill the brooder, who was obsessed with the antinomies of human existence. Correspondingly, the passage of day to night, and vice versa, in O'Neill's plays verge from effects which are pure theatricality to a blend in which the theatricality suggests a moral mood or even a metaphysic as well. An early one-act play, *The Rope,* takes place at sundown, and the deepening scarlet of the evening is meant to provide a sinister backdrop for the sinister events of the play wherein at the end one man is preparing to torture another man by holding a red-hot file against the soles of his feet. At other times these risings and settings are purely spectacular; for example, the sunset at the opening of the gate in the Great Wall of China in Act I, Scene 5, of *Marco Millions.* Or they are meant to signify a human discovery, as in *The Fountain* when the discovery of land by Columbus' ship coincides with sunrise (II), or, as in *Days Without End,* when the light of the rising sun strikes the gigantic representation of the crucifixion simultaneously with the regaining of his faith by John Loving. Again the very transitory or indefinable character of a sunrise or a sunset may be used to suggest a kind of moral murk in the human

events that are being enacted. The rebellion in *The Fountain* (VI) happens in a stiflingly hot and purple twilight.
Yank in *The Hairy Ape* dies at the hands of the gorilla at
twilight. The climactic act of *Dynamo*, Act III, begins at
evening, against "a darkening crimson sky." The repeated
sunsets of *All God's Chillun Got Wings* suggest the inevitable tragedy of the characters. Sunsets and dawns
punctuate and dramatize the tragedies of *Desire Under the
Elms* (predawns and dawns) and *Mourning Becomes
Electra* (sunsets and twilights). The characteristic movement of each act of *The Great God Brown* is a journey
into night. Sometimes a sunset is used ironically, as in
*Beyond the Horizon*, where in Act I the young lovers,
Robert Mayo and Ruth Atkins, whose marriage is to be
such a horror, plight their troth in a beautiful twilight,
which then is the realm of illusion. A correlative of this
concept is the conventional notion that dawn, the light of
dawn, brings the truth. Thus the final act of *Beyond the
Horizon* takes place in the cold, pitiless light of an October
morning which throws its watery glance on the human
wreckage that the Mayos have become. In *The Iceman
Cometh* dawn coincides with the arrival of Hickey (I),
the truth-teller and the dispeller of illusions.

The most spectacular and effective "truth-telling" dawn
occurs in *A Moon for the Misbegotten* in the last act when
the sleeping Jamie Tyrone and the waking Josie Hogan
await the coming of dawn and do, in fact, see the sun rise,
as, in the light of that rising sun, the two lovers take their
final leave of one another. O'Neill sets the scene: "*The two
make a strangely tragic picture in the wan dawn light—
this big sorrowful woman hugging a haggard-faced, middle-
aged drunkard against her breast, as if he were a sick
child.*" When Josie's father appears, she tells him a miracle
has happened: "A virgin who bears a dead child in the
night, and the dawn finds her still a virgin. If that isn't a
miracle, what is?" Some old echo of *Hedda Gabler* must
have remained in O'Neill's memory at this point, for he
has Josie, whose eyes are "*fixed on the wanton sky*," re-
strain herself from waking Tyrone until the sky is properly
"beautiful," that is, "glowing." Meanwhile she pronounces
her—and O'Neill's—benediction on James Tyrone (Jamie
O'Neill): "I thought there was still hope. I didn't know
he'd died already—that it was a damned soul coming to

me in the moonlight, to confess and be forgiven and find peace for a night." "Dawn" had always been the key and shattering experience in life for Jamie Tyrone: waking up, hungover, in bed with an unknown whore and with the knowledge that all dawns are "gray." But this night he has had no nightmares, and he awakes in peace and at peace, for Josie, the priestess in the confessional, has given him, for once, a clean dawn. If the moon in Act III of the play created the atmosphere for the confession of his sins, the sun in Act IV provides the background for his absolution and also for the return to reality: the knowledge on the part of both characters that theirs is an impossible love and that Jamie has one last reality to face and undergo: death.

A corrclary use of cosmic rhythms by O'Neill was the day-night cycle. *Lazarus Laughs* begins at twilight of a certain day; each scene in the play thereafter occurs at night, at a later hour each time. The last scene occurs just before dawn. Thus, although the action of the play is spread out over months, the time cycle is that of twilight to predawn. Furthermore at the end, as the play reaches its climax, Act III, Scenes 1 and 2, and Act IV, Scenes 1 and 2, the time sequence is continuous, all events occurring in the same early morning hours of the same day. Thus this pageant of human cruelty has as its backdrop the dark watches of the night. *The Emperor Jones*, of course, follows the cycle quite explicitly, beginning in the afternoon (confidence), night (terror, disintegration, retrogression), dawn (retribution). The day-night cycles recur throughout the trilogy of *Mourning Becomes Electra*, as they do in *The Iceman Cometh*, where, as in *A Moon for the Misbegotten*, daylight is reality. *A Moon* follows the same time sequence as *The Emperor Jones*: afternoon to the following dawn. *Ah, Wilderness!* is, roughly, in the same mode as *The Iceman Cometh*, a two-day cycle. O'Neill's most Aristotelian plays are *Long Day's Journey Into Night* and *A Touch of the Poet*. Sure here of his own powers, he used the morning to post-midnight cycle but forewent any spectacular sunrise or sunset. In both plays the journey into night is a journey into the hell of "truth," and each reaches its tragic climax when its tortured protagonist, deep into night, has lost his or her own identity: the proud Con Melody turned into a leering, brogue-speaking peasant, the white-haired Mary Tyrone, drowned in morphine, back in her virginal childhood; for the journey into night is also a journey into the past: Con has become his father, the thievin' shebeen keeper, and Mary has become her childhood. Night then is a backward journey, the inescapable past become alive once more. If dawn is reality, sunset is memory: both are insupportable, and only alcohol, dope, or a loss of identity can make them so.

## III  Land and Sea

If the human imagination first experienced cosmic terror at the electrical displays of God the Father, it probably conceived its first sense of the almost inexhaustible plentitude and variety of terrestrial existence in the polarity between land and sea. Thus it was that O'Neill's imagination, always partially archaic, instinctively seized upon this elementary and primordial antithesis for the background of so many of his plays and thus it was too that as a young man he had lived the sailor's life. At least twenty of his plays, and the majority of the early one-acters by which he gained his first fame, take place on or near the sea. Moreover, many plays that take place on land have as an integral part of their symbolism, themes, and meaning the folklore, mythology and appurtenances of sea life. For example, the sea and its accoutrements, fog, a foghorn, and ships' bells, are very much a powerful part of the total effect of the last act of *Long Day's Journey Into Night.* Sailing and the sea life is integral to *Mourning Becomes Electra*; the climactic murder of Adam Brant occurs aboard ship; Brant himself is a spokesman for two mystiques of the sea: the beauty of clipper ships and the warm lure of the South Seas, and it is on a visit to these same South Seas that Lavinia Mannon sheds her Puritan inhibitions. The Mannon fortune was based upon shipping; the sea chanty "Shenandoah" is the theme song of the play. Throughout the trilogy the sea is always "the other," the place of freedom and beauty, opposed to the dark, prison-like existence of nineteenth-century New England Puritanism. Even in *Ah, Wilderness!* the sea is a presence, for the romantic scene in Act IV between Richard and Mildred is played on a moonlit beach on Long Island Sound.

The sea in O'Neill's plays is employed in two ways: first, as a world in itself, with its own meanings, beauties, and defects, and, second, as a place that provides a general contrast to the land and its way of life. O'Neill thought sea chanties, like "Shenandoah," the most rhythmic of musical compositions. Moreover, the sound of the sea itself was inherently rhythmical and was often used by O'Neill as background music in the early plays, e.g., *The Rope*: "*From the rocks below the headland sounds the muffled monotone of breaking waves.*" In *Where the Cross Is Made* is heard, "*An insistent monotone of thundering surf, muffled and far-off.*" Or, conversely, land sounds, such as the songs of the natives in *Moon of the Caribbees*, can come drifting over the sea to an anchored ship.

But the genuine beauty of the sea was embodied in the sailing ship, especially the clippers. O'Neill put this mystique of the clippers in the dialogue of Adam Brant in *Mourning Becomes Electra*, but the most extended exposition of it is given to Paddy in Scene I of *The Hairy Ape:*

> (*With a sort of religious exaltation*) Oh, to be scudding south again wid the power of the Trade Wind driving her on steady through the nights and the days! Full sail on her! Nights and days! Nights when the foam of the wake would be flaming wid fire, when the sky'd be blazing and winking wid stars. Or the full of the moon maybe. Then you'd see her driving through the gray night, her sails stretching aloft all silver and white, not a sound on the deck, the lot of us dreaming dreams, till you'd believe 'twas no real ship at all you was on but a ghost ship like the *Flying Dutchman* they say does be roaming the seas forevermore widout touching a port.

This rhapsody goes on at length, until rudely interrupted by Yank. Paddy's chief point is: " 'Twas them days a ship was part of the sea, and a man was a part of a ship, and the sea joined all together and made it one." This lyric of the sailing ship recurs throughout O'Neill's works, most notably in Edmund Tyrone's attempt at it in Act IV of *Long Day's Journey Into Night*, when he tries to describe to his father the sense of mystic oneness that he felt on a sailing vessel at night.

But the sea also has negative rhythms, mostly made by man the mechanic, as, for example, that oppressive, insistent foghorn that sounds the crack of doom for the haunted Tyrones during the last part of *Long Day's Journey*, or the periodic blast of the ship's whistle that announces the impending death of Yank in *Bound East for Cardiff*. Thus the sea really has two great contrasting rhythms, the "natural" movements and sounds of the sea and of sailing vessels, and the "mechanical" movements and sounds of steam vessels and other modern man-made devices. Thus in *The Hairy Ape*, against Paddy's dream of the lyrical, sailing past is posed the ugly, machinelike reality of the present in the stokehold of the modern steamer, with Yank's gutteral shouts and the engineer's whistle relentlessly driving the Neanderthal men to their onerous task at the fiery, clanging furnaces. Even in relaxation these men are not men but machines. Their very words (*"a brazen metallic quality"*) and their laughter (*"hard, barking"*) are mechanized. This change in the rhythm of the sea from the natural to the mechanical underlies *Beyond the Horizon*, which spans that era in history when on the sea the sailing ship began to give way to the steamer and on land the horse-drawn carriage was displaced by the automobile. These symptomatic changes are meant to underline the steadily deepening tragedy of the lives of the principals, who fall from Eden into Hell.

In the land-sea antithesis the principal movement or rhythm is embodied in the alternation between the two. It is difficult to say what the sea finally means in O'Neill's plays, for, as in *Moby Dick*, it means everything: rapture, beauty, terror, danger, adventure, isolation, renewal, immolation, union, death, peace, boredom, and so on. In his own life O'Neill is said to have cherished his own period as a sailor as his best and proudest memory. Among other things, sea life signified a completely unconventional existence, free of social hypocrisy and the entanglements of woman, punctuated by orgies, sexual and alcoholic, with always the purificatory sea to return to. Actually, in the plays as a whole there is no single, simple antithesis between the land and the sea, although it can always be confidently asserted that whatever the sea means—and it means different things in different plays—the land has hardly anything, ever, to recommend it. The most nearly unalloyed use of the myth of the sea as rhythmical and beautiful and the land as mechanical and ugly (which is a version of the antithesis between sail and steam) is in

*Mourning Becomes Electra,* in which through Brant we are told of the beauties of the clippers, "tall, white," like beautiful, pale women and of the beauties of the lands where only the clippers can transport you, the South Seas, with their eternal sunshine, lovely people, and sinless sex, the place where, as Lavinia says in *The Haunted,* "Love is all beautiful" (I, 2). Moreover, the sea is the home of authentic masculinity. As Brant says to Christine, with the fates closing in on them and Brant about to be murdered by the avenging Lavinia and Orin, "The sea hates a coward" (*The Hunted,* IV). But even in *Mourning Becomes Electra* the sea life is not pure idyl, for the sea meant the slave trade, upon which the Mannons based their fortune, and even at the historical date of the play, 1865–66, the steamship was beginning to drive out the sailing vessel. Still, land meant the bloody Civil War, Lincoln's assassination, the nosy, gossipy neighbors of the Mannons and, above all, the Mannon household and the Mannons themselves: doomed, cruel, puritanical, constricted, dark, sin-ridden, murderous, and suicidal.

In other plays the sea is not always expressive of the rhythm and beauty that Paddy or Brant or Edmund Tyrone attribute to it. It can also be the home of isolation, stagnation, and maddening monotony (*Ile, Thirst,* or *Fog*); or the home of violence and hardship (*Anna Christie* or *The Long Voyage Home* or *Bound East for Cardiff*). Beautiful or dangerous, it usually signifies the call of adventure and the far-away. In this aspect it is the motivating force of *Beyond the Horizon,* for it is the dream of the sea, "beyond the horizon" (in Act II, Scene 2, which takes place on the top of a hill, the sea can actually be seen in the distance), that gives content to the vague, beautiful, doomed idealism of Robert Mayo. Equipped with a "touch of the poet," Robert feels the call of the beyond, "the beauty of the far off" and "the mystery and spell of the East" (I, 1). The play is a tragedy and a prolonged irony, and he never does see the fabled East, but his brother Andrew does and finds "the mystery and spell of the East" to be composed of "filthy narrow streets with the tropic sun beating on it" (II, 2). Finally, the sea can mean, simply, a clean, uncomplicated, and healthy existence, as it does for Anna in *Anna Christie* in which, for her at least, life on board her father's barge is purifying.

Always associated with the sea is the fog, that gray

nothingness that envelopes everything and blurs all distinctions, even the basic ones between night and day and land and sea. Fog for O'Neill had something mystifying and supernatural about it, and in the early one-acter *Fog* there is an explicitly miraculous event: the drifters in the lifeboat in the fog are saved by the fact that a passing steamer hears the cry of a child in the boat when, in fact, the child is already dead. Fog is also background for *Anna Christie*, where it is purificatory; immersed in the fog, Anna feels an entirely new combination of feelings: it makes her feel old, that is, as if she had been living a long time; it seems that at last she has found something in life that she had missed and for which she had been looking; finally, it makes her feel, for the first time, clean and happy.

The most powerful and somber evocation of fog and its spell occurs, as with so many other of O'Neill's devices, in *Long Day's Journey Into Night*, where fog is a palpable ambiguity. On the one hand fog, in *Long Day's Journey*, is a profound, brooding, and steadily deepening, natural backdrop for the various tragedies of the Tyrones; even though it is not seen, its eerie companion, the foghorn, the most lonely and mournful of man-made sounds, repetitiously broods over the last part of the play. On the other hand, fog also represents that blessed loss of identity for which all the main characters, the father excepted, are seeking. Edmund explains the mystique of immersion in the fog to his father in Act IV:

> Everything looked and sounded unreal. Nothing was what it is. That's what I wanted—to be alone with myself in another world where truth is untrue and life can hide from itself. Out beyond the harbor, where the road runs along the beach, I even lost the feeling of being on land. The fog and the sea seemed part of each other. It was like walking on the bottom of the sea. As if I had drowned long ago. As if I was a ghost belonging to the fog, and the fog was the ghost of the sea. It felt damned peaceful to be nothing more than a ghost within a ghost.

In Act III his mother, from whom he derives his essential nature, tells Cathleen, "I really love the fog. . . . It hides you from the world and the world from you. You feel that everything has changed, and nothing is what it seemed to be. No one can find or touch you any more." But that terrible foghorn is always sounding a counterpoint: "It's

the foghorn I hate. It won't let you alone. It keeps reminding you, and warning you, and calling you back." Thus it
is that in the final act of O'Neill's finest tragedy the great
antitheses between land and sea and day and night, which
underlay so many of his plays, become dissolved into fog
whose only rhythm is the repetitious moan of the foghorn
and the occasional tinkle of ships' bells. Still, as Edmund
Tyrone would indicate, the fog is not a nothingness. It is
another world where, like Melville's Pip at the bottom of
the sea, that most profound of fogs, one can see God's foot
on the treadle of the loom.

## iv  City and Country

As immemorial as the antithesis between land and
sea is the one between city and country, which constitutes
yet another fundamental geographical polarity in O'Neill's
plays. As in the biblical legend, where Cain, the fratricide,
is reckoned the founder of cities, the city in O'Neill's plays
is the place of corruption, evil, despair, loneliness, and
heartlessness. In one sense the city is the dead end of life.
Especially is this true of a city slum, such as that which
contains Harry Hope's saloon. As Larry, the philosopher of
*The Iceman Cometh*, explains it: "It's the No Chance
Saloon. It's Bedrock Bar, The End of the Line Café, The
Bottom of the Sea Rathskeller! Don't you notice the beautiful calm in the atmosphere? That's because it's the last
harbor. No one here has to worry about where they're going
next, because there is no farther they can go" (I).
But the city, by which is meant the megalopolis, is a
monstrosity, considered at any level, from top to bottom.
In its lower reaches it spawns those ferocious racial hatreds
and embroglios that form the substance of *All God's
Chillun Got Wings* and *The Dreamy Kid*. Upper middle-
class life, as presented in *Days Without End*, is equally
appalling in its way, for here is only mindless, joyless, aimless adultery and drink, peopled by lacerated hearts and
frayed nerve-ends. Worst of all, this existence is finally just
plain dull, a ceaseless round of witless parties. In Act II of
*Days Without End*, Lucy, the unhappy wife of a faithless
husband, describes to the heroine, Elsa, John Loving's
wife, a typical New York party given by her husband and

how she got her revenge on her husband by being unfaith-
ful to him, and that with a long-time, and happily married,
friend (unbeknownst to Elsa, the man is John Loving).
The party is made up of "would-be" Bohemians, vulgar,
cynical, poisonous, sneering at anything decent. Her husband was drunk and flagrantly pawing his latest mistress,
with whom he finally left the party. Thus, out of a desire
for revenge, she seduced the old friend, hating herself and
the whole incident all the while, motivated only by a desire to smash a happy marriage.

New York generally means dissipation and interruption
of work. When Stephen Murray, the protagonist of *The
Straw*, returns to the sanitarium after a sojourn in New
York, he is well and expensively dressed, but a "great
change is visible in his face," which is thinner, sallow,
puffy, and dissipated (III). He complains to Eileen, the
heroine, "in New York it's so hard. You start to do one
thing and something else interrupts you." "There's so little
time to yourself once you get to know people in New
York." In *Welded* it is the web of past love affairs in The
City that threatens the union of Michael and Eleanor
Cape. Even New York at its best, Fifth Avenue on a fine
Sunday morning, is somehow tawdry; thus in Scene V of
*The Hairy Ape*, Fifth Avenue is described as *"cheapened
and made grotesque by commercialism,"* despite the
natural beauty of the Sunday morning. Moreover, the city
is the home of the mechanization of human life. The people that Yank encounters on Fifth Avenue are lifeless
marionettes, with *"something of the relentless horror of
Frankensteins."* For the rhythm of the city is totally
wrong: it is mechanical, ever more progressively so as it
becomes modernized.

*All God's Chillun Got Wings,* for example, covers some
sixteen or seventeen years, during which New York passes
from the nineteenth into the twentieth century, a transition from the organically rhythmic to the mechanically
rhythmic. Rhythm, both alternation and repetition, is of
the essence in *All God's Chillun.* In Act I, Scene 1, two
streets are seen: one is all black and the other all white.
It is late in the afternoon and as the scene progresses twilight comes on. The Negroes laugh frankly and freely; the
whites awkwardly and constrainedly. The Negroes sing,
"I Guess I'll Have to Telegraph My Baby"; the whites,

"Only a Bird in a Gilded Cage." At the end an organ-grinder appears and plays "Annie Rooney." These alternating rhythms, always getting sadder, are repeated in Scenes 2 and 3. Scenes 1, 2, and 3 of the play span fourteen years, during which the city becomes mechanized. In Scene 1 the repetitious rhythms are the roar of the Elevated, the puff of the locomotive, and the "*lazy sound of a horse-car, the hooves of its team clacking on the cobbles.*" But nine years later, in Scene 2, "*The street noises are now more rhythmically mechanical, electricity having taken the place of horse and steam.*" Scene 3, five years later, begins at night in what is now the enormous and indifferent modern megalopolis: "*The arc-lamp discovers faces with a favorless cruelty. The street noises are the same but more intermittent and dulled with a quality of fatigue. Two people pass, one black and one white. They are tired. They both yawn, but neither laughs. There is no laughter from the two streets.*" Thus as the happy children of Scene 1 grow up to their dark adulthood, the city itself darkens and becomes increasingly mechanical.

*The Great God Brown* touches on big-city architecture, which, of course, is shown to be fraudulent. The only group of decent big-city people in O'Neill's world are the whores and the down-and-outers, in short, characters such as those of *The Iceman Cometh.* As with all other O'Neill themes, the evil of the city receives its most powerful evocation in the late plays, especially *Long Day's Journey, A Moon for the Misbegotten,* and, above all, *Hughie.* In Act IV of *Long Day's Journey* Edmund tells his father that although Baudelaire was French and never saw Broadway and died before Jamie Tyrone was born, he knew Jamie's "Little Old New York" just the same. He then recites Symons' translation of Baudelaire's "Epilogue":

> *With heart at rest I climbed the citadel's*
> *Steep height, and saw the city as from a tower,*
> *Hospital, brothel, prison, and such hells,*
>
> *Where evil comes up softly like a flower.*
> *Thou knowest, O Satan, patron of my pain,*
> *Not for vain tears I went up at that hour;*
>
> *But like an old sad faithful lecher, fain*
> *To drink delight of that enormous trull*
> *Whose hellish beauty makes me young again.*

*Whether thou sleep, with heavy vapours full,*
*Sodden with day, or, new apparelled, stand*
*In gold-laced veils of evening beautiful,*

*I love thee, infamous city! Harlots and*
*Hunted have pleasures of their own to give,*
*The vulgar herd can never understand.*

Jamie himself in *A Moon for the Misbegotten* explains to Josie Hogan that the city is EVIL and demonstrates that it perverts that most basic and beautiful of urges, sex; thus when in Act III the gigantic virgin offers herself to him, drunk as he is, he immediately turns into a leering Broadway "sport" with his tart: "Sure thing, Kiddo.... I know what you want, Bright Eyes...." She is repelled, and when he comes back to his real self, he remarks: "Believe me, Kid, when I poison them, they stay poisoned!"

The most concrete and somber picture of the city is in *Hughie*, which, strangely enough, is in its totality one of the most optimistic plays that O'Neill ever wrote. *Hughie* is Night and the City, one of the most powerful brief evocations of the loneliness, boredom, and despair of the bottom-dog in the modern city in the language. Only Melville's *Bartleby* is comparable. All rhythms are mechanical and repetitious, each harsh sound indicating the alexandrine crawl of time, dragging its snaky length slowly along. As Erie Smith, small-time Broadway "sport," carries on his monologue in a shabby hotel on the West Side of Manhattan at three o'clock of a hot and humid morning in the summer of 1928, we are, by a series of stage directions that amount to a stream of consciousness, allowed into the "consciousness," if it can be called that, of the night clerk, with his greasy, pimply face, and his aching feet. Except for some Walter Mitty-esque overtones and urges, the inner "life" of the night clerk is a stream of nothingness, beyond and below despair. It is all described by O'Neill with great wit, irony, and power.

The night clerk is initially described as neither thinking nor sleepy, *"He simply droops and stares acquiescently at nothing."* His sole occupation is telling time by the sounds of the darkened street. In fact, such thoughts as he has—until near the end of the play when he comes alive, so to speak, and enters into a human relationship with Erie—are set off only by these periodic noises. It is true that his

aching feet remind him that he should get a new pair of
shoes and that he has not enough money to buy them, but
this train of thought is ended abruptly by a kind of supreme theistic Stoicism, *"Get a pair when he goes to
heaven."* The last time he had been able to *"feel despair"*
was back around World War I when he was temporarily
out of work. His enemy is Time, and sounds are his
weapons against it—for a sound means some time has
passed. Thus when the garbage men, clanging cans, pass
on, *"Time is that much older,"* and the repeated roar of
the El even offers *hope. "But there is hope. Only so many
El trains pass in one night."* So the night recedes; only so
many sounds can happen, night after night, until *"Nirvana,
the Big Night of Nights. And that's life."* When his wife
nags him, this is always his reply, *"That's life."* He is
hardly aware of the voluble Erie, and answers him only
automatically, *"as his mind tiptoes into the night again."*
When Erie begins talking of the beauty of horses, the
night clerk vaguely wonders what horses have to do with
anything, *"or for that matter, what anything has to do with
anything."* The sound of a passing policeman penetrates
the consciousness of the night clerk. *" 'If he'd only shoot it
out with a gunman some night! Nothing exciting has happened in any night I've ever lived through!' "* A streetcar
is faintly, distantly heard: *"It* [the sound] *is still lost in
the night. Flat wheeled and tired. Distant the carbarn,
and far away the sleep."* An ambulance screams in the
night, and the night clerk ruminates: *" 'Will he die, Doctor, or isn't he lucky?' "* A fire engine wails: *" 'Will it* [the
fire] *be big enough, do you think?' " " 'I mean, big enough
to burn down the whole damn city?' "* But the imaginary
fireman replies in the negative, "Sorry"—too much stone
and steel.

Even more appalling are the city's silences: *"His mind
has been trying to fasten itself to some noise in the night,
but a rare and threatening pause of silence has fallen on
the city."* It is at this point, when fear has replaced nihilism, that he becomes genuinely aware of Erie: *" 'I should
have paid 492* [Erie's room number] *more attention. After
all, he is company. He is awake and alive. I should use
him to help me live through the night.' "* The silence begins to be unbearable: *"Outside, the spell of abnormal
quiet presses suffocatingly upon the street, enters the de-*

*serted, dirty lobby. The Night Clerk's mind cowers away from it."* At this point he asks his first sincere question of Erie, who was at the point of giving up, in despair, of making a contact with the clerk. Erie is transformed and embarks on the telling of some grandiose lies for the now enchanted night clerk. A human bond, founded on an illusion, is formed: two humans will help one another get through the night, as they must, night after night, until the coming of Nirvana, the Big Night, and the Last. Meanwhile they must hold at bay the great, somber, monotonous, heartless, roaring, silent City, "Where evil comes up softly like a flower." Thus it is that O'Neill's most powerful prophet, Lazarus, should urge his followers to go out into the woods, under the sky, for "Cities are prisons wherein man locks himself from life" (II, 1).

If city life is usually inhuman, its antithesis, farm life, is by no means paradisical, and comes equipped with its own horrors. Only in the opening part of *Beyond the Horizon* do we get a glimpse of an orderly, well-run, handsome New England farm, with the commanding father, the obedient family, the freshly plowed fields, the checkerboard hills and valleys divided by neat stone walls, the distant hills rimmed by the setting sun. But after this in the play, and in O'Neill's plays as a whole, farm life means narrowness of outlook, or moral degeneracy, or financial ruin, or brutality, or back-breaking work, or sexual repression, in short, a distinctively unlovely way of life.

Degeneracy is the theme of his first farm play, *The Rope*, which besides its unsavory plot (the proposed torture of an old miser by his son in order to get his money) and its gruesomely ironic ending (while the torturers heat up an iron file, an idiot girl has discovered the moneybag and is scaling the coins out into the sea) contains about as unappealing a group of characters as O'Neill ever assembled: the ten-year-old idiot girl, Mary; the old, thin, weak-eyed, biblical-speaking miser, Abraham Bentley, who has put up a rope in the barn so that when his prodigal son, Luke, comes home, Luke can hang himself on it; Annie, Abraham's slovenly, worn-out, sullen daughter; her husband, Sweeney, a drunken, cunning, avaricious lout; and Luke, the prodigal son, tall and strapping but shifty and shiftless, who proposes at the end of the play to torture his father, after he has refused his father's invitation to hang himself.

*Beyond the Horizon* is about the narrowness of New England farm life, its terrible demands, and its final failure as a way of life. It is as Emerson described it in "Farming": "continuous hard labor ... and small gains." For Robert Mayo the hills surrounding the Mayo farm are a physical symptom of the restrictions, the limitedness, and the monotony of farm life itself. "Beyond" them lies adventure and romance, so he thinks. Those hills finally turn into his prison house, as both his marriage and his farm go to wrack and, finally, to ruin. That last watery dawn of Act III, Scene 1, of that bleak October morning, faintly illuminates the last remnants of what had been once a primary force in American history, the healthy existence of the small independent farmer, of which we have caught a glimpse in Act I when the elder Mayo is still alive and vigorous. But now the farmhouse is sunk in a poverty and neglect so profound that it is no longer "*ashamed or even conscious of itself.*" The curtains are torn and dirty; dust is everywhere; blotches of dampness disfigure the wallpaper; the faded carpet shows trails leading to the kitchen and outer doors. Spilt food, unwashed dishes, an unblacked stove, a shadeless lamp, all these constitute the setting for the human wreckage, the dying, consumptive Robert Mayo and his deathly pale, listless, aged wife.

*Anna Christie* while not a farm play has a farm background for its heroine, Anna. This play is tendentiously critical of both the myth of the sea and the myth of the farm. Chris Christopherson, who from bitter experience hates the sea for its dangers and treachery, decides to have his daughter Anna brought up by some cousins in the "bucolic" atmosphere of a Midwestern farm. But what Anna finds on the farm is endless work, beatings, and, at the age of sixteen, seduction, which starts her on her way to becoming a prostitute.

In *Desire Under the Elms* there is once more the Bible-quoting, tyrannical father and the rebellious sons. Added is the picture of volcanic passions and lusts and insensate greed, precariously controlled at best, and, in the action of the play, an infanticide. The general run of farming people who gather at Ephraim's celebration for the birth of "his" son are mean, petty, envious, and malicious. But the genuine essence of farm life as dramatized by *Desire Under the Elms* is back-breaking labor, and its proper symbols are the rocky soil and the stone walls which have been made of components extracted from that soil. It is all summed up in the monody on stones given by Ephraim in Part III, Scene 2, to his unattentive and preoccupied wife. Many years before, Ephraim had gone West and seen with his own eyes the rich, black, stoneless soil which would have made farming easy. But this was immoral, and unbiblical: "God's hard, not easy! God's in the stones! Build my church on a rock—out o' stones an' I'll be in them! That's what He meant t' Peter! (*He sighs heavily— a pause*) Stones." Year after year he had picked them up and piled them into walls. The years of his life could be read in the walls, with every day a hefted stone. He had, like God, made something out of nothing, a rich farm out of the bleak stony earth. It was hard, and God had made him hard to do it.

The only other substantial treatment of a farm in O'Neill's plays is Phil Hogan's establishment in *A Moon for the Misbegotten*, where the picture is comic, practically a parody. There, amidst poverty, a shack for a house, pigs, rocks, ticks, lice, poison ivy, and so on, the wily Phil Hogan and his doughty daughter, Josie, eke out their precarious existence. Thus if farming and farm life are a tragedy in O'Neill's first major play, they finally become a farce in his last major play. Farm life is also one of the running jokes—and one of the "pipe dreams"—of *The Iceman Cometh*, for it is the "dream" of Chuck, the bartender, and Cora, the tart, to marry and settle down on a farm, where, as Pearl and Margie say, it would be a moot point whether Cora knows which end of the cow is which, and where, as Rocky says, the silence and the chirping of the crickets will drive them both crazy.

The bridge between the city and the country is the suburb. Several of O'Neill's plays take place in a suburb although the only ones that can properly be called "suburban" plays are *The First Man* and *Ah, Wilderness!*, both taking place in suburban Connecticut. As usual, we find in these plays two antithetical extremes, the one an attack on, the other an apotheosis of suburban life. *The First Man* (1921) is a bitter, blunt, and not very skillful attack on suburban conventionality and hypocrisy. Curtis Jayson, an anthropologist, breaks entirely with his smug family, of Bridgetown, as his wife dies giving birth to their son (the rhythm of repetition here is the groans and shrieks of the laboring wife). The attack is a familiar one, and stems back to Flaubert (or Chaucer): the bourgeoisie are crooked in business, smug, philistine, mean, petty, conventional, and given to gossip. The title of the play has a twofold reference: Curtis Jayson is slated to go on an anthropological expedition to Asia to find "the first man"; but, second, his son is going to be a "first man," in that he is not going to be brought up side by side with the Jaysons, or Joneses, in Bridgetown—"You're like a swarm of poisonous flies." Rather, as Curt Jayson says, "When he's old enough, I'll teach him to know and love a big, free life" (IV). In the suburban-rural contrast in this play there is a kind of Wordsworthian flavor, for at the end of the play Curtis, who is off to Asia, leaves his son in charge of his aunt, Mrs. Davidson, a *grande dame*, therefore not a bourgeoisie, and an actual dweller in the countryside. Mrs. Davidson is charged with keeping the boy and bringing him up "out there" in the country—never to let him know "this obscene little world." This bucolicism, however, is only the concluding falsity of a very weak play.

But, finally, everyone must have, back in a pocket of the past, a golden age and a golden place: it is one of the historic necessities of the human mind and imagination, and O'Neill is no exception. His national idyl, his *Pickwick Papers*, is of course his other suburban play, *Ah, Wilderness!*, a charming, heart-felt comedy which is about the pangs of adolescence, but which is also a sustained paean of praise to suburban American life in 1906: northern East Coast, Protestant, middle-class, a way of life that O'Neill later said he would have liked to have had for his own growingup period. (*Ah, Wilderness!* will be discussed in Chapter 2, Sec. iii.) However, *Ah, Wilderness!* excepted, the life of man in O'Neill's world on land or on sea, in the city or on the farm, or in the suburb—is not a happy one.

O'NEILL, while we think of him as a playwright of the
contemporary American scene, was actually as much or
more, and increasingly so during the latter part of his
career, an historical dramatist. Indeed it could be argued
that his best plays are the historical ones. Practically all
of his early one-act plays dealt with contemporary life although almost always in an unusual or exotic setting: an
open boat, the bowels of a tramp steamer, and so on.
His first full-length, produced play, *Beyond the Horizon*
(1917–18), is not precisely dated but it must be taking
place very early in the twentieth century. Of all the plays
he wrote after this only a few can be described as contemporary, i.e., as dealing with life contemporaneous with the
time of the writing itself. The principal ones in this category are (assumed date of composition given) *The Straw*
(1918–19), *Anna Christie* (1920), *The First Man* (1921),
*The Hairy Ape* (1921), *Welded* (1922–23), *Strange Interlude* (1926–27), *Dynamo* (1928), and *Days Without
End* (1931–34). *All God's Chillun Got Wings* (1923)
and *The Great God Brown* (1925) also deal with modernity, but have their beginnings and roots set back in
the late nineteenth or early twentieth century. It hardly
needs to be remarked that in this group are O'Neill's worst
plays: *The First Man, Welded,* and *Days Without End;*
in fact the closer O'Neill got to wrestling with "serious"
modern ideas and problems, as in *Days Without End,* the
worse he became as a dramatist.

Considered as a unit, O'Neill's history plays fall into
three groups. First and furthest back in time are the
historical exotics, *The Fountain, Marco Millions,* and
*Lazarus Laughed,* which take place, respectively, in the

late fifteenth and early sixteenth centuries, late thirteenth and early fourteenth centuries, and *circa* A.D. 37 (the date of the death of the Emperor Tiberius). A second group of history plays occur in America in the nineteenth or early twentieth century: *A Touch of the Poet* (1828), *Desire Under the Elms* (1850), *Mourning Becomes Electra* (1865–66), the first half of *Diff'rent* (1890), *Ile* (1895), *Where the Cross Is Made* (1900), *Gold* (*ca.* 1900), and *Beyond the Horizon* (early twentieth century). The projected cycle of nine history plays, of which only *A Touch of the Poet* and *More Stately Mansions* survive, would have covered American history from the late eighteenth to the early twentieth centuries but the majority of them would have, obviously, taken place in the nineteenth century. The third group of history plays are not "history" in the same sense as those listed above; they are rather a dramatization of O'Neill's own "remembered" past (the two dates after each play signify, respectively, the date of composition and the imaginary date of the play): *Ah, Wilderness!* (1932; 1906), *The Iceman Cometh* (1939; 1912), *Long Day's Journey Into Night* (1940–41; 1912), *Hughie* (1941; 1928), and *A Moon for the Misbegotten* (1943; 1923).

In many respects as a writer O'Neill was a throwback to the nineteenth century and, especially, to the nineteenth-century novelists, Scott, Hugo, Dickens, Lever, and others, all of whose books were in his father's library and which he had read as a child. In using a "remembered" past for the background of his late plays O'Neill would be in the best Victorian tradition, for the best and most characteristic efforts of the major Victorian novelists are in this genre, the retrospective novel which takes place in a period the writer had known in his own lifetime but which had receded far enough to be seen clearly, if mellowly: with Dickens, *Great Expectations* (1860–61; England in the 1820's); with George Eliot, *Middlemarch* (1871–72; England around the time of the Reform Bill, *ca.* 1832); with Thackeray, *Vanity Fair* (1847–48; England from the Waterloo era up through the 1820's).

The key figure and influence here on modern literature generally was Scott, in whose train the Victorian novelists followed. Scott's first novel *Waverley*, published in 1814 and concerned with events in 1745, was subtitled *Tis Sixty*

*Years Since,* or, in other words, the events being described could have either been seen by the author (*Waverley* was published anonymously and no general reader knew who the author was), or the author could have known older people who had seen or participated in these events. The best of the Waverley novels occur in this time-realm, just within or just beyond personal memory, and Scott was at his worst in dealing with the present (*St. Ronan's Well*) or the medieval past (*Count Robert of Paris*). Leslie Stephen in his discussion of Scott makes the essential point: the present is too harsh, confused, and grating to be captured and shaped; the far past is lost, drowned in darkness; but there is a twilight zone where memory could operate and recapture the essence of things and could even operate and recapture an age just behind one's own lifetime, as in *Waverley.* Then following Scott came the Victorian novelists, who habitually set their fictional histories back in time, ten, twenty, thirty, forty, even sixty years.

Now O'Neill had tried the far past in *The Fountain, Marco Millions,* and *Lazarus Laughed* without notable success; he had tried the present many times, disastrously so in *Dynamo* and *Days Without End.* But by the time of the first production of his first major memory play, *The Iceman Cometh,* in 1946, he had come around in these matters to the point of view of the Victorians: "I do not think that you can write anything of value or understanding about the present. You can only write about life if it is far enough in the past. The present is too much mixed up with superficial values; you can't know which thing is important and which is not. The past which I have chosen is one I knew." [1] The people of the projected cycle of plays about American history he could not have known, of course, but he knew the country, America, where the action was to occur, and he knew the cultures, New England Puritanism and New England Irish-Catholicism, which were to shape his cast of characters, and, in the cycle as a whole, he was finally to come down into the twentieth century. In a sense, then, the cycle was to be a series of memory plays too. Certainly they were to be of a different order, as *A Touch of the Poet* attests, from the O'Neill plays of the far past, *The Fountain, Marco Millions,* and *Lazarus Laughed.*

## 1 *Ancient and Renaissance*

For his histories of the far past O'Neill, like Scott once more, seems to have instinctively chosen historical periods when mankind was about to embark on some irreversible course, some critical juncture in human history which, once passed, would commit man to a new future. Conflict then is of the essence in these plays. Then within the framework of this historical period there were the various clashes of the races, cultures, and beliefs that make up the substance of the plays. For example, *The Fountain*, the first of this group of plays, takes place from 1492 (Columbus' first voyage and the expulsion of the Moors from Spain) to *circa* 1514. It begins in Granada and recounts the defeat of the Moors by the Spaniards. Scene II takes place on Columbus' ship on the second voyage to the New World in 1493. The rest of the play and time-span are concerned with the dealings of the Spanish with the natives of Central America. Thus we have the most powerful country of the world at the time, Spain, casting off an Eastern invader and turning to the New World as invader herself.

The bulk of the play is made up of polar conflicts between various cultural and religious forces. The initial one is between proud defeated Moslems and proud triumphant Spaniards. Scene II, on Columbus' ship, introduces the major conflict of the play, between the Spaniards and the Indians, for Columbus is bringing back with him some Indians that he had previously taken to Spain. But the specific conflict in this scene is between Columbus, who represents the religious aspirations of Spain, or, in other words, its past; and Juan Ponce de Leon, who embodies Spain's secular aims, or its future. Columbus is presented as being a tall, commanding, ardent, religious devotee, one of the "unworthy servants of God's Holy Will." He has promised the Pope to raise "the last Crusade," with fifty thousand men and four thousand horses, a like force to follow five years later. But Juan exclaims, "The Crusades are dead," and proclaims himself as "a soldier of the present, not the ghost of a Crusader!" He stigmatizes the motives of most of the other voyagers: adventurers lusting for loot, nobles itching for wealth, monks eager to use the rack, and at their head a leader who will pillage to resurrect the Crusades. "We will loot and loot and, weakened by looting, be easy prey for stronger looters," says Ponce de Leon; whereas he, Ponce de Leon, wishes to make Spain the mistress of the world. And as the inevitable sunrise occurs and as land is sighted, Columbus kneels to the cross and Ponce de Leon to the sword.

Twenty years or so elapse between Scenes II and III— years of conflict between Spaniard and Indian and Spaniard and Spaniard. Among the Spaniards there is a twofold conflict: one between the secular arm (Ponce de Leon) and the religious arm (the evil Franciscan monk, Menendez); and one within the religious arm itself, between the gentle, charitable Dominican order, which Ponce de Leon's friend Luis joins, and the fanatical, blood-thirsty Franciscans. Thus Juan complains about the Franciscans that he fights the battles and they steal the spoils; he seeks to construct, they to destroy. In his turn Juan is involved in several personal contrasts and struggles, not to mention the various struggles going on in his own split personality, which is half self-confident and ambitious leader and half dreamy poet. Of the exterior contrasts, two are unfavorable to him, and two are favorable. The favorable ones are to Columbus and Menendez. Columbus is presented as a man who pursued chimeras over South and Central America and never mentioned in his dispatches the name of Ponce de Leon, who had fought all the battles, held the outposts, and suffered the wounds and the fevers. Menendez is presented as totally evil, changing only from a rigid fanatic to the "not less cruel," "oily intriguer of Church politics," and is always Juan's opponent about the proper way in which to treat the natives. Ponce de Leon is compared, to his disfavor, with his friend Luis, once drunken poet and gambler, by now (Scene III) a Dominican with a "calm, peaceful expression," "at last in harmony with himself"; and to Nano, the noble-savage Indian, whose refusal to tell Juan where he can find the Fountain of Youth reduces Ponce de Leon to his most barbarous action of the play, torture: "Juan Ponce de Leon—to torture a helpless captive! Why did you bring me to such shame?" (V). *The Fountain* reaches its climax in some rather murky religious symbolism in Scene X, when the wounded Juan sees visions in the Fountain in the clearing in the wilds of

Florida, and when all the discords of his life and time are meant to be dissolved into some misty, rhythmical, transcendental One. As Juan exclaims: "All is within! All things dissolve, flow on eternally!" "All faiths—they vanish —are one and equal—within—." But the play ends, of course, in sunset and "rhythm"; the old and dying Don Juan, in a Cuban sunset *of infinite depth glow*[ing] *with mysterious splendor,* listening to Beatriz, the heroine, and her young intended sing the Fountain song (love), while the Dominicans chant vespers (religion).

O'Neill's researches for *The Fountain* led him to the story of Marco Polo and finally to the play, *Marco Millions,* simultaneously a funnier and a more serious play than *The Fountain,* which, with its blend of history, romance, shallow characters, and stale rhetoric is the most insubstantial and the weakest of O'Neill's first group of history plays. *Marco Millions* is a rather amusing satire— O'Neill's *Babbitt*—on contemporary American business superimposed upon another great historical turning point in world history, the first longitudinal trip by European man across Asia to China, and one of the first cultural and commercial interchanges between East and West. Marco Polo is thus modern American business and Western greed, set off against the wisdom and the exquisite aestheticism of classical China. The play also contains some rather amusing satire on contemporary America, beyond the business interest. For example, on his return to Venice (III, 1) Marco Polo makes a homecoming speech to his fellow citizens and is described as striking a good listening attitude, so that he will be sure *not to miss a word his voice utters.* Again in Act II, Scene 1, when he enters into the presence of the Kaan his face is described as having the grave and responsible expression of an American Senator from the South who is about to propose a constitutional amendment *restricting the migration of non-Nordic birds into Texas,* or forbidding the operation of the *laws of biology within the twelve-mile limit.* In this same scene Marco boasts of how he has "Americanized" a Chinese province during his term as its governor: "democratic" taxes, that is, taxes for all, including beggars; suppression of free speech ("every citizen must be happy or go to jail"); appointment of five hundred committees to carry on his work when he is gone; suppression of vice; and, his mightiest accomplishment, the invention of paper currency and gunpowder. As he explains it to the Kaan, you conquer the world with the one (patting the gun) and you pay for it with the other (he pats the currency). You become the bringer of peace on earth and good-will, without it costing hardly a yen. And he offers these priceless gifts to the Kaan for only a million yen.

But despite the fact that all businessmen in the play, and all nations produce them, are shown always to be incurious, cynical, callous, vulgar, and grasping, O'Neill, like Sinclair Lewis—and *Babbitt* is certainly a palpable influence here—finally fell in love, as he admitted, with his own creation, who is finally shown to be a sturdy, essentially decent fellow, like Babbitt. The great question for O'Neill in determining human worth comes down to whether the individual has "soul." It turns out that Marco does have, vestigially anyway, a "soul," at least, according to Kukachin. In Act II, Scene 1, Kukachin testifies that she has seen him bind up her dog's leg and play with a slave's baby; she had heard him sigh when he heard music over the water, and looked at the sunrise, the sunset, and the stars. Each time he had remarked that Nature was wonderful. But, to put the other side of it, the wise old Kaan, Kukachin's grandfather, remarks that men like Marco Polo (i.e., businessmen) memorize everything and learn nothing; look at everything and see nothing; lust for everything and love nothing. What they have, only, is a shrewd and crafty greed. And, according to *Marco Millions*, the only truly international phenomenon, common to all nations, are war, greed, and lust; as the prostitute, who turns up everywhere and in all lands, remarks: "I sell to all nations" (I, 3).

Within the over-all polarity between American-Western greed and materialism and classical Chinese wisdom and beauty, there are various other antinomies: the Christian vs. the heathen; two contrasting wise men: Tedaldo, the Papal legate at Acre, who is to become Pope Gregory X, and the Great Kaan; the various formal religions, Christian, Buddhist, Taoist, Persian, Moslem, set off against the wisdom of the Kaan; Christian Westerners set off against Persians, Indians, and Chinese.

The rhythm of the play as a whole, as is the case with so many of O'Neill's plays, is split between the tragic and the comic. In O'Neill's later plays the rhythmic movement tends to run from the comic, at the beginning, to the tragic, at the end. But in *Marco Polo* the two strains run side by side; and thus alongside the satire on Marco Polo, unfolds the tragedy of Princess Kukachin and her grandfather, the comic and the tragic sides being united by Kukachin's hopeless love for the unaware Marco. Thus the last act contains both the most hilarious moment in the play and the most sadly poignant one. The hilarity is provoked by a vision, seen through the Kaan's crystal ball, of the triumphant return to Venice of the now wealthy Polos and the elaborate banquet they provide for their fellow Venetians. This scene, which has many analogies to the triumphant part of Leopold Bloom's hallucination in the Night-Town scene in *Ulysses*, concludes with a speech by Marco about the financial possibilities of the silk industry—"millions upon millions upon millions of millions of worms!"—which is gradually drowned out by the noise of voracious Venetians gluttonously devouring the banquet the Polos have served, this uproar finally being only faintly punctuated by Marco's voice: "millions! . . . millions! . . . millions! . . . millions!" But in the scene that immediately follows, the funeral scene of Kukachin, the mood and tone are tragic, with the wise old Kaan trying to find some meaning to a life so cruel as to destroy his little flower, Kukachin. Accordingly, he turns for an explanation to the various eastern religions: Confucian, Taoist, Buddhist, and Moslem. A priest of each can tell him only, "Death is." Only the Kaan can rise above this negativity to make the play's affirmation, in one of O'Neill's rather vague, turgid, and paradoxical statements about the "meaning of life": "Be exalted by life! Be inspired by death! Be humbly proud! Be proudly grateful!" Like Hamlet, the Kaan professes not to know what lies beyond the brink of the grave, and he concludes that it is "nobler not to know!"

The Kaan's gnomic wisdom immediately calls to mind *Lazarus Laughed*, in which the Kaan figure, the wise man, becomes a literal and joyous prophet and moves to the very center of the play. Throughout O'Neill's dramatic career one can see this same process again and again: a character or an idea or a situation which is treated in a minor or secondary way in one play becomes dominant in a succeeding play. Especially is this true of the sequence, from 1923 to 1926, of *Marco Millions, The Great God Brown,* and *Lazarus Laughed,* which have all kinds of cross references and common themes. These plays constitute what might be called the "apocalyptic" phase of O'Neill's career.

*Lazarus Laughed* is the last of the O'Neill history plays of the distant past; it is also the most serious, profound, original, and distinctive work of this genre, as much an advance, in seriousness and originality, over *Marco Millions,* as *Marco* was over *The Fountain. Lazarus Laughed* is also placed the furthest back in time (*circa* A.D. 37) of all of O'Neill's plays and centers on what has been, so far, the most crucial period in Western history when a Hellenized but corrupt Rome was witnessing the birth pangs of Christianity. It is also O'Neill's most explicitly "Christian" play since, like *Paradise Lost,* it is, in essence, an enormous, imaginative expansion on a brief biblical text, John XI. *Lazarus Laughed* is also one of the most profoundly rhythmic of O'Neill's plays: death vs. life; hate vs. joy; despair vs. ecstasy; Jew vs. Nazarene; Lazarusites vs. Orthodox Jews; Jews vs. Greeks; Romans vs. Greeks and Jews; Lazarus vs. humanity; and so on. The whole edifice of the play is erected on a paradox: the dead man, Lazarus, has come to life (and is indeed the very embodiment of LIFE—he grows steadily younger as the play progresses) and becomes the prophet to the living, who are really the dead. Verbally, the play is a prolonged irony or antithesis, with Lazarus expressing, hyperbolically, religious paradoxes: "Are you a speck of dust danced in the wind? Then laugh, dancing! Laugh yes to your insignificance! Thereby will be born your new greatness! As Man, Petty Tyrant of Earth, you are a bubble pricked by death into a void and a mocking silence! But as dust, you are eternal change, and everlasting growth, and a high note of laughter soaring through chaos from the deep heart of God!" (II, 1).

Unlike any other character created by O'Neill, Lazarus is released from his own past, the toils of history, the fear of death, and the loneliness of the self. At the same time he has passed the threshold of godlike thought and has access to some kind of timeless but still human wisdom which he expresses in gnomic aphorisms: "I know that age and time are but timidities of thought" (IV, 1); "If

you can answer Yes to pain, there is no pain!" (*ibid.*);
"Life is for each man a solitary cell whose walls are mirrors" (II, 1). Mankind, however, is not yet ready for his
wisdom although by the end of the play he has half converted the half-mad Caligula who, left alone on the stage
at the end of the play, with Lazarus, Tiberius, and Pompeia dead, finds himself speaking of his mortal enemies, the
people of Rome, in Lazarus-like paradoxes: "O my good
people, my faithful scum, my brother swine . . ." Similarly,
the pangs of life—all except Lazarus suffer from them—are
presented by other characters in the play and by the chorus
in bitter paradoxes that have in them some of the spirit
of the terrible nullifications of the slogans of George Orwell's super-state in 1984: "Life is a fearing, / A long dying,
/ From birth to death! / God is a slayer! / Life is death!"
(I, 2).

Strictly human wisdom, such as Tiberius possesses, is
based not on intuition, as is that of Lazarus, but on experience, and that experience is invariably sad and lonely.
As Tiberius explains it to Lazarus, "I know it is folly to
speak—but—one gets old, one becomes talkative, one
wishes to confess, to say the thing one has always kept
hidden, to reveal one's unique truth—and there is so little
time left—and one is alone! Therefore the old—like children—talk to themselves, for they have reached that hopeless wisdom of experience which knows that though one
were to cry it in the streets to multitudes, or whisper it in
the kiss to one's beloved, the only ears that can ever hear
one's secret are one's own!" (IV, 1). Thus all the characters are poised between absolute alternatives; on the one
hand, there are: experience, Caesar, the State, death, torture, fear, loneliness, lust, greed, satiety, innervation, sexual
inversion, night, terror, wakefulness, despair (this is the
world most of them occupy); on the other hand, there
is: the intuitive, blessed, happy, natural, organic, affirmative, individualistic but nonegotistical life that Lazarus
embodies and offers. As the play goes on, and as Lazarus
becomes progressively younger, the stage directions describing him take on a D. H. Lawrencean flavor with the
repetition of such words and phrases as "recurring seasons," "processes," "eternal growth," "sap and blood and
loam," "triumphant," "blood-stirring call," "ecstatic affirmation," and so on. With his instinctive sense for the

polar, O'Neill, in doing research for the play, went to Mommsen's history of Rome (for his Roman characters and for Roman corruption) and to Frazer's *The Golden Bough* (for the character of Lazarus and for fertility rites), and these two poles provide the backdrop for the play.

As might be expected, human character itself is split in this play. The characters of *Lazarus Laughed* fall into two categories: inner characters and outer characters. The outer characters are all masked types, and they are typed in three ways: according to age, of which there are seven; according to character, of which there are seven; and according to race, of which there are three: Jew, Greek, and Roman. By blending his three basic types in various and changing ways O'Neill manages to suggest a great human world which is at one and the same time universally typical and infinitely varied—the play requires four hundred costumes and three hundred masks—and the masks, far from depersonalizing the people of the enormous chorus, individualize them in a peculiarly dramatic fashion. Thus the sixty Roman Senators of Act II, Scene 2 are all generalized by having the Roman mask, which suggests both nobility and corruption; but within this generalizing principle there are two individualizing principles at work: three periods of age—middle age, maturity, and old age; and five types of character—the self-tortured introspective, the proud self-reliant, the servile hypocritical, the cruel revengeful, and the resigned sorrowful. The possibilities for variation here—three ages, five types, sixty people—are enormous. But among the sixty there are certain blocks or units, suggesting once more the human tendency for any large body of men to divide into groups. Thus the Chorus of Senators, seven in number, are identical, each in double-sized masks of the servile, hypocritical type of old age.

These are the outer characters. The inner characters, Lazarus, Miriam, Caligula, Tiberius, Pompeia, are set off, except for Lazarus who is unmasked, by the fact that they wear half-masks on the upper part of their faces. Again these masks are not meant to depersonalize but to characterize and individualize in an extraordinarily telling and graphic manner. Lazarus alone is unmasked, which means that he is a complete, unified, and harmonious human being. Miriam's upper face is masked but there is no great discrepancy between her upper mask and lower face, which means that she is, though a lesser being than Lazarus, still a harmonious one. The three most interesting inner charac- ters are Caligula, Pompeia, and Tiberius, each of whose personalities, as their respective half-masks indicate, is radically split. Interesting conceptions as they are in them- selves in this play, these three characters are doubly inter- esting in a consideration of O'Neill's whole career in that they are the first clear and convincing—*The Great God Brown* is finally only confusing—indication of the "split- character" psychology that O'Neill was to employ, without masks, so effectively in *Long Day's Journey Into Night* and the other late plays.

Caligula, Tiberius, and Pompeia are half-masked, like Miriam, but unlike her there is in their physiognomies a great discrepancy between the upper mask, the face that they show to the world and the person that experience has made them into, and the lower face, the face they do not show to the world, the person they had once been before life took its toll, the person that they still are, vestigially; in short, the lower face is the "real" self from which experience has permanently separated them. In his description of the upper masks O'Neill's stage directions suggest with considerable power the terrible attritions that life, especially the life of power in a cynical and corrupt society, can wreak. Caligula *"wears a half-mask of crimson, dark with a purplish tinge, that covers the upper part of his face to below the nose. This mask accentuates his bulg- ing, prematurely wrinkled forehead, his hollow temples and his bulbous, sensual nose. His large troubled eyes, of a glazed greenish-blue, glare out with a shifty feverish sus- picion at everyone"* (II, 1). In Act III, Scene 2, Pompeia and Tiberius are introduced. Pompeia *"wears a half-mask on the upper part of her face, olive-colored with the red of blood smoldering through, with great, dark, cruel eyes —a dissipated mask of intense evil beauty, of lust and per- verted passion."* Tiberius is: *"An old man of seventy-six, tall, broad and corpulent but of great muscular strength still despite his age, his shiny white cranium rises like a polished shell above his half-masked face. This mask is a pallid purple blotched with darker color, as if the imperial blood in his veins had been sickened by age and debauch- ery. The eyes are protuberant, leering, cynical slits, the large nose, once finely modeled, now gross and thickened, the forehead lowering and grim."*

But underneath each of these monstrosities—and ultimately O'Neill was an optimist about the human race—is a human "soul," if in Caligula's case a rather troubled and ambiguous one. For Caligula's face is actually rather childish: "*spoiled, petulant, and self-obsessed, weak but domineering.*" Pompeia is, in reality, pale of complexion, with a "*gentle, girlish mouth . . . set in an expression of agonized self-loathing and weariness of spirit.*" In short, in the depths of her there is, in T. S. Eliot's phrase, "some infinitely gentle / Infinitely suffering thing." And beneath Tiberius' mask is another Tiberius: the thin, stern, self-contained mouth of an able soldier and a statesman of integrity, with a severe, forceful chin, and the healthy complexion of an old campaigner.[2]

Lazarus, then, is the catalyst that makes the "real" self come to the fore although only momentarily. For the theme or message of the play is "not yet," or "too soon." It is in the mood of the conclusion of Shaw's *St. Joan* when Joan, having returned from the dead and found herself most unwelcome, asks God how long it will be before the beautiful earth is ready to receive its saints: "How long, O Lord, how long?" Thus in Lazarus' actual presence, or, more precisely, at the sound of his laugh, Caligula can turn true believer, Tiberius can trust other men, and Pompeia can turn from lust to love, but these are only partial, fleeting revelations. And Pompeia must finally turn on Lazarus, Tiberius must torture him and burn him alive, and Caligula must perform the *coup de grace* on the dying Lazarus and kill Tiberius to gain the throne. Lazarus, nevertheless, is not without his victories and effects. The remorseful Pompeia immolates herself on the flames that are destroying Lazarus, and Caligula, alone at the end, is left wavering between Caesarism and Lazarus-ism, berating himself for having killed Lazarus and so proving there was death: "Fool! Madman! Forgive me, Lazarus! Men forget!" which are the last words of the play.

*Lazarus Laughed* has its shortcomings, the chief of these being the abstract and colorless language, especially of Lazarus, and the terrible necessity for the recurrent laughter by Lazarus and by others, though it is a matter of record that when the Pasadena players produced the play in 1928, the actor Irving Pickel, according to one observer, was able to play the role of Lazarus—including one four-minute bout of laughing—"superbly." [3] O'Neill himself is reported to have said he knew of no actor who could play the role of Lazarus.

On the printed page, however, it is a play of great interest and force. While O'Neill's first historical play, *The Fountain*, was superficial and conventionally romantic, this last is profound and biblical. It is quite obviously a very deeply felt play, so much so that it prefigures in some ways *Long Day's Journey Into Night* in which split personalities abound.

Act IV, Scene 1, of *Lazarus Laughed* takes place after midnight; on stage are three men, one old and two young, and one woman who is the paramour of the older man; all, except Lazarus, have been drinking. The older man (Tiberius) recounts how he has been trapped by his own past, especially by a parent, namely, his mother. When the older man is off stage one of the young men (Caligula) dances a grotesque, hopping dance and sings snatches from a bawdy song:

> A Roman eagle was my daddy
> My mother was a drunken drabby
> Oh march on to the wars!

The other young man (Lazarus) is given to rhapsodic and mystic utterances on Unity and the All. The woman (Pompeia), who had in the scene before been filled by loathing for what she has become, thinks to realize her true self once more through love of Lazarus. But, rebuffed, sexually anyway, by him, she too realizes that there is no escape from experience and by the end of the scene she has plunged back into her hated role of the cruel courtesan. By all this one is reminded, inescapably, of Act IV of *Long Day's Journey Into Night*: late of an alcoholic night, with James Tyrone telling how his father's desertion of his family had made him, irrevocably, what he is; Edmund Tyrone describing his mystic feeling of unity while aboard a sailing vessel; Jamie Tyrone staggering around the stage shouting scraps of poetry and bawdry; and Mary Tyrone plunging further into the recesses of her hated vice. It is not often that one's own family bulks so large as to provide the cast of characters for the rulers of the Roman Empire, but such was the case with the O'Neills. At this point in his life, however, he could only approach them obliquely, by way of Rome in A.D. 37.

Besides the fact that these first history plays by O'Neill

all deal with decisive moments in history and with great cultural contrasts and clashes, they tend to be alike also in two other respects, each respect embodying a different side of O'Neill's complex experience and imagination. On the one hand, each play is a great pageant, romantic-religious in *The Fountain* and *Marco Millions*, religious in *Lazarus Laughed*, with crowds, color, song and vivid stage effects, all of which constitute a reminder that, on one side of him, O'Neill was of the school of David Belasco, who had staged in grandiose fashion Salmi Morse's *The Passion* for James O'Neill in San Francisco in 1879 and who, many years later, took an option on Eugene O'Neill's *Marco Millions* although he never finally acted upon it.[4]

On the other hand, and despite their historicity, each of these plays is an allegory of, or a parable about, modernity. *Marco Millions* is, of course, explicitly a satire on modern America, but the tortuous straining after a meaning for human life that occurs in *The Fountain*, in the serious side of *Marco Millions* and in *Lazarus Laughed* is meant to apply to human life in general, modern as well as Renaissance and Ancient. In short, they are "message" plays and, as such, are a reminder that besides being a student of Belasco, O'Neill was also a student of *Thus Spake Zarathustra*, whose gnomic outpourings are one of the literary sources for those of Lazarus.

But in the next group of history plays, about the New England nineteenth century, pageantry, for obvious reasons, disappears, as do "messages." It is not that his New England characters are not given to statements about the "meaning of life," but the observations are those of the characters and do not necessarily represent the sentiments of the playwright himself, as they so palpably do in *The Fountain, Marco Millions*, and *Lazarus Laughed*. In brief, the closer O'Neill got to home, in time and space, the more genuinely dramatic became his plays, concerned not with "the meaning of life" but with dramatizing human nature at a certain time and in a certain place.

## II *Nineteenth-Century New England*

The second group of history plays, those about the New England nineteenth century, not only dispense with the pageantry and the "messages" of the first history plays but also make a different assumption about the nature of history. The assumption underlying *The Fountain, Marco Millions,* and *Lazarus Laughed* is that history is a circular process, the endless repetition of the same human experiences, problems, hopes, defeats, answers, dreams, all no different in A.D. 1920 America than in A.D. 37 Rome. Thus Lazarus speaks to all men at all times. In the New England plays history is not circular, but evolutionary, a cultural line declining (*Mourning Becomes Electra*) or a cultural line emerging (*A Touch of the Poet*). These plays catch this evolutionary process at a certain point in time and dramatize it in the context of that time, without attempting to make this unique and peculiar situation emblematic of the universal human condition. Naturally, there is a common residuum of irreducible humanity in all human situations at any place or any time, and what I am pointing out here are degrees of emphasis rather than absolute distinctions. In *The Fountain, Marco,* and *Lazarus* it is the universality of human nature that is being emphasized; in the New England plays what is stressed is the uniqueness and distinctiveness of human groups at a certain time and in a certain place.

For his knowledge of the background for this second group of history plays, O'Neill was dependent on books, as with the first group. But the second group take place in New England in a landscape and climate O'Neill knew and had lived on and in; further, the various kinds of people, attitudes, religions, outlooks, and ways of life that O'Neill was acquainted with in twentieth-century New England were the direct descendants of their various counterparts in nineteenth-century New England. So that while the imaginary events of *A Touch of the Poet* or *Mourning Becomes Electra* take place long before O'Neill was born, he still had an intuitive feeling for what these people were actually like. Like Scott writing in the nineteenth century about Scotland in the eighteenth century, O'Neill had to make only the slightest of imaginative efforts to project himself back into a not-too-remote past. It is true that three of these nineteenth-century plays, *The Rope, Gold,* and *Where the Cross Is Made* take place in California (*The Rope* is not specifically "placed" by O'Neill; since, however, the sun is setting in the sea, it must be the

Pacific), but the characters in these plays are unmistakably transplanted New Englanders, especially Isaiah Bartlett and his wife in *Gold* and *Where the Cross Is Made* and Abraham Bentley in *The Rope*.

If one considers all of O'Neill's land plays as a single entity, set off from the sea plays, they fall naturally into two contrasting groups: about half the land plays have as their setting the island of Manhattan; the rest occur in New England, whose various moral struggles O'Neill once said constituted his real cultural center. If the emphasis in the New York plays is on the moral laxity and corruption of the City, the emphasis in the New England plays is on the moral, social, religious, and cultural struggles between the conflicting forces of historical New England culture. In a rough and general way this split between New York and New England has some historical justification. In the nineteenth and early twentieth centuries, anyway, it was a generally accepted cultural truism that New York City was pagan while New England was Puritan. A. Oakey Hall, who was the Mayor of New York for Boss Tweed in the late 1860's, when Tammany corruption was at its height, once responded to a toast to "The City of New York" at a New York dinner for the New England Society with a long speech, whose chief point was: "And especially do we admire the taste you have displayed in quitting that part of the United States, where, as we Knickerbockers believe, New Englanders continue to persecute each other for opinion's sake. Here you enjoy extensive freedom—freedom in newspaper abuse; freedom to gamble in Wall Street; freedom in marriage; freedom in divorce; free lager; free fights; free voting; free love!" [5] New York then was free sin, while New England was moral conscience or, its converse, hypocrisy.

In O'Neill's New England plays nearly all the important New England moral preoccupations and struggles and activities appear. In the group concerned with the nineteenth century: the rise and incipient decline of the Protestant-Puritan aristocracy (*Mourning Becomes Electra* and *A Touch of the Poet*); whaling (the first part of *Diff'rent* and *Ile*); shipping and sailing (*Mourning Becomes Electra, Gold, Where the Cross Is Made*); sex and greed on the farm (*Desire Under the Elms*); identification of New Englander and Greek (*Mourning Becomes Electra*); rural degeneracy (*The Rope*); the conflict of Irish with Yankee, and Thoreauesque idealism (*A Touch of the Poet*). In the twentieth-century New England plays: suburban hypocrisies (*The First Man*); the ruin of the New England farm (*Beyond the Horizon*); Ivy-League academicism (the first part of *Strange Interlude*); Ivy-League athletics (the last part of *Strange Interlude*); post-World War I moral decay (the second part of *Diff'rent*); working-class life (*The Straw* and *Dynamo*); last-gasp fundamentalism (*Dynamo*); Irish-Catholic stresses and strains (*Long Day's Journey* and *A Moon for the Misbegotten*); and "nice" suburban middle-class Protestant life (*Ah, Wilderness!*).

*Ah, Wilderness!* excepted, the picture of New England is bleak, and O'Neill's New England plays are, by and large, in the vein of the second stanza of Edward Arlington Robinson's "New England":

> *Passion is here a soilure of the wits*
> *We're told, and Love a Cross for them to bear;*
> *Joy shivers in the corner where she knits*
> *And Conscience always has the rocking chair;*
> *Cheerful as when she tortured into fits*
> *The first cat that ever was killed by care.*

In short, with a dramatist's instinct, O'Neill saw New England as the place of struggle, contrast, and vivid background. Writing to William James in 1908, Henry Adams had made the criticism of the American scene that its literary creators could not "get your contrasts and backgrounds." [6] But America's greatest playwright was to find backgrounds vivid in contrast for his greatest plays in the Adams' ancestral home, New England, which, ironically enough, Adams himself called the home of contrasts.

Sounds from American history at large echo in these plays: Ephraim Cabot of *Desire Under the Elms* had once gone West and had fought Indians; the Jackson-John Quincy Adams presidential contest of 1828 is background for *A Touch of the Poet*; Ezra and Orin Mannon of *Mourning Becomes Electra* had fought in the Civil War, and in the Mannons' study are portraits of George Washington, Alexander Hamilton, and John Marshall. Still these are only echoes and the subject matter of these plays is New England in the nineteenth century.

What attracted O'Neill to New England were two
clashes: first, the inner conflicts of New England Puritanism, with its official code fighting a losing battle with its
animal instincts; second, the clash between the Anglo-
Protestants and the Irish-Catholics, in which he was involved in his own early life. He was fascinated also, like
Melville, with the powerful characters, physically and emotionally, that arose from these various matrixes. *Ile,
Diff'rent, Gold,* and *Where the Cross Is Made* all have
at their center the Ahab-figure, the powerful New England
sea captain with a drive, sometimes monomaniacal, to pursue or possess something. In *Ile* the parallel to *Moby Dick*
is almost precise. Captain Kearny, a great, strong hulk of a
man, commands a steam whaler, caught in the ice in the
year 1895. With his hold empty, his near mutinous crew
and his near insane wife begging him to return—they have
been out two years—the captain still refuses to start for
home. Like Ahab, he is driven not by greed but by pride,
for he has never put back to port empty-handed. He for-
cibly puts down a mutiny and almost gives in to his young
wife; but the ice breaks up, a school of whales is sighted,
and he drives forward after them, while his now insane
wife wildly plays an organ. Captain Isaiah Bartlett of *Gold*
and *Where the Cross Is Made* is similarly and monoma-
niacally possessed of the dream of retrieving a South Sea Island treasure horde, which in reality is a fake. In pursuit of
his illusory treasure he permits the murder of two men,
estranges himself from his wife, and almost drives his own
son crazy. Caleb Williams, the whaling captain, of *Dif-
f'rent* represents a different, and milder, kind of obduracy,
namely, lifelong fidelity to Emma Crosby, who broke their
engagement because she found out he had been seduced
by a brown-skinned maiden when the whaler had anchored
near a South Sea Island. Caleb nevertheless remains faithful, and hopeful, for thirty years. But when, in Act II,
thirty years after the breaking of the engagement, he sees
Emma, now transformed into a pathetic coquette and
proposing to marry his worthless nephew Benny, Caleb
kills himself (in what is a most improbable ending). And
O'Neill evidently thought that the character and fate of
Caleb were in the Melvillean tradition and said of him:
"he dies because it is not in him to compromise. He belongs to the old iron school of Nantucket–New Bedford

whalemen whose slogan was 'A dead whale or a stove boat.' The whale in this case is transformed suddenly into a malignant Moby Dick who has sounded to depths forever out of reach. Caleb's boat is stove, his quest is ended. He goes with his ship." [7]

But the resolute or monomaniacal ship captain of the New England nineteenth century is, in O'Neill's career as a whole, a minor concern. Much more important are life on the farm, *Desire Under the Elms;* Anglo-Protestant inner conflicts and incipient external decline, *Mourning Becomes Electra;* and Irish vs. Yankee, *A Touch of the Poet;* his three best and most comprehensive plays about nineteenth-century New England.

There is a link between the sea captain plays and *Desire Under the Elms* in the character of Ephraim Cabot who in sheer power, both physical and emotional, is the rural equivalent of Captain Kearney. *Desire Under the Elms,* despite the starkness of its outline and the simplicity of its plot, is a rather complex play. At first glance it seems to be simply in the tradition of late nineteenth- and early twentieth-century "exposure" literature, like Edith Wharton's *Ethan Frome,* Ed Howe's *The Story of a Country Town,* Edgar Lee Masters' *Spoon River Anthology,* or Harold Frederic's *Seth's Brother's Wife,* the anti-Wordsworthian genre which purported to tell the reader what *really* went on behind the trim, neat walls of the American farmhouse. And, in fact, *Desire Under the Elms* is one of the best in this genre, having the advantage over most of the other treatments in that it is more compressed and is outrageously funny in some parts and melodramatically powerful in others. On the other hand, it is also the story of the star-crossed lovers, Abbie and Eben, their affair, and the murder of their child, with a Dostoevskian conclusion, as they are marched away by the sheriff—a world well lost— to face together their punishment. Abbie and Eben are, nevertheless, rather simple as characters—despite the fact that Eben is supposed to be a blend of his mother and father—almost stock types: Abbie is *sex* and *greed* ennobled finally by love. Eben is *revolt against the father,* once more ennobled finally by love. Most things about them are literal and obvious. Thus on a hot Sunday afternoon Abbie begins her seduction: "(*She laughs a low humid laugh without taking her eyes from his. A pause—her body squirms de-*

*sirously—she murmurs langorously*)." There follows a
series of ejaculations on her part about the hotness of the
sun, "burnin' " into the earth; about Nature, "makin'
thin's grow—bigger 'n' bigger—burnin' inside ye"; and
how all this will make Eben "grow bigger—like a tree—
like them clumps." She finally tells him that "Nature'll"
beat him (Part II, Scene 1), and by the end of Scene 3
"(*Their lips meet in a fierce, bruising kiss*)."

But the play really belongs to Ephraim Cabot, a great
grotesque, a powerful buffoon in the tradition of the elder
Karamasov, an almost endearing old miser and lecher who
has an apt biblical quotation for every misdeed he performs. Historically, he is based on the small New England
farmer of whose almost absolute individualism and flinty
cantankerousness Cabot is the heightened and dramatized
embodiment. When he is first introduced, he resembles,
unmistakably, a Grant Wood portrait: tall, angular, with
weak eyes set close together. But the essence of his character is not dryness and narrowness; on the contrary, he is
complex and expansive. A note of pathos, still grotesque,
is introduced by his love of cows. He can talk to the cows,
he says, for they know the farm and him. In his fierce pos-
sessiveness he would like to burn down the farm, and everything on it, so that it would not pass on to anyone else, but
he would turn the cows free. When his suspicion that
something is wrong in his house grows to the point where
he can no longer sleep, he takes to sleeping in the barn
with the cows: "They'll give me peace." It is this aspect
of his character that comes out occasionally in a facial expression that has a *strange, incongruous dreamy quality*
(Part II, Scene 1). And he has a genuinely somber side
as well: "God's hard, not easy!" and life is "lonesome,"
as he keeps repeating.

But he has an ego of monumental proportions and is,
in fact, that very God he keeps referring to and calling
upon. For what he really represents is pure power, physically and emotionally. His great dramatic moment occurs
when he explodes in Scene 1 of Part III at the party celebrating the birth of "his" son and when the gaunt old
man of seventy-six outdrinks and outdances all the younger
men in the room. Here he takes on epic proportions and
joins the American folklore tradition of Paul Bunyan and
John Henry, the mythical and legendary strong men who

perform superhuman feats. In the midst of his wild dance, leaping, capering, prancing, kicking, which he steadily speeds up until the fiddler is exhausted, he bellows out the story of one of his legendary feats, namely, how when he was out West, he was attacked by Indians, shot in the backside by an arrow, and chased by the whole tribe, which he outran. He returned, and took his revenge—"Ten eyes for an eye, that was my motto"—and scalped the dead Indians. And he is, of course, as hard as nails, and at the end, all his sons gone, his wife a murderess, he goes off to round up the stock. Of all O'Neill characters Cabot is the one who comes closest to suggesting a great natural force and who is a complete stranger to guilt. He is the New England farmer raised to mythic proportions, and without him *Desire Under the Elms* would be only a well-contrived melodrama or another expression of "exposure" literature.

The two most comprehensive O'Neill plays about the New England nineteenth century are *Mourning Becomes Electra* and *A Touch of the Poet*. As history, they are complementary, and contrasting, accounts of similar historical events: the decay of the Anglo-Puritan aristocracy (treated in both plays); and the emergence of the Irish-Catholic underdogs (*A Touch of the Poet*).

In *Mourning Becomes Electra* the sinister, scarlet sunset is ubiquitous. The first scene of the first act of the first play, *Homecoming*, opens in the afterglow of a sunset, with the white porticos of the Mannon temple bathed in a "crimson" light. This is to be the chief "light" of the trilogy. This recurring crimson sky, always steadily deepening, in *Mourning Becomes Electra* signifies one thing: death. Underneath the play's Freudianism; its analogizing to Greek myth; its recurrent incest motif, generation after generation; its contrast between the uninhibited sexuality of the South Seas and the rigid prudery of New England and the accompanying contrast between the freedom, rhythm, brightness, and beauty of life at sea and the restrictions, mechanization, darkness, and dreariness of life on land; underneath all these devices and themes is the ubiquity of death. This is not only a question of the two murders (those of Ezra Mannon and Adam Brant) and the two suicides (Christine Mannon and Orin Mannon), but of the very fabric of the thought of the play, wherein

the characters are not only trapped by their own dead but
are also continually, tortuously meditating upon death. No
one ever reaches a conclusion; all they know, with any certainty, is that death is surely, inexorably devouring the
Mannons, their power, and their way of life. In Act III of
*Homecoming* the newly returned Ezra Mannon, home
from the war, cannot stop talking about death, despite his
wife's pleas that he cease: "That's always been the Mannons' way of thinking. They went to the white meeting-
house on Sabbaths and meditated on death. Life was a
dying. Being born was starting to die. Death was being
born." But the war, seeing too many white walls splattered
with blood "that counted no more than dirty water,"
made all this seem meaningless, "so much solemn fuss over
death!" Real death has taught him the meaninglessness of
imagined death, the Mannon obsession. But by dawn he
will be death's victim, murdered by his wife. Ironically, he
had earlier observed to his wife: "All victory ends in the
defeat of death." But he does not know if defeats "end in
the victory of death."

Death symbols and themes are woven into the play in
all kinds of ways. For example, the ancestral Mannons,
whose portraits glare down from the walls of the house,
were "witch-burners." Again, the black-white symbolism
that is endemic in O'Neill's plays, and in American literature generally, is pervasive in *Mourning Becomes Electra:*
the white faces set off by black clothing; the white porticos
of the house dimming into darkness; and so on. And as in
Melville, white does not signify purity; rather it means
the charnel house. The sound effects concur. The first song
heard is "John Brown's Body." The theme song of the
play, "Shenandoah," is meant to signify the more somber
aspects of the sea (*"a song that more than any other holds
in it the brooding rhythm of the sea"*). The drunken
chantyman of Act IV of *The Hunted* staggers off singing
"Hanging Johnny." Even American history plays a role
in generating this aura of the charnel house, for the seminal national events in the background of the play are the
Civil War, the greatest carnage experienced on American
soil, and the assassination of Lincoln, its greatest single
political tragedy. Moreover, beautiful, rhythmic ways of life
are dying too, with the clipper giving way to the steamer.
As the chantyman drunkenly and lugubriously laments to

Adam Brant, the owner of a beautiful clipper: "Aye, but it ain't fur long, steam is comin' in, the sea is full of smoky tea-kettles, the old days is dyin', and where'll you an' me be then? (*Lugubriously drunken again*) Everything is dyin'! Abe Lincoln is dead."

*Mourning Becomes Electra* is not only O'Neill's "death" play; it is also, and logically, his "war" play. The Civil War is, of course, the chief agent in the plot, for it is Ezra and Orin's absence in the war that allows the conditions for the tragedy to emerge.

O'Neill on several previous occasions had dealt with that other great contrast in which mankind seems to be permanently involved, war and peace. An early one-acter, *The Sniper*, is a not very skillful anti-war propaganda tract. And the naturally corrupt Benny of *Diff'rent* had been even further corrupted by reason of having been in the American Expeditionary Force in World War I (safely behind the lines). Nina of *Strange Interlude* had lost her Gordon in World War I. But it is in *Mourning Becomes Electra* that O'Neill treats of war most extensively and somberly. If peace, in O'Neill's world, is hell, war is worse. On battle itself O'Neill was of Tolstoi's school: individual engagements are a series of accidents whose only meaning is the irony of human affairs. Orin, who is the spokesman for the hatred of war, blunders in war and becomes, naturally and logically, a hero. In Act III of *The Hunted* he explains how it happened. He had been in the trenches at Petersburg, had not been able to sleep, and felt "queer" in the head. Like a good soldier, he thought that generals were stupid and he wished that the soldiers on both sides would suddenly throw down their weapons, shake hands, and laugh. So he did, in fact, begin to laugh and walk toward the Southern lines with his hand out. What he got for his pains was a wound in the head, which drove him temporarily mad. He ran on yelling, wanting to kill somebody. This excited a lot of "our fools" and they went crazy too, following Orin and capturing a part of the Southern line they had not dared tackle before. He had acted in all this without orders, but his father, the General, decided it would be better to overlook this and let his son be a hero. "So do you wonder I laugh!" But by and large war is not a joke, and the war itself is never over, "Not inside us who killed!" (*The Hunted*, III). Still, the Civil

War became the Mannons. In Orin's words, as he surveys the dead body of his unlamented father: "Who are you? Another corpse! You and I have seen fields and hillsides sown with them—and they meant nothing!—nothing but a dirty joke life plays on life! (*Then with a dry smile*) Death sits so naturally on you! Death becomes the Mannons!" (*ibid.*). Significantly, the only positive Mannon accomplishment in the war was negative. Grant had nicknamed Ezra Mannon "Old Stick," an abbreviation for "Stick-in-the-Mud," for while General Mannon was worth nothing on offence, he could hold ground forever, "until hell froze over!" (*ibid.*).

In a queer, complicated Mannon way the killing of others is in reality a form of self-destruction. Orin says in Act III of *The Hunted* that in the war he had the "queer" feeling that he was murdering the same man over and over again and that he would discover in the end that the man was really himself. After he kills Brant, his mother's lover, and notices Brant's Mannon countenance, a masklike look that always appears to be fighting life, he exclaims on the resemblance of Brant to his father and to that "man" that he had killed over and over again in the war. The man's face had a habit of changing into that of his father and finally of himself, and in killing Brant he thinks that maybe he has "committed suicide."

This is the real meaning of the trilogy considered as an historical document: the Puritan aristocracy willing its own destruction. And one does not in this world have to have been in the war to be obsessed with and dominated by death. The very mansion is infected by the taint of mortality. As Seth, the hired hand, says in the first scene of *The Haunted*: "There's been evil in that house since it was first built in hate—and it's kept growin' there ever since, as what's happened there has proved." There is in the trilogy the usual hint, in the imagination of a woman, that some kind of evil and implacable deity is behind it all. This notion—the Mary Tyrone speech—is given to Christine Mannon in Act I of *The Haunted* in a dialogue with Hazel, the "nice" young lady of the play. Christine too had once been innocent and loving and trusting, like Hazel, but "God won't leave us alone"; He tortures and wrings and twists human lives with "others' lives until—we poison each other to death!" But, as in most of O'Neill's tragedies, no exact balance is ever struck between fate and free will. And the men, on their part, think, simply, that a Mannon is a Mannon and this signifies death. Thus Orin sets out to write a history of the Mannon family in order to trace out to its secret hiding place the evil destiny that has dominated the Mannon family. He finds no answer and can only make the observation to Lavinia that he finds her the "most interesting criminal" of them all. And he concludes too that the Mannons are not special in any way but are only mankind writ large. He thus takes himself, prematurely aged, guilt-ridden, sitting in a dark room and writing about sin and death by a dim lamp, to be a symbol of man's fate—"a lamp burning out in a room of waiting shadows!" (*The Haunted*, II).

Furthermore, where death's dominion leaves off, there begin the tortures of guilt. In Orin's words: "The only love I can know now is the love of guilt for guilt which breeds more guilt—until you get so deep at the bottom of hell there is no lower you can sink and you rest there in peace!" (*ibid.*, III). Ironically, the last Mannon, Lavinia, is not given the blessed relief of death but is doomed, instead, to a continued existence of death-in-life: "I'm not asking God or anybody for forgiveness. I forgive myself! (*She leans back and closes her eyes again—bitterly*) I hope there is a hell for the good somewhere!" "Love isn't permitted to me. The dead are too strong!" "I'm the last Mannon. I've got to punish myself!" "It takes the Mannons to punish themselves for being born!" (*ibid.*, IV). These mortal sentiments of Lavinia bring the thought of the play back full circle to her father's original remarks on the Mannon preoccupation with death. She then withdraws into the mansion, which will be boarded up, with a "*strange cruel smile of gloating*" over the coming years of self-torture.

The pendant and companion piece to *Mourning Becomes Electra* is *A Touch of the Poet*, which is once more about the incipient decline of an aristocratic New England family. But it differs radically from *Mourning Becomes Electra* in two important respects: it shows the beginnings of the social climb of the Irish Catholics, and the over-all theme of the play is not death but its opposite, love. So while the dramatic movement of *Mourning Becomes Electra* is a narrowing and constricting, back to death and extinction, the total movement—despite Con Melody's tragedy—of the dramatic action of A *Touch of the Poet* is a broadening out and a leap forward, as Sara Melody makes the jump into an aristocratic New England family, from which union will follow, in effect, a new race, the Anglo-Irish, just as the end of *The Haunted* signifies the end of a Yankee genetic strain. This is not a question of personal happiness, and in *More Stately Mansions*, which shows Sara married, this particular Cinderella does not live happily ever after. Rather it is initial release of a pent-up race and culture. To underline the theme of Yankee decline, O'Neill chose as his historical background for A *Touch of the Poet* the 1828 presidential contest between Andrew Jackson and John Quincy Adams, by which a "common man" became President, and the Adams family, *the* New England aristocratic family, was ushered off the national scene, even though John Quincy Adams was to return to Washington as a congressman.

In most respects these two New England plays are diametric opposites. As *Mourning Becomes Electra* is about, among other things, female destructiveness, A *Touch of the Poet* is in part about female creativity, the somewhat Barryesque notion that romantic love is not only woman's creation but does not even depend on its supposed source and object, the beloved male. Men, so the play implies, are all for pursuing ideas or forms to some inhuman extreme and for knocking heads together and trying to kill one another in the name of their impossible pride, but women, like "God's glue," hold it all together, whatever the men may think is happening. In the last act of the play Sara makes the discovery, after her successful and satisfying seduction of Simon Harford, that her mother's undying love for her impossible husband, Con, is not folly, as she had thought, but wisdom: "Sure, I've always known you're the sweetest woman in the world, Mother, but I never suspected you were a wise woman too, until I knew tonight the truth of what you said this morning, that a woman can forgive whatever the man she loves could do and still love him, because it was through him she found the love in herself; that, in one way, he doesn't count at all, because it's love, your own love, you love in him, and to keep that your pride will do anything" (IV). Men would be shamed, in their boasting and vanity, if they but knew that women are not the slaves of men but the slaves of love itself. If a woman, Lavinia, is the worst criminal of all in *Mourning Becomes Electra*, a woman, Nora, is the best person in *A Touch of the Poet*. In Act I she is described as lovable, simple, sweet, charming, and dauntless, with a never-quenched spirit.

If the memories of the Civil War that play so important a role in *Mourning Becomes Electra* are to the effect that "war is hell," the war memories of the Napoleonic era that operate in the background of *A Touch of the Poet* imply that battle is a glorious thing: brilliant uniforms, cavalry charges, heroism, and glory.[8] Only his memories of his triumphs at the battle of Talavera, in Wellington's Peninsular Campaign, and his splendid officer's uniform, barely sustain the character of Con Melody throughout most of the play, whereas in *Mourning Becomes Electra* Orin Mannon's war memories are only another aspect of his obsession with, and descent to, death.

*A Touch of the Poet* was part of a planned cycle of plays on American history that O'Neill projected and, in some form, wrote. Only *A Touch of the Poet* and the "makings" of another, *More Stately Mansions*, recently edited and performed in Sweden and published in the United States, are extant. The rest O'Neill and his wife tore up, the last ones in a Boston hotel just before he died. His disease had rendered him physically helpless; further writing was out of the question. Fearful that someone else might try to finish the plays, O'Neill deliberately destroyed them with a ghastly ceremoniousness. According to Mrs. O'Neill: "He could only tear a few pages at a time, because of his tremor. . . . So I helped him. We tore up all the manuscripts together, bit by bit. It took hours. After a pile of torn pages had collected, I'd set a match to them. It was awful. It was like tearing up children" (Gelbs, p. 938). In a life that had contained much destruction, including some torn children, this was the last destructive act. According to Jordan Y. Miller,[9] the projected series, about an Anglo-Irish family that is begun by the union of Sara and Simon in *A Touch of the Poet*, would have covered American history from its founding, as the United States of America, to the twentieth century and was to be called "A Tale of Possessors Self-Possessed." Nothing is certain here, but the plan seems to have been as follows:  1]

(The) Greed of the Meek, 1776–93; 2] And Give Me (Us) Death, 1806–7; 3] A Touch of the Poet, 1828; 4] More Stately Mansions, 1837–42; 5] The Calms of Capricorn, 1857; 6] The Earth's the Limit, 1858–60; 7] Nothing Lost Save Honor, 1862–70; 8] (The) Man on Iron Horseback, 1876 93; 9] (The) Hair of the Dog, 1900–32. Facts about these projected plays are meager. In 1934 O'Neill was reported to be working on "The Life of Bessie Bowen (Brown, Bolen)," which was then incorporated into "Hair of the Dog"; and this was supposed to have been concerned with the American automobile industry. He also was reported to have been at work on a play called "The Last Conquest" or "The Thirteenth Apostle," which was to include the figures of Christ and Satan, which would have dramatized the greatest polarity of all.

As with all his history plays, O'Neill chose a seminal and crucial moment in history for his background for the cycle plays. In fact the cycle plays would have encompassed one of the most fateful moments of all in Western history, the era of the French Revolution and the industrial revolution, the founding and emergence to world power of the United States, the meteoric career of Napoleon, the Civil War in America, World War I, the Russian Revolution, and so on.

O'Neill, like his father, was very much under the spell of *The Count of Monte Cristo*, which in its first act had evoked, in a very positive fashion, the name and image of Napoleon, now defeated and exiled at Elba. It is for stopping at Elba and acting as a courier for a secret Napoleonic missive, of a revolutionary nature, that Edmund Dantes gets into trouble with the reactionary State and is subsequently imprisoned. Now as *Monte Cristo* was fake history attached to real history through the evocation of Napoleon, O'Neill's cycle was intended to be imaginary (although "real," psychologically, socially, and morally) history, but attached to actual history through the recreation of the American past. And Napoleon was to have played an important role too. One of the early plays in the cycle was to have taken place in both Rhode Island and Paris, with one scene occurring on the day of Napoleon's coronation (March 18, 1804).

Indeed, it would seem that Napoleon, as he was a tutelary figure in the early part of *Monte Cristo*, was also to be a tutelary figure in the early plays of O'Neill's cycle.

(One is reminded that Ella Quinlan, Mrs. O'Neill to be, first saw James O'Neill in a play about the French Revolution.) The Harford family are described in A *Touch of the Poet* as extravagant admirers of Bonaparte, in his role as the light-bringer and herald of freedom. The whole family, Mrs. Harford tells Sara, had accompanied her and her husband to Paris on their honeymoon: "to Paris to witness the Emperor's coronation." Con Melody had fought in the Napoleonic Wars; and of this Sara says to Mrs. Harford: "I've always admired him [Napoleon] too. It's one of the things I've held against my father, that he fought against him and not for him" (II). It is impossible to estimate the number of times Eugene O'Neill had witnessed, or played in, *The Count of Monte Cristo*, but that first-act invocation of the great Emperor with its resultant sense of attaching the imaginary event, the play, to a luminous historical figure and to tumultuous and stirring times (before war became "hell")—the Napoleonic era, certainly remained with him, to emerge and become explicit in his mightiest projected imaginative effort.

A *Touch of the Poet* pits two families, and through them, two cultures, against one another, and not in a simple conflict. It is much like the conflict or contrast between the Earnshaws and Lintons in *Wuthering Heights*. The Melodys, like the Earnshaws, have great vitality and good looks. Like the Earnshaws too, they have a crude side. The mother, Nora Melody, is a once beautiful Irish peasant; the father likewise is a handsome peasant but has had the background of a gentleman and officer; the daughter is a crossbreed:

> *Sara is twenty, an exceedingly pretty girl with a mass of black hair, fair skin with rosy cheeks, and beautiful deep-blue eyes. There is a curious blending in her of what are commonly considered aristocratic and peasant characteristics. She has a fine forehead. Her nose is thin and straight. She has small ears set close to her well-shaped head, and a slender neck. Her mouth, on the other hand, has a touch of coarseness and sensuality and her jaw is too heavy. Her figure is strong and graceful, with full, firm breasts and hips, and a slender waist. But she has large feet and broad, ugly hands with stubby fingers [I].*

Hers is the victory: by a peasant ruse—she seduces him, as had her father her mother—she is to marry Simon Harford, against the wishes of both of his parents. But, we may assume, she will play the role of the great lady with propriety, as her face forecasts. The defeat is Con's, who thinking, as an officer and a gentleman, he will have a duel with Simon's father, is, instead, treated as a drunken, Irish peasant (to which he reverts at the end of the play), and is beaten by Harford's servants.

The Harfords are an analogously complex blend, somewhat like the Lintons to the Melodys' Earnshaws. The father and son are never seen, but we may assume that the father is a materialistic businessman. The mother is an aristocrat, finely drawn, to the edge of decadence (only Con's full-blooded mare is so delicate):

> She is small, a little over five feet tall with a fragile, youthful figure. One would never suspect that she is the middle-aged mother of two grown sons. Her face is beautiful—that is, it is beautiful from the standpoint of the artist with an eye for bone structure and unusual characters It is small, with high cheekbones, wedge-shaped, narrowing from a broad forehead to a square chin, framed by thick, wavy, red-brown hair. The nose is delicate and thin, a trifle aquiline. The mouth, with full lips and even, white teeth, is too large for her face. . . . She has tiny, high-arched feet and thin, tapering hands. Her slender, fragile body is dressed in white with calculated simplicity [II].

The Harford son, like Sara, is a blend of his parents. From his retiring, ironic, book-reading mother, he receives his "touch of the poet," and his Thoreauesque side which leads him to live alone in the wilderness, in order to write a book about human freedom. But he has a "touch" of his father as well, a will of his own and some business ability. As the character of Simon would indicate, O'Neill's picture of the Harford family was not to be a simple one; in fact, compared to the Harfords the Mannons are simplicity itself.

In Act II of A Touch of the Poet Mrs. Harford gives Sara a rather extended account of the familial complexity. Simon, she tells Sara, is a great dreamer, a quality that he inherits from her although she adds that the Harfords are great dreamers too; even her own husband is, in "a conservative, material" way. Simon's great-grandfather, Jonathan, had been killed at Bunker Hill. His own particular

war had been for "pure freedom," as was the war of
Simon's grandfather, Evan, a fanatic in the cause of "pure
freedom." Evan had become scornful of the American Revolution and had gone to France and become a rabid
Jacobin, a worshipper of Robespierre. He escaped execu-
tion only by oversight and neglect. He then returned to the
United States to live in retirement, spending much time
in a little Temple of Liberty which he constructed in a
corner of what is now Mrs. Harford's garden. He frequently wore his uniform of the French Republican National Guard. Mrs. Hanford remembered him as a "dry,
gentle, cruel, indomitable, futile, old idealist." Mrs. Harford goes on to say that one can have no idea what "revengeful hate" the Harford pursuit of freedom imposed
upon "the women who shared their lives." All this time
the Harford wealth, through privateering, the Northwest
trade and the slave trade, was being built up as a triumphant climax to their overriding aim "to escape the
enslavement of freedom by enslaving it." Their women
were inevitably drawn into the familial ambitions, although
Deborah herself escaped. She says that "they," the Harford women, would have approved of Sara for her strength,
courage, and ambition, and would have welcomed her into
their "coils," smiling like "senile, hungry serpents." The
only bond in common that Deborah had with "them" was
an admiration of Napoleon whom they "idolized." Napoleon, they said, was the only man they would have
married, and Deborah herself says she used to dream she
was Josephine, "even after my marriage."

Thus with the union of Sara and Simon quite a few
complexities, powers, and qualities were to be inter-
mingled. One of the few things that O'Neill believed
in was the power of biological inheritance; and it is a great
loss to American literature and to dramatic literature that
we do not have the whole story of "A Tale of Possessors,
Self-Dispossessed." But it must all remain an American
"Kublai Khan," merely a splendid possibility.[10]

## III *Early Twentieth-Century America*

O'Neill's finest histories are autobiographies as
well, and take place in the "remembered" past, in the early

twentieth century: *Ah, Wilderness!, The Iceman Cometh, A Long Day's Journey Into Night, A Moon for the Misbegotten,* and *Hughie*. Even though O'Neill never completed his consciously planned cycle of plays on American history, he did nevertheless, albeit unconsciously, finally leave an "American" cycle if we look at the nineteenth- and twentieth-century American plays as an historical unit and sequence, despite the fact that only in *Long Day's Journey Into Night* and *A Moon for the Misbegotten* is there a carry-over of characters. The sequence would cover exactly one century, from *A Touch of the Poet* (1828) to *Hughie* (1928), from the era of Adams-Jackson to that of Hoover. The historical character of most of these plays is underlined by the fact that they seldom take place in a vacuum. The Adams-Jackson presidential contest is as integral to the background of *A Touch of the Poet* as the Great Depression is to *Hughie*. Even the apolitical and asocial *Long Day's Journey* and *A Moon for the Misbegotten* remind us, if ever so slightly, of the existence of, and the wealth of, the Standard Oil Company.

The twentieth-century plays in the historical category divide themselves into the directly autobiographical, *Long Day's Journey* and *A Moon for the Misbegotten*, about O'Neill and his family; the obliquely autobiographical, *Ah, Wilderness!*, based on a family the O'Neills knew in New London; *The Iceman Cometh*, dealing with characters O'Neill knew in his down-and-out days in New York; and *Hughie*. (I do not know, nor does any student of O'Neill as yet, so far as I know, the living sources for the characters and conceptions in the last. If such exist I suppose some day a scholar will identify them). If sorrow envelopes *Long Day's Journey* and *A Moon for the Misbegotten* and pathos is the note of *Hughie*, it is nostalgia that envelopes *Ah, Wilderness!* and, less obviously and less inconclusively, *The Iceman Cometh*. The various tragedies, and the themes, of *The Iceman Cometh* are so bleak that as the humor of the play is almost completely overlooked, so its nostalgic elements are set aside or unremarked. Yet *The Iceman Cometh* is, in part, a companion piece for *Ah, Wilderness!*, looking back from the middle of the twentieth century at pre-World War I America and seeing it through the indulgent, but not falsifying, haze of nostalgia. Nostalgia is the only kind of sentimentality that is honest and, in the later plays, this is the only sentimentality in which O'Neill indulged.

The nostalgic element in *The Iceman Cometh* is rather complicated by the fact that, though the time of the play is 1912, the characters are practically all living in the past, in most cases a long-ago past; so that the nostalgia is really about the late nineteenth century. Larry, for example, had left "The Movement" (anarchism) eleven years before, or in 1901, but he had been in it for thirty years, which means he joined it in 1871. Harry Hope had not been out of his saloon for twenty years, or since 1892. The song sung in Acts I and II, "She's the Sunshine of Paradise Alley" (the melody of which was taken from Mascagni's *Cavalleria Rusticana*), about which Cora exclaims, "I've forgotten dat has-been tune," was composed by Walter H. Ford and John W. Bratton and became popular in 1895.[11] The Boer War, which figures so prominently in the memories and motivations of Wetjoen and Lewis, took place in 1899–1902. Hickey's story of his life —the forty-five minute monologue that forms the climax of the play—has, in great part, nineteenth-century America for its backdrop since he is about fifty and therefore must have been born around 1862. In fact about the only way that the America of 1912 gets into the play is in references to the I.W.W. and to "de Bull Moosers" mentioned in Act I by Margie and Pearl, and the bombing in which Parritt's mother was involved. But the New York that Joe, Harry, and the other New Yorkers remember and dote upon is the good old days—"Dem old days!"—richly, unashamedly corrupt, automobile-less, peopled with such giants as Richard Croker, "Big Tim" Sullivan, John L. Sullivan, and Jim Corbett, whose framed photographs are seen over the mirror behind the bar in Act III, and with Harry's termagant wife, now deceased, transformed into a loving spouse. Even the fall of Oban's father, the King of the Bucket Shops, must go back five years or so to 1907. Bucket shops, which first came into existence after the Civil War, were sham stockbrokerages which really gambled in the stock market. Their first big heyday was from 1900 to 1907. A financial panic wiped them out in 1907, but they had their greatest, and final, resurgence from 1917 to 1929.

In other words, the days most of the New Yorkers are

talking about are those of the 1890's, one of the most flourishing periods of Tammany Hall [12] when Richard Croker, the most autocratic and ruthless of the Tammany bosses and the one who dominated the organization from 1886 to 1902, had corruption organized on a hitherto unparalleled scale. "Big Tim" Sullivan, also known as "The Big Feller," was the political boss of the Sixth District of Manhattan, the East Side below Fourteenth Street, but he was such a power in Tammany itself that he was one of the real leaders of the organization as a whole, so much so that no one could be the boss of Tammany without his consent and support. The conjunction of the two prize fighters, John L. Sullivan and Jim Corbett, with the two politicians, Croker and Sullivan, was not fortuitous, for both Croker and Sullivan were known for, and got their political start with, their prowess with their fists; in the "good old days" this was how an aspiring young politician first made his mark.

By 1912, when *The Iceman Cometh* takes place, Croker had long since retired from the scene, and in that year "Big Tim" Sullivan went insane and was confined. Sullivan, whatever his sins and they were many, up to and including the direction of organized crime, was one of the most colorful and likable of the old leaders and was, in fact, the last of the important "old-style" leaders, who kept a saloon, knew everybody personally, led parades, provided Thanksgiving and Christmas dinners for the poor, had a taste for public sentiment and melodrama, and so on.[13] The year 1912 also witnessed the notorious Blumenthal murder which publicly exposed New York police corruption and eventuated in the setting up of a commission, the Curran Committee of the Board of Aldermen, to investigate the police. At least one old-time New York "character," "Big Dick" Butler, thought that 1912 marked the real end of the "good old days." [14] Since 1902 the boss of Tammany had been Charles Murphy, sometimes known as "Sir Charles" or "Charles I," a closemouthed man who lived on a dignified estate on Long Island, complete with a nine-hole holf course. While in town he could be met, by those he really wanted to see, only by his summons to a luxurious suite on the second floor of Delmonico's restaurant. At the Hall he was seen by those who requested to see him. Since the décor of the establishment at Delmon-

ico's was red, it was known as "The Scarlet Room of
Mystery." With reference to Murphy's previous life as a
ward leader, Gustavus Meyers remarked: "Mr. Murphy's
habits as a leader at this time were in singular contrast
with those of years previously when, as a district leader,
he had made his hailing place a lamp post. He now used a
luxurious suite of rooms at Delmonico's fashionable restaurant" (p. 355). The mayors of New York at this time, the
first decade of the twentieth century, were by and large
respectable. The most important change in Tammany was
that some of the visitors to "The Scarlet Room of Mystery"
were powerful and respectable, nominally anyway, finan-
ciers and businessmen with whom Murphy carried on business within the law. In short, the façade of Tammany had
become respectable and many of its dealings had the odor
of sanctity, because, as M. R. Werner says, Murphy taught
Tammany that "more money could be made by a legal
contract than by petty blackmail" (p. 557). Not that
Tammany's connections with vice and corruption had disappeared by 1912; to the contrary they flourished, but in a
more discreet, less open, fashion. (Police corruption had
in fact actually been curtailed somewhat, in the large
sense.) Twice in *The Iceman Cometh* McGloin, who had
been thrown off the Police Force in "the good old days"
for being *too* greedy, speaks longingly of what is going
on in the "reformed" present: "Man alive, from what the
boys tell me, there's sugar galore these days" (II). And
Rocky must pay the police to protect his two tarts, Pearl
and Maggie. Still, as Larry says to Parritt in his characterization of McGloin in Act I, McGloin's day was "back
in the flush times of graft when everything went." Then
when the usual reform investigation came, McGloin was
caught red-handed and thrown off the Police Force. After
describing McGloin, Larry nods at Joe Mott and remarks
that Mott had "a yesterday in the same flush period. He
ran a colored gambling house."

Through Mott's reminiscences in Act I we have a concrete vignette of what the flush period was like, as he
describes how he was permitted to set up his gambling
house. He had saved his money and had gotten a letter
to "de Big Chief" from Harry, who at that time was a
minor Tammanyite and knew the Chief. "De Big Chief"
in the play is called "Big Bill," but in reality it must have

been "Big Tim" Sullivan, whose special province was control of gambling and gambling houses during the Croker
period.[15] Of the physical size of "de Chief" there can be
no doubt, for Joe Mott dwells on it: sitting down, "big
as a freight train"; standing up, "big as two freight trains";
and with a fist "like a ham." He roars at Joe to scare him
and then gives quiet permission to open, and, as Joe says,
"I run wide open for years." For the flush times were the
years of the magic "word": no laws, documents, or formal
agreements, just the personal say-so from the right person.
As McGloin puts it in Act III: "All I've got to do is see
the right ones and get them to pass the word. They will,
too. They know I was framed. And once they've passed
the word, it's as good as done, law or no law." Harry himself was once, in Larry's phrase, a "jitney Tammany politician" whom in 1892, the year of Bessie's death, "the
boys" were going to nominate for Alderman: "It was all
fixed" (I). Almost immediately though, and in characteristic *Iceman Cometh* fashion, it is suggested that "the
boys" were going to run him only because they knew they
were going to lose the ward anyway. Still, Harry had once
known the right people, as Joe Mott attests; and, as the
general stage directions say, he still possesses friends, sufficiently so for him to evade the technicalities of present-
day laws, such as the Raines Law.

The Raines Law itself is one other roadblock that stands
between Harry Hope's saloon and the good old days. The
implication generally, in the reminiscences of Harry, Joe
Mott, Mosher, McGloin, and some of the others, is that
in the 1890's Harry Hope's saloon was a relatively prosperous place; as Joe Mott says, "Dis was a first-class hangout
for sports in dem days" (I). Most aspiring Tammany politicians had gotten their start not only because of their
fistical prowess but by running a saloon, as had "Big Tim"
Sullivan; hence the talk of running Harry for alderman of
the ward, a small affair but a not at all impossible post
for the well-liked owner of a "first-class hangout for
sports." But in 1912 Harry Hope's saloon is decayed, seedy,
the tavern of the lost, and is described by O'Neill as having become a "Raines-Law hotel of the period."

The Raines Law,[16] so called after the prohibitionist
Senator Raines, who was its sponsor, was passed by the
New York Legislature in 1896. The intent of the law was

twofold: to increase the excise tax on the sale of liquor and to cut down the number of dealers in liquor in the state of New York. To effect these two changes the law declared that in the licensing of an establishment which dispensed liquor to be consumed on the premises, there should be no distinction between the types of establishments, as there had been hitherto. Under the Raines Law, hotels, restaurants, public houses (bars in today's parlance), and ordinary beer saloons were charged the same price, a high one, for their licenses. The distinctions that were made were statewide and were made on the basis of population, that is, the higher the population of the city or town wherein the establishment was located, the higher the price of the license. Therefore the real tax increase fell on the proprietors in New York City, and the smallest proprietors there carried the heaviest burden. When in 1903, for example, seven years after the Raines Law was enacted, the taxes were increased once more, four hundred small beer saloons were wiped out. But small proprietors in Harry Hope's class, who dealt in spirits, suffered grievously too. George Washington Plunkitt was especially incensed by the Raines Law because it discriminated against the small and poorer saloonkeeper, as contrasted to the hotelkeeper. Plunkitt claimed to have known personally of a half-dozen small saloonkeepers who, unable to pay the enormous license fee and faced with the loss of their business, committed suicide. He had heard of others: "Every time there is an increase of the fee, there is an increase in the suicide record of the city" (Riordon, pp. 113–14). Whether this assertion is true cannot be proved, but certainly the enactment of the Raines Law in 1896, and its further implementation in 1903, must have seriously contributed to the decay of Harry Hope's saloon.

The Raines Law had two side effects that were not anticipated in the original legislation and that play some role in *The Iceman Cometh*. There was written into the statute a Blue Law aimed expressly at the saloons, to the effect that only hotels could serve liquor after hours and on Sundays, the times at which the saloons did some of their best business. Accordingly, every saloon that could manage to do so immediately turned itself into a "hotel restaurant," by renting rooms upstairs and by putting on the tables, in O'Neill's words, "a property sandwich . . . an old desiccated ruin of dust-laden bread and mumified ham or cheese." The most profitable thing to do with the rooms usually was to rent them out for sexual intercourse, the result being that many of the saloons became, in effect, brothels (Werner, p. 405). Now Harry Hope is still holding up his head in two respects: first, he still has enough connections at the Hall to dispense with putting out the property food on the tables (*"except during the fleeting alarms of reform agitation"*), and, second, although he has tarts rooming at his establishment, they do not carry on their trade there. As Harry says in Act I, "Never thought I'd see the day when Harry Hope's would have tarts rooming in it. What'd Bessie think? But I don't let 'em use my rooms for business." Still, he and his kind have fallen on evil times, and most of the New York characters in the play, while they lament and glorify their individual mistakes and past, are also paying a collective obsequy to the "good old days," the 1890's, when giants walked the earth, when corruption was direct, open, and simple, when "de Chief," whoever he was, was tangible and approachable, and when they were respectable "middle-class" (neither powers nor riffraff) members of the Tammany organization. The circus, and its ways, have provided the same frame of memory for Mosher.

This collective nostalgia blends into the private nostalgia of each character, New Yorker or not. It is, I think, an oversimplification to say that all these characters are special cases of preoccupation with the past because they are failures and down-and-outers; rather they represent, each in his own way, the real vagaries of the human memory, which must both simplify and glorify, if ever so slightly in a more happy and healthy climate than that of *The Iceman Cometh*, the past. It is not that all men have been fired from their jobs as drunks and thieves, as have some of the characters in *The Iceman*, but all men have done things they would like to forget and they all have at least some happy memories, which they would like to be even happier, and simpler, and to have bulked larger, in time and importance, than they actually had done in reality. It is by use of an artistically, artificially shaped past that man defends himself against the threatening present and the ominous future. A man is only genuinely lost when the past contains something mortal and deadly, like

Hickey's murder of his wife and Parritt's betrayal of his mother. Almost anything else memory can take care of.

Music is, of course, the great evocator of memory, and especially in middle-class and lower-class America is popular music expressive of certain sentimental certainties that the memory would like to believe in and re-embrace, hastening back over the years to simpler and happier times and occasions. This is why popular songs plays a role in *The Iceman Cometh* and even more of a role in *Ah, Wilderness!*

Popular songs gravitate between the bawdy and the sentimental; thus the two songs sung in *The Iceman Cometh* are Oban's "Sailor Lad" ditty (bawdy) and "She's the Sunshine of Paradise Alley" (sentimental). The choruses of songs dealt out to the various characters at the end, with Hickey gone, the "booze" working again, the present and future banished, were carefully chosen to perform two nostalgic functions: first, to awaken memories in the minds of the older people in the audience of the 1940's who saw the play performed for the first time and who, like the playwright, had memories of pre-World War I America, and, second, to invoke nostalgia in the minds of the characters in the play, whose memories extend back into the nineteenth century.

Although O'Neill chose his songs with extreme care for their historical date, he did commit one anachronism, a perfectly understandable one. This occurs in the musical medley at the end when Chuck is given "The Curse of an Aching Heart." Actually this song, by Henry Fink and Al Piantadesti, was not published until 1913 and could thus not have been known by people in 1912. However, the song itself was a purposeful anachronism and is made up of, in Sigmund Spaeth's phrase, "the maudlin absurdities" of the 1890's. Thus for the characters in the play it does invoke nostalgia. All the other songs sung at the end fall into one of two basic categories: either they are songs that were popular around 1912, or they are songs from the past.

"A Wee Dock and Doris," Jimmy Tomorrow's song, was published by Harry Lauder and Gerald Grafton in 1911; "Everybody's Doing It," appropriately given to Pearl and Margie, was published by Irving Berlin in 1911; "The Oceana Roll," Cora's, was done by Roger Lewis and Lucien

Denni in 1911; and Rocky's "You Beautiful Doll" was perpetrated in 1911 by A. Seymour Brown and Nat Ayer. These songs, presumably, would be remembered by many of O'Neill's audience. All the other songs, however, like "She's the Sunshine of Paradise Alley," are nostalgia-invokers for the members of the cast. Wetjoen's "Waiting at the Church" (also sung in *Ah, Wilderness!*) by Fred Leigh and Henry E. Pether, was vintage 1906; Joe Mott's "All I Got Was Sympathy" (actually the song was entitled "Sympathy"; O'Neill is using the first line of the lyrics) was put together by Kendis and Pauley in 1905; "Tammany," sung, appropriately, by McGloin, was an affectionate but lively satire on Tammany politics concocted by Gus Edwards and Vincent P. Bryan in 1905.

"Tammany" in particular, and the circumstances under which it was written illustrate most concretely what Harry Hope, Joe Mott, McGloin, and the rest mean by New York's "good old days," the time when they were part of a political corruption which was not only open, and cheerfully so, but had such a sense of humor about itself as to make it almost endearing. According to a tradition run down by Sigmund Spaeth, "Tammany" was composed under the following circumstances (whether this story is true or not, it should be): Edwards and Bryan were invited to entertain the members of New York's Democratic Club at a smoker. They had planned to introduce their new song, "In My Merry Oldsmobile," the best of many of the transportation songs of the day. But when they arrived at the smoker, the orchestra was playing a medley of the Indian songs that were so popular at the time, and so they decided, on the spot, to compose a burlesque of this type of music which would also be a poltitical satire on Tammany, whose name was Indian in origin. The two retired to a room and worked out the chorus and two verses, with Edwards putting down the notes as fast as Bryan could write the words. In the lyrics there are references to *Hiawatha* and *Navaho*, all building up to "Big Chief Tammany." They tried out this song first on a small group of important Tammanyites, including Charlie Murphy and "Big Tim" Sullivan. With their approval, Edwards and Bryan then presented it to the whole group. It was a great and immediate success and later became the official anthem of the Tammany Society (Spaeth, pp. 347–48).

After these songs, however, we are back in the nineteenth century: Ed Mosher's "Break the News to Mother," by Charles K. Harris, was a Spanish-American War song, vintage 1897; Harry Hope's "She's the Sunshine of Paradise Alley (1895); Oban's "Sailor Lad" ditty (the sea) is an immemorial folk song, as is Captain Lewis' "The Old Kent Road" (the land); and, of course, with Hugo's "Carmagnole" we are back to the French Revolution. As Hickey and Parritt go to their deaths, all of the other happy sinners, Larry excepted, are sinking gratefully back into nostalgia, alcoholic and tuneful.

*Hughie*,[17] through Erie's memories, likewise takes place in a corrupt, but somehow glorious, New York. Erie, speaking his monologue in 1928, has been coming to the seedy West Side hotel, on and off, for fifteen years, or, since 1913; thus his reminiscences span an era when Broadway was peopled by "frails" from the Follies, Scandals, and Frolics and by such legendary "big shots" and gamblers as Arnold Rothstein, who is invoked at the end of the play.[18] Historically considered, *The Iceman Cometh* and *Hughie* are companion pieces: as "Big Tim" Sullivan is a tutelary presence in the beginning of *The Iceman Cometh*, Arnold Rothstein is an unseen but Olympian presence at the end of *Hughie*; as Sullivan went insane in 1912, the fictional date of *The Iceman Cometh*, so Arnold Rothstein was shot and killed in November 1928, the fictional date of *Hughie*, which takes place sometime in the preceding summer of that same year. Indeed the connection in the two plays are surprisingly close, despite the disparities in their fictional dates. "Big Tim" Sullivan was not only the imaginary benefactor of the imaginary Joe Mott and Harry Hope but was also the real benefactor of the real Arnold Rothstein. Rothtsein at the age of sixteen, in 1898, got his first glimpse into the amenities of power, money, and corruption by hanging around the headquarters of Sullivan, who considered him a very promising young man, besides being very useful in dealing with the Jewish constituency. This *Iceman Cometh-Hughie* world was tied into O'Neill's New York memories in other ways. For example, when Arnold Rothstein was getting his start with Sullivan he was also having his first experience with gambling in the prop room of Hammerstein's Theatre. Among the patrons of the game were the Hudson Dusters, a gang of toughs, whom O'Neill himself was to know later in his

Greenwich Village days. The backgrounds of the two plays correspond in other ways not indicated by O'Neill. For example, Arnold Rothstein was deeply implicated in the second wave of "bucket shop" operations (1917–29) whose first wave (1900–1907) gave birth, and finally ruin, to the empire of Willie Oban's father. Rothstein, who had connections with anything and everything in the vast New York underworld—he "popped up everywhere," "an underworld bus boy," said one investigator—was also deeply involved with Tammany, often acted as the middleman for Charles Murphy and was, evidently, one of the welcome in "The Scarlet Room of Mystery."

Historically considered, *The Iceman Cometh* and *Hughie* are separated only by time: *Hughie* in 1928 looking back on the era from the first World War to the 1920's, *The Iceman Cometh* in 1912 looking back on the 1890's and the early years of the twentieth century; and by space: *The Iceman* is the Bowery; *Hughie* is Broadway. Both deal with essentially the same world, which fascinated O'Neill and which as the son of a famous actor he would have had some acquaintance with and some access to, a world composed of New York eminences from various activities, sometimes only analogous, sometimes intimately interrelated: the stage, sports, journalism, politics, shady finance, gambling, and gangsterdom. At one end of the spectrum, the stage, sports, journalism, and politics, this world was reasonably respectable (if less so in politics), although, collectively, these pursuits had not the impeccability of inherited wealth, business proper, high finance, banking, and the professions; but at the other end of the scale were gangsters and hoodlums. *The Iceman Cometh* is an underdog look at this world from the political side (Tammany); while *Hughie* is an underdog look at it from the gambling side (Arnold Rothstein). Erie Smith and the habitués of Harry Hope's are blood brothers: the little men who once had a glimpse of glory and who ever since use that memory to warm themselves.

But pathos is the real note of *Hughie*, for Erie had never had any real status in the world of Broadway, as had Harry Hope, Joe Mott, and McGloin in the old Bowery. He imagines, for himself, for Hughie, and for Charles Hughes, a glory that never was. Furthermore, this world itself is a colder, crueler world than that of old-time Tammany corruption. This New York was inhabited by real gangsters like Legs Diamond, who was first employed by Arnold Rothstein ("Hughie wanted to think me and Legs Diamond was old pals"), and at its top is not the ebullient Big Tim Sullivan doing a political favor but the cold Arnold Rothstein, who "wouldn't loan a guy like me a nickel to save my grandmother from streetwalking"; "Sure I know the bastard. Who don't on Broadway? And he knows me—when he wants to. He uses me to run errands when there ain't no one else handy." As in all other O'Neill worlds, so with New York: the more modern it is, the colder, the more mechanical, and the more ruthlessly efficient; the more old-fashioned it is, the warmer, the more illogical, the more personal. The only genuinely beautiful thing in Erie's world are the horses, the bangtails: "I tell you, Pal, I'd rather sleep in the same stall with old Man o' War than make the whole damn Follies." Heroism and romance finally exist only in the imagination of the Night Clerk, whose dream of paradise would be to face poker-faced Arnold Rothstein over a pile of chips, won by himself on a royal flush over Rothstein's four aces and say, "Okay, Arnold, I'm a good sport, I'll give you a break. I'll cut you double or nothing. Just one cut. I want quick action for my dough." And then he would cut the ace of spades and win again. Yet his longings are real enough: gambling, gangsters, blondes, crap games with thousands of dollars on the table, "big deals," "action"— this Broadway, like the old Bowery, was colorful and exciting in its harsher, more glittering way. Of all this Erie had once caught a glimpse, but the Night Clerk must live it only vicariously, getting a slight interest on the small capital of Erie.

If *The Iceman Cometh* is, in part, New York nostalgia for the old Bowery and *Hughie* a pathetic longing for the bright lights of Broadway, *Ah, Wilderness!* is middle-class New England refracted through an unqualifiedly benign haze. *Ah, Wilderness!* is soaked in a nostalgia to a degree that even the most acute observer might not appreciate without some historical context. As in *The Iceman Cometh*, the several songs that are sung in the play were chosen with great care for the date at which they were published and first became popular. The play takes place in the year 1906 and, historically, the songs "Waltz Me Around Again

Willie" (Will Cobb and Ren Shields), "Waiting at the Church," and "Poor John" (both by Fred Leigh and Henry E. Prether) were all first published and played in 1906. The rest of the songs in the play, as in *The Iceman Cometh*, reach further back and are thus evokers of nostalgia even in the year 1906. One of the reasons that Belle, the prostitute of Act III, Scene 1, says that the large small-town in Connecticut where the play takes place is a "burg" is because "Bedelia," the song ground out by the player piano in this scene, is popular there when, in fact, "Bedelia" (William Jerome and Jean Schwartz) is of 1903 vintage. As Belle says, "Say, George, is 'Bedelia' the latest to hit this hick burg? Well, it's only a couple of years old! You'll catch up in time!" "Bedelia" then is the "Sunshine of Paradise Alley" of *Ah, Wilderness!* "Bedelia" was highlighted by O'Neill for two other reasons. First it employed actual Irish folk material, both in verse and music, and is thus, along with Norah, the serving girl, the only conscious or visible "Irishism" in what is otherwise a completely Yankee play. The second reason was that "Bedelia," like so many saccharine popular songs, easily lent itself to *double-entendre* and bawdy reversals. Belle tells Richard of one such version of "Bedelia" which has a line, "Bedelia, I'd like to feel yer." [19]

"Dearie" (III, 2), by Clare Kummer, is only a little dated—1905—but the other songs in the play reach back further in time. In Act I there is a brief (and bad) punning reference by Uncle Sid to "Mighty Lak a Rose," which was composed by Ethelbert Nevins in 1901. Sid's short version goes:

> *"Dunno what ter call 'em*
> *But he's mighty like a Rose——velt."*

"In the Sweet Bye and Bye," sung alcoholically by Sid in Act II, is a venerable Salvation Army hymn which takes us back in memory into the nineteenth century. "Then You'll Remember Me" (Act III, 2) is from *The Bohemian Girl*, by William Balfe and Alfred Bunn, which was first produced in England in 1843. What is suggested by all this is a solid, Victorian, family-based culture, all grouped around the piano and singing a song either sentimental or—and this is often overlooked—funny. "Waiting at the Church," for instance, is not sentiment but British music-hall humor. The male protagonist in this song cannot get to the church because "My wife won't let me." When Arthur and Mildred sing it in Act III, Scene 2, Sid exclaims, "You ought to hear Vesta Victoria sing that! Gosh she's great! I heard her at Hammerstein's Victoria." Vesta Victoria (1873?–1951) was, in fact, a famous English comedienne of the day, and "Waiting at the Church" was written expressly for her. These songs then are meant to carry the Millers, and the audience, back into a past that is marked by its simple sentiment and simple humor.

Another important atmospheric device in the play is created by having it take place on July 4. Independence Day—although only a shade of the fervor and activities that used to go into it still remain—is the greatest secular holiday in America and is observed in all the states and territories. Since it signified the break of the United States with England, and the triumph over England in the Revolutionary War, it had a double claim upon an Irish-American whose middle name was "Gladstone." Thus for his play about his love affair with pre-1917 American culture, O'Neill chose its greatest and most significant "day."

In the present writer's childhood July 4th ranked almost with Christmas in importance, which, in its turn, was of much greater significance, and less commercialized, than it is now. "The Fourth," as it was known, was always—so it seemed—an excessively hot day. (Thus in Act I of *Ah, Wilderness!* Mrs. Miller exclaims, "Phew, I'm hot, aren't you? This is going to be a scorcher.") In the morning there was a parade down the Main Street and patriotic speeches in front of the City Hall, followed by Gargantuan meals, either at home or on a picnic. Watermelon and corn on the cob (neither of which are even mentioned in *Ah, Wilderness!* in which, since it takes place in a city on Long Island Sound, they have a sea-food dinner) were the special delicacies. For devotees of Bacchus, as is Sid in *Ah, Wilderness!*, the Fourth was an annual Saturday-night that could go on all day long.[20] For the young people it was a day and evening to "date." For the very young it was firecrackers from early morning (the rhythm of repetition in Act I of the play is Tommy's firecrackers) until noon; at night it was fireworks. In short, the day was conceived of in the terms first suggested for it by John Adams in his famous letter to Abigail: "I am apt to believe that this day will be celebrated by succeeding generations as the great anniversary festival. It ought to be commemorated as the day of deliverance, by solemn acts of devotion to God Almighty. It ought to be solemnized with pomp and parade, with shows, games, sports, guns, bells, bonfires and illuminations, from one end of the continent to the other, from this time forward forevermore." In O'Neill's early days in New London, further back than mine, July 4th was an even more protracted holiday, and the display of fireworks began on midnight July 3 and continued to the night of July 4.

The spirit of "the Fourth," then, animates most of the characters in the play—Aunt Lyly perhaps excepted—all of whom think that this is no ordinary day, or even an ordinary holiday. Richard's family are not even more angry with him for his nocturnal adventure with Belle and drink because it all happened on the Fourth. In Act II, Nat Miller declares, "Fourth of July is like Christmas—comes but once a year." In Act III, Scene 2, while the Millers are anxiously awaiting the return of their wayward son, Miller again says that their son's return is not "so late—when you remember it's Fourth of July." At which his wife explodes: "If you don't stop talking Fourth of July—! To hear you go on, you'd think that was an excuse for anything from murder to picking pockets!"

There are, to be sure, touches of the O'Neillian gloom in the play, and some of O'Neill's favorite somber themes are touched on. The "afraid of life" speech of Dion Anthony of *The Great God Brown* is given by Richard in his description of Mildred who, he says, is afraid of "everything," love, life, "her Old Man," people, and so on. The sad figure is Aunt Lyly, the sweet and gentle spinster who will never allow herself to marry the irresponsible Sid; and to her is given, indirectly, the Mary Tyrone speech about the inexorability of the consequences that flow from past actions. Thus in a discussion of Fitzgerald's *Rubaiyat*, she unerringly gravitates to:

> "The Moving Finger writes, and having writ,
> Moves on: nor all your Piety nor Wit
> Shall lure it back to cancel half a Line
> Nor all your tears wash out a Word of it."

Likewise, Sid's habits and hyberbolical jokes are undoubtedly based on Jamie O'Neill's habits and japes, but the cynicism, malice, and bottomless nihilism of the real Jamie have been expunged entirely.

But the idyllic quality is not only generated by July 4, it is also generated by 1906, or the early twentieth century in America. Historically, if one belonged to the right class and lived in the right place, this era in American history was in many respects a national idyl. Like the middle-class Englishman of the mid-nineteenth century, with Napoleon fifty years behind him and Kaiser Wilhelm fifty years ahead of him, the Northern American middle-class man could honestly think that war was a thing of the past. For this hypothetical Northerner the Civil War had long since been concluded, victoriously from the Northern point of view, and the Spanish-American War was only an interlude with comic opera overtones. Involvement in a general European war was virtually unthinkable, as was a Russian or Chinese revolution or the idea that such revolutions, if they did occur, could have any conceivable effect upon the United States. Only eight years away from the year 1906 lay the outbreak of World War I and the beginning of America's finally total and agonizing involvement with the rest of the world. But in 1906 and on July 4, Europe was the severed past, three thousand miles away. Internally, things were equally placid, and there was no economic depression. Accordingly, in good (old) American fashion, public life, or politics, is a kind of joke, as with the above-mentioned amalgam of Theodore Roosevelt and "Mighty Lak a Rose." Nat Miller remarks, after a radical outburst on the part of his son, "I've always found I've had to listen to at least one stump speech every Fourth." Nevertheless, Richard's speech—"I'll celebrate the day the people bring out the guillotine again and I see Pierpont Morgan being driven by in a tumbril"—is a reminder that this same period saw a great deal of social ferment, for this was the era of the Progressivists, one of the great reform movements in American history.

Besides this social and political vigor there was a great deal of cultural and intellectual ferment as well, for these were also the years when late nineteenth-century European culture was having its first real impact upon American culture which, on its part, was about to emerge into a second literary flowering, beginning with the renaissance of 1912 in poetry and the Armory Show in 1913. Something of the intellectual excitement of those days is suggested by Richard's other consuming passion, literature: "The days grow hot, O Babylon! / 'Tis cool beneath thy willow trees!" (Carlyle's *French Revolution*); Oscar Wilde's *Picture of Dorian Gray* and *The Ballad of Reading Gaol*; Shaw's plays and *The Quintessence of Ibsenism*; Ibsen, the "greatest" playwright since Shakespeare; Swinburne's *Poems and Ballads*; Fitzgerald's *Rubaiyat*. But American literature itself was in the doldrums, still in the fag end of the nineteenth century (Percy MacKay's *The Scarecrow* was first performed in 1906). The only intellectual excitement in *Ah, Wilderness!* is in the imagination and the growing pains of an adolescent, who will, presumably, get over it all and go on to Yale, like his brother, Arthur. For everything finally is solidly encased in a thick, warm, bourgeois domesticity, and Richard always remains a "nice" boy. The whole outlook is epitomized by Nat Miller's closing words: "Well, Spring isn't everything, is it Essie? There's a lot to be said for Autumn. That's got beauty, too. And Winter—if you're together."

A final and also important manner in which *Ah, Wilderness!* looks back in the direction of another era was the way in which O'Neill wove into it many of the stock situations of nineteenth-century vaudeville comedy. George M. Cohan, who knew whereof he spoke and who played the first Nat Miller, was not much impressed by the play, because, he said, it was full of old vaudeville jokes that had been done over and over again.[21] Whether one agrees with Cohan that an old joke is not a good joke, it is true that *Ah, Wilderness!* runs on time-honored rails. The sustaining joke is, of course, Richard's growing pains. Adolescence, while painful to the young person undergoing it, is, or used to be in "the good old days," inexpressibly funny to the observing adult. Thus Richard on the beach at night, waiting for the fifteen-year-old Mildred and declaiming:

> "Nay, let us walk from fire unto fire
> From passionate pain to deadlier delight—
> I am too young to live without desire,
> Too young art thou to waste this summernight—"

Or when his mother rebukes him for sending the Swinburne poems to Mildred, Richard quotes from *Candida* in a "hollow" voice, "Out then into the night with me!"

and stalks out of the house, slamming the door behind him. Or he is given a mispronunciation, as, for example, he pronounces "Reading Gaol" as it is in the word, "goal post." The cast of characters is standard: Sid, the drunken clown, Norah, the good-natured but stupid serving girl, Arthur, the stuffed-shirt, Essie, the bustling, good-natured mother, these are all familiar types, despite the fact that the Miller family was based on the real McGinley family that the O'Neills knew in the New London days. "My purpose," O'Neill said, in a much-quoted statement, "was to write a play true to the spirit of the American large small-town at the turn of the century. Its quality depended on atmosphere, sentiment, an exact evocation of the mood of a dead past. To me, the America which was (and is) the real America found its unique expression in such middle-class families as the Millers, among whom so many of my own generation passed from adolescence into manhood."

The two other plays of early twentieth-century America, A *Long Day's Journey Into Night* and A *Moon for the Misbegotten*, are also memory plays in the most literal sense although social background does not count for so much in these plays as it does in *Hughie, The Iceman Cometh,* and *Ah, Wilderness! Long Day's Journey* was O'Neill's "confession, absolution, and penance" for his family, his sins against them and theirs against him; A *Moon* performs this same function for the most disastrous of that disaster-ridden family, his brother Jamie. I wish to reserve more general discussion of these plays for later parts of the book and will confine myself here to a few remarks about their genesis.

Three great, and productive, cultural agonies of the twentieth century have been those of O'Neill in his late plays (he is reported to have often wept when composing *Long Day*), of Joyce, and of Proust, and in each case a good deal of the agony, and the resultant power, arose from the fact that their works were based on their own memories and that they were always wrestling with these memories, or their respective pasts, and hence themselves; it was like self-directed psychoanalysis which, as Freud said, is the most difficult art of all. Proust was much the most self-conscious about this, as contrasted to Joyce or O'Neill, but since his explicit theory about art was that it *was* memory, his remarks on the process have considerable validity for the case of O'Neill who, unconsciously, was doing what Proust was doing in a more conscious fashion.

Both O'Neill and Proust came from, each in his own way, very strong families from which neither escaped, nor, for that matter, wished to escape. Each man was deeply attached to his mother, and each had experienced a serious illness which turned him even more introspective than he was by nature and had a determining influence on his desire to be a writer. Proust began, in *Remembrance of Things Past*, by writing about his family and then proceeded to write *away* from them. O'Neill began by writing about other matters and peoples, though his family often entered in in disguised fashion, sometimes disguised to himself, but finally, consciously and explicitly, he wrote his way *back* to family. O'Neill approached his family obliquely, beginning with an idyllic inversion of it in *Ah, Wilderness!* and getting closer and more serious with his own "bottom-dog" experiences in New York in 1912 in *The Iceman Cometh*. Then he could finally bring himself to do the family as a whole in *Long Day's Journey* and then—perhaps the most difficult of all—his brother Jamie in *A Moon for the Misbegotten*. For both men, in their greatest work, art was memory. Thus Proust's statements on the psychology of the process, especially in the conclusions about the nature of art which the narrator finally arrives at in *The Past Recaptured*, after which he will presumably start writing the novel *Remembrance of Things Past*, that we have just read, are not only definitive for the nature of his own art but very suggestive for O'Neill's.

In *Guermantes Way* (the Scott-Moncrieff translation) Proust had remarked, in a vein familiar to all students of O'Neill, "The past not merely is not fugitive, it remains present" ("The Wit of the Guermantes"). And thus the whole enormous edifice of *Remembrance of Things Past* was spun out of its author's memory or his past. Furthermore, according to Proust, it was only the sad memories that had any artistic validity: "It is our moments of suffering that outline our books and the intervals of respite that write them" ("The Princess de Guermantes Receives"). Again in *The Past Recaptured*: "Happy years are wasted years; we wait for suffering before setting to work." Or—prophetically describing what happened to O'Neill as he got older—Proust says: "Our sorrows are obscure, despised servants, whom we struggle against but who gain more and more dominion over us, wretched but irreplaceable servants, who lead us by subterranean passages to the truth and to our death" (*ibid.*). Whether O'Neill had savored a *madeleine* soaked in lime-flower tea, or stepped on a stone, or heard a spoon struck against a plate, and thereby "recaptured" his past, as did Proust, I do not know, but the general psychology projected here by Proust is certainly an exact description of the emotional processes by which *Long Day's Journey*, *A Moon*, *The Iceman Cometh*, and probably *Hughie*, got written. It was all put, in Proustian fashion, by Jamie Tyrone in Act III of *A Moon for the Misbegotten* when he says to Josie Hogan, "It was long ago. But it seems like tonight. There is no present or future—only the past happening over and over again—now."

But surely also, and despite his personal agonies, O'Neill must have felt Proust's overwhelming sense of control and power once he had recaptured and artistically re-embodied his own past. As the narrator says in *The Past Recaptured:* "The date when I heard the sound—so distant and yet so deep within me—of the little bell in the garden at Combray was a landmark I did not know I had available in this enormous dimension of Time. My head swam to see so many years below me, and yet within me, as if I were thousands of leagues in height" (The Princesse de Guermantes Receives"). And so too *The Iceman Cometh, Long Day's Journey Into Night, Hughie,* and *A Moon for the Misbegotten* constitute an American quintet that could justly be entitled "Remembrance of Things Past." Certainly their effect upon the observer or the reader is precisely what Proust described as the effect of all great art in *The Sweet Cheat Gone:* "certain novels are like great but temporary bereavements, they abolish our habits, bring us in contact once more with the reality of life" (Mademoiselle de Forcheville"). This is precisely the point made about *A Moon for the Misbegotten* by Nicola Chiarmonte,[22] who says of the play that "it gives, in fact, such an impression of probability that we lose all sense that it is a play. But we lose at the same time the sense of artistic convention": we *are* in Connecticut in America in 1923; these *are* real people.

It should first be emphasized, of course, that although Proust and O'Neill are the clearest cases of great modern

writers for whom art and autobiography are one, they are
not the only ones. It could be argued that most serious
imaginative writers in the post-1800 era who did anything
on a large scale and in a dramatic fashion, i.e., created
characters and social worlds, have tended to write about
their own past, or that of their family and friends, or that
of their culture, or all three. This generalization holds even
for what we might think of as the more objective art of
the European nineteenth-century novel. Most every great
novel of the nineteenth century, be it *Middlemarch* or
*War and Peace*, is not spun out of whole cloth but is
based on real people and on remembrance of things past.
Tolstoi's wonderful Natasha was taken from the life as
was the domesticity of the opening pages of *War and
Peace*, not life literally, but life as the basis in reality for
the superstructure of artistic creation and imagination.[23]

It sometimes takes generations of scholarship to prove
it,[24] but it usually turns out that most of the major characters in works such as these are based either directly on
the author himself, as Pierre and Andrew in *War and
Peace* represent two sides of Tolstoi, or as Dorothea
Brooke and Mary Garth in *Middlemarch* represent two
sides of George Eliot; or on someone the author knew
well, as John Dickens is the basis for Mr. Micawber of
*David Copperfield*; or is based on some individual the
author knew and who then becomes the archetype for a
whole progeny of variations, as Henry James's cousin,
Minny Temple, became the mythological mother for an
entire series of representations of that "heiress of all the
ages," the American girl; or on a crossbreeding or com-
posite of several people the author had known, or known
of, as Thomas Mann's Peeperkorn is supposed to be a
blend of Tolstoi and Gerhart Hauptmann, among other
things. Furthermore the fictional "world" itself, the social-
moral-cultural background of these works, tends to be
based on memory as well. Humphrey House has shown in
*The Dickens World* that the background for most of
Dickens's novels is that of his own childhood. House in-
vokes Proust explicitly: "It is astonishing, with a writer
of Dickens's fertility and scope, to see how his first book,
the *Sketches*, forms a prospectus of what he was to do for
the next thirty years. There is no need to emphasize any
more that he used the years of his youth with a persistence

and confident exactness unequalled by any other writer whose youth was not, like Proust's, his one chosen subject. The truth recurs throughout Forster's biography, and has been reiterated by all biographers since." [25] *Middlemarch* is directly based on George Eliot's girlhood memories. With Samuel Butler's *The Way of All Flesh* (1901) the novel became explicitly a way of settling accounts with one's self and one's family. In the twentieth century, with such directly autobiographical works as *Portrait of the Artist as a Young Man, Sons and Lovers, In Our Time,* Thomas Wolfe's entire production, and at least the first work of almost every modern writer, fiction and autobiography have become inextricably welded. But the difference between these admitted "confessions" and the mode of James or Dickens or Eliot or Tolstoi is one of degree, not of kind. Still it should be noted that seldom, even in the avowed confessions, are the autobiographical revelations so direct and literal as they are in *Long Day's Journey Into Night*.

O'Neill, then, was not an initiator of this tradition but a culminator of it. The hoots of derision that greeted Wordsworth's thousands of lines about himself were directed at what was to become a new and major mode of literary expression in the next two centuries of Western literature. Chiarmonte cites Maurice Blanchot on Rousseau (the French counterpart of Wordsworth, or vice versa), to the effect that Rousseau is the seminal figure for modern literature since he, rebelling against artifice, invented "sincerity" under which dispensation all art becomes "confession." The significant difference, according to Chiarmonte, between these two great, sad, mad writers, Rousseau and O'Neill, resides in the fact that O'Neill could never believe, as could Rousseau, that it was all—the whole, dark plight—*"the fault of others."* [26] Honesty, then, is at the root of O'Neill's power, but it must be added that only the naturalistic-realistic drama, the fourth wall removed, real people saying real things, could provide this ultimate illusion of reality and validity.

But having said this, we immediately encounter an ambiguity which necessitates a qualification, namely, that autobiographical art is not literal autobigraphy. In the first place—although this has nothing to do with *Long Day's Journey Into Night* as a play per se—life itself considerably

mitigated the implications of that tragic fourth act of
Long Day's Journey: it was almost as if Dickens had taken
over to write an Epilogue. Edmund-Eugene was only
slightly ravaged by consumption, which was soon arrested,
and he became eventually, after many other vicissitudes,
a great playwright. Mrs. O'Neill did overcome her dope
addiction ("Tiny Tim did get well"), and with the help
of nuns at that, for her cure was effected by a stay at a
nunnery, not a sanitarium. After James O'Neill's death, his
eldest son stopped drinking and remained abstemious for
two years. (Although when his mother became mortally
ill he began drinking once more, and continued to, until
his early death.) Moreover, at the time of the production
of Beyond the Horizon, the family, especially Eugene,
James, and Ella—Jamie at this time was still unregenerate
—came together in a harmonious unit, and the father had
the pleasure of seeing one son a very great success and,
like himself, in connection with the theater. When James
O'Neill became ill, Eugene O'Neill wrote to George Tyler,
an old family friend, "This sickness of the Governor's is
really hell to me. The thought that there is a chance of
losing him just at the time when he and I, after many
years of misunderstanding, have begun to be real pals—
well, you can imagine" (Gelbs, p. 419).

These details are irrelevant to Long Day's Journey Into
Night considered as a dramatic document although they
cast back some ironic light upon it as an autobiography.
Much more interesting, relevant, and puzzling are the actual facts of the life of the O'Neill family in 1912 when
Long Day's Journey takes place. The puzzles multiply
because the autobiographical facts do not square, in very
important ways, with the play itself, and because the
three big biographies, Croswell Bowen's, Doris Alexander's
and Barbara and Arthur Gelb's, do not always square with
one another.[27] There is a further complication in that none
of these biographies is documented. And to compound
confusion they are all based both on interviews with people
who knew O'Neill, and were thus depending on memory,
a notoriously unreliable repository for facts, and on documents which, on their part, cannot be evaluated properly
unless their source, condition, and so on, are cited. Miss
Alexander promises complete documentation with the
publication of her second volume; this will then be the

first scholarly biography of the subject, which is not to imply that the student of O'Neill should not be grateful for
the labors of Bowen and, especially, the Gelbs. Because
of their labors both the general outline and many details of O'Neill's life at this time are clear and reliably
reported.

Eugene O'Neill did fall ill in 1912, not in August but
in October, while living at the family summer place in
New London where he was a reporter on a local newspaper. He had already been married, had fathered a son,
and had been divorced—an interlocutory decree—on June
10, 1912. He had been seeing regularly, and was very serious about, a young New London lady, who was a "nice"
girl, from a "nice" family and whom he treated with the
greatest respect. James O'Neill disapproved of the relationship because he thought the young lady was too good
for his at that time disreputable son. During this same
period Jamie O'Neill was in a sanitarium taking "the cure."
James O'Neill was, except for week ends, in New York,
where he was making a movie of *Monte Cristo* for Froh-
man and Zukor's Famous Players Film Company. Eugene
was examined by a doctor, or doctors, all respectable, diagnosed as tubercular, and confined to bed, with a regis-
tered nurse chosen by himself in attendance. On December 9, after carefully outfitting Eugene with a new suit at
New London's best tailor, James O'Neill took his ailing
son to Shelton, Connecticut, to the Fairfield County State
Tuberculosis Sanitarium, at that time state supported and
commonly regarded as a paupers' institution. Eugene
O'Neill lasted only two days in these dismal surroundings
and among these dismal people. He came to New York
on December 11 and, after some wrangling with his father,
was examined again by a doctor, or doctors, very reputable
once more. He finally went to Gaylord Farm Sanitarium
in Wallingford, Connecticut, which was a reputable, successfully experimental, partially state-supported institution, in which the patients paid a small amount of money
if they could afford it. From a financial point of view—
since this is such an issue in *Long Day's Journey*—Gaylord
Farm was neither that expensive private institution that
the sons in the play think Edmund should go to, nor was
it the "pauper's grave" that Shelton evidently was and to
which James O'Neill had initially taken his son. The fol-

lowing spring he was released from Gaylord Farm as an arrested case, and had by then determined to be a writer. Such is the chronology of events that O'Neill telescoped, in part, into one day in August, 1912.

There are other discrepancies between life and art to be found in the play. The O'Neill summer home in New London was by no means the claptrap affair that it is implied to be in the play. In 1883 it had cost something like $40,000 to build. It was spacious, and the wood used in it was so fine that years later when a back wing was torn down the contractor offered to do the job free, in order to keep the beautiful wood (Alexander, p. 12). It was perhaps modest in comparison to the authentic mansions of the millionaires who summered in New London, but by the O'Neills' Irish relations it was thought to be very comfortable and certainly more than adequate for the four O'Neills. By the Irish anyway, Ella O'Neill was regarded as somewhat of a snob. One relative interviewed by the Gelbs said that Ella would "never have allowed her husband or sons to keep a whiskey bottle on her living-room table" (Gelbs, p. 93). In the eyes of these people the O'Neills were affluent, with a chauffeur and a coachman, the boys in their tailor-made suits and the mother in her beautiful and expensive clothing. Although the family car was secondhand, it was a Packard, which in those days was a vehicle beyond social reproach. Even the turning out of the electric light bulbs, which plays such a role, both comic and serious, in Act IV of the play, was not evidence of pure penury, as the play implies. According to the Gelbs, this habit was a crotchet of the period, even among genuinely wealthy people who were offended by extravagant rates that the electric power companies, in their hurry to get back their capital investment, were charging (Gelbs, p. 219).

With the characters of the O'Neills themselves, we are on even shakier ground, no matter how many biographies have been, or will be, written. In fact, the only rule or generalization that clearly emerges is that, as most serious art of the past two centuries is in great part autobiography, whether announced as such or not, explicitly autobiographical art, such as *Long Day's Journey Into Night*, is hardly ever, strictly speaking, "true," for the literary characters and events hardly ever correspond exactly and precisely with the actual characters and events. Here again *The Way of All Flesh* is the classic instance of the genre. When Butler's novel was first published, and for generations after, the book was taken, at least by the general reader, as a literal and accurate picture of the Butler family. Two recent collections of Butler letters, however, show quite clearly that neither his father, nor his sisters and brother, nor himself were, in the life, identical to the characters in *The Way of All Flesh*, nor was the general situation identical.[28]

And there is always the further complexity and irony that complicated characters, such as the O'Neills, would not lend themselves to any kind of clear photography. Nor, finally, does it all matter: the O'Neills have all gone to their graves; while the play remains. The interesting aspect with *Long Day's Journey* is that seldom in literature, if ever, have we had a conjunction of such a nakedly autobiographical work juxtaposed with such an abundance of detailed knowledge about the people upon whom the play is based; and no doubt in the future there will be still more factual knowledge.

Besides the discrepancy between the rather shabby summer home of the imaginations of Mary, Jamie, and Edmund Tyrone in the play and the rather solid one of reality, there are various other, and curious, discrepancies between the play and reality: Edmund-Eugene's marriage and son are never mentioned, nor is his rather serious involvement with a "nice" girl, such as Mary Tyrone laments in the play her sons will have nothing to do with, nor they with her sons. With Mary Tyrone–Ella O'Neill, there are several discrepancies. The little shrine of Our Lady of Lourdes that Mary Tyrone remembers praying before at her school was not at her school at all but at Eugene's own, Mount St. Vincent, which he attended from 1896 to 1900. Mary Tyrone's recollection of her father being on the scene when she married James Tyrone is also wrong, for Thomas Quinlan, Mary Ellen Quinlan's father, died of consumption, aggravated by alcoholism, three years before the event. Not all of Ella's girlhood and school friends dropped her or snubbed her after her marriage to the actor, James O'Neill. The Mother Elizabeth that she mentions was not an innocent, unworldly woman, as James Tyrone declares, but was a very shrewd person who noted that, besides her musical talent, Mary Ellen Quinlan had some talent for self-dramatization and who, when Ella felt the "call" and talked of becoming a nun, told the girl, wisely, to wait and think it over.

The O'Neill's themselves are, like all human beings worthy of the designation, impossible to type or categorize, although there are degrees in this matter, as in all other things. The least gap between the reality and the dramatization seems to be in the picture of Jamie, who appears to have been in life just about what he is in the play: cynical, libidinous, alcoholic, rebellious, passionately attached to all the other members of the family but especially to his mother; a monumental failure of considerable charm; simultaneously devoted to and jealous of his talented younger brother—and yet withal, and under all the bravado and verbal fireworks, a lost soul with some last traces of boyish sweetness, headed only, and as surely as Hickey of *The Iceman Cometh*, to extinction. Perhaps only his mother and his brother knew of the "soul" still there, which was why O'Neill could not let his portrait in *A Long Day's Journey Into Night* stand as definitive but had to go on to the portrait in *A Moon for the Misbegotten*, which by Acts III and IV he becomes, in effect, a little boy crying in the dark.

With Edmund (himself), O'Neill effected some suppressions both of fact and of character traits. The suppression of the marriage and the fact of his current romance have aready been mentioned. In addition, like Joyce with his self-portrait in Stephen Dedalus, O'Neill emphasized his own somber, brooding and poetic side, to the exclusion of his extroverted, bawdy, outgoing side, for the existence of which, as with Joyce once more, there is plenty of evidence. It perhaps could be argued that this side would not show itself on such a day as the one described in *Long Day's Journey*, just as Stephen Dedalus can do nothing but brood over his sins against his dead mother on June 16, 1904 (the day of *Ulysses*). Nevertheless, there was a certain ruthlessness about O'Neill, as his conduct in his first marriage would indicate, that is absent from the character of Edmund Tyrone, the young poet perhaps facing extinction and therefore a figure of more pathos than the real Eugene O'Neill seems to have been. Likewise, at least so it seems to me, he is the one character in the play who is more sinned against than sinning, betrayed alike by his father, who will skimp on his medical care, his brother, who will try to make him fail, and his mother, who will re-shatter the image of motherly purity by taking dope. His own aggressions against them are, more or less, minimized although he does once mention the "rotten" things he has done to his father; he does not, however, get specific about these matters.

The most problematical characterizations are those of the father and mother. Almost everybody who knew James O'Neill, who was legendary for his good-looks, charm and generosity, was outraged by the portrait of him in *Long Day's Journey Into Night*.[29] Yet it is a fact of life, as Samuel Butler's father (who was held in great esteem by his fellow citizens) attests, that a man may present one face to the world and another face to his family. It is also quite possible for a man, especially a self-made man, to be an inexplicable combination of generosity and penuriousness, to squander thousands in real estate and always stand drinks for the house, as James O'Neill used to do, and pinch pennies in other areas, in the home, for example. Still it would seem that as O'Neill gave himself the better of the deal, morally speaking, he gave his father the worse, for the fact would seem to be that the father was not the almost total skinflint that he is made out to be in *Long Day's Journey Into Night*. O'Neill would not allow his father to be a "good Catholic" either. In the play it is said that he never attends church but, in fact, he was a regular Mass-goer (Gelbs, p. 219). There are still further complications. O'Neill *did* let his father off the hook, morally speaking, on the worst charge of all, which in reality did eventuate, of placing his ill son on public charity. In the play the father promises not to do this. But, further complications, the fact of his having done just this in reality, by, initially anyway, putting Eugene O'Neill into the state hospital at Shelton, was not the mercilessly penurious act that it might seem. Tuberculosis in those days was the leading killer, of all diseases, and its onslaught was invariably fatal. Especially was this true of the Irish. Thomas Quinlan, the maternal grandfather, had died of it and Edward O'Neill, the paternal grandfather, may have died of it. Croswell Bowen (p. 62) quotes a specialist on this subject, the Irish and tuberculosis: "Treating an Irishman for t.b. is extremely complicated. You are not only dealing with the disease and fear of it, normal in any patient, but you have to deal with a patient who thinks he has the disease because God is punishing him for something he has done. Often the patient is ready to accept it as fatal and is ready to lie down and die, right then and there. You can't convince him he is not doomed." It is this kind of "bog-trotter" fatality about consumption that Jamie Tyrone attributes to his father, which he probably did share. In 1912 his income from *Monte Cristo* was ended, and the money he had was entangled and overcommitted in property. As far as he could foresee at this point, the only thing that he could confidently expect from his sons was that they would cost him money and repay him with insults. To the thousands he had spent on his wife's cures at sanitariums, he could expect, at this time, only to add many more. He bore many burdens and he bore them well; and he may perhaps have sincerely thought he would be wasting still more money by sending Eugene to an expensive private sanitarium.

But, it should be said, the play itself finally does full justice to James O'Neill, and I think his defenders often overlook or minimize this. In the great fourth act certainly his essential decency, and his charm, are convincingly dramatized, as is the very real motivation for any penuriousness that he may have had. If Eugene O'Neill had done in his early years some "rotten" things to his father, as he had, he more than made up for it in writing this play. And in *A Moon for the Misbegotten* he has Josie Hogan, whose words we may take for true metal, give a brief, but splendid, encomium to the character of James O'Neill.

The most shadowy figure in the play and the most shadowy figure in the family was the mother, Mary Tyrone–Ella O'Neill. There seems to have been some basis for this elusiveness in reality; what the Gelbs found in their extensive researches, interviewing people who had known, or should have known, Mrs. O'Neill, was that nobody did seem to know her. Her Irish relatives tended to think of her as "stuck-up." She also evidently remained aloof from the world of actors and actresses that her husband introduced her to. She was automatically shut out from the world of the wealthy New Londoners. Her morphine addiction would tend, of course, to make her even more of a pariah. That, isolated as she was, she tended to dwell upon the past would seem to be indubitable. Cancer and the removal of a breast at the age of twenty-nine could hardly have encouraged her to be optimistic and forward-looking. She was pretty and loved beautiful things. She was deeply loved and cherished by her "three men." For two of them, James and Jamie, she was enough for a lifetime. For her turbulent sons and her earthy husband she represented something indefinably feminine and delicate, if desecrated when taking "the poison." James O'Neill put her on a pedestal, from the day they were married, and she seems to have remained there. Again that fourth act, with the three men downstairs, drinking, wrangling, reminiscing, and the ghostlike mother rumaging around, set off and alone, on the second floor, must have some wide-ranging significance for the whole relationship. She had, when she wanted to, a good deal of charm, like the rest of the family. This quality is shown briefly in Act I of the play, and it was attested to by people who had met her, as, for example, when she is described by Agnes Boulton in *Part of a Long Story* (New York, 1959). She was somewhat of a Mona Lisa in life, and she is certainly the Mona Lisa of the play, aloof, apart, lost in a glorified and sentimentalized past. As Jamie is as gross and clear as earth, she is somnambulistic, wraithlike, disembodied.

As far as one can tell at this point, then, O'Neill in writing this play telescoped events, suppressed some facts, distorted others, invented some more, and transferred some others (the Lady of Lourdes incident). He seemed to have both simplified and heightened characters, Jamie perhaps excepted. He presented Jamie as is, or was, selected one side of himself and one side of his father and presented them in a rather exaggerated fashion; he made his mother shadowy and insubstantial, as was only fitting for someone existing in the twilight zone of a morphine stupor. He cut the O'Neill family off from the social connections they did have. He picked the year, 1912, when his father's career ended and his own began, or was at least determined on. Finally, he did not "blame" anybody, neither God, nor History, nor Man; and thus the play is, in a good sense, morally relativistic. Each of the characters is on some kind of treadmill that they did not create but which they certainly freely stepped on to. If I may be allowed to quote myself, from a previous essay on *Long Day's Journey*, "Nothing is to blame except everybody." [30]

## 3    MANKIND

O'NEILL'S CHARACTERS exist on various levels, or rather on a spectrum that has race or culture or civilization or class at one end and pure individuality at the other. O'Neill wrote surprisingly seldom of the American middle-class of the twentieth century. Significantly, when he did, as in *The First Man*, *Welded*, or *Days Without End*, he was usually at his worst, with characters that do not come alive, dialogue that is banal, and dramatic clashes that fail to engage any deep interest. His most powerful plays dealing with this class are *The Great God Brown* and *Strange Interlude*, and they are powerful precisely because the one, *The Great God Brown*, is really about religion, or at least, the religious impulse, and the other, *Strange Interlude*, is really about the sexual impulse. His only fully successful play about the American middle-class, *Ah, Wilderness!*, is frankly a comedy of sentiment which deals with life's surfaces, not with its depths.

His first great successes, the one-act sea plays, were concerned with "melting pot" crews of sailors, that is, a medley of races engaged in a sub or marginal or exotic occupation. Practically all his most distinctive and original plays are concerned with specific racial or cultural strains engaged in out-of-the-way activities: A Negro adventurer in the Caribbean (*The Emperor Jones*), a stoker in a "melting pot" crew on a trans-Atlantic steamer (*The Hairy Ape*), American Negroes (*All God's Chillun Got Wings*), "melting pot" down-and-outers (*The Iceman Cometh*), a small-time New York gambler (*Hughie*), middle-class Irish-Americans of an acting family (*A Long Day's Journey Into Night*), and middle-class and lower-class Irish-Americans (*A Moon for the Misbegotten*).

And, of course, in the history plays he dropped out of twentieth-century America altogether, and, correspondingly, race or culture became that more important.

What he seemed to feel was that the generic American type, Anglo-Protestant, middle class, business-oriented, lacked individuality and color. In addition, his rhetoric was at its worst in normative American middle-class speech; he was much more at home and at ease with a Swedish or Negro dialect or an Irish brogue. Finally, as a dramatist, he instinctively reached out to the situation in which there was a profound and built-in clash between opposing and differing outlooks and ways of life, as, for example, the American Negro and the American white (*All God's Chillun*) or the Anglo-American and the Irish-American (*A Touch of the Poet*). Furthermore, like Whitman and Melville, his imagination was captured by the idea of America as the "melting pot," and one of his ideal dramatic situations (the steamer's hold in *The Hairy Ape* or Harry Hope's bar in *The Iceman Cometh*) is a cacophony of accents rising to a kind of universal din, as they do in the scraps of American popular songs that are sung at the end of *The Iceman Cometh*, or as they do in the drinking scene in *The Hairy Ape*. Nothing was too large a subject, he thought, for the stage; nothing less than to suggest the continual discord and concord of mankind itself in all its cultural and racial variousness.

Man as a purely social being, that is, as a representative of a special social class or occupation and hence largely defined by that social class or occupation, did not really interest him, despite the fact that *The Hairy Ape* was hailed, when it first appeared, as a masterpiece of proletarian literature. But in the play itself Yank either eschews social protest or is rebuffed by organized labor (the IWW) and at the end of the play is, so to speak, alone in the universe. What he is seeking, and does not find, is some kind of relationship between himself and life itself, a condition of feeling at home in the universe, of "belonging" in some way. O'Neill's own way of putting this preoccupation of Yank was to say that as a playwright he was not so much interested in relations between man and man, the social nexus, as in those between man and God.

The existential psychiatrists [1] have a theory about the levels on which humans exist which is useful here: first, there is the *Umwelt*, the biological world of environment, the world of instinct, the unconscious, in short, the world of Freud; second, is the *Mitwelt*, the world of relationships with one's fellow man, the interaction of human beings upon one another; and, third, the *Eigenwelt*, or "own-world," inhabited by a kind of metaphysical self, an "I" or an "I am," a distinctive, unique, uncertain dweller in the universe, an amateur, unconscious ontologist, a student willing or unwilling of the self in relation to the self, a reluctant contemplator of the nature of reality.

O'Neill's chief, though not sole, interests, are the *Umwelt* and the *Eigenwelt* rather than the *Mitwelt*. The *Umwelt*, being instinctual, includes the sexual impulse and thus the sexual relationship between male and female. At the center of most of O'Neill's plays is the male-female relationship, considered from every conceivable angle or level, from the grossly animal, not to mention the commercial (the woman as object), to a sacramental concept of marriage (the woman as idea). Thus a torrent of sexual energy and romantic and marital love, thwarted, displaced, fulfilled, runs throughout his plays, and is, like power in history, the force that makes the world go round; passions spin the plot. The story of the male and the female, how they came together, how they torment one another or fulfill one another, or both, is told again and again in the plays, from differing points of view, sometimes that of the woman (Nina in *Strange Interlude*); sometimes that of the man (Dion Anthony in *The Great God Brown*); sometimes both (*Welded* and *Days Without End*). It is a panorama, by and large, of sorrow, frustration, and suffering, with interludes of felicity (*Ah, Wilderness!*, or the "good" moments and certainly the good memories of James and Mary Tyrone in *Long Day's Journey*). As such, O'Neill's plays could have served John Jay Chapman's illustrative purposes when he was trying to explain, by graphic illustration, what was missing in Emerson's world. The legendary man from Mars, said Chapman, could read all of Emerson's essays and still not have an inkling of what human life was basically about; whereas a glance at an Italian opera, the male and the female in vocal rapture or rupture, would tell him what was what. A glance at an O'Neill play would serve the same purpose.

Finally man or woman is alone, staring into a mirror, wondering what he or she is. In two of O'Neill's late plays, A *Touch of the Poet* and *The Iceman Cometh*, two ambiguous characters, Con Melody and Theodore Hickman, have a preoccupation with mirrors. Throughout A *Touch of the Poet* Con continues to look at himself in the mirror, and Hickey speaks of having done so ("I'd curse myself for a lousy bastard every time I saw myself in the mirror"—IV). When they look into a mirror they are, of course, searching for themselves, looking to see if they can see what they are. This is the realm of the *Eigenwelt*. Its problems, concerns, and perplexities are best illustrated by parables, one by Pascal and one by Plato. In Section 199 of "Of the Necessity of the Wager," Pascal presents a parable about the inevitability of death. "Let us imagine a number of men in chains, all condemned to death, where some are killed each day in the sight of others, and those who remain see their own fate in that of their fellows, and wait their turn, looking at each other sorrowfully and without hope. It is an image of the condition of man." In the opening part of Book VII of *The Republic* in the parable of the Cave, Plato also talks of a number of men in chains. By a flickering light they see on the wall of the cave images which they take for reality, while in truth they are only seeing shadows. On the scale of Plato's fourfold level of perception they dwell on the lowest level, the perception of shadows. Further, they are habituated to their semi-blind condition and would be not only resentful of but hostile toward the philosopher who would force them out of the dark cave and up the rugged ascent to the light of the sun and reality. Most of them anyway will never make the journey. For, as they fear death, they are at home in the ambiguous darkness of the cave (or the bar) and ill at ease in the open and in the sun of reason.

Fearing death, shunning the light, men also suffer from a cosmic loneliness and a corresponding doubt as to who and what they are. In Pascal's words: "I know not who put me into the world, nor what the world is for, nor what I myself am. I am in horrible ignorance of everything. I know not what my body is, nor my senses, nor my soul, not even that part of me which thinks what I say, which reflects on all and on itself, and knows itself no more than the rest" ("Of the Necessity of the Wager" —194). In such a world—death, darkness, and doubt— illusion is the only protection and hence O'Neill's plays, at their deepest level, are concerned, tormentedly and complexly, with the endless ambiguities of the relationship between illusion and reality. Moreover, there is no final "message" about this problem: man must, and must not, live upon illusions.

Not all of O'Neill's characters are concerned with these problems, at least not explicitly. Their common lot, however, is unhappiness. In the early plays there are a few happy, intelligent, and committed people usually doctors or nurses, such as Dr. Stanton and Miss Gilpin in *The Straw*, but they disappear in the major and later plays. There are also characters who are wise, like the Great Kaan in *Marco Millions*, but those that are, are unhappy, like the Kaan. Some of these wise people, like Larry Slade in *The Iceman Cometh* or Mrs. Harford in *A Touch of the Poet*, try, usually unsuccessfully, to withdraw from the race (both senses meant). Withdrawn or committed they are all trapped, like George Eliot's characters, in an inexorable moral machine that hardly ever lets its transgressors escape the consequences of past misdoings. Many of them live in the past, endlessly ruminating over their sins, or, paradoxically, celebrating the imagined and departed glories of this same past. Life for all of them is a "strange interlude" in which "we call on past and future to bear witness we are living" (*Strange Interlude*, VIII).

## 1 *The Races*

In practically all of O'Neill's history plays the rhythm of the races is one of the primary polarities, and in his career as a whole two racial-cultural polarities loom the largest: Irish vs. Yankee in New England and Negro vs. white in New York City. During their summers in New London the O'Neill family had experienced the anti-Irish prejudice of the more wealthy and long-established Protestants. And because James O'Neill was an actor, the family perhaps suffered under a double onus. However, another wealthy actor, Richard Mansfield, who spent his summers in New London, was not only *au courant* with the native aristrocracy but even *he*—much to James O'Neill's amusement—would have nothing to do socially with the O'Neills. In the words of Mrs. E. Chappell Sheffield, daughter of the Chappels (the "Chatfields" of *Long Day's Journey*), who were the very embodiment of New London snobbery, "We considered the O'Neills shanty Irish . . . and we associated the Irish, almost automatically, with the servant class" (Gelbs, p. 95). All this seemed not to have bothered James O'Neill at all, nor Jamie O'Neill. But it wounded Mrs. O'Neill, who laments the O'Neill isolation in *Long Day's Journey*, and it smoldered for some time in the memory of Eugene O'Neill, who once told an old New London crony: "You know, I always wanted to make money. My motive was to be able, someday, to hire a Tally-Ho and fill it full of painted whores, load each whore with a bushel of dimes, and let them throw the money to the rabble on a Saturday afternoon; we'd ride down State Street . . . and toss money to people like the Chappells. Now that I've made as much as I need, I've lost interest" (Gelbs, p. 95).

But in his plays he never did lose interest and in them he defeated the Yankees again and again. According to Frank Budgen, Joyce finally came to feel that the English had occupied Ireland for all those terrible centuries in order that finally out of the nightmare of his country's history would come *Dubliners*, *A Portrait of the Artist as a Young Man*, *Ulysses*, and *Finnegans Wake*. By the same token, and in a smaller way, all literate Americans—not to mention the Swedes, the Germans, the Russians, and so on—owe a debt to those New London snobs, for they provided both social background and character motivation for some of O'Neill's best and most powerful plays, namely, *Mourning Becomes Electra*, *A Touch of the Poet*, *Long Day's Journey Into Night*, and *A Moon for the Misbegotten*.

While the Irish are not mentioned in *Mourning Becomes Electra*—although the drunken chantyman of Act IV of *The Hunted* is probably one—the picture of the Mannons: black, grim, repressed, powerful, humorless, unyielding, puritanical, hypocritical, doomed, death-obsessed, wealthy, tenacious, for whom life is some terrible burden imposed upon them by a narrow-minded, wrathful, and pitiless God who has chosen them to be His earthly instruments to stamp out any elements of freedom and joy that may persist in human life—all this is unmistakably the traditional Celtic view of the English. Cromwell and his soldiery were "Mannons" to the seventeenth-century historical Irish. But whereas Cromwell was triumphant, the Mannons are doomed. To at least one European observer this aspect of the play constituted its real cultural significance. In the words of Camillo Pellizzi: [2]

> In this ancient tragic chain, seeming strangely audacious in these times, the Catholic, anti-Puritan Irishman is revealed again, the enemy of the Anglo-Saxon race and religion, which dominated in Ireland, the country of his origin, and predominates in his adopted country. The terrible Mannons, whom such a pitiless nemesis seems to overshadow, are really representative of the oldest race of English Nonconformist settlers, transplanted centuries ago into New England, and uncompromising in their religious, social and economic dogmas; they are the "man-eaters" of the new America, the tyrants who are always thinking of death and pray to God according to Calvin. It is not that O'Neill has quarrels to pick, or social arguments to support; nevertheless, he always remains the best exponent of the rebellion of a new America, more original and eclectic, against the old, on which certain imprints received at the time of its origin are still deeply stamped.

An analogous picture is set up in *A Touch of the Poet*, only this time with the Irish at the center of the stage and the Yankees, with the exception of Mrs. Harford, off stage. In this play the Yankees are explicitly defeated by the Irish through Sara's seduction of Simon Harford, even though Con Melody himself is defeated.

The Irish in the play constitute a racial spectrum—ranging from peasants, the crude, ignorant, drunken, hangers-on, like O'Dowd and Roche, up to Sara and Con, who are half peasant and half aristocrat. Thus they are lower on the evolutionary scale than the Harfords but, for this very reason, have what the Harfords lack, sexual vitality. In Act II Con exclaims against the pale, inhibited Yankees that when it comes to making love, they are "clumsy, fish-blooded louts" who know nothing about women. And to prove it he almost seduces the aristocratic Yankee matron, Mrs. Harford; that is, before she smells the whiskey on his breath.

*Long Day's Journey* and *A Moon for the Misbegotten* both take up the Irish-Yankee conflict in the "pigs-in-the-pond" episode that opens each play. Since the time is the twentieth century and the battle is won, what was once tragedy, as in the case of Con Melody, can now be comedy. For this comic victory O'Neill availed himself of two "myths"; [3] first, the legendary "terrible tongue" of the Irish; and, second, the legendary weakness and neuroticism of the second generation of a wealthy American family. In *A Moon for the Misbegotten* Hogan, the Irish peasant of the play, keeps pigs (of course) and has allowed them to wallow in the ice pond on the property of one Harder, scion of Standard Oil money. Since the pond is used to make ice in winter, Harder comes to protest to Hogan who, along with his daughter, proceeds to rout the innocuous and vapid American by the power of his terrible tongue and by the threat of his and his daughter's superior physical power. [4]

*Long Day's Journey Into Night* employs the Irish material with greater frequency and greater power. It directly parallels *A Moon* in that the "pigs-in-the-pond" incident occurs again, only it takes place off stage, with Hogan's name changed to Shaughnessy and Harder's name changed to Harker, and is related to the Tyrone family by Edmund, to their mutual delight. Dramatically, this is the one moment in the play when the characters are all united, happy, and laughing, mutually enjoying a vicarious victory over "the stranger":

> Then he [Shaughnessy] accused Harker of making his foreman break down the fence to entice the pigs into the ice pond in order to destroy them. The poor pigs, Shaughnessy yelled, had caught their death of cold. Many of them were dying of pneumonia, and several others had been taken down with cholera from drinking the poisoned water. He told Harker he was hiring a lawyer to sue him for damages. And he wound up by saying that he had to put up with poison ivy, ticks, potato bugs, snakes and skunks on his farm, but he was an honest

man who drew the line somewhere, and he'd be damned
if he'd stand for a Standard Oil thief trespassing. So
would Harker kindly remove his dirty feet from the
premises before he sicked the dog on him. And Harker
did!

[*He and Jamie laugh.*]

MARY [*Shocked but giggling.*] Heavens, what a terrible tongue that man has!

TYRONE [*Admiringly before he thinks.*] The damned
old scoundrel! By God, you can't beat him! [*He laughs
—then stops abruptly and scowls.*] The dirty black-
guard! He'll get me in serious trouble yet. I hope you
told him I'd be mad as hell—

EDMUND I told him you'd be tickled to death over the
great Irish victory, and so you are. Stop faking, Papa.

TYRONE Well, I'm not tickled to death.

MARY [*Teasingly.*] You are too, James. You're simply
delighted!

But such felicities can never last with the Tyrones, and
Edmund continues:

I told Shaughnessy he should have reminded Harker that
a Standard Oil millionaire ought to welcome the flavor
of hog in his ice water as an appropriate touch.

TYRONE The devil you did! [*Frowning.*] Keep your
damned Socialist anarchist sentiments out of my affairs!

And almost immediately after the anecdote is told we
are in a world of wrangling: Jamie's nasty tongue, Edmund's "cold," Mary's nervousness and general apprehen-
sion, as the long day's journey begins, on the heels of the
opening of the comic interlude.

Equivalent to the off-stage Shaughnessy is the on-stage
Cathleen, the bumptious, ignorant, cheerful, Irish-peas-
ant serving-girl. Her presence underlines the pitiable isolation of Mary Tyrone, whose only real companion is
Cathleen, and in Act III she is reduced to giving Cathleen drink, in order to have someone to talk to. Through
Cathleen, too, we get a glimpse of bottom-dog Irish life
in the early twentieth-century. As Cathleen explains it to
Mary Tyrone, Smythe, the Tyrones' chauffeur, can't keep
his hands to himself and is always pinching her leg or,
"you-know-where—asking your pardon, Ma'am, but it's
true." But *Long Day's Journey* also contains a somber,

and historically accurate, picture of the fate of the Irish peasant who immigrated to America in the nineteenth century. This occurs when the father in Act IV tells Edmund the story of his life, which, roughly, was the life of the real James O'Neill. This story of racial discrimination, hardship, grinding work, always on the verge of starvation, evictions, with Tyrone becoming the man of the family at ten years of age, finally explains Tyrone's penuriousness and land-hunger, which, according to other members of the family, is the cause of their various tragedies.

Then comes the moving story of his rise and fall as an actor. On the verge of becoming one of the great Shaksepearian actors of the nineteenth century, in the tradition of Booth, he was trapped by the commercial success of *The Count of Monte Cristo*, and his real ambitions were never realized. This narrative is of considerable importance in the moral calculus of the play, which is rather complex. Up to this point James Tyrone has been the target for all the others' accusations and gibes, the "cause" of the family's various tragedies. But his own story extends the moral spectrum of the play into another dimension and puts the father in a new and sympathetic light. He is finally "motivated" and can take his particular place in that world the others inhabit: in Mary Tyrone's words: "None of us can help the things life has done to us."

EDMUND [*Moved, stares at his father with understanding—slowly.*] I'm glad you've told me this, Papa. I know you a lot better now.

For the father had been, in part anyway, a victim of racial intolerance.

But in the plays as a whole O'Neill does not let his Irishmen go scot free, nor are they idealized. Ella Downey, the white heroine of *All God's Chillun Got Wings*, married to the Negro Jim Harris, is the most racially prejudiced person in the play; in fact, the villain of the play, if it can be said to have one. As her name indicates, she is of Irish extraction, and she thus constitutes O'Neill's reminder that the discriminated-against Irish were as racially intolerant, sometimes more so, than their oppressors. Again, Bill Carmody, the gross parent in *The Straw*, is an Irishman: a heavy-set body, with a ponderous face and a complexion freckled, streaked with purple, and mottled-red; a loud, hoarse voice; and small blue eyes that betoken only a selfish cunning. Mike Hogan, Josie's brother in *A Moon for the Misbegotten*, is described in Act I as a "New England Irish Catholic Puritan, Grade B." Sweeney in *The Rope*, is the same type, only worse: "*mean cunning and cupidity about his mouth and his small, round, blue eyes.*" The bartender of *Ah, Wilderness!* is of this same ilk. And into the mouth of his most Irish Irishman, Con Melody, O'Neill put the following sentiment: "Ireland? What benefit would freedom be to her unless she could be freed from the Irish?" (I). This, of course, is the observation of a patriot.

In all his dramatizations of Irish-Yankee conflicts O'Neill availed himself of two of the oldest myths of mankind, used by the Jews against the Egyptians, the Trojans against the Greeks, the Greeks against the Romans, the Irish and the Indians against the British, the American Indians against the American Caucasians, and the American Negroes against the American whites, namely, that the captive race, the people in bondage, are really superior, both inwardly and outwardly: they have "soul" and they have superior physical beauty and vitality. Small, beset, enslaved, they yet are the Children of God, while their captors are gross materialists, and usually decadent as well. These themes animate the entire structure of *Ulysses*. In the newspaper-room scene in *Ulysses* Professor MacHugh contrasts the shining Greeks and the holy Jews to the dull, crude Romans and English: "What was their [Roman] civilisation? Vast, I allow: but vile. Cloacæ: sewers. The Jews in the wilderness and on the mountaintop said: *It is meet to be here. Let us build an altar to Jehovah.* The Roman, like the Englishman who follows in his footsteps, brought to every new shore on which he set his foot (on our shore he never set it) only his cloacal obsession. He gazed about him in his toga and he said: *It is meet to be here. Let us construct a watercloset.*" Or, as the British are described in "Oxen of the Sun" in *Ulysses*: "Beer, beef, business, bibles, bulldogs, battleships, buggery and bishops." With affluence, according to the myth, goes decadence, and the essence of Harder-Harker in *A Moon for the Misbegotten* and *Long Day's Journey* or Mildred Douglas in *The Hairy Ape* or Mrs. Harford in *A Touch of the Poet* is that they constitute a decadent, played out genetic strain. Thus James Tyrone has an iron constitution, and thus it takes all the Harford servants, plus clubs and police, to subdue Con Melody and Cregan.

But if the Yankee-Irish clash could finally end in the twentieth century in triumph and comedy, the other racial clash that interested O'Neill, white vs. colored, could not so end, for obvious reasons. O'Neill himself had had just enough insight into racial intolerance to have some sense of what the much more deeply beset Negro was up against. In a rough and general way in his Negro plays the Negroes are to the whites what the Irish were to the Yankees in the Irish plays. This analogy is suggested in various ways in different plays. Thus in *All God's Chillun Got Wings* the Irish heroine, Ella Downey, embodies the same attitude toward the Negroes that Mr. Harford had toward the Irish in *A Touch of the Poet*. Or in *The Emperor Jones* Brutus Jones is physical power and vitality, like Con Melody or Phil and Josie Hogan, set off against the physical decadence of Smithers. Or in the stage directions of *All God's Chillun Got Wings* it is suggested that the Negroes are uninhibited and gay, while the whites are constrained and nervous.

It is often overlooked or forgotten that O'Neill, along with Twain and Faulkner, is one of the great white writers on the subject of the American Negro. As Faulkner's novels constitute an epic on the Negroes in the South and Twain's a kind of bitter (*Pudd'nhead Wilson*)-sweet (*Huckleberry Finn*) comedy of the same situation, so O'Neill is the dramatist of the Negro ghetto of the northern megalopolis. Van Wyck Brooks in *The Confident Years* entitled his chapter on O'Neill, "Eugene O'Neill: Harlem" and cited James Weldon Johnson to the effect that the Provincetown Players were the first and the greatest force in opening the way for the Negro on the serious stage in America.[5] When O'Neill's *The Dreamy Kid*, an early one-act play about a Negro gangster, was produced in New York in 1919, it was the first serious play by a white producing company that used Negro actors (hitherto colored roles had been played by whites in black-face).[6] *The Emperor Jones*, O'Neill's first full-length Negro play, is not only an exciting piece of theatrically, it is also an impressive monument in the history of enlightened attempts by enlightened white Americans to lend a helping hand in the Negroes' fearsome struggle. In the year 1920 when *The Emperor Jones* was first produced no Negro had ever played a major role in the American theater. The Provincetown Players decided that only a Negro should play the role of Brutus Jones. (According to the Gelbs, O'Neill had first agreed to a white in black-face for the role; others determined on a Negro for the role and O'Neill concurred.) Thus, Charles Gilpin, who had once been, like Brutus Jones, a Pullman porter was chosen for the role.

*The Emperor Jones* was such an instantaneous success that it was moved from the Players' theater in the Village to Broadway, where on December 27, 1920, for the first time in American history, a serious play by a serious playwright about a "human" Negro, intelligent and resolute, was played by a Negro before a white audience on Broadway. But, of course, like all initial attempts to breach an almost impassable situation, the whole affair was fraught with ironies and ambiguities. Gilpin himself said: "I am pleased ... especially with the generous praise of the critics. But I don't fool myself about the stone walls that are in my way. Mr. O'Neill made a breach in those walls by writing a play that had in it a serious role for a Negro. The Provincetown Players gave me the chance to do the part. But—what next? If I were white, a dozen opportunities would come to me as a result of a success like this. But I'm black. It is no joke when I ask myself, 'Where do I go from here?' " (Gelbs, p. 448). So it was; there were no more jobs forthcoming. The Drama League invited Gilpin to their annual dinner as an "honored guest," upon which some members of the League objected to dining with a Negro, and the League withdrew the invitation from Gilpin. Furious, O'Neill, accompanied by Kenneth Macgowan, who did the talking, went around to other actors who had been asked, told them what had happened, and asked them to decline their invitations, which they did; as a result Gilpin was reinvited, and the affair was a great success.

But the strain was too much on both men. Gilpin began to drink heavily, performance or not, and began to edit the play; he could not, understandably, continue to utter the word "nigger" every night and began to substitute euphemisms, such as "black baby." If anything, once more understandably, was calcuated to infuriate O'Neill it was this: tampering with his hard-won dialogue. One night he went backstage and said to Gilpin: "If I ever catch you rewriting my lines again, you black bastard, I'm going to beat you up" (*ibid.*, p. 449). Gilpin was neither asked to play in the English production nor to appear in the New York revival. O'Neill said: "Honestly, I've stood for more from him than from all the white actors I've ever known—simply because he was colored! He played Emperor with author, play and everyone concerned. There is humor in the situation but I confess mine has worn out" (*ibid.*). Meanwhile O'Neill had discovered another young Negro—"with considerable experience, wonderful presence and voice, full of ambition and a damn fine man personally with real brains—not a 'ham'" (*ibid.*), for the role, namely, Paul Robeson. The rest of the story is sad enough. Gilpin got no more parts, went back to a farm in New Jersey, and died at fifty-one. He had some final, wistful remarks to make about *The Emperor Jones:* "I created the role of the Emperor. That role belongs to me. That Irishman, he just wrote the play" (*ibid.*, p. 450).

Gilpin too probably resented the play's atavism, whereby the terrors of the jungle night reduce the proud Jones to a cringing, crawling African savage, just before his end. But this was precisely the point of O'Neill, who was himself an atavist and who therefore thought that the real cultural roots of the Negro lay in Africa where, in fact, in the nineteenth century the Negro had been an aboriginal, who, to reverse the order of the sequence of the play, had come from the primeval jungle (Scene VII), across the Atlantic Ocean in slave ships (VI), to the auction block in the United States (V), to, later on, prison gangs (IV), to subjobs as Pullman porters and to orgiastic outlets, such as gambling, for his intolerable situation (III), and, to therefore, a kind of built-in psychic instability (II), and to advancing himself in anyway he could, if strong enough and clever enough, like Jones (I). But to go to his death if his power weakened (VIII). The other racial point, made in Scene I, is quite clear. Jones, the Negro, is tall, powerfully built, strong of will, self-reliant, keen and cunning in intelligence, and has a certain grandeur. Like Mark Twain's Jim and Melville's Queequeg, although with none of their natural sweetness, Jones is a kind of noble savage. Smithers, the white cockney, is stoop-shouldered, with a pasty face, with *"little, washy-blue eyes ... red-rimmed ... dart[ing] about him like a ferret's."* He presents an expression of *"unscrupulous meanness, cowardly and dangerous"* (I). So much for white natural superiority. The grandeur of Jones even elicits some grudging praise on the part of Smithers, who remarks, with real admiration, that Jones is a "cool bird."

The black-white polarity fascinated O'Neill, as it does, understandably, most American writers, and it carried over to a second play, *The Hairy Ape*, written after *The Emperor Jones*, where, as in *A Moon for the Misbegotten*, brute power faces neurasthenic, second-generation, American wealth. *The Hairy Ape* itself is full of the black-white symbolism. For example, Mildred, who is dressed in white, looks up at a smoke stack and remarks: "How the black smoke swirls back against the sky! Is it not beautiful?" (II), but the central confrontation occurs in the stokehole between the terrified, slender, white-skinned, white-clad Mildred and the black, half-clad, muscular brute, Yank, the Hairy Ape. This would suggest a familiar theme in the American racial situation, or at least one popular version of it, which comes to the surface in O'Neill's next Negro play, *All God's Chillun Got Wings*, namely, that black stands for animal vitality, while white signifies frayed nerves.

The classical O'Neill play about the American Negro, and one of the best on the subject, is *All God's Chillun Got Wings*, and since it is one of the most serious, compassionate, and profound artistic treatments of the racial problem in America ever written, comparable to *Huckleberry Finn* or *Pudd'nhead Wilson* or *The Sound and the Fury*, it has caused the most furor. With a prescience and boldness unusual for the 1920's O'Neill, in *All God's Chillun Got Wings*, went right to the heart of the racial matter, the sexual relation and miscegenation and presented a black-white marriage, in which at the end of the play the white actress (Mary Blair) kissed the hand of the Negro actor (Paul Robeson). When these "horrors" were bruited about—the play was published before it was performed—there was a national outcry comparable to that about the Scope's trial although O'Neill's material was much the more incendiary. John S. Sumner of the Society for the Suppression of Vice, said the play should be suppressed; the Mayor of New York received so many complaints about it that he ordered an investigation; there were poison-pen letters, threats from the KKK, and threatened law suits; O'Neill was denounced by the Irish Catholics as a disgrace to their race. Perhaps no play in history received such advance publicity. The company even received a bomb warning. By opening night it had been "legally" established that the white children could not play the opening scene with the colored children (Jimmy Light, one of the Provincetown Players, read that particular scene on the opening night, which was overseen by the police). To O'Neill's disappointment, really, there were no incidents to mar the occasion of the first performance.

As befitting a black-white play, *All God's Chillun Got Wings* is rampant, literally, with the contrasting rhythms of sounds and songs: street noises, popular songs, an organ grinder, and so on. Brooding over the entire play, like the fog horn in *Long Day's Journey*, is a Negro spiritual, sung just before the climactic moment of the play, the marriage of Ella and Jim:

> *. . . a Negro tenor sings in a voice of shadowy richness—*
> *the first stanza with a contented, childlike melancholy—*
> > Sometimes I feel like a mourning dove,
> > Sometimes I feel like a mourning dove,
> > Sometimes I feel like a mourning dove,
> > > I feel like a mourning dove.
> > > Feel like a mourning dove.
> *The second with a dreamy, boyish exultance—*
> > Sometimes I feel like an eagle in the air,
> > Sometimes I feel like an eagle in the air,
> > Sometimes I feel like an eagle in the air,
> > > I feel like an eagle in the air.
> > > Feel like an eagle in the air
> *The third with a brooding, earthbound sorrow—*
> > Sometimes I wish that I'd never been born,
> > Sometimes I wish that I'd never been born,
> > Sometimes I wish that I'd never been born,
> > > I wish that I'd never been born.
> > > Wish that I'd never been born.

This is the black rhythm; then comes the white rhythm: *"one startling, metallic clang of the church-bell."* At the sound the blacks and whites pour forth and form into two racial lines facing one another, staring at each other with *"bitter hostile eyes."*

Some of the points about the racial situation in *All God's Chillun* are fairly obvious; some less so. The obvious one is, of course, that the children, colored and white, who play happily together in Act I, Scene 1, must, as they grown up, diverge into hostile groups. But most of the other characters and situations in the play have some of the irony and subtlety of *Huckleberry Finn* in which two characters, Huck and Jim, have come together as human beings but who have been so profoundly, overwhelmingly stamped with racial categories that these categories have become Kantian configurations in the mind, like the ideas of space and time. By helping Jim, whom he loves, Huck thinks he will go to hell because he helped a "nigger." Jim, on his part, can never think outside of racial terms: "I'd bust him over de head, dat is, if he warn't a white man." As with Twain, the point that O'Neill makes in *All God's Chillun,* is that the problem is almost insuperably complex for *any* individual, white or colored, who is involved in it. For the heart of the play resides in the fact that it is not about the economic and legal barriers that impede the rise of the Negro; to the contrary, Jim's father was a successful businessman. Jim is able to go to law school with white students and to take the examinations; he can marry, and in a church at that, a white woman; he can go to live in France with her, to escape. But he can't escape, and has to return, for the play is about inescapable states of mind created by an impossible situation, under which no individual can have the strength and dignity to be himself. Practically all the characters, white or colored, pay some terrible price for a situation they have not personally created.

As *Long Day's Journey Into Night* shows degrees of assimilation of the Irish—from the crude peasant Shaughnessy up through the sensitive educated "poet," Edmund Tyrone—so *All God's Chillun* shows the degrees of assimilation of the much more deeply set apart and less assimilable Negro. The only well-adjusted Negro character is Jim's mother, and adjusted precisely because she has completely accepted her prescribed role as a "Negro," an "Aunt Jemima," a different order of being from the whites;

there is, she says, one road for the whites and another for the blacks. Farther up the scale is the furious Negro whose fury is directed at his fellow Negro who is trying to get ahead in the white man's world and in the white man's way, as Jim is. This is Joe of Act I, Scene 2:

> . . . [*In a rage at the other's* (Jim's) *silence*] You don't talk? Den I takes it out o' yo' hide! [*He grabs* JIM *by the throat with one hand and draws the other fist back*] Tell me befo' I wrecks yo' face in! Is you a nigger or isn't you? [*Shaking him*] Is you a nigger, Nigger? Nigger, is you a nigger?
> JIM   [*looking into his eyes—directly*]   Yes. I'm a nigger. We're both niggers. [*They look at each other for a moment.* JOE'S *rage vanishes.* . . .]

But even when one is intelligent and educated, there is still no escape from the psychological malaise. Jim's sister Hattie is described as a woman of thirty, intelligent, courageous, even powerful, but high-strung and dressed in a severe and mannish manner. She has achieved something, but at the price of chronic nervousness and the loss of her very femininity. And although a schoolteacher, and presumably a good one, she must endure the indignity of the indifferent scorn and sense of superiority of the white ex-prostitute, Ella, whom her brother has married. Thus for Hattie the whites must always be "them." All Negroes, no matter how determined, fall under the mother's somber generalization: "Dey ain't many strong. Dey ain't many happy neider" (II, 1).

The only person in the play who almost escapes racial prejudice or hatred is Jim, named, I am sure, for his prototype, the Jim of *Huckleberry Finn*. But again at a terrible price: the inability to sustain himself and his integrity in the presence of whites. He does not have hatred to back him up. He is intelligent, well-educated, unaccented, and hard-working, the equal to any of his white counterparts, but he cannot pass the law examination because (I, 3):

> . . . I swear I know more'n any member of my class. I ought to, I study harder. I work like the devil. It's all in my head—all fine and correct to a T. Then when I'm called on—I stand up—all the white faces looking at me—and I can feel their eyes—I hear my own voice

sounding funny, trembling—and all of a sudden it's all gone in my head—there's nothing remembered—and I hear myself stuttering—and give up—sit down— They don't laugh, hardly ever. They're kind. They're good people. [*In a frenzy*] They're considerate, damn them! But I feel branded!

ELLA    Poor Jim.

JIM    [*going on painfully*]    And it's the same thing in the written exams. For weeks before I study all night. I can't sleep anyway. I learn it all, I see it, I understand it. Then they give me the paper in the exam room. I look it over, I know each answer—perfectly. I take up my pen. On all sides are white men starting to write. They're so sure—even the ones that I know know nothing. But I know it all—but I can't remember any more— it fades—it goes—it's gone. There's a blank in my head —stupidity—I sit like a fool fighting to remember a little bit here, a little bit there—not cnough to pass— not enough for anything—when I know it all!

And when the uncomprehending Ella tells him to give it up, he replies: "I need it more than anyone ever needed anything. I need it to live."

The point that O'Neill is making is that the genuinely intolerable thing about a racial situation is not laws and overt taboos—in the long run these can be overcome—but attitudes; and that the well-meaning white, who still thinks in his heart of hearts that he is a different, and better, being than the Negro, is in some ways harder to bear than the outright racist, who, at least, can be hated. And even Jim himself cannot completely escape the racial habit of mind; thus when in the last scene of the play his by now practically insane wife goads him beyond endurance, it is her very whiteness that is part of her evil, and he calls her a "white devil woman."

The most deeply ingrained racist is the white heroine, Ella Downey. Again the point O'Neill makes with her is acute, especially for the 1920's. Although, as an individual, she loves Jim, her white racial consciousness cannot accept him sexually. Thus she turns sexually inhibited and neurotic and finally almost insane. As with all O'Neill tragic protagonists, her only escape finally is in loss of identity, in her case escape into the past of her childhood when race did not matter. Thus the last scene of the play comes full circle to the first, with Ella once again the innocent little white girl playing with Jim, the innocent little black boy, as in Scene 1. In the words of the last lines of the play:

ELLA  [*jumping to her feet—excitedly*]  Don't cry, Jim! You musn't cry! I've got only a little time left and I want to play. Don't be old Uncle Jim now. Be my little boy Jim. Pretend you're Painty Face and I'm Jim Crow. Come and play!

JIM  [*still deeply exalted*]  Honey, Honey, I'll play right up to the gates of Heaven with you! [*She tugs at one of his hands, laughingly trying to pull him up from his knees as the curtain falls.*]

And behind it all is a primitive sexual-racial fear. Hattie tells Jim that Ella is afraid to have a child by him "because it'll be born black—!" (II, 2).

The point made with Jim is that, because of skin pigmentation, he must be subjected to endless, piled-up humiliations and frustrations. No other character in all of O'Neill's plays, where humiliations and frustrations constitute the web of life, undergoes so many. In Act II, Scene 2, his sister Hattie enumerates for him his sorrows and burdens: that he himself is liable to break down; that his wife, Ella, will be sick a long time; that she, Ella, should go to a sanatorium; that she, the demented Ella, hates, in part anyway, her husband and calls him "Black!" Black!"; that she, Hattie, must leave and that Jim, while trying to study for his law examination, must himself now nurse Ella; that Ella will not have a baby by him, her husband; and that Ella should be sent to an asylum or they will probably both go together. After this harrowing series of prophecies Ella herself comes on the stage, carrying a carving knife and calling him, "Nigger." In the last scene of the play, after he announces that he has again failed the law examinations, the happy and triumphant Ella exclaims: "Oh, Jim, I knew it I knew you couldn't! Oh, I'm so glad, Jim! I'm so happy You're still my old Jim—and I'm so glad" It is at this point that he calls her a "white devil."

As in *The Emperor Jones*, and in the other racial plays, atavism plays a powerful role, although, as contrasted to *The Emperor Jones*, its role in *All God's Chillun Got Wings* is a positive rather than a negative, the idea being

that the African Negro had a culture of his own, worthy
of aesthetic comparison to white Western culture and
that, when he was torn loose from it, and transplanted
to America, he not only lost his genuine cultural roots but
was subjected to taking on only the farcical trappings,
the parody of his "adopted" culture. Thus in Act II, Scene
1, the apartment of Jim's mother is described: "*On one
wall, in a heavy gold frame, is a colored photograph—the
portrait of an elderly Negro with an able, shrewd face but
dressed in an outlandish lodge regalia, a get-up adorned
with medals, sashes, a cocked hat with frills—the whole
effect as absurd to contemplate as one of Napoleon's Mar-
shalls in full uniform.*" In short, Jim's father gets only a
parody of Western culture. But: "*In the left corner, where
a window lights it effectively, is a Negro primitive mask
from the Congo—a grotesque face, inspiring obscure, dim
connotations in one's mind, but beautifully done, conceived in a true religious spirit.*" It is this mask, which
signifies Negro creativity and sense of beauty, that Ella
fears and detests. As the tragedy deepens and as, to suggest this, O'Neill's stage directions have the room shrink-
ing, the mask "*look[s] unnaturally large and domineering*"
(II, 2). When Jim announces his failure in the law examinations, Ella grabs the mask from the wall, places it
on a table, and plunges a knife through it. The symbolism
of the act is fairly obvious, as she explains: "It's all right,
Jim! It's dead. The devil's dead. See! It couldn't live—
unless you passed. If you'd passed it would have lived in
you. Then I'd have had to kill you, Jim, don't you see—
or it would have killed me. But now I've killed it (*She
pats his hand*) So you needn't ever be afraid any more,
Jim" (II, 3).

In O'Neill's deterministic world, the most beset figure
is the long-suffering black man, Jim Harris. Joe Mott of
*The Iceman Cometh* can escape into alcohol and dreams
of glorious yesterdays. Dreamy, of *The Dreamy Kid*, represents the other side of the coin, of which Jim Harris is
one side, for he turns, not Christ-like, but fierce and cruel
and a killer. Thus at the end of the play, as his dying
Mammy (his grandmother) tells Dreamy how he got the
name "Dreamy," in the good old days before they came
"No'th" to the ghetto which has turned him into a criminal and when Dreamy's boyish eyes were "jest a-dreamin'

an' a-dreamin'," the grown-up Dreamy, armed and like a caged tiger, waits for the police to close in on him. But Jim Harris has not even this precarious freedom: "We're never free—except to do what we have to do" (I, 3).

Ironically, it is only back in history, in slavery times, that O'Neill can conceive of the existence of a "free" Negro. This is Cato, the Harford's coachman in *A Touch of the Poet*; as Mrs. Harford describes him: "Cato will be provoked at me for keeping him waiting. I've already caused his beloved horses to be half-devoured by flies. Cato is our black coachman. He also is fond of Simon, although since Simon became emancipated he has embarrassed Cato acutely by shaking his hand whenever they meet. Cato was always a self-possessed free man even when he was a slave. It astonishes him that Simon has to prove that he —I mean Simon—is free" (II).

But in the modern megalopolis, no such racial felicity is attainable: to exist with dark skin is to suffer, and to exist with white skin, in proximity to the dark, is to suffer too. O'Neill was sure that *All God's Chillun Got Wings* was one of his "most misunderstood" plays but that some-day it would come into its own.[7] What he really meant by its being misunderstood was that in the last analysis, and in its full scope, the play was not a racial play or about the "race problem" but about two human beings and their tragic struggle for happiness;[3] that by the last act Jim and Ella are mankind and its problems. He puts these sentiments into Jim's mouth in Act II, Scene 2: "She's all I've got! You with your fool talk of the black race and the white race! Where does the human race get a chance to come in?" In other words *All God's Chillun* was writ-ten in the same spirit as James Baldwin's *Go Tell It on the Mountain*, which, its author claims, is not a "Negro" novel, despite the fact that the principal characters are Negroes. At least one contemporary reader caught O'Neill's ultimate meaning here, and that was T. S. Eliot, who reviewed an O'Neill volume consisting of *All God's Chillun, Desire Under the Elms*, and *Welded* for *The Criterion* in April 1926. Singling out *All God's Chillun* as the most impressive and interesting of the three plays, Eliot said that it had its weaknesses but that O'Neill had got hold of a "strong plot," and had succeeded in giving the problem universality. In *"this"* respect, said Eliot,

O'Neill had been more successful than the author of *Othello*, for O'Neill had finally arrived at the "universal problem of differences which create a mixture of admiration, love, and contempt, with the consequent tension." At the same time O'Neill had never deviated from an exact portrayal of a "possible Negro" and the ending was "magnificent." The other dean of twentieth-century American criticism, Edmund Wilson, was equally enthusiastic about the play—which he saw performed—on its first level, as a racial document, which he called "one of the best things yet written about the race problem of Negro and white and one of the best of O'Neill's plays." [9] With such testimonials as these, it is to be hoped that history itself will someday catch up with the play.


## II *Male and Female*

O'Neill's various dramatizations of the primary polar relationship, that between the sexes, gravitates, as might be expected, between two extremes, a fervent idealization of its blisses and a mordant critique of its insuperabilities. Under the one dispensation, marriage or love, is a perpetual felicity; under the other they are both impossible; and of course, the two polar attitudes often merge in the same play, as they do in *A Touch of the Poet* and *Long Day's Journey Into Night*. Then subsumed under this general antithesis, there are three kinds of sexual relationships in O'Neill's plays: intercourse with whores, love affairs, and marriages.

O'Neill's prostitutes diverge into two polar types, or rather, constitute a spectrum, with the philosopher-whore, a romantic convention, at one end, and a fairly realistic representation of twentieth-century, American streetwalkers, at the other. The contrast can be seen at its most obvious between Cybel, the earth-mother-goddess of *The Great God Brown*, and the feather-brained young ladies of the evening of *The Iceman Cometh*. Cybel is strong, calm, junoesque, with a fresh and health complexion; she moves slowly and languorously, chews gum like a "sacred cow," and seems to stand outside time and to have access to some kind of rare and profound instinctual life, as her dreamy eyes indicate. Thematically, *The Great God*

*Brown* embodies two trains of thought or feeling, a negative and a positive. The negative theme is expressed, and lived out by the men, who, alone and afraid in a world they never made, torture themselves to death by their inability to bridge the gap between the real and the ideal. But to the women is given a vision of the world as a recognizable and unambiguous monolith, with certain recurring and basic repetitions, which one simply accepts. For this outlook the bovine Cybel is the spokeswoman, explicitly in her repetitious speech at the end of the play (see above, Chapt. I, Section i) and implicitly throughout the play as a whole, in which she is given various lines of gnomic wisdom as "Life's all right, if you let it alone" (I, 3).

As against the philosophical prostitute, we have the young ladies of *The Iceman Cometh*, described by O'Neill as "street walkers" and by themselves as "tarts," not "whores." They come not out of romantic literature but off the streets of New York in 1912. Pearl and Margie are described in Act I as typical dollar streetwalkers: each with a vestige of youthful freshness but each beginning to acquire the hard and worn expressions of the trade. They are sentimental, silly, giggly, lazy, good natured, and contented. Real too, no doubt, is "Fat Violet," the pachyderm of Mamie Burns's whore house in New London, described by Jamie Tyrone in Act IV of *Long Day's Journey Into Night*. So, too, is Belle, the prostitute in *Ah, Wilderness!* who tells Richard that he can do a lot with her for five dollars but that the one thing he can't do is to reform her. All these young ladies are no doubt closer to reality than is Cybel. In Act IV of *Long Day's Journey*, that great penitential outpouring and confession, O'Neill has Jamie Tyrone tell Edmund that one of the many sins he has committed against his younger brother is to have built up in his brother's mind the image of whores as romantic and glamorous, instead of showing them as they really are, poor, diseased "slobs." In the late plays generally the picture of the prostitute tends to be, like all the other pictures, a literal transcription of reality, untinged by the slightest trace of invention, convention, or romanticism. Instead of fairly grammatical, philosophic meditations on the meaning of life, Margie and Pearl are given to more earthy distinctions and descriptions (I):

MARGIE    Anyway, we wouldn't keep no pimp, like we was reg'lar old whores. We ain't dat bad.
PEARL    No. We're tarts, but dat's all.

O'Neill's most famous prostitute, Anna Christie, is a blend of these polar types. Like Cybel, she is in the Franco-Dostoevskian tradition, the prostitute with the heart of gold, who, while defiled physically, is still a virgin soul. And she finally has a wildly improbable happy ending with the wildly improbable stage-Irishman, Matt Burke. On the other hand, her account of how she became a member of the world's oldest profession is quite realistic and authentic, as is her attitude toward her customers: "Men, I hate 'em—all of 'em!" (I). This same combination of romanticism and realism is put together in the prostitute in *Welded*, who is known only as WOMAN. Like the realistic whores of the late plays she is rather stupid and not at all glamorous, but, like Cybel, she is, at a lower level, a philosopher of the Stoic variety, "You can get used to anything, take it from me!" (II, 2).

The male attitude toward these ladies of the evening varies by about the same ratio that the women themselves do. Cybel has possession of life's meanings, and therefore all men seek her out, not only for sexual satisfaction but for the sense of tranquility that she alone can give. Only in her presence can Dion Anthony take off his mask and be himself. But in the bulk of the plays, first and last, although especially last, the representations of whores and the male attitude toward them are more realistic. In *The Iceman Cometh* Margie and Pearl are the object of a good-natured and kindly contempt and are never taken seriously, no more so than the native women who come aboard ship in *The Moon of the Caribbees* or the London tarts who help to shanghai Olson in *The Long Voyage Home*, or the Broadway "dolls" that Erie Smith of *Hughie* used to bring to the hotel. In this sexual underworld the men are usually crude, and between them and the whores there is a kind of freemasonry; thus in *Ah, Wilderness!* when the salesman comes into the barroom, Belle looks at him and he at her, exchanging in an instant, "a glance of complete recognition," for they know each other by heart, in advance. We may also assume, from fairly explicit hints in other parts of the play, that Uncle Sid is a member of the same sorority-fraternity.

For the more intelligent and complex males the prostitute means two complementary but contrasting things: first, bawdy and therefore enjoyable conversation; and, second, guilt-ridden sexual intercourse. It is in the late plays, as always, especially with Hickey of *The Iceman Cometh* and with Jamie Tyrone of *Long Day's Journey* and *A Moon for the Misbegotten*, that this paradox receives its fullest and darkest expression. Both Hickey and Jamie have come out of puritanical societies, Hickey from nineteenth-century fundamentalist, Middle-Western America, Jamie from early twentieth-century Irish Catholic New York and New England; in both cultures there was a firm distinction between "nice" girls, to whom certain words were not said, and "bad" girls, with whom anything went. In his long monologue in Act IV Hickey explains this side of the attraction. In his puritanical home town there had been one "hooker shop" and, as a boy, he liked to sit around in the parlor and joke with the girls. And they liked it too because he could "kid 'em along and make 'em laugh." But Evelyn, the "nice" girl and his future wife, does not like this kind of talk; thus even before their marriage Hickey lives in and gravitates between two incompatible realms.

By the same token Jamie's wild adventure with "Fat Violet" on the night of the "long day's journey" was motivated not only by a sexual urge but by a desire for some mocking and bawdy conversation. He tells Edmund how he took "Vi" upstairs to have "a little heart-to-heart talk concerning the infinite sorrow of life," how he recited poetry and talked "seriously" with her until she got good and mad and insulted and said that she was better than any drunken bum who recited poetry. He then had to tell her he loved her and make love to her. This finally led to a tearful farewell between the two of them, which convinced Mamie Burns that he, Jamie, was "bughouse." Jamie continues, intoxicated by now with his own bizarre, verbal high jinks: "I shall give the art of acting back to the performing seals, which are its most perfect expression. By applying my natural God-given talents in their proper sphere, I shall attain the pinnacle of success! I'll be the lover of the fat woman in Barnum and Bailey's circus!"

But all this Rabelaisian wordplay is finally only a veneer

or surface behind which Hickey and Jamie suffer, for to them prostitutes are not only bought flesh but are also instruments by which these sinners torture themselves, piling guilt upon guilt. Both are trapped in the familiar O'Neill moral impasse described by Orin Mannon in Act III of *The Haunted:* "The only love I can know now is the love of guilt for guilt." For both men there is an undefiled woman in the background: for Hickey, his wife Evelyn; for Jamie, his mother, Mary. And it is because of their feelings of guilt toward these chaste women that the two men punish themselves with whores although they themselves are not always conscious of this paradox. What Hickey thought he wanted was "some tramp" that he could be himself with, tell a dirty joke to, and not be ashamed. Actually what he was doing was piling up guilt for himself and hate for his wife; until, "There's a limit to the guilt you can feel and the forgiveness and the pity you can take!" So he finally shoots her, in order, he thinks, to save her from her sufferings. But when he tells this story to the denizens of Harry Hope's saloon, his unconscious motive bursts out, uncontrollably: "Well, you know what you can do with your pipe dream now, you damned bitch!" And he is taken off by the police, a broken man, not knowing himself whether in the last analysis he hated her or loved her. So, too, Jamie Tyrone symbolically "murders" his dead mother, the devotee of the Virgin Mary, the symbol of sexual chastity, by his conduct on the train when he is bringing her body back to the East Coast from Los Angeles. He stayed drunk and had a nightly assignation with a tough, blonde, fifty-dollar whore, and sang scraps from an old "tear-jerker" ballad: "And baby's cries can't waken her / In the baggage coach ahead." Both men go from these desecrations to their death, in a sense to their suicides: Hickey to the electric chair which is his destination, as he knows, after murdering Evelyn; and Jamie to the slow and prolonged suicide of alcoholism. In the deepest pits of O'Neill's secular hell are those for whom sex is guilt and for whom guilt is death.

O'Neill's treatment of romantic love tends to diverge in two directions: pictures of wildly romantic—"the world well lost"—love affairs, of couples who literally give their all for one another; and the opposite, pictures of frustration and subsequent humiliation. The paradigm for the romantic love affair in O'Neill's plays is first sketched in jejeune fashion in *Recklessness,* an early one-act play concerned with the love affair between Mildred Baldwin, married to a crude businessman, and Fred Burgess, their handsome young chauffeur. Some of the qualities, or lack of them, of this play can be gauged from the dialogue. Thus Fred: "As soon as I've passed those engineering examinations—and I will pass them—we'll go away together." But, as in *The Great Gatsby,* the automobile is used as an executioner, and Arthur Baldwin arranges for Fred to be killed while driving the car. Life not being possible without Fred, Mildred shoots herself as the play ends. As romantic in its way is *Anna Christie,* which turns on "love at first sight." Matt Burke has hardly come completely to his senses, after his terrible experiences in the lifeboat, when he is proposing to Anna. He has been telling Anna how he would like to settle down and has selected her to do it with: "Tis you, I mean." When in Act III he hears that she has been a prostitute, his whole world collapses and he breaks into an Irish wail of lamentation. But true love can conquer all and even wipe out the past, no matter how unsavory. When the lovers are reunited in Act IV, Burke exclaims: "(*simply*) For I've a power of strength in me to lead men the way I want, and women, too, maybe, and I'm thinking I'd change you to a new woman entirely, so I'd never know, or you either, what kind of woman you'd been in the past at all." And this statement is the meaning of the play, despite O'Neill's attempt to make it all questionable by giving old Chris the final, somber words of the play.

The "world well lost" theme reappears, in varying ways, in *Desire Under the Elms, Mourning Becomes Electra,* and *Strange Interlude,* in which men and women either ruin their lives or go to their deaths because of a consuming passion. In *Desire Under the Elms* it is death. Eben could escape at the end of the play but he will not, for, as he explains to Abbie, he could never forget her and he must share everything with her, "prison 'r death 'r hell": then he will not be lonesone. In *Mourning Becomes Electra* it is the woman, Christine Mannon, who loses the world for love.

The most complex and sustained picture of a man ruining his life because of a woman in O'Neill's plays is that of Darrell in *Strange Interlude* and here, as in so many ways, O'Neill is a continuator of some characteristic themes of the nineteenth-century novel. In the nineteenth-century novel the most well-known instances of men of great intellectual ability and great ideals being ruined by infatuations with beautiful women are doctors, namely, Turgenev's Bazarov and George Eliot's Lydgate. The resemblances between their characters and fates and that of Darrell, also a doctor, are striking. Both Bazarov and Lydgate are strong, tough, resolute, dedicated men, with twin and complementary ambitions: to do medical research and promote social reform. The irony of their fates —Lydgate turned into a society doctor by the demands of his wife, Bazarov a conscious-unconscious suicide because of his hopeless passion for Madame Odintsov— arises from the fact that each, supposedly completely self-sufficient and wholly dedicated, has, unbeknownst to himself, a weakness for beautiful women. When Bazarov first sees Madame Odintsov he thinks, "What a magnificent body. Shouldn't I like to see it on a dissection-table." But he is soon interested in that same body in a most unscientific manner; it becomes his romantic obsession and finally his ruination. So Darrell in *Strange Interlude* is first introduced as the coolly self-sufficient, emotionally self-contained man of science. He is handsome, intelligent, supremely analytical and uncommitted to anything save his work. As with Bazarov, even his sexual feelings are a scientific phenomenon to be observed dispassionately. But after his love affair with Nina he is trapped ("her body is a trap!"—V). A trip to Europe, other women, dissipation, none of these escapes can quell the all-consuming passion. In Act VI he returns, haggard, worn, dissipated, his pride gone, hopelessly and permanently in love with Nina. He then settles down to his official, but secret, occupation as Nina's lover, and eleven years later has grown stout, jowly, puffy, aimless and unambitious. He has become solely a cotquean or, in George Eliot's phrase, Nina's "basil plant." (Near the end of *Middlemarch* with Lydgate conquered by his wife Rosamond and merely existing as a fashionable doctor, he remarks to her that she has been his basil plant. When she asks what this is, Lydgate answers that a basil plant is a plant "which had flourished wonderfully on a murdered man's brains"—Finale.)

Darrell, however, is spared total extinction, and in Scene
VIII is reintroduced after eight years away from Nina;
these eight years of scientific research have restored him
to leanness and to *"the air of the cool detached scientist."*
But the obsession really never dies, and he almost falls
prey to Nina's body once more. Looking at her, he thinks,
"but she's kept her wonderful body ... how many years
since? ... she has the same strange influence over me."
Old as they are, she almost captures him again. It is the
sudden appearance of Marsden, drunk—they are on a yacht
at Poughkeepsie—that breaks the spell. Darrell pushes the
almost-triumphant Nina away from him and thinks:
"Marsden again! ... thank God! ... he's saved me!" Still,
she has dominated his life, and he can never claim his
son by her. In the last act he is finally left alone with his
"cells"; as he walks off stage at the end, the oblivious Nina
does not even hear his last words, for she is staring at the
airplane which is carrying away their love-child, now grown
and married.

O'Neill's other subject in the area of romantic love was
frustration, both masculine and feminine, although the
feminine frustrations are more numerous and more harrowing. The most sustained pictures by O'Neill of male
frustration are Yank in *The Hairy Ape* and Jim in *All
God's Chillun Got Wings*. It is true that neither of these
dramatizations of humiliation is caused by sexual rebuffs,
pure and simple. In *All God's Chillun Got Wings* there
is the racial issue, and in *The Hairy Ape* there are a lot
of other issues—but in each case it is a light-colored
woman facing and scorning a dark-colored man that sets
off the machinery of humiliation and self-doubt and which,
with Yank, leads to final immolation. In Scene I of *The
Hairy Ape* Yank, the brutelike leader of the stokehole
gang, has a simple and perfect metaphysic: everything in
the world moves, but nothing moves unless moved by
"somep'n else." If this chain of cause-and-effect movements is followed out, one finally arrives at Yank, who
is thus at the center of things. Then in Scene III occurs
the confrontation with Mildred Douglas, the neurasthenic
heiress. In a career given to dramatizing startling contrasts,
O'Neill in this scene gave one of his most startling:
woman vs. man; white vs. black; top-dog vs. bottom-dog;
frayed nerves vs. brute power; the slight vs. the muscular;

civilization vs. the jungle: as the snarling, ferocious, ape-like, crouching beast-man, his lips drawn back over his teeth, his little eyes gleaming like those of a jungle animal, whirls and faces—his eyes boring into hers—the slight, high-strung, decadent young woman who is crushed, paralyzed, almost turned to stone, by the unimaginable figure of brutality, power, and ferocity that stands before her. But at her outcry of horror Yank's mouth falls open and his eyes begin to grow bewildered. He has started down the road to self-extinction.

The frustrated male appears in many of O'Neill's plays: *The Fountain, The Great God Brown, Strange Interlude, Mourning Becomes Electra, Ah, Wilderness!* and, most powerfully, in *A Moon for the Misbegotten*. In *The Great God Brown* and *Strange Interlude* he is also the humiliated man and must experience the contempt of his loved one. In *Strange Interlude* Marsden must endure Nina's calling him "good old Charlie." Brown of *The Great God Brown*, having assumed the dead Dion Anthony's mask and thus his position as Margaret's husband, must actually listen to Margaret express her distaste for Brown and her description of him as a "stupid old fool" (III, 3).

The classic instance of male frustration is Jamie Tyrone in *A Moon for the Misbegotten* where Jamie's physical desire for Josie is absolutely dammed up by his feelings of guilt, and even the basic desire to communicate with her, simply to talk honestly and without evasion, is almost so. That he desires her there can be no doubt, but he cannot think of sexual relations except in terms of debasement and defilement followed by a gray, "hung-over" dawn, and Josie is, in his words, "real and healthy and clean and fine and warm and strong and kind—" (III). Thus he could not bring himself to desecrate her. If a physical union is impossible, their emotional union is almost as difficult. Jamie wishes to "confess" to her, but he delays coming to their nocturnal and prearranged meeting. She finally concludes that he will not come at all, and he does not arrive until very late and is, of course, quietly drunk. Even then it takes almost a whole act before they can grope their way to an honest emotional relationship. Only more whiskey and an agonized recital of Tyrone's sins and transgressions can finally bring the two together in any significant way. I know of no finer description of this tortuous process than that by Nicola Chiarmonte: [10] "I cannot remember any comparable passage in any work of literature: nowhere else is the almost insurmountable difficulty preventing two human creatures from communication as such, expressed with like violence, with like torment, with a like rough, wordy and disorderly confession, but with like moving authenticity." Chiarmonte continues: "We are present not at a dialogue but at a struggle in the dark. We emerge exhausted and, if not moved, at least shaken." Josie, at least, finally does understand what happened between them and realizes that her presence—for she mostly listens—has been for Jamie as "a promise of God's peace in the soul's dark sadness" (III). Jamie also, through the haze of alcohol, recognizes that for once he has come together in an honest, human relationship with a woman other than his mother. But it can only be temporary communion and her final words to his departing figure are "May you have your wish and die in your sleep soon, Jim, darling."

Feminine frustration and humiliation loom even larger in O'Neill's dramatic world, right from the beginning of his career. In *Moon of the Caribbees* Smitty repulses and thus humiliates a native girl. In *In the Zone* Driscoll reads to the sailors, who mistakenly think Smitty a spy, a letter written by Smitty's ex-fiancée, Edith, who charges him with having wrecked both her life and his own because of his drunkenness. Edith is the archetype for a whole series of women in O'Neill's plays who must endure humiliation and frustration at the hands of the man they love. *Beyond the Horizon* is the first large-scale picture of the frustrated and humiliated woman, Ruth Mayo. Having married the wrong Mayo Brother, Robert, whom she thought she loved, rather than Andy, who loved her, she must see her marriage fall apart, along with the farm. Her consolation is that the absent Andy still loves her and that he will be a final refuge for her. But this consolation is taken away from her by Andy himself and in a most humiliating fashion. Three years have passed and Andy has returned. Dressed in her best white dress, Ruth is alone with him on a sun-lit hilltop, and she takes the opportunity to sound him out, to let him know, although he did not know it, that she really loved him all along.

But he quite unconsciously and brutally lets her understand that he does not love her any longer, describing himself at the time when he did love her as a "dumb fool." She tries to stop the conversation after this, but the obtuse Andy blunders ahead, unconsciously twisting the knife, until laughing hysterically, she commands him to stop talking.

The classic instance of the humiliated heroine in O'Neill's early plays is Eileen Carmody of *The Straw*. *The Straw*, which takes place in a tuberculosis sanatorium, is not a good play in its entirety although there are some good things in it, such as the poignancy of the heroine's plight. Eileen Carmody is the sweet and sensitive child of a mean and stupid father. Her mother is dead and her siblings, save one, are like her father. Tubercular, she must keep the house and try to maintain in it some order and decency. The young man who supposedly loves her promptly becomes uneasy when she is diagnosed as tubercular. Her unfeeling father does not want to spend any money on her, but an angry doctor forces him to pay part of the expenses when Eileen is finally sent to a sanatorium as a partial charity case. When she is brought to the sanatorium by her father and her now reluctant fiance, both behave characteristically. The young man cannot get away fast enough, for good, and the father is openly drinking from a bottle in the waiting room of the sanatorium. She learns from her father that a brutal older woman, a Mrs. Brennan, who is later to marry her father, is to take her place in the household and to "bring up" the children. Her young man is afraid to kiss her goodbye for fear of catching consumption. At the sanatorium she meets and falls in love with a young newspaper man, Stephen Murray, who does not reciprocate her feelings. She encourages him to write, which he does, and as he gets better in health and succeeds in getting some stories accepted for publication, her health declines. As he prepares to leave to return to normal life, she is on the verge of being sent to another sanatorium where the hopeless cases are sent to die. The night that Stephen leaves, they have an assignation in the forest where she realizes that he does not love her, and she forgives him for this last, and what may prove to be fatal, blow (II, 2):

EILEEN  Then I want to say—I know your secret. You
don't love me—Isn't that it? [MURRAY *groans*] Ssshh!
It's all right, dear. You can't help what you don't feel.
I've guessed you didn't—right along. And I've loved you
—such a long time now—always, it seems. And you've sort
of guessed—that I did—didn't you? No, don't speak!
I am sure you've guessed—only you didn't want to know
—that—did you?—when you didn't love me. That's why
you were lying—but I saw, I knew! Oh, I'm not blaming you, darling. How could I—never! You mustn't look
so—so frightened. I know how you felt, dear. I've—I've
watched you.

Her explanation continues at further length, punctuated
only by groans of guilt and self-accusations on the part
of Murray. She concludes, brokenly:

Sshh! Let me finish. You don't know how alone I am
now. Father—he'll marry that housekeeper—and the children—they've forgotten me. None of them need me
any more. They've found out how to get on without
me—and I'm a drag—dead to them—no place for me
home any more—and they'll be afraid to have me back—
afraid of catching—I know she won't want me back.
And Fred—he's gone—he never mattered, anyway. Forgive me, dear—worrying you—only I want you to know
how much you've meant to me—so you won't forget
—ever—after you've gone.

The language here is perfectly commonplace and could
have been written by any reasonably competent soap-
opera writer. What gives the passage its force is its context which has been described in detail above. In the
play as a whole the portrait of Eileen gathers even more
force because of the lack of sentimentality in the drawing
and the absence of self-pity in the heroine, who just suffers. Her humiliations continue to heap up. In Act III she
is visited by her father, her new stepmother, and Mary,
her favorite sister, who had once, under Eileen's influence,
been sweet but who is now possessed of "a hangdog
sullenness." Eileen has to endure recriminations from
her stepmother and is repulsed when she tries to embrace Mary. There is finally an ambiguous mitigation at
the end of the play when Murray returns and declares
his love her for, but she is on the verge of death and
what they both are left with finally is a "hopeless hope,"
an illusion that their love will restore her ravaged lungs.

In the other plays variations on this same theme constantly recur. In *Diff'rent* Emma Crosby turns into a hideous old frump and grotesque coquette because of sexual repression. In *Marco Millions* Kukachin dies of a broken heart because the unfeeling Marco neither sees nor responds to her love for him. In *Lazarus Laughed* Lazarus repulses Pompeia. In *Dynamo* Reuben Light merely uses Ada Fife as a sexual object and will have no talk of "love." In *Ah, Wilderness!* Lily must remain a spinster because Sid is not to be trusted. In *A Moon for the Misbegotten* Josie Hogan can never have the man she loves because he is already a walking corpse.

The subject of love affairs in O'Neill's plays can hardly be separated from the subject of marriage, although I have done so here for purposes of discussion. The two become one in the figure of the sorrowing or frustrated or humiliated and/or guilty women who crop up in practically all of O'Neill's plays, whether they are concerned with a love affair or a marriage.

As for marriage, one might think, initially anyway, with such plays as *Strange Interlude, Mourning Becomes Electra, Desire Under the Elms,* and the like, that O'Neill is the dramatist of misogamy, which he is in part. On the whole however, and especially in the late plays, he is the celebrator of the values of wedded love, as well as the analyst of its complications. Almost alone among modern writers, he has presented marriages which are believable, durable, and positive, without being idealized and romanticized. This ability to portray such matches came from direct observation, for whatever was wrong with the lives of James and Ella O'Neill, there was never anything wrong with their marriage, which was the most durable possession of the O'Neill family.

In a general way O'Neill's picture of marriage evolves from the early plays, where it is usually pictured as an unmitigated disaster, through a middle period where it is a conflict between idealism and realism, to the final period when it tends to be creative and positive, though not without its stresses and strains. For O'Neill's own long journey finally took him back to the only certainty he ever knew: the lifelong love affair of his mother and father.

One of the first plays, if not the first, that O'Neill wrote was about marriage, namely, *A Wife for a Life,* and it

concludes with O'Neill's most bathetic single line, which
is also a remark about a marriage. A *Wife for a Life* takes
place in Arizona and concerns two prospectors, Jack and
"The Older Man." Unbeknownst to them the same
woman has been the badly treated wife of "The Older
Man" and the lover of Jack. At the beginning of the
play a telegram from her arrives for Jack, bidding him
to come to her. The point of the play is that "The Older
Man" gradually realizes who the woman is, but Jack
never knows that "The Older Man" is the husband.
Swallowing his jealousy, "The Older Man" keeps his
silence and lets Jack go back to HER. At the end of the
play "The Older Man" is left dolefully alone on the
stage, saying: "Greater love hath no man than this that
he giveth his wife for his friend."

Another early play, *Servitude*, is an Ibsenesque exploration of the ambiguities in the married life of a writer,
specifically, a playwright. It ends happily, as the "Other
Woman" straightens out the egotistical playwright. But
after this play, marriage in the early O'Neill plays is
liable to be a disaster: a shrewish wife (*Before Breakfast*
and *Beyond the Horizon*); a tyrannical and older husband
(*Ile* and *Desire Under the Elms*); a horde of unwanted
and undisciplined children (*Warnings* and *The Straw*);
or, from the children's point of view, stupid or unfeeling
parents (*The Straw, The Great God Brown,* and *Dynamo*). Only *The First Man,* of these earlier plays, exhibits a happy marriage, but the wife dies in child-
birth, the implication being, as if, on a variation on the
old saw, "Only the good die young," "Only the stupid
marriages can last." Thus all the other marriages in the
play are presented as decidedly unloving and unlovely.
In Act IV the bereaved husband, Curtis Jayson, rasps
out at his married sister, Emily, some epithets on "your
little rabbit hutch emotions" and "bread-and-butter passions—." Lurking behind all this cynicism and disillusionment about marriage is, as might be expected, a fervid
idealism about the same institution. Thus in the plays of
the twenties marriage, its nature and its problems, came
to the fore in a kind of running debate, notably in *Welded*
and *Days Without End,* but also in *The Great God
Brown, Strange Interlude, Dynamo,* and *Mourning Becomes Electra.*

The "marriage plays" proper, where marriage is discussed and dramatized at length, are *Welded* and *Days Without End*, both, significantly, dreadful plays, two of O'Neill's worst in banality, stale rhetoric, inconclusive characterization, and a kind of embarrassing, even at this date, outpouring of the author's own thoughts and desires. But it was probably necessary for O'Neill to write these plays, in order to cast off their burdens, so as to go on and write the last masterpieces. However, these two plays are not without their interest, intellectually anyway.

*Welded* was obviously based on O'Neill's marriage to Agnes Bolton. O'Neill went so far as to have Michael Cape, the male protagonist, resemble himself in appearance and be a playwright, while Eleanor Cape, the female protagonist, looks like Agnes Bolton but is changed from a writer, which the real Agnes Bolton is, to an actress (in O'Neill's terminology a word of opprobrium, even contempt: at the height of their argument in Act I he cried "(*furiously*) Good God, how dare you criticize creative work, you actress!"). Actually, the first act of *Welded*, with its discussion of the problems of a marriage between a sensitive and idealistic writer of genius and a rather prosaic woman with a career of her own, living together in New York, where both had lived before, and thus living amidst the tangible remains of past love affairs, is quite acute and is perhaps a discussion of the essential problems of all marriages, only here heightened and highlighted.

Michael Cape is an implacable and impossible idealist who demands that marriage be a total and perpetual romance, a continuously ecstatic union. The mood of the opening Act I is tender, with a dialogue that sounds ominously like Joyce's parody of this very kind of sentimentalism in the "Nausicaa" section of *Ulysses*, as when, for example, Gertie McDowell dreams of her ideal marriage:

He would be tall with broad shoulders (she had always admired tall men for a husband) with glistening white teeth under his carefully trimmed sweeping moustache and they would go on the continent for their honeymoon (three wonderful weeks!) and then, when they settled down in a nice snug and cosy little homely house, every morning they would both have brekky, simple but perfectly served, for their own two selves and before he went out to business he would give his dear little wifey a good hearty hug and gaze for a moment deep down into her eyes.

But O'Neill really *meant* it. At the opening of the play Michael has just returned after a brief absence:

CAPE  [*straining her in his arms and kissing her passionately*]  Own little wife!
ELEANOR  Dearest! [*They look into each other's eyes for a long moment.*]
CAPE  [*tenderly*]  Happy?

He notices a letter on the floor, and it turns out that, although they have been married for five years, she still reads his old love letters. But soon we find out that they quarrel repeatedly and both nag at one another for past affairs. A casual visitor, an old friend of Eleanor, drops in, and this is enough to set off Cape. Two spotlights shine always on these two egotistical lovers as they argue about marriage, which is their universe, in the light of the "Grand Ideal" for marriage that Michael Cape proposes. It soon settles down to a rather interesting *débat*, between a masculine "relentless idealist" and a woman of common sense. The arguments of each, because true, are unanswerable by the other, and marriage is shown to be a clearly impossible institution if compromises are not made. Here is the substance, not the complete dialogue, of the argument:

HE  More and more frequently. There's always some knock at the door, some reminder of the life outside which calls you away from me.
SHE  It's so beautiful—and then—suddenly I'm being crushed. I feel a cruel presence in you paralyzing me, creeping over my body, ... my soul—demanding to have that, too!
HE  I've grown inward into our life. But you keep trying to escape as if it were a prison.
SHE  Why is it I can never know you? I try to know you and I can't. I desire to take all of you into my heart, but there's a great alien force—
HE  At every turn you feel your individuality invaded— while at the same time, you're jealous of any separateness in me. You demand more and more while you give less and less.

SHE    You insist that I have no life at all outside you. Even
my work must exist only as an echo of yours. . . . You're
jealous of everything and everybody. [*Resentfully*]    I
have to fight. You're too severe. Your ideal is too inhuman.

The argument soon turns heated, to put it mildly.

SHE    Your egotism is making a fool of you! You're becoming so exaggeratedly conceited no one can stand you!
Everyone notices it!

A little later, "*with a snarl of fury*," he attempts to
throttle her. The play is a failure from here on, in terms
of dramatic interest and conviction as, in the next two
scenes, each of the protagonists tries to go to bed with
another mate, but they cannot bring themselves to go
through with it. In Act III they are back in their own
apartment wrangling in a lower key. The resolution comes
when they both accept marriage as a love-hate relationship. Cape declares that they will torture and tear and
clutch at one another, that they will fight and hate and
fail, but that they will "fail *with pride*—with joy!" As she
stands with her arms in the shape of a cross, the play
ends on a note of love.

The Great God Brown continues the *débat* on marriage, from an even more negative and almost exclusively
male point of view. If Welded was about the love-hate
aspect of marriage, The Great God Brown is about the
inability of man and wife, and child and parent, simply
to communicate with one another. In this play no one
ever really knows who or what the other person is, although they may have a preconceived theory of their
own about the nature of the partner. The theory is
usually wrong, but they cling to it despite any evidence
to the contrary. Thus in the Prologue when Dion tears
off his laughing, satirical, sensual Pan mask and displays
his somber, spiritual face, Margaret is frightened of him:
"Don't! Please! I don't know you! You frighten me"
Thus she marries her conception of him rather than the
real Dion. Years later, the by now alcoholic and ever
more tormented Dion exclaims against the domestic
diplomacy of marriage, whereby each partner communi-
cates by code and neither knows the other's key. In the
beginning of the play Margaret's mask is an abstraction

of her face, but as the play goes on her real face becomes
worried and haggard, while her mask becomes a "brave
face" that she turns to the world. Thus her children
never really know her because they see only the mask,
not the face. In Act II, Scene 2, when Dion takes off
his mask and shows her his real face, *"radiant with a
great pure love for her and a great sympathy and tenderness,"* she is horrified and screams that he is a "ghost."
She raises her mask to ward off his face and falls, fainting,
and when her three sons come in they find, along with
their strange father, a strange woman, who is not restored
to their mother until Dion puts her mask back on. The
play is full of such contretemps, with everyone, except
Dion and Cybel, a stranger to one another. The themes
of this aspect of the play are summed up by Dion in his
comments on his father and mother (I, 3):

> What aliens we were to each other! When he lay dead,
> his face looked so familiar that I wondered where I had met
> that man before. Only at the second of my conception.
> After that, we grew hostile with concealed shame. And my
> mother? I remember a sweet, strange girl, with affectionate,
> bewildered eyes as if God had locked her in a dark closet
> without any explanation. I was the sole doll our ogre, her
> husband, allowed her and she played mother and child with
> me for many years in that house until at last through two
> years I watched her die with the shy pride of one who has
> lengthened her dress and put up her hair. And I felt like
> a forsaken toy and cried to be buried with her, because her
> hands alone had caressed without clawing. She lived long
> and aged greatly in the two days before they closed her
> coffin. The last time I looked, her purity had forgotten me,
> she was stainless and imperishable, and I knew my sobs
> were ugly and meaningless to her virginity; so I shrank
> away, back into life, with naked nerves jumping like fleas,
> and in due course of nature another girl called me her
> boy in the moon and married me and become three moth-
> ers [their three sons] in one person, while I got paint on
> my paws in an endeavor to see God!

*Strange Interlude* continues the debate on the nature
of marriage, only now the viewpoint is almost exclusively
feminine, that of the interesting but impossible Nina.
*Strange Interlude* is concerned with the perplexities of
marriage and also with the need of the female to have
multiple male relationships. This multiplicity in marriage

makes the play the opposite to *Welded*, where an absolute one-to-one union is the ideal. In Act VI of *Strange
Interlude*, after Nina has had her baby by her lover
Darrell, and Darrell himself, hopelessly in love with her,
has returned to join the ever faithful Marsden and Nina's
husband, Sam, Nina is triumphant: a lover, a husband,
a father, all attached to her. It is at this point in the play
that she makes her famous "My three men!" speech, to
which she soon after adds a fourth, her son, the "little
man." She should be, she says, the happiest and proudest
woman in the world. Of the men only Marsden, the most
feminine, senses what has happened to them all: that
somehow Nina has "strange devious intuitions that tap
the hidden currents of life," which have entrapped each
of them and which make it almost as if "her child is the
child of our three loves for her."

But since one of the themes of the play is the instability of human relations, Nina's felicity cannot last, and
if she is always the magnet for the males, the steel fillings
are always, kaleidoscope-like, rearranging themselves. The
lover must break off and exit finally as only an old friend;
the husband must die; the son must grow up, marry, and
go away; and Nina must be left finally with only "good-
old" Charlie. And her marriage to a man that she did
not love, Sam Evans, has meant over the years only endless emotional strain. The triumph of Act VI is replaced
by: "These men make me sick! . . . I hate all three of
them! . . . they disgust me!" (VII).

The debate about marriage, as with so many other of
O'Neill's concerns and themes in his first career, closes
with *Day's Without End*, which is not only about religion but is also about marriage, especially as it is related
to the problems of religious faith, to adultery and its consequences, and to the concept of one male playing all the
roles necessary to the woman (the reverse of the situation in *Strange Interlude*). The marital theme and the
religious theme are linked by the fact that "Loving," the
cynical, skeptical side of John Loving makes "John" commit adultery with the old friend of his wife, in order to
wreck his own marriage which is "too happy" to be possible in a meaningless universe. "John" had not always
seen the universe as meaningless, however, for as a child
he had believed in the merciful and beneficent God taught

to him by his beloved parents; the "God of Punishment" taught at school had made little impression on him, as he could not reconcile it with the God of his parent's faith. But after his father died he came to believe in a "God of Vengeance," and upon the death of his mother when he was fifteen years old even this God ceased to exist, and he "promised his soul to the Devil"; thus was created "Loving." His "John" side is still a believer in religion and is faithful in his marriage. The action of the play dramatizes the ultimate healing of the break between man and God and man and wife, and the annihilation of the agnostic-adulterer "Loving." The psychology is unmistakably Catholic. Choosing his wife and a priest, Father Baird, as his priestly confessor, John obliquely but unmistakably "confesses" his sin to them. Shattered, his wife becomes ill, to the verge of death, which event her husband's skeptical side desires. But after they have suffered long enough, there is atonement. When he rushes out to the Catholic Church to regain his faith and to destroy "Loving," he also regains his marriage as well, for his wife recovers.

The play then is Dickensian in its wildly improbable happy ending. It was in fact the "happiest" happy ending of the few happy endings O'Neill ever devised, for the marriage of the Lovings is, once the adulterous stain has been exorcised and John becomes one of the faithful once more, that perfect union that the man and wife of *Welded* strove in vain to achieve, and Nina attained only momentarily and precariously. John is simultaneously Elsa's husband, lover, father, and child, and their marriage is not a prison but, in Elsa's words to a friend, "freedom and harmony within ourselves—and happiness" (II). The fact that the woman she tells this to is the woman with whom John committed adultery provides a large irony, but only a momentary one, which is to be flooded away by the ocean of bathos that is released at the end of the play. O'Neill probably reached the low point of his dramatic career at the end of this play when the now whole John Loving stands at dawn in the church before the crucifixion, with the impossible Father Baird purring in the background, his prodigal son finally come home. One can almost agonize with O'Neill as he gropes for his affirmative words to close the play. Perhaps some old memory of Alyosha's speech at Ilusha's stone at the end of *The Brothers Karamasov* remained in his memory, for, like Dostoevski, he tried to conclude his bout with God and the demon of unbelief on a note of New Testament sweetness and joy, emphasizing the childlike happiness of true faith. Unfortunately, O'Neill had not constructed beforehand an immense and complex dialectic of good and evil, as had Dostoevski in his novel, so the final words of *Days Without End* are as banal and sentimental as is the play as a whole: "Life laughs with God's love again! Life laughs with love!"

Ironically, right in the middle of his tortuous struggle to write the unsuccessful *Days Without End*, O'Neill composed in almost instantaneous fashion his successful comedy, *Ah, Wilderness!*, which, along with *Marco Millions*, constitutes his comic love letter to America. According to his own account, he dreamed the whole play one night in September, 1932, after having just completed a third and unsatisfactory draft of *Days Without End*. Within six weeks *Ah, Wilderness!* was completed in its final, and present, version. Thus *Ah, Wilderness!* was the "comic relief" for the absolutistic romanticisms that O'Neill was so unsuccessfully wrestling with in *Days Without End*.

*Ah, Wilderness!* is also about a felicitous marriage but one that is presented in perfectly prosaic, realistic, and common-sense terms, without a shade of the harrowing idealism that pervades *Welded* and *Days Without End*. In a sense *Ah, Wilderness!* says, in Delmore Schwartz's phrase, "A child is the meaning of this life," for Mr. and Mrs. Miller live principally for their children of whom there are six, although only four, Arthur, Mildred, Richard, and Tommy, appear on the stage in the play. Like the American family of today, the chief concern of the Millers is the education of their children. They are a family of readers and one of the opening stage directions, as in *Long Day's Journey Into Night*, describes bookcases filled with books, "*the family really have read.*" In the play they discuss or refer to Carlyle, Wilde, Shaw, Ibsen, Swinburne, Shelley, and the *Rubaiyat*. Arthur goes to Yale and is, indefatigably, a "Yale man." When the play gets serious at the end, after Richard's indiscretion, the big question is how he is to be punished. The ultimate punishment that Nat Miller can think of for his erring son is to threaten him with not going to Yale. When he suggests this, his indignant wife explodes: "Not go to Yale! I guess he can go to Yale!" And Miller has hastily to assure her that this is only a threat.

The Miller marriage is saved from being sentimentalized by certain realistic touches that O'Neill carefully inserts. Thus when Nat returns, mellowly alcoholic, from the Fourth of July picnic, he jokes with his wife and then *"slaps her jovially on her fat buttocks."* She, on her part, cheerfully perpetrates a long-standing deception on him, namely, serving him for years bluefish (under the name of "whitefish") about which he has an obsession that it contains an oil that is poisonous for him. When the deception is found out at dinner, she laughs with the others at her wounded husband. She also presumably joins in the general hilarity at the rather cruel mockery by Sid when Miller begins to tell his oft-told story of how, as an adolescent, he had saved another boy, named Red, from drowning. But when she sees Miller is genuinely hurt, she comes to his rescue and silences Sid. Again in Act III, Scene 2, when they are sitting up waiting for the erring Richard, the Millers, as parents will do, turn upon one another with mutual irritation: when Mrs. Miller tells Tommy that it is way past his bedtime, Tommy appeals to his father's often repeated theme that anything goes on the Fourth of July, and Mrs. Miller giving her husband an accusing stare, erupts: "There! You see what you've done? You might know he'd copy your excuses!"

*Ah, Wilderness!* is the idyllic prelude to the more troubled but equally firm marriages that occupy the scene in the late plays. *Hughie* and *The Iceman Cometh* are companion pieces in that in each play a long-suffering wife, who never herself appears on the stage, is yet fully characterized by a male speaker. In *Hughie*, through Erie Smith's monologue, we get a fairly detailed picture of the wife of Hughie, the night clerk, now deceased, who had preceded the night clerk of the play, Charlie Hughes. It seems that Erie had once gone to dinner at Hughie's flat and met his wife and children. But when Erie told the children an anecdote about a race horse, Hughie's wife turned cold to him, in order to protect the children from a baneful influence. As Hughie says, rather wistfully: "I coulda like her—a little—if she'd give me a chance." By Erie's random remarks we get a picture of a dauntless, if drab, woman, the wife of a bottom-dog, carrying on. In *The Iceman Cometh* her pendant as a character is Hickey's wife, Evelyn, who will never renege on, and always will forgive, her ever erring husband. Through drunken bouts, through the infection of a venereal disease, she remains steadfast, until her husband comes to hate her and finally kills her.

The final and most complex marriage plays by O'Neill are *A Touch of the Poet* and *Long Day's Journey Into Night*. Nora Melody of *A Touch of the Poet* is a sister to Evelyn Hickman, the martyr-wife, who will love her ambiguous husband in any form he assumes, be it officer and gentleman or brogue-speaking peasant. Having lost her youthful beauty by the passage of time and having been reduced to a slattern because of the drudgery to which she is committed by the necessity of her impecunious husband to keep up his "grand" appearances, Nora is ennobled, even transfigured, by the magnanimity of her devotion to her impossible husband. Melody is a question mark to himself and to everybody else in the play, except his wife, who alone understands that he is a completely isolated human being, that the only human relationship he has is to her, and that without her he would cease to exist. Near the end of the play when the proud Major has turned himself into a crude peasant, Nora is disturbed not at all. When at the very end of the play Con goes off to join the shanty Irish roistering at the bar, she remarks: "Well, why shouldn't he if it brings him peace and company in his loneliness? God pity him, he's had to live all his life alone in the hell av pride. *Proudly*. And I'll play any game he likes and give him love in it. Haven't I always?" The daughter now for the first time understands her mother and realizes that she is, in effect, supporting the life of another human being, and she declares: "You're a strange, noble woman, Mother. I'll try and be like you."

*Long Day's Journey Into Night* picks up two of the most persistent themes or subjects in O'Neill's lifelong preoccupation with the relations betheen the sexes; the rock-bound, if storm-tossed, marriage, and the sorrowing, humiliated, guilty woman, and gives them their most complex and complete dramatization. The only stable element in *Long Day's Journey* is the permanent love affair between James and Mary Tyrone which is impervious to his penuriousness, nomadism, social isolation, and heavy drinking, or to her dope addiction, continual complaints about the present, and persistent lament for her lost, virginal, happy childhood. The only unambiguous emotional relationship in the play is theirs, as is the only unalloyed tenderness. No matter what happens, the handsome young actor and the beautiful schoolgirl who fell in love at first sight never quite disappear. In Act I, with "Irish blarney," he tells her that her eyes are "beautiful" and adds—as a reminder to her that she is not a nun *manqué*, as in her darker moments she would like to think, but a beautiful and charming woman, full of life and love—"and well you know it." And this statement, followed by a kiss, brings forth the radiant schoolgirl who, it seems, is always there just below the surface: *"Her face lights up with a charming, shy embarrassment. Suddenly and startingly one sees in her face the girl she had once been, not a ghost of the dead, but still a living part of her."* There follows some more blarney and badinage about the beauty of her hair, and this interchange has enough warmth and good feeling in it to wipe the sneer off Jamie's face, who only at this moment in the entire play is described as showing a countenance that is *"cleared"* and exhibiting *"an old boyish charm"* and *"a loving smile."* O'Neill's career is full of paradoxes, and nowhere more so than in his greatest play and tragedy, wherein is presented the most sincere, unambiguous, and believable picture of marital love, as romantic as the impossible *Days' Without End*, as real as the prosaic *Ah, Wilderness!*, as tortuous and problematical as the excruciating *Welded*, as long-suffering as the agonized *A Touch of the Poet*, or as wistful as *Hughie*. There is no attempt to explain marriage in the sense that it is "explained" in *Welded* and *Days Without End*. It exists like the weather or like life itself.

*Long Day's Journey Into Night* ends with Mary Tyrone at the front-center of the stage, falling once more in love in the spring with the Shakespearian actor, James Tyrone. In the last lines of the play she says she was "so happy

for a time." Then came life and suffering which is what
*Long Day's Journey* is about; indeed all the late, great
plays are in great part about feminine suffering: Nora
Melody, Hickey's wife, Parritt's mother, Hughie's wife,
Mary Tyrone, and Josie Hogan, who is the final and, literally, the largest, dramatization of feminine frustration,
sorrow, and humiliation. Rendered a freak by nature, Josie
is doomed to act out a robustious role in life that is absolutely at odds with her lyric, virgin soul. Forever cut
off from her doomed love, James Tyrone, she is allowed
only a night holding the sleeping, drunken Tyrone in her
arms and a sorrowful parting at dawn—he going to his
death sooner or later—and a final benediction and wish
on her part that his death come soon and painlessly.

Men—sons, husbands, lovers—and whiskey, these are
the sources of feminine sorrow in O'Neill's world. And at
the end of the long, dark tunnel of the long day's journey
into night stands a wounded woman, grieving at what
time has done to her, at her present sorrows or lost
felicities, of life's general impossibilities.

This was Joyce's subject as well. Gretta Conroy at the
end of *The Dead*, Molly Bloom at the end of *Ulysses*,
and Anna Livia Plurabelle at the end of *Finnegans Wake*
are the sisters of Nora Melody, Josie Hogan, and Mary
Tyrone. As a master of language, O'Neill was no match
for Joyce, but I am sure that if O'Neill had ever looked
at the last part of *Finnegans Wake* when Anna Livia is
slowly coming to consciousness, along with the dawn,
that he would have instantly perceived that Joyce had
struck off beautifully in his invented language the most
poignant of O'Neill's themes:

> My great blue bedroom, the air so quiet, scarce a cloud. In
> peace and silence. I could have stayed up there for always
> only. It sometimes fails us. First we feel. Then we fall.
> And let her rain now if she likes. Gently or strongly as
> she likes. Anyway let her rain for my time is come. I done
> me best when I was let. Thinking always if I go all goes.
> A hundred cares, a tithe of troubles and is there one who
> understands me? One in a thousand of years of the nights?
> All my life I have lived among them but now they are be-
> coming lothed to me. And I am lothing their little warm
> tricks. And lothing their mean cosy turns. And all the
> greedy gushes out through their small souls. And all the
> lazy leaks down over their brash bodies. How small it's all.

Like *Finnegans Wake, Long Day's Journey Into Night*
is cyclical, a circle of sorrow, and the end is as the beginning, the radiant schoolgirl falling in love with the
brilliant actor. But in between is, "a hundred cares, a
tithe of troubles and is there one who understands me?"
Or, as Mary Tyrone protests: "Why? How can I? The
past is the present, isn't it? It's the future, too. We all
try to lie out of that but life won't let us" (II, 2).

## iii *The Individual*

In matters of individual characterization Proust is
once more a supremely self-conscious commentator on an
outlook that O'Neill instinctively and intuitively shared.
Of all great modern writers, Proust and O'Neill tend to
believe the least in the power of environment and to
believe the most, almost mystically and certainly atavisti-
cally, in the force of heredity, conceived of both as a
racial-cultural general inheritance and as an individual
specific inheritance. So strong are family ties in the works
of both men that grandparents play a potent role in the
lives of their grandchildren. As Proust's grandmother is
a living and forceful presence in the early part of *Remembrance of Things Past,* so in *Long Day's Journey*
both the maternal and paternal grandparents, while in
fact dead, have been such seminal forces on their children that they, in a sense, are a dominant force on their
children's children.

It could be argued that Tyrone's father and his wife's
father are, like Hardy's heath country in the Wessex
novels, the motivating forces in the play. It was Tyrone
Senior's desertion of his family that projected James Tyrone, his mother, and his siblings into the subrole of
penniless Irish immigrants in nineteenth-century America
and that left James Tyrone with a permanent fear of the
poorhouse, and a concomitant hunger for land, and a
general penuriousness that causes so much trouble for
his family. In her turn, Mary Tyrone was spoiled by her
father and because of him has retrospectively sentimentalized him and her childhood to the point where her own
past and dope become the avenue for escape from present
realities.

In either Proust's world or O'Neill's, one is never related to anyone with impunity. In *Cities of the Plain* when Saint-Loup is beginning, at long last, to resemble his uncle, the Baron de Charlus, Proust remarks (in the Scott Moncrieff translation): "We are not always somebody's nephew with impunity. It is often through him that a hereditary habit is transmitted to us sooner or later. We might indeed arrange a whole gallery of portraits, named like the German comedy: *Uncle and Nephew,* in which we should see the uncle watching jealously, albeit unconsciously, for his nephew to end by becoming like himself" ("The Princess de Guermantes Entertains"). With parents and children, of course, this phenomenon in inescapable. In *Within a Budding Grove* when the narrator observes Gilberte, the child of Odette and Swann, he can see both parents, physically, in their joint creation, wherein the two natures of M. and Mme. Swann "ebb and flow, encroaching alternately one upon the other in the body of this Mélusine" ("Madame Swann at Home").

Correspondingly, O'Neill's stage directions in any play that deals with the generations, and many of them do, are studded with similar descriptions. To cite only one, when Richard Miller first appears on the stage in *Ah, Wilderness!* we are told that he, going on seventeen, is such a perfect blend of his father and mother that each parent is convinced that their child is the exact image of the other. He has his mother's hair and his father's eyes. In height, weight, and general appearance he is perfectly average. He has one aspect that sets him off from both parents, that is, an extreme sensitiveness. But in Act IV, Scene 1, when Miller is preparing to chastise his erring son, Mrs. Miller reminds him that even the sensitivity is hereditary by cautioning him to be careful because their son is just like his father, "too sensitive for his own good." Such biological-psychological sketches constitute the substance of O'Neill's characterology: the determinism of heredity. Similarly, Proust in *The Guermantes Way* after remarking, apropos of Swann's fatal disease, that the same malady had killed his mother and that she had first been attacked by it at the precise age that Swann had arrived at, goes on to conclude: "Our existences are in truth, owing to heredity, as full of cabalistic ciphers, of horoscopic castings as if there really were sorcerers in the world. And just as there is a certain duration of life for humanity in general, so there is one for families in particular" ("The Red Shoes of the Duchess"). In like manner, in *Long Day's Journey* Mary Tyrone's remembering that her father had died of consumption doubles her fears for the fate of the consumptive Edmund.

Both writers, naturally, varied the genetic patterns considerably. In an O'Neill play, if there is a progeny, the various children very often take after one parent or the other, as, for example, in *Long Day's Journey* Edmund is a variation on his mother while Jamie is more of the father, just as the two Mayo boys in *Beyond the Horizon* diverge, the one by way of the mother, the other by way of the father. Some times a man may be like his father, but, instead of having added positive qualities to the already positive inheritance, like Richard Miller, he may lack something his father has. For example, Nat Bartlett in *Gold* looks like his father but has not his father's health and great strength. Or a sibling may resemble a parent who has died, thus leaving the sibling stranded, so to speak. This situation is the basis for the pathos of the position of Eileen Carmody in *The Straw*, Sweet, gentle, and sensitive like her dead mother, she lives in the midst of coarse and insensitive creatures, her siblings, who resemble her father. The one exception, a sister, is brutalized by the rest of the family when Eileen is away at the sanatorium. She thus loses her last link with her mother. This same situation, only presented with much greater force and with an element of the grotesque, reappears in *A Moon for the Misbegotten*. Josie Hogan's stature and strength, which makes her, in effect, a freak, had been passed on to her by her now deceased mother.

But there are also genetic sports and freaks in O'Neill's works. Gordon Evans in *Strange Interlude* resembles neither his mother nor his biological father (Darrell) and seems "*to have sprung from a line distinct from any of the people we have seen*" (VII). For reasons of plot, of course, he could not resemble Darrell. Nonetheless, the biological mystique is still there, and Gordon, who consciously hates Darrell, as the other man in his mother's life, feels, in spite of himself, an intuitive attraction to him as well, an attraction he cannot rationally understand.

Similarly, Dion Anthony of *The Great God Brown,*
while he possesses a partial resemblance to his mother,
is in reality like neither his mother nor father physically
or emotionally; and this constitutes a part of his tragedy:
he begins as a "stranger" and continues to remain so.
Reuben Light, in *Dynamo,* similarly and tragically, is a
stranger to both his father and his mother. Friends or
strangers, child and parent seldom mesh, especially father
and son; as Marsden puts it in *Strange Interlude:* "What
son can ever understand . . . always too near, too soon,
too distant, or too late!" (I).

O'Neill shared with Proust several, sometimes contradictory, assumptions or ideas about the nature of character moving through time: identity, multiplicity, and process and change. To take the last category first: in *Within
a Budding Grove,* after describing the great alteration in
Swann's character—the one time *boulevardier* has become
now solely, almost professionally, "Odette's husband"—
Proust observes: "we must bear in mind that the character which a man exhibits in the latter half of his life is
not always, even if it is often his original character developed or withered, attenuated or enlarged; it is sometimes the exact opposite, like a garment that has been
turned" ("Madame Swann at Home"). Thus O'Neill's
extended plays are populated by characters who change
in both appearance and personality, *Strange Interlude* and
*The Great God Brown* being the classic examples. For
example, in *The Great God Brown* Billy Brown, the all-
American boy and after that the all-American businessman, finally becomes, after donning Dion Anthony's mask
and persona, a tortured, ascetic believer, who dies with a
version of a Beatitude on his lips: "Blessed are they that
weep, for they shall laugh!" (IV, 2). Most of the other
characters in the play, as well as most of the characters in
*Strange Interlude,* undergo similar metamorphoses.

On some occasions what appears to be process and
change in characters may simply mean they are turning
into their parents. Proust's world is full of such phenomena. In *Cities of the Plain* ("The Heart's Intermis-
sions") the narrator observes that his mother is gradually
but surely turning into his grandmother, now that the
grandmother, her mother, is dead:

Once she is dead, we should hesitate to be different, we begin to admire only what she was, what we ourselves already were only blended with something else, and what in future we are to be exclusively. It is in this sense ... that we may say that death is not in vain, that the dead man continues to react upon us. He reacts even more than a living man because, true reality being discoverable only by the mind, being the object of a spiritual operation, we acquire a true knowledge only of things that we are obliged to create anew by thought, things that are hidden from us in everyday life. ... Lastly, in our mourning for our dead we pay an idolatrous worship to the things that they liked.

By the time of *The Captive* the narrator himself is beginning to turn into all his dead relatives, taking on his father's obsessive interest in the weather; his Aunt Léonie's passion for seclusion in a room. Proust explains the psychology of this process with his customary acumen: "When we have passed a certain age, the soul of the child that we were and the souls of the dead from whom we spring come and bestow upon us in handfuls their treasures and their calamities, asking to be allowed to cooperate in the new sentiments which we are feeling and in which, obliterating their former image, we recast them in an original creation. ... We have to give hospitality, at a certain stage in our life, to all our relatives who have journeyed so far and gathered round us" ("Life with Albertine").

The hold of the dead upon the living in O'Neill's plays need hardly be remarked upon—it is one of his central subjects—and the same kinds of ancestor-worshipping transformations that Proust has just described occur frequently in O'Neill's plays. Like Marcel's mother, Lavinia Mannon of *Mourning Becomes Electra* turns into her mother (although her motive for so doing is quite different from the filial obeisance that Proust's mother was paying). In *The Haunted*, the last play of the trilogy, the thin, colorless Lavinia has become voluptuous and colorful and bears a "striking" resemblance to her dead mother. In fact, it could be argued that this is precisely the tragic fate of the Mannons: they keep turning into their father and mother, as their father and mother had turned into their father and mother, and so on, in an endless chain of biological doom that stretches all the way back to those witch-burning ancestors, whose pictures hang from the walls of the study, but that comes to an end with Lavinia, the last of the Mannons. Only death released one from the hereditary tyranny. So, too, among the many laments that the O'Neill women have is the one that the beloved son finally turns into his father. Thus Nina, in Act IX of *Strange Interlude*, having just lost her son to another woman, his wife: "Sons are always their fathers. They pass through the mother to become their father again."

Or people may be inherently multiple in character, irrespective of process and change or parentage. In *The Sweet Cheat Gone* the narrator says that Andrée, whom he had known for many years, really has three natures, and each is not of the same value. This, he continues, is a "thoroughly objective truth too, to wit, that each of us is not a single person, but contains many persons who have not all the same moral value" ("Grief and Oblivion"). In the plays of his maturity practically all of O'Neill's characters have this multiplicity and are split into halves, thirds, or more, as is shown by masks or otherwise. Con Melody, like Proust's Andrée, has three "characters," none of which is wholly the "true" or the "real" Melody. On the one hand he plays the role of the somber and proud gentlemanly officer, a role that has become so real that it has taken almost complete control over him. (And it is not all play-acting either, for he had been a hero at Talavera.) On the other hand, biological fatality dictates that he shall have in him—lurking under the Major's handsome exterior—his father: a coarse, crude, crafty, leering, unscrupulous, bog-trotting, Irish peasant, a character that comes to the fore at the end of the play. In between this polarity there is a "nothingness" that constitutes a third character and that occasionally rises, wraithlike, to the surface. In Act II, standing alone on the stage, he tries to strike the pose of the Byronic hero, but with no audience to sustain him, he cannot. Sagging, defeated, solitary, staring at the table, a still different look comes over the ruined and handsome face, "a trace of real tragedy." It is this third character that reappears again at the end of the play when he is determined to be a peasant, and his daughter is trying to force him into being the Major once more. The third character, speaking neither the Irish brogue nor the courtly rhetoric of the Major, begs Sara in plain English, "Let me go—!" At the mother's intervention, the daughter desists, and Con falls into the brogue once more.

Yet, it should be reiterated, there is always a kind of identity or integrity to human character in O'Neill's plays. In the Epilogue of *The Great God Brown* the wildest of O'Neill's plays, with characters changing as though in a kaleidoscope, the last words are given to Margaret, who has seen and suffered so much change: "And yet I'm still the same Margaret. It's only our lives that grow old." For character, whatever its complexities and contradictions, is like an arrow pointed at an ultimate destiny, and in its complex evolutions and devolutions, so bewildering moment by moment, or even year by year, it is actually flying unerringly to the mark. As Hickey says at the beginning of the long story of his life in Act IV of *The Iceman Cometh*: "Well, it's all there, at the start, everything that happened afterwards."

It is doubtful, and happily so, that O'Neill had any formula or abstraction or fundamental assumption about human nature per se. His characters are, by turns and sometimes simultaneously, monolithic, contradictory, split, fluid, self-contained, and interacting. They are not rationally conceived but *felt*, and, as such, are maelstroms of powerful emotions. Their emotions are so strong that these characters are always striving at overleaping the bounds of rationality into an area that suggests—but only suggests—a belief in the existence of supersensory perceptions and powers. Intuitions, for example, in both men and women tend to be both powerful and accurate. In *Desire Under the Elms* the cuckolded Ephraim Cabot senses "somethin'" in the house and turns to his cows ("cows is queer") for peace and consolation. In their burning sense of one another Abbie and Eben can almost see through the walls (II, 2). In *Strange Interlude*, in Act III, Nina senses that there is something "wrong" with the Evans' house. In Act V, observing Darrell and Nina, Marsden feels something: "Darrell! . . . and Nina! . . . there's something in this room! . . . something disgusting! . . . like a brutal hairy hand, raw and red, at my throat! . . . stench of human life! . . . heavy and rank!" In *Mourning*

*Becomes Electra* practically everyone in the play senses that there is something wrong and evil in the Mannon house. The more intelligent characters in the later plays practically run on their intuitions. Hickey's entire life as a successful salesman has been built upon the ability, the "game," of "sizing people up quick, spotting what their pet pipe dreams were" (IV). And when he sees Parritt, one look convinces him that they are members of the same "lodge," that is, betrayers and murderers. When Hickey announces Evelyn's death, Larry exclaims: "Be God, I felt he'd brought the touch of death on him!" (II). Like Ephraim Cabot and Hickey, Larry can sense things.

If O'Neill's characters can intuit the feelings of others, they can also at times transfer their own emotions or feelings to others. For example, one can transfer one's will temporarily to another person, although at great emotional cost. In *All God's Chillun Got Wings* (I, 4) after their marriage Jim and Ella must walk from the church to the street between the two hostile lines of whites and Negroes. Ella is overcome with fear and nervousness, but Jim wills her through although he himself almost collapses by the time they get to the curb. In Act I, Scene 2, of *The Haunted*, Lavinia wills the uncertain Orin into submission to her. But, *"the strength she has willed into him has left her exhausted."* In the Poughkeepsie crew race of *Strange Interlude* Gordon Evans, a stellar oarsman, wills a faltering fellow crewman through the race and then collapses at the conclusion, as had, many years before, Gordon Shaw, Nina's lost love. O'Neill, without doubt, would like to have believed in ghosts; in *A Moon for the Misbegotten* he has Jamie Tyrone say: "Wish I could believe in the spiritualist's bunk." And, in the late plays he came upon what can be called a "ghost" psychology which suggests but never affirms the existence, psychologically speaking, of a suprareal or suprasensual realm, a kind of Melvillean whiteness or blankness, a gray somnambulist purgatory through which pass the wraithlike psyches of his characters who have split into a reality and a shade, with a palpable body on the stage but a psychic identity that is lost in the dead past or only hovering fitfully around the tremulous present, cut off from the living and the real. Thus a *Moon for the Mis-*

*begotten*, *A Touch of the Poet* and, especially, *Long Day's Journey Into Night* are psychological ghost stories, peopled by characters so haunted that they seem to have split into a reality and a shade that haunts the reality. "Ghost" is, in fact, the key word in both Tyrone plays. In Act III of *A Moon for the Misbegotten* Jamie Tyrone explains to Josie that he is haunted, and haunted by the worst ghost of all, "your own," by which he means his various "might-have-beens." And Josie in Act IV, says that Tyrone has already "died" and that the man who has come to see her and confess in the moonlight is a "damned soul." So, too, Con Melody in *A Touch of the Poet* describes himself as a "ghost haunting a ruin."

*Long Day's Journey Into Night* exists precisely in a split world, so full of gross reality, on the one hand, so ghostly, foggy, nebulous, on the other. For there is "real" life aplenty: whiskey, curses, whores, laughter, poetry, card games, work, arguments, laughter, confessions, disease, doctors, drugstores, servants, food, electric light bulbs, trolley cars, the sea, the foghorn, the ships, the house itself in all its substantiality. On the other hand, and increasingly so as the play goes on and as the fog closes in, the characters, the mother the most, the father the least, tend to move, psychologically speaking, into a shadowy realm in which, as the fog has blurred all distinctions between night and day and land and sea, human memory and human hurt blur the distinctions between the past and the present and the living and the dead. Mary Tyrone's white hair, so much remarked upon, is emblematic of that white, somnambulist world which finally engulfs all the characters. The play becomes, in fact, by Act IV, a ghost story with the drugged Mary, out of sight but always a heard presence, rummaging around the upper floor and fulfilling her husband's grim prophecy of Act III that before the night was out she would be like "a mad ghost." And Edmund remarks to his father in Act IV that Mary Tyrone moves, "above and beyond us, a ghost haunting the past." The ghost metaphor inevitably blends into and turns into the dead metaphor. Both images are contained in Edmund's parable of the three Gorgons and Pan: "You look in their faces and turn to stone. Or it's Pan. You see him and you die—that is, inside you—and have to go on living as a ghost"

(IV). Jamie, by his own admission, is half dead. "You think I'm going to die," says Edmund, bluntly, to his father. Only the father still has an anchor in reality but even he must describe, in his way, the shadowy realm into which the Tyrones have drifted. Characteristically, he employs Shakespeare and calls it neither Hades nor Death but Sleep: "We are such stuff as dreams are made on, and our little life is rounded with a sleep."

The only other conclusion in modern literature comparable to Act IV of *Long Day's Journey Into Night* is the ending of Joyce's *The Dead* where the all-enveloping snow plays the same role as the fog in *Long Day's Journey*. It is true that *The Dead* ends quietly and elegiacally, instead of dramatically and tragically, as does *Long Day's Journey*. Nevertheless, the psychology behind the two works as well as the symbolism in each is remarkably similar. In both cases the woman is reminded of her past, especially of a man; with Mary Tyrone it is her father, with Gretta Conroy it is Michael Furey, the boy who died—of consumption—for her love. In both cases this past was better than the present; for Mary it was happier; for Gretta it was more romantic. In each case this fixation of the woman on the past, which was more beautiful and happy and free than the present tragedy or dreariness, excludes the men entirely and sets them to thinking of the mutability of all things and the ubiquity of death. They feel themselves passing into the realm of a white nothingness. In Joyce's words: "One by one, they were all becoming shades." Then Gabriel Conroy at the end of *The Dead* walks to the hotel window to hear the snow in the darkness outside: "falling faintly through the universe and faintly falling, like the descent of their last end, upon all the living and the dead." O'Neill conceivably could have had Edmund say something like this, but it is late and all the men are sodden. Instead he has Jamie recite, seriously and well, three stanzas from Swinburne's "A Leavetaking." The men then lapse into silence as Mary Tyrone relives her past; each is alone, a solitary in the universe. Night, fog, ghosts, sleep, the past, dreams, elegy, loneliness: this is how O'Neill's world ends in *Long Day's Journey*. In the coda and epilogue to his dramatic career, *A Moon for the Misbegotten*, the same pattern evolves. Beginning in daylight laughter, engrossed in the substantiality of the commonplace, whiskey and pigs and crude jokes, *A Moon* finally exhibits at its climax a ghost in the moonlight and a dead man at dawn. It is as if, in Melville's words in *Pierre:* "It is all a dream—we dream that we dreamed a dream."

Every serious dramatist is finally a Prospero and like Prospero must finally break his staff, foreswear his magic, make his "retraction," and ask the pardon of God and man for his audacity at playing the Creator; in Prospero's, and Shakespeare's, last words: "As you from crimes would pardon'd be, / Let your indulgence set me free" (Epilogue, *The Tempest*). So O'Neill in the dedication to his penultimate and greatest tragedy, *Long Day's Journey Into Night*, asks for forgiveness not only for his family but for himself in this play *"written in tears and blood"* and *"with deep pity and understanding and forgiveness for* all *the four haunted Tyrones."*

But O'Neill always saw human experience as dialectical and polar, and not all of his late plays are peopled by death-obsessed and somnambulistic individuals. Thus the picture of this greatest period of his dramatic career is incomplete and decidedly one-sided if *Hughie,* the least generally known of his late plays, is not taken into consideration. For *Hughie* is the proper pendant and companion piece to *Long Day's Journey Into Night* and *A Moon for the Misbegotten.* If *Long Day's Journey* and *A Moon* are the ghost plays, *Hughie* is the life play, and as *Long Day* and *A Moon* go from life to death, *Hughie* goes from death to life, beginning as elegy for the dead and ending in a wistful hope for the living. Both plays deal with one of O'Neill's central themes: the necessity for individuals to have shared illusions upon which to live. The two plays differ diametrically on this issue, and in most other respects as well. To enumerate some: *Long Day's Journey* is a four-act tragedy, *Hughie* a one-act comedy; in *Long Day's Journey* the characters speak standard, middle-class American speech, with an infusion of slang, *Hughie* employs the patois of the underworld of the New York of the 1920's; *Long Day's Journey* takes place in a summer home on Long Island Sound, *Hughie* in the lobby of a run-down hotel in mid-town Manhattan; *Long Day's Journey* is a quatrologue, *Hughie* virtually a monologue; *Long Day's Journey* is about an extraordinarily close-knit and intimate family, *Hughie* is peopled by two strangers; in *Long Day's Journey* people fall apart, in *Hughie* they come together. *Long Day's Journey* says that human illusions cannot withstand the monstrous invasions of reality; while *Hughie* says that a shared illusion can make life bearable, livable, and, at moments, happy.

From the exposition of *Hughie*, all contained in Erie Smith's monologue, we learn that Erie and the now deceased Hughie had once been human beings together, and human precisely because they shared an illusion, namely, that Broadway gangsterdom is glamorous and that Erie was an important part of that glamor. So, too, the "raw babes" that Erie brings to his room become, in the imagination, "dolls."

The action of the play is like a V. Erie, who is "drying out" after a drunk, his way of mourning for Hughie, begins his monologue with the full assumption that his glib tongue will soon captivate the new night clerk and that he will soon have a "Hughie" relationship with him. But the utter, bottomless apathy of the new night clerk, awake only to the noises of the night, comes close to defeating him. Jaunty at the beginning of the play, Erie slides down gradually into desolation, his luck gone, his pal, Hughie, dead, the new night clerk indifferent, his confidence gone, he himself broke and in debt, and dangerously so. In order to give Hughie a proper send-off to the next world Erie had sent to the funeral an elaborate wreath, which he purchased by borrowing money from Broadway sharpies, some of whom are "dead wrong G's" who unless they get their money back by next Tuesday will probably put Erie in the hospital. As his forlorn recital goes on, he becomes more apathetic, more oblivious of the night clerk, and they stand as strangers still, as far apart as Mary Tyrone and her men in Act IV of *Long Day's Night*. Erie loses the bouyancy that presumably had kept him afloat all those years of his hanger-on existence, and he begins to envy Hughie who is "out of the racket. I mean, the whole goddamned racket. I mean life." But even at his lowest ebb O'Neill says there is "*something pathetically but genuinely gallant about him.*" Then the night clerk, out of his deep need for communication, asks a question about the legendary Arnold Rothstein. Erie immediately embarks on his monologue about high-life in the gangster world and brings out the dice: "It will give me confidence." He turns from death and the past to life and the future: "Y'know, it's time I quit carryin' the torch for Hughie." Thus while the last act of *Long Day's Journey Into Night* says: we are the dead, *Hughie*, at the end, says: we are the living. It is somehow appropriate that O'Neill should have chosen for his only affirmative male in the late plays, a Broadway hanger-on, a little, pathetic, soiled, and faded flower growing up in the dunghill of lower depths Broadway. I would hesitate to extract a "message" or a "moral" from such an organic masterpiece as *Hughie*, and I am sure O'Neill intended none. Nevertheless, Erie is endowed with certain qualities that enable him to cope with life, as the Tyrones, the father excepted, never can. First, negatively, he is less intelligent and sensitive than they. But, positively, he is endowed, both by the stage directions and by the words in his mouth, with "sentimentality," that is, a genuine and unambiguous feeling for other people, and with "gallantry," the courage to carry on. He is neither so wise nor so tough as he thinks he is—his illusion, for all men must have them—but he can roll with the punch, and, perhaps, this is the secret of survival. I would not argue that *Hughie* cancels out, or even modifies *Long Day's Journey Into Night*, but rather is its complement in that ceaseless dialectic about human affairs that O'Neill created and re-created, always from a different angle, all his writing life.

For the individual in O'Neill's world as a whole there are both prior ambiguities and ultimate ambiguities. The ultimate ambiguities deal with such basic questions as fate and free will, reality and illusions, and so on, but before the individual can confront these final perplexities, he finds his whole existence hemmed in with anterior problems. There is the thought, first, that all human existence may be basically insane and that the earth is one vast lunatic asylum. Such is the conclusion of the long-suffering Caleb of *Diff'rent*, who must endure thirty years of frustration, only to see the love of his life, Emma Crosby, turn into a bizarre old frump contemplating marriage with the despicable and corrupt Benny. As he departs the scene, and he is soon to commit suicide, he exclaims to Emma: "You used to say you was diff'rent from the rest o' folks. By God, if you are, it's just you're a mite madder'n they be! By God, that's all!" (II). Or if human existence is rational, it has been so arranged that stupidity, rather than intelligence, is the single virtue, and the obtuse will inherit the earth. In the words of the Kaan of *Marco Millions*: "Life is so stupid, it is mysterious" (II, 1). Thus, if there is a Deity, He has made avoidance of thought the summit of human wisdom, and stupidity the moving force in His empire.

Or, perhaps, we are not even alive but are ambulatory corpses. The night clerk of *Hughie* lives, ordinarily, a life-in-death existence. When trying to rouse himself to life and enter into some kind of communication with Erie, he is described as speaking *"In the vague tone of a corpse which admits it once overheard a favorable rumor about life."* If anything he would prefer not to *see*, that is, to be alive, and when he looks at Erie, he is purposely myopic, *"with vacant, bulging eyes full of vague envy for the blind."* The only sadly hopeful thing he can drudge up is the sententious statement: "But they say most of the things we worry about never happen," and this bottom-dog is not exceptional in his death-in-life existence. "Men call life death and fear it," says Lazarus. "They hide from it in horror. Their lives are spent in hiding. Their fear becomes their living. They worship life as death!" (II, 1). In *Days Without End* John Loving, another O'Neill Everyman, describes himself as having been born with "a horror of death" and "a dread of life." And when he falls in love, marries, and is happy, he is afraid of his own happiness (III, 1).

Even if man can escape, or thrust back into the hinterlands of his consciousness, such concerns as the rationality or irrationality of life and the stark ubiquity of death, he is still faced, aways, with a series of self-defeats. If he fights the good fight, he is liable to find that he has wasted himself on trivalities. In the words of the aged Ponce de Leon in *The Fountain*: "I am too weary. I have fought small things so long I am small" (III). If love is one's passion, then its relationship to hate is always the gargoyle in the fountain. " 'Twould take a wise man to tell one [love or hate] from the other [hate or love]," says Paddy, the wise old man of *The Hairy Ape* (IV). Happiness is something surreptitious, to be stolen and enjoyed in secret, like a thief with his ill-gotten spoils ("but we must all be crooks where happiness is concerned! ... steal or starve!"—Marsden in Act I of *Strange Interlude*). Healthy, happy "normality" is liable to be only a veneer or exterior over guilt. When in *The Great God Brown* Dion Anthony asks Cybel, the omniscient, what she thinks of the simple, straightforward, healthy, successful, good-looking businessman, William Brown, she says, simply, "He's healthy and handsome—but he's too guilty" (II, 1). Most hopes are, in fact, hopeless and are called such in *The Straw* where the impossible desire of the two lovers to live their lives together is described as the "hopeless hope" (III). Even suffering has no clear-cut meaning and no compensations. At the end of *Beyond the Horizon* the long-suffering hero protests, impotently, against this final injustice: "Life owes us some happiness after what we've been through. (*Vehemently*) It must! Otherwise our suffering would be meaningless—and that is unthinkable" (III, 1). But he is about to die, leaving his ruined farm, his prematurely aged wife, and his unsuccessful brother, his beloved and sickly daughter having already died. And almost everyone's life is haunted by "might-have-beens." In the hopelessly ambiguous characters, like Con Melody in *A Touch of the Poet*, the basic emotions themselves become hopelessly entangled and working at cross purposes, as, for example, in Act I he is described as being "*ashamed of being ashamed.*" Perhaps then man could be punished into being happy or good, but the answer to this is given by Uncle Sid, the decayed Peck's Bad Boy of *Ah, Wilderness!*: "If you remember, I was always getting punished—and see what a lot of good it did me!" (IV, 1). It is true that the dreamers in their dreams escape; thus the uncomprehending Bill Carmody of *The Straw* complains against his now deceased wife and his daughter, Eileen, his wife's legacy: "They [his wife's family] was dreamin' their lives out" (I, 1).

So life can be supportable only as it leaks away in dreams or drink or both. O'Neill's stages of the life of man have only three acts and are described by Hugo in *The Iceman Cometh*: "So ve get drunk, and ve laugh like hell, and den ve die; and de pipe dream vanish" (II).

Below and beyond these more obvious obfuscations are ultimate antinomies of human existence in which every individual is finally involved and which always come down to certain basic, and sometimes overlapping, antithetical categories of being: freedom or determinism, reality or illusion, courage or fear, commitment or withdrawal, communion or solitude; to be forgiven, no matter what one has done, or to be damned, no matter what expiation one tries to make. While personal happiness is out of the question, even in the first realm, human integrity would consist of existing, or at least having the illusion of existing, on a plane of experience that is purposive: to be free, courageous, forgiven, committed to reality and to one's fellow man, and in communion with others. The damned then would be the predetermined, fearful, guilt-ridden solitaries, who live on illusions, are committed to nothing, and are unforgivable. Yet the power of O'Neill's plays consists in the fact that neither realm can be called O'Neill's ontology, for the two realms are never presented as they have been here, as pure and abstract antitheses between which one consciously chooses, but as a muddled blur of human possibilities, a booming, buzzing confusion into which every individual is thrust, willy-nilly, and like a mole or like the prisoners in Plato's cave, he can hardly see or only dimly see what the issues themselves are: what is illusion and what is reality, or what is freedom or what is slavery. Much less is he able to make any wise or conscious choice between them. As Dreiser put it in *The Titan:* "Woe to him who places his faith in illusion—the only reality—and woe to him who does not."

O'Neill in his great plays is the dramatist of night, and the obscurity of the cosmos is nature's equivalent to man's confusion, as he gropes about in his moral and intellectual night. For man is always in a moral realm like that of *Don Quixote* where we finally do not know who is in possession of the truth, the idealistic Don Quixote or the practical Sancho Panza or the world which each opposes, and where any adjudication involves us in the quintessential paradox that Américo Castro said [11] is at the heart of Cervantes' novel: "In the supreme repertory of axiological themes that is *Don Quixote* is presented the problem of which of the two is preferable—the pain of the hare or the pleasure of the wolf that eats it."

Nevertheless, despite these final ambiguities, characters are faced with limited choices and possibilities, and at the heart of O'Neill's world are three ambiguities and one permanent problem. The ambiguities are all interrelated: is man free or determined? should he live by reality or illusion (assuming he can distinguish between the two or that a distinction does exist)? should he be committed or uncommitted? His permanent problem is his own loneliness, and its concomitant, his fear of death. Each of the serious plays touches on one, or more, or all of these ambiguities and this problem, and no two of them exactly agree either on the formulation of the ambiguities and the problem or on the answers or nonanswers to them.

As in life itself, O'Neill's characters are both free and unfree, depending on one's angle of vision. Their agony is so great precisely because they are caught in the paradox of Mary Tyrone, who simultaneously takes full responsibility for her sins, and berates herself morally, as much as she laments her fate, and at the same time blames mighty, obscure, occult forces—"God," "Life," "Time"— for making her their victim. Hickey and James Tyrone are male representatives of the same moral paradox. Thus the characters as a whole are given to heartfelt statements on both sides of the question of freedom, sometimes in the same play. In *Anna Christie* Anna speaks for individual helplessness: "It ain't your fault, and it ain't mine, and it ain't his neither. We're all poor nuts, and things happen, and yust get mixed in wrong, that's all" (IV). But Matt Burke, her prospective husband, says: "For I've a power of strength in me to lead men the way I want, and women, too, maybe, and I'm thinking I'd change you to a new woman entirely" (IV). Criticized for his happy ending in this play, O'Neill claimed that he meant the ending to be ambiguous but with a strong suggestion that fatality and unhappiness would finally win the day. He had once thought of calling the play "Comma" and, as it was, he gave the last lines of the play to gloomy old Chris, murmuring of the dark power of that "ole davil sea."

The idea of absolute, unqualified freedom is preposterous; that of complete, utter determinism is emotionally and intellectually insupportable; thus man is condemned to live in the middle, both determining and determined. In ages of religion man could locate his freedom in God; in a secular age he must somehow find it in himself, hesitantly, obscurely, blindly, unsurely, but, nevertheless, unmistakably, for he cannot find it in history. O'Neill's characters, usually existing in secularity, occupy precisely this middle realm. They are very often, of course, borne down by fate or the idea of fate. In *Long Day's Journey* each character thinks he or she is bearing his parents, his grandparents, his race, history, life itself on his back, hopelessly stumbling along and always tied by an invisible but unbreakable umbilical cord to both his own past experiences and the generations behind him. At the same time these same characters are always blaming one another for being pessimists and fatalists. James Tyrone condemns equally the cynicism and pessimism that one son (Edmund) got from books and the other (Jamie) got from Broadway: "There's little choice between the philosophy you learned from Broadway loafers, and the one Edmund got from his books. They're both rotten to the core" (II). But Jamie speaks contemptuously and angrily of his father's "Irish peasant idea [that] consumption is fatal," which leads the father to assume that Edmund is going to die, no matter what kind of medical aid he gets. Thus while they can bear the thought that possibly they themselves are unfree, they cannot contemplate the thought that others are similarly driven, and none of the men can accept the fact that the mother must continue in her dope addiction. She should have more will power, they think. In the last analysis, O'Neill's characters, by and large, cannot really believe that any absolute determinism always governs themselves either. Thus in the late plays, so grim and so enveloped in a hopeless sense of fatality, some character is always throwing off the shackles of destiny, metaphorically speaking, and announcing his or her own freedom and responsibility. Even the denizens of Harry Hope's saloon are given to such candid insights and declarations. In Act III of *The Iceman Cometh* Harry Hope, having retreated from his excursion into the streets of New York because of his fear of nonexistent automobiles, exclaims: "All a lie! No automobile. But, bejees, something ran over me! Must have been myself, I guess." "Must have been myself, I guess" is a thought that occurs to other characters as well, in intervals between those almost continuous declamations against the Powers that rule. And in the final reckoning, no matter how terrible have been the attritions of life, they believe somehow that they have earned their destiny. As Melville put it in *White Jacket,* concluding a discussion of the omnipotent neutrality of fate: "Yet though all this be so, nevertheless in our own hearts, we mould the whole world's hereafters; and in our own hearts we fashion our own gods. Each mortal casts his vote for whom he will to rule the worlds; I have a voice that helps to shape eternity; my volitions stir the orbits of the furthest suns. In two senses we are precisely what we worship. Ourselves are Fate" (LXXV).

Freedom and fate are all tied up with reality and illusion, as both are with happiness and unhappiness. The ambiguities of truth and illusion, reality and appearance, were one of O'Neill's major concerns; and its paradoxes appear again and again, often in different ways, in his plays as a whole from beginning to end. His early and complementary plays about an illusory treasure, *Gold* and *Where the Cross is Made,* are concerned with just this problem. Like Hickey in *The Iceman,* Captain Bartlett in *Gold* and *Where the Cross is Made* finally cannot tell the difference between truth and illusion. When, in Act IV of *Gold* his daughter begs him to tell his now-obsessed son the truth, namely, that there is no treasure, Bartlett exclaims: "The truth? It's a lie." In *Where the Cross is Made* O'Neill wished to involve the audience in the illusion of the mad Captain who sees ghosts on the stage. But in *A Touch of the Poet* a daughter begs a father to reassume and continue being his illusion. Thus in Act IV of the play when Melody has lapsed to an Irish peasant, Sara Melody says: "Listen! Forgive me, Father! I know it's my fault—always sneering and insulting you—but I only meant the lies in it." But her father begs to be left alone in his new simple reality. Thus men must and must not live on illusions. Whichever way one turns, honesty is next to impossible. As Nina in *Strange Interlude* says: "L-i-i-e! Now say life. L-i-i-f-e! You see! Life is just a long drawn out lie with a sniffling sigh at the end" (II).

The great, and the most complex, O'Neill play on all these final issues is *The Iceman Cometh,* in many ways his grimmest play of all, concerned as it is with murder, suicide, loneliness, guilt, fear of death, the problems of identity, the necessity for illusions, the ambiguities of pity, the nature of "truth," and the paradox of commitment. Like the other late plays it seems to take place on the bottom of the sea. When Wetjoen is described in the opening stage directions he is said to have *"a suggestion of old authority lurking in him like a memory of the drowned."* The ships of all the denizens of the saloon, says Larry, "are long since looted and scuttled and sunk on the bottom" (I). As in the other late plays, ghosts edge, crabwise, along the bottom of this sea. Jimmy Tomorrow's speech, for example, has only *"the ghost of a Scotch rhythm in it."* The over-all dialectic of the play is concerned with the separate but allied problems of reality vs. illusion and commitment vs. noncommitment, with reality-commitment set off against illusion-noncommitment. The play provides no answers to anything, but states insoluble problems: it says, through most of the characters, that man cannot face reality or commitment, but, through Larry, that he cannot escape from them either; finally however, through Hickey, it says that man probably cannot tell what reality is; he therefore cannot tell either what he should be—or thought he was—committed to. Thus the classic adage to "Know Thyself" is clearly impossible in this world although there are several different ways of realizing its impossibilities. The only moment of complete self-realization belongs to Larry at the end of the play, but his is the brute realization that he is, in truth, only going to die. When the well-intentioned but merciless Hickey tells him in Act II, "You'll say to yourself, I'm just an old man who is scared of life, but even more scared of dying. So I'm keeping drunk and hanging on to life at any price, and what of it?"—he is incensed and frightened. At the end of Act III he says to Hickey in an ironical and rhetorically defensive manner: "I'm afraid to live, am I?—and even more afraid to die!" But by the end of the play, having given permission to Parritt to commit suicide, he has finally and completely faced the central fact of life: death. "Be God, I'm the only real convert to death Hickey has made here. From the bottom of my coward's heart I mean that now!"

If the characters in *The Iceman Cometh* are all faced with the same problems, they do not collectively constitute a democracy with all men equal and of equal value. Rather, like human society itself they constitute a hierarchy, both as to their worth and as to their function. There is first, and representing mankind in the mass, the majority of the roomers of Harry Hope, the derelict alcoholics; second, there is the outsider and moral leper, Parritt; third, there are the two observers or commentators, Rocky and Larry, who split the world between them in Cervantine fashion with Rocky playing Sancho Panza and Larry a disillusioned Don Quixote, for while they are members of the cave-world, they yet can view it with some objectivity. Fourth and finally there is the reformer and manipulator, Hickey.

To begin with the lowest figure on the moral scale, Parritt, who, of all the haunted, haunting ghosts that people O'Neill's late plays, can never be forgiven and pardoned, even temporarily, as is Jamie Tyrone in *A Moon for the Misbegotten*. In O'Neill's plays as a whole contemptible people are rare; even murderers, like Christine Mannon in *Mourning Becomes Electra*, are sympathetic and at the end of their lives genuinely pitiable. But there are in the O'Neill world some Smerdyakovs, of which genus Parritt is the most fully drawn. He does, however, have some ancestors: Mrs. Rowland in *Before Breakfast*; the shanghaiers in *The Long Voyage Home*; Sweeney and Luke Bentley in *The Rope*; Benny in *Diff'rent*; the relatives and in-laws of Curt Jayson in *The First Man*; Hutchins Light in *Dynamo*, and others. In *The Iceman Cometh* Parritt in unlike anyone else in the play: he is *"unpleasant,"* with *"a shifting defiance and ingratiation in his light-blue eyes and an irritating aggressiveness in his manner"* (I).[12] In the play as a whole O'Neill's stage directions for Parritt have a note of absolute condemnation and moral repulsion that seldom appears elsewhere in his plays. Thus when he confesses to Larry that he betrayed his mother for money to spend on a whore (which is a lie), he is described as having *"the terrible grotesque air, in confessing his sordid baseness, of one who gives an excuse which exonerates him from any real guilt."* A penny-pincher (perhaps *the* sin against the Holy Ghost in a roomful of thirsty alcoholics), a coward, and a betrayer, out of hatred, of his mother, Parritt has only one mission in life: to get out of it. He is such a moral leper that even that great sinner, Hickey, who can forgive everybody—except himself—cannot even consider absolving Parritt. One of the few times in the play that Hickey becomes genuinely irritated is when Parritt attempts to identify himself with

Hickey, who tells Larry to get rid of him (IV). What Parritt then represents is the unforgivable sin and the complete failure of nerve, with consequent total disintegration of personality. As for his act of betrayal he finally passes judgment on himself when at the end of the play he says to Larry, "You know I'm really much guiltier than he [Hickey] is. You know what I did is a much worse murder. Because she [Hickey's wife] is dead and yet she [Parritt's mother] has to live." And, unlike the unsure Hickey, Parritt is certain that he committed his act out of unalloyed hatred. He is thus beyond the pale: "He's licked, Larry"; "He's lost all his guts" (Hickey). "Yuh're a soft old sap, Larry. He's a no-good louse like Hickey. He don't belong" (Rocky). If Larry's realization is that all men must die, Parritt's is that he, alone, can expiate his crime only by his own immolation. For, morally, O'Neill is an intentionalist, and anything is forgivable except an evil motivation.

The bulk of the characters, however, are not moral lepers, no matter what their past transgressions. But within this group there is a hierarchy as well. The three people whom Hickey wants most to "save" are Harry, Jimmy Tomorrow and Larry, who are, respectively, the most generous, the most sensitive and the most intelligent of the inhabitants of the cave. The rest constitute a kind of middle class, not too good, not too bad, not too intelligent, not too obtuse. Two of them, Larry and Rocky, are set apart in that while each has an illusion—Rocky that he is not a pimp, Larry that he is uncommitted to man and unafraid of death—they are more attached to reality than the rest and they have no illusions about their fellow-inhabitants. They are the "spokesmen" in the play as a whole, summing up characters and puncturing balloons of fancy, Rocky from his worldly-wise point of view, Larry from his philosophical, or "foolosophical," one.

Standing outside this world and trying to manipulate it is Hickey who, like so many of O'Neill's characters at the climacteric and at the end of their lives, has become his own father, the preacher, who shows the way, or purports to show the way, to salvation. Besides being the most ambiguous character in the play, in his dual role as murderer-reformer, Hickey stands in a completely different sphere from all the other characters (in a much less clear-cut way Parritt is in this same sphere). First, Hickey has just murdered someone and is accordingly himself facing death. Thus while most of the others live on illusions, he is living on the most powerful, elemental, and terrifying of realities: the memory of a murder and the expectation of extinction (Parritt has not committed an actual murder and does not know he is going to die until the end of the play). Thus Hickey is in possession of certain certainties although, characteristically, O'Neill takes these certain certainties away from him by the end of the play, leaving the meaning of the play, in Larry's phrase, "all question and no answer" (I).

The two things that the inhabitants of Harry Hope's fear the most are two realities: a time-sequence and the light of day. Hickey is the bringer of both. Most of the characters in the play have no sense of temporality, immersed as they are in a glorified past: "Isn't a pipe dream of yesterday a touching thing?" (I). And vaguely ruminating about an impossible future, "The tomorrow movement is a sad and beautiful thing, too" (I). The present, then, is an endless repetition, every day precisely like the day before and the day to come: drink, talk, memories, dreams, and the final annihilation of drunken sleep. Only death, which is unthinkable (except for Larry at the end), could alter the sequence and reintroduce a real past and a real future. But such is not the case with Hickey who is facing not only reality, but a real past and a real future. He thus can think in terms of change. He seems in fact to some of the others to exist in another world from theirs, a world not only real but inhumanly so. As Parritt says, "There's something not human behind his damned grinning and kidding" (II).

Moreover, Hickey's sense of time is extraordinarily heightened by his own situation. For while he is facing extinction and thinks he has not much time at his disposal, actually his moment-by-moment sense of time has been enormously expanded, so much so that only a few hours, he thinks, will suffice to "reform" the barnacle-encrusted inhabitants of Harry Hope's. According to Dostoevski, who knew what he was talking about in these matters, the imminence of death has the effect of greatly enlarging the content of time. At the beginning of *The Idiot* Prince Myshkin tells what must have been Dostoevski's own psychological experience when he faced a firing squad in 1849. Myshkin tells of a man, under sentence of death for a political offense, who is led out to the scaffold. Twenty minutes later a reprieve was read and another punishment was passed on the prisoners. The man later said he would never forget those twenty minutes because they were so full. When the time was down to five minutes, the same feeling persisted: "He told me that those five minutes seemed to him an infinite time, a vast wealth; he felt that he has so many lives left in those five minutes that there was no need yet to think of the last moment" (chapt. 5, Garnett translation). Down to two minutes he still felt mentally omnipotent: he thought of existence and nonexistence and the relationship between the two: "He meant to decide all that in those two minutes!" It is this apocalyptical sense that sustains Hickey in the face of all his lack of success and the churlishness of his reformees, and makes him feel God-like in his omniscience and omnipotence as he bustles around in his role as Saviour: "He's been hoppin' from room to room all night. Yuh can't stop him. He's got his Reform Wave goin' strong this mornin'!" says Rocky in Act III.

If Hickey would push them back into a genuine time sequence, he would also thrust them into the light of the sun, for the morning of "reform" day is hot and sunny although the sunlight itself barely penetrates the recesses of The Last Chance Saloon. Here then, at the heart of the play, is O'Neill's own ironical dramatization of Plato's parable of the cave, in which the philosopher drags protesting mankind, content to live in semidarkness, satisfied with his own ignorance, never knowing the real nature of anything, out into the bright and merciless light of the sun. Only in O'Neill's play the philosopher is a salesman who has just committed a murder and "mankind" is a motley collection of alcoholic derelicts. The point, however, of both Plato and O'Neill is identical: eyes accustomed to darkness do not want to see the light: "And suppose [says Plato] once more that he [man] is reluctantly dragged up a steep and rugged ascent, and held fast until he is forced into the presence of the sun himself, is he not likely to be pained and irritated? When he approaches the light his eyes will be dazzled, and he will not be able to see anything at all of what are now called realities" (*The*

*Republic,* Bk. VII, Jowett translation). Thus the *"blind"* Harry Hope forces himself out into the sunlight but scurries right back, as do the others at greater leisure.

One of the pleasures of the darkened cave is that in it nothing is quite certain or clear-cut, even the names of objects. As Plato says, "And if they [the inhabitants of the cave] were able to converse with one another, would they not suppose that they were naming what was actually before them?" And they would, of course, be misnaming everything.

So in *The Iceman Cometh* names are both highly important and highly problematical. Like the blind, or like primitive man, the characters can only perceive something by attaching a name to it, but the name, like its object, is often shifting and ambiguous in meaning. The ambiguous but all-important question of nomenclature is carried throughout the play by two of its sustaining jokes: Larry as the old "Foolosopher" (fool and/or philosopher); whether Pearl and Margie are "tarts" or "whores." Names take on an almost totemistic power: you are what you are called (although you may not be in truth what you are called). Furthermore, there is a kind of insane "logic" operating about names. They are like assumptions in a mathematical equation: given one name, other names must follow. Thus Pearl to Rocky: "Aw right, Rocky. We're whores. You know what dat makes you, don't you?" Margie: "A lousy little pimp, dat's what." Pearl: "A dirty little Ginny pimp, dat's what!" This name-calling orgy of derogation spreads out to include his race as well: "yuh poor little Ginny," "yuh little Wop!" (II). But when the reconciliation occurs at the end of the play, after Hickey's departure, Rocky becomes once more, "Our little bartender" and "a cute little Ginny at dat!" (IV). The ambiguities of the various appelations of Joe Mott, the "black" man who is morally "white," likewise run throughout the play. A "dinge," a "black bastard," a "doity nigger" when the others are enraged at him, he is a "white" man in the stretches of peace.

The point is, of course, that no one is quite sure who or what he or she is, and the single most ironical speech in the play is, appropriately, Joe Mott's: "Don't you get it in your heads I's pretendin' to be what I ain't, or dat I ain't proud to be what I is, get me?" (II). As in so many major documents by major American writers, some—in this case most—of the characters in the play have deep-set doubts about their own identity.

Moreover, Hickey's panacea for the discovery of the true self and the real identity by destroying both the past and the future is deeply dubious as well: "You'll be in a today where there is no yesterday or tomorrow to worry you" (II). "No," says Larry to Rocky in Act IV, "it doesn't look good, Rocky. I mean, the peace Hickey's brought you. It isn't contented enough, if you have to make everyone else a pimp, too." And as they all cry out, after having been jarred back into a time sequence, seen the sun, inspected reality, and destroyed the lies about the past and smashed the daydreams of the future: "We can't pass out! And you promised us peace!"

For Hickey's "message" is, as Larry says in Act II, equivocal: "Be God, its a second feast of Belshazzar, with Hickey to do the writing on the wall" (II). But there is no Daniel to interpret the cabalistic hieroglyphics. In so far as Hickey's "message" is understandable or realizable, it is wholly negative and destructive, despite its admonition to face the "truth." [13] Again Larry gives the key: "Be God, it's not to Bakunin's ghost you ought to pray in your dreams, but to the great Nihilist, Hickey! He's started a movement that'll blow up the world!" (II). As the historical Nihilists would have destroyed the past of mankind, Hickey would destroy the past of the individuals in the play. By Act IV, he himself is apprehensive of his own "cure" and is nervously exhorting the depressed patients to be content: "Can't you see there is no tomorrow now? You're rid of it forever! You've killed it! You don't have to give a damn about anything any more!" But man needs his past and his future, no matter how illusory, for he is incurably lonely. In Lazarus' millennium there will be no more loneliness: "Lonely no more! Man's loneliness is but his fear of life! Lonely no more! Millions of laughing stars are around me!" (III, 2). But the human condition, before this millennium, is inescapably solitary, more so as one gets older. This is why the elderly talk and confide; they can no longer endure being locked up with their own secrets. As Tiberius describes the phenomenon to Lazarus (see Chapter 2, Sec. i above), the old must talk because they cannot bear their own solitude. And the loneliness is always fearful. In *Strange Interlude* when Darrell meets Marsden and speculates why a man of Marsden's intelligence and talent does not go deeper into the problems of human existence in his novels, he concludes that Marsden is afraid to, "afraid he'll meet himself somewhere" (I). Very often man's only companions are his own past and his own future, chimerical as they may be.

O'Neill was dialectical in his thinking, and he had already "answered" Hickey in an earlier play, *The Hairy Ape*. O'Neill said that Yank in *The Hairy Ape* was not a stoker but an Everyman who fell from innocent certainty to complex incertitudes, or, as the play puts it, to "not belonging," the ultimate human frustration and humiliation and the essence of loneliness. Further, the fall made "thought," always torturous, inescapable. Thus in Scene IV Yank is sitting in the exact pose of Rodin's "The Thinker" and exclaims to his bemused fellow-Neanderthals, "Can't youse see I'm tryin' to tink?" Whether O'Neill knew that "The Thinker" was originally meant to be a representation of Dante I do not know, but his choice of this piece of sculpture was particularly apt. Thus in Scene VIII, looking at the gorilla, himself in the Dantesque pose, Yank says, "I ain't on oith and I ain't in heaven, get me? I'm in de middle tryin' to separate 'em, taking' all de worst punches from bot' of 'em. Maybe dats what dey call hell, huh?"

Like Jim in *All God's Chillun Got Wings*, Yank suffers one rebuff and humiliation after another, until he begins to feel like a Kafka hero whose only sin was being born. When a policeman sends him on his way after he has been thrown out of the I.W.W. local meeting house, Yank explains that he has done enough to get "life": "I was born, see?" (VII). He has only one glimpse of what it is like "to belong," when he is sitting peaceably one morning in the Battery watching New York harbor: "Sure. I seen de sun come up. Dat was pretty, too—all red and pink and green. I was lookin' at de skyscrapers—steel—and all de ships comin' in, sailin' out, all over de oith—and dey was steel, too. De sun was warm, dey wasn't no clouds, and dere was a breeze blowin'. Sure, it was great stuff. I got it aw right—what Paddy said about dat bein' de right dope [see above, Chapter 1, Sec. iii]—on'y I couldn't get in it, see? I couldn't belong in dat" (VIII). Earlier in the play he had contemptuously dismissed Paddy for "Hittin' de pipe of de past, dat's what he's doin' " (I). But "de pipe" of the past is a human necessity, and Yank's real tragedy is to have been thrust into the condition of existing in what Hickey describes as the panacea for man, existing solely in the present, without a past or a future, in a kind of ultimate "not belonging." At the end of *The Hairy Ape* Yank realizes the extent of this total isolation and sees that his final solitude is precisely the inhuman predicament of having neither a past nor a future. Just before his death (VIII) he says exactly this: he has no past to "tink in" and he does not know what is coming. He knows only "what's now—and dat don't belong." Hickey's heaven is Yank's hell.

The quintessential O'Neill character can neither *be* nor *not be*. He longs for an indifferent existence which he cannot have and would not rest in content if he could. All these characters share Dion Anthony's "hopeless hope." "But to be neither creature nor creator! To exist only in her indifference" (II, 3). Indifference, however, cannot be, and to exist is to be both self-destructive and destructive of others. Again a key line is in *The Great God Brown* in Act IV, Scene 2, when Brown points at the mask of Dion Anthony and exclaims: "I am his murdered and his murdered." Most O'Neill characters are "*tortured with torturing others*" (II, 3).

And thus at the end of the long dark tunnel at the end of the long day's journey into night stands, along with the grieving woman—although she cannot see it or hear it—the lonely self of mankind, shouting noiseless Promethean threats, crying soundlessly in the dark, huddling over the faint, flickering light of an illusion, clinging to his past and future as a kind of ultimate identification. Slave or free man, illusionist or realist, solitary or fraternalist, guilty or innocent, all he finally knows is that he must be an "I" and have an ego, no matter the number of assaults by reality upon it and no matter the number of illusions it must feed upon.

# *4*   THE FORM

ANY PLAY, formally considered, is made up of its dramatic structure or organization and its language, both stage directions and dialogue. Considered either as a dramatic architect or as a writer of dramatic prose, O'Neill is a protean figure, remarkable for his range, his daring, and his originality. Looked at casually, his plays seem to represent a bewildering display of artistic pyrotechnics, as he constantly varies both their form and their language. On closer inspection, however, and as I hope to show, there is going on a continuous and chartable evolution which is to culminate in plays that are remarkable for the compressed unity and explosive power of their structure and for the appropriateness and the verisimilitude of their language. Of other American writers only Henry James can be said to have undergone such a lengthy, continuous, and finally triumphant artistic evolution.

## I *Structure*

In *The Captive* of *Remembrance of Things Past* Marcel (Proust) wiles away the hours with the captive, Albertine, by giving her informal lectures on the nature of art. He explains to her that the great writers have never created more than a single work, or "rather have never done more than refract through various mediums an identical beauty which they bring into the world ("Flight of Albertine"). He explains by concrete examples, beginning with "that stonemason's geometry in the novels of Thomas Hardy":

Do you remember the stonemasons in *Jude the Obscure*, in *The Well-Beloved*, the blocks of stone which the father hews out of the island coming in boats to be piled up in the son's studio where they are turned into statues; in *A Pair of Blue Eyes* the parellelism of the tombs, and also the parallel line of the vessel, and the railway coaches containing the lovers and the dead woman; the parallelism between *The Well-Beloved*, where the man is in love with three women, and *A Pair of Blue Eyes* where the woman is in love with three men, and in short all those novels which can be laid one upon another like the vertically piled houses upon the rocky soil of the island. I cannot summarize the greatest writers like this in a moment's talk, but you would see in Stendahl a certain sense of altitude combining with the life of the spirit: the lofty place in which Julien Sorel is imprisoned, the tower on the summit of which Fabrice is confined, the belfry in which the Abbé Blanès pores over his astrology and from which Fabrice has such a magnificent bird's-eye view.

In many of the pictures of Vermeer (Proust's favorite painter), Marcel continues, one finds always fragments of an identical world: the same table, the same carpet, the same woman, the same novel and unique beauty. In Dostoevski it is the face of a beautiful and enigmatic woman and an enormous old house, especially in *The Idiot*, "the masterpiece of the House of Murder in Dostoevski, that sombre house, so long, and so high, and so huge, of Rogojin in which he kills Nastasia Philipovna. That novel and terrible beauty of a house, that novel beauty blended with a woman's face, that is the unique thing which Dostoievski has given to the world." A unique and distinct human face; a particular place, a certain setting; an unmistakable atmosphere, terrible and beautiful; a certain arrangement of peoples and things, houses or tombstones or railroads or tables or carpets: this is the figure in the carpet of all great artists, according to Proust. Each has seized out of the enormous flux of experience some basic picture which stands as metaphor for the whole human condition. Like the phrase from Vinteuil's music in *Remembrance of Things Past*, this metaphor, orchestrated, sounds throughout the whole length and breadth of the author's corpus, as he tells his same unique story, again and again, continually changing the names but never the essence.

O'Neill's figure in the carpet in his best and most characteristic plays is the grieving woman and the lonely self of mankind. The setting is a ship or a bar or a home. The house has columns in front (*Mourning Becomes Electra*) or a porch or piazza (*Desire Under the Elms, Long Day's Journey Into Night, Ah, Wilderness!*) or a front stoop (*A Moon for the Misbegotten*). His greatest plays, *The Iceman Cometh* (the lonely self) and *Long Day's Journey Into Night* (the grieving woman) take place, respectively, in a decayed bar and in a middle-class home. These two habitations were the polar places of existence in O'Neill's world: the bar signifying drink and song, artificial conviviality, penitential outpourings, the racial and cultural melting pot, the masculine world, and the world of down-and-outers. It plays the role in the later plays that the ship had in the earlier ones. The house, on the other hand, was the place where memory, etched into the walls, the furniture, the books, was almost tangible, the place where the family was thrown back on itself and each member on himself or herself with an explosive power. This world of middle-class home and often shabby barroom was James O'Neill's world and, in all his early life, the world of Eugene O'Neill. A *Touch of the Poet* combines both worlds, weaving together the bacchanal of the barroom and the excruciating tensions of the family. *Long Day's Journey Into Night, A Moon for the Misbegotten*, and *Ah, Wilderness!*, while taking place in or before a house (or shack), have the bar in the background as the place where the males go to escape the proprieties and the entanglements of the home. Men drinking, not very happily; women waiting or weeping: this is the primordial O'Neill situation. Throughout his writing career his imagination carried him and his dramatic world over vast reaches of space and time: across Asia, back to the Roman Empire, through jungles, New York apartments, farms, sanitariums, dynamos, hotels, but the home and the bar were like Hardy's stones or Dostoevski's houses or Vermeer's tables and carpets, the quintessential and emblematic background for his most powerful dramatic creations.

This is the picture; the mode is contrast and repetition. In the organization of all of O'Neill's plays the molecular unit, the thumbprint of the playwright as it were, is that most simple, basic, and elementary of artistic devices, contrast, which operates both in the briefest vignette and in the total structure of the plays. Day and night, land and sea, city and country, New England and New York, the old and the new, heat and cold, organic order and mechanical order, white and Negro, male and female, all these great contrasts, the entire Manichaean universe of O'Neill, is the macrocosm to the innumerable microcosms of sharp, single, visual images: the black face of Mammy against the white pillow in the darkened flat of *The Dreamy Kid*, or Eileen Carmody's white face in the obscurity of the forest at midnight in *The Straw*, or the great black trunk of the pine tree standing parallel, like a Hardy stone or casket or like the Vermeer tapestry, to the white columns of the portico of the house of Mannon, or the white hair, white face, and white dress of Mary Tyrone in the darkened house in New London, or Jamie Tyrone's "haggard, dissipated face...like a pale mask in the moonlight—" in Act III of *A Moon for the Misbegotten*.

The impulse toward contrast tends to be more obsessive in the earlier plays and is often schematic, as in *Beyond the Horizon* or *All God's Chillun Got Wings*. *Beyond the Horizon* begins in happiness in a warm sunset in the spring; it ends in tragedy on a cold dawn in the fall; in between is the heat—and scenes of anger—of the summer. The individual scenes alternate, in precise order, between the indoors and outdoors. Most of the play takes place in a valley, but the surrounding hills are always being looked at and remarked on, and in one scene (II, 1) the action takes place on top of one of these hills. Though it is a farm play and concerned with the land, the sea can be seen from the top of this hill. The characters divide into those who are attached to the farm and those who travel by sea to foreign parts, and the plot is propelled by the periodic returns of the travelers. The characters are arranged in schematic fashion: the two brothers, one sensitive, sickly, idealistic (Robert Mayo), the other solid, simple, healthy (Andrew Mayo); the two older men: the one vigorous and irascible (James Mayo), the other vigorous and hearty (Captain Scott); the two older women: the one gentle and sensitive (Mrs. Mayo), the other peevish and durable (Mrs. Atkins). Or the contrast, instead of being pervasive and schematic as it is in *Beyond the*

*Horizon,* is located in one central disparity that entails a series of correlative contrasts. Such is the situation in *All God's Chillun Got Wings* in which, at the center, is the contrast between the white and the Negro. From this follows all else: they look different, talk different, live on opposite sides of the street, sing different songs, live in a different manner; each is forced by terrible pressures to live opposite but complementary lives of intensity and emotional torture. Again the contrast can be temporal, as the tone or mood of a play successively changes. *Moon of the Caribbees* begins in an atmosphere of tranquility with a melancholy chant drifting over the water to a ship on which the sailors are talking desultorily; a tension gradually builds up as the girls and the liquor arrive, develops into a bacchanal, erupts into violence with the flash of the knife in the moonlight, and just as quickly subsides into a somber silence, with only the original sound of the brooding music drifting across from the shore.

Practically all of O'Neill's characteristic methods and devices appear in the late plays, only in a simple and elemental, and hence unobtrusive, form, the effect of these plays being so overwhelmingly "real" and lifelike that the form itself tends to disappear, dissolved by the vitality of the drama. Yet these plays too are founded on contrast of various kinds, the most basic being the temporal passage from comedy (the morning) to tragedy (the night); *The Iceman Cometh, Long Day's Journey Into Night,* and *A Moon for the Misbegotten* follow this pattern, beginning in laughter and ending in sadness and tears. To a lesser degree, this is true also of *A Touch of the Poet* which opens with some broad badinage between Cregan and Malloy.

Running through the contrasts, from first to last, are repetitions: sounds, songs, snatches of poetry, themes, and phrases. Again and again there is the obsessive, binding reiteration: of a word or phrase or of a visual image: the gray stone and the white columns of the Mannon mansion in the crimson sunset in *Mourning Becomes Electra,* the dawn coming up over the rocky farm in *Desire Under the Elms;* or of a sound: the organ grinder of *All God's Chillun Got Wings,* the water lapping at the piles and the music in the air in the Prologue and Epilogue of *The Great God Brown,* the jabbering, human, and the jabbering, simian, that opens and closes *The Hairy Ape*, the successive pistol shots in *The Emperor Jones*, with the infernal tom-tom beat slowly but steadily building up in the background, the indescribable laughter in *Lazarus Laughed*, the crash and then the hum of Promethean fire at the beginning and the end of *Dynamo*. Drinking, which occupies so much time in the late plays, is itself a rite of repetitions.

Human experience in all these plays has an almost ritualistic flavor, as if the explosive and anarchistic emotional forces unleashed could somehow be ordered and controlled by repeated incantations. O'Neill liked to think of the incantatory aspects of his plays as their musicality, the motifs and the leitmotifs by successive iteration building up in the play horizontal lines of force which, like the Vinteuil phrase in *Remembrance of Things Past*, become in their mute but expressive monotony the very essence and emblem of the meaning of the play in which they occur. Or, to put it another way, these reiterations show the inevitable limitations of the life of each character, hemmed in as he is by certain inescapable boundaries, condemned, because of what he is, to say the same things, hear the same sounds, react to experience in all its variety and complexity in a certain, fixed, unalterable way. Each man has his own passport to eternity, his own, sole way of handling the enormity of experience. More often than not it involves simply thowing up the hands, figuratively speaking, and repeating one's own phrase, "Well, that's life" (*Hughie*), "Dat ole davil sea" (*Anna Christie*), "Laugh!" (*Lazarus*), "Bejees" (*The Iceman Cometh*). For it is doubtful if most people, throughout no matter how long a life, do much more than repeat themselves. Moreover, consciously-unconsciously, humans possess an archaic belief that words are a kind of magic, never more so than in their incantatory aspects, and instinctively believe that they can somehow tame the terrors of their existence by reducing each, unique onslaught into a protective phrase or word or sound. By the same token, they take satisfaction in hearing sounds repeated, for it means they are still themselves, no matter what life has done to them. When in the Epilogue to *The Great God Brown* Margaret hears the music in the night and the water lapping at the piers and sees the moon in the sky over the sea, she knows that she is "still the same Margaret," despite the fact that "the nights are so much colder than they used to be." For some things must somehow stay the same—"Bejees, what did you do to the booze, Hickey?" —or total chaos is come. As Freud put it in *Civilization and Its Discontents*: "Order is a kind of repetition—compulsion by which it is ordained once for all when where and how a thing shall be done so that on every similar occasion doubt and hesitation shall be avoided." [1]

Finally, repetitions are deeply satisfying aesthetically, no matter what O'Neill's detractors may have said. O'Neill's own feeling was that these reiterations satisfied a primordial aesthetic need and desire. The instinct for "rhythm," Aristotle had said in the *Poetics*, is, along with the instinct for imitation, at the root of our love of art. And thus Stark Young in a review of *Mourning Becomes Electra* said that in this play O'Neill "has come to what is so rare in Northern art, an understanding of the depth and subtlety that lie in repetition and variations on the same design." [2]

EACH OF THESE formal devices by O'Neill, the quintessential picture, the contrasts, the repetitions, are all part of an over-all temporal order, for a play, like a narrative, is above all an ordering of human experience in time. Considered as temporal units the plays fall into four, at times overlapping, groups. The four groups comprise plays with long time spans; those with medium time spans; those with time spans in an indeterminate realm between the medium and the brief; and the brief or Aristotelian. (I exclude from these considerations the one-act plays which are of necessity Aristotelian.) Roughly speaking, the long- and the medium-sized predominate in O'Neill's early career which opens with *Beyond the Horizon* in 1918 and closes in the late 1920's and early 1930's when he composed the third, or indeterminate, group of plays. The fourth, and Aristotelian, phase occurs in the final and culminating career, of the late 1930's and early 1940's.

The elongated group is comprised of *Beyond the Horizon*, eight years; *All God's Chillun Got Wings*, seventeen or more years; *The Great God Brown*, some eighteen years plus *"some"* weeks; *The Fountain*, twenty-two years or more; *Marco Millions*, twenty-three years plus; *Strange In-*

*terlude,* twenty-seven or -eight years; and *Diff'rent,* thirty years. Side by side with these temporal monsters is the second, or medium-sized group: *Anna Christie,* nineteen days or so; *The Hairy Ape,* seven weeks and three days; *The First Man,* eight months or so; *The Straw,* eight months and one week: *Desire Under the Elms,* eleven or twelve months; *Lazarus Laughed,* some months (indefinite); *Gold,* a year and a half; and *Dynamo,* some nineteen months. Twice during this same period in his career, in 1920 with *The Emperor Jones* (twelve to fourteen hours), and in 1923 with *Welded* (one night), O'Neill abandoned both the elongated and the medium-sized time span for a modified Aristotelian form. Neither *The Emperor Jones* nor *Welded* have unity of place although both have unity of time and action. These plays, however, are the exceptions in this period; furthermore, pure Aristotelian plays, with all of the three unities observed, are reserved for the late and final career. After *Strange Interlude,* there is an abrupt turn toward economy in time. *Dynamo* takes some nineteen months, but after this the years disappear altogether. From this point on the longest time gap, and the only sizable one, in an O'Neill play is the one month that elapses between Act I and Act II of *The Haunted,* the last play of *Mourning Becomes Electra.*

By this period (*circa* 1929–32) in his writing career O'Neill was in his indeterminate phase: *The Haunted,* one month and three days; *Days Without End,* one week; *The Hunted,* three days; and *Ah, Wilderness!,* two days and two nights. The fourth and last stage, beginning with *A Touch of the Poet,* seventeen hours, and *The Iceman Cometh,* two days, two nights, and the early morning of the third day, culminates in *Long Day's Journey Into Night,* sixteen hours or so, and *A Moon for the Misbegotten,* eighteen hours or so.[3]

Such groupings as this are, of course, artificial in the sense that they may give the impression of symmetry, where, in fact and moment by moment, no such symmetry exists. Thus the period in O'Neill's career from 1918 to about 1928 shows him oscillating wildly in the choice of time-span for the successive plays. For example, from 1920 to 1923, the time chart runs: *Gold,* one and one-half years; *Anna Christie,* nineteen days; *The Emperor Jones,* twelve to fourteen hours; *Diff'rent,* thirty years; *The First*

*Man,* eight months or so; *The Hairy Ape,* seven weeks and three days; *The Fountain,* more than twenty-two years; and *Welded,* one night. The only patterns discernible are that in the middle and late twenties and in the elongated plays, the time span tended to become longer and longer: thus *All God's Chillun* (seventeen years); *Marco Millions* (twenty-three years); *The Great God Brown* (eighteen plus years), and *Strange Interlude* (twenty-seven plus years), and that, over all, the plays as a whole gravitate from longer time spans in the early career to shorter time spans in the later career.

The impulse in his earlier career to spread his dramatic action over a long period of time arose, in a general way, from O'Neill's novelistic impulse, the Proustian urge to dramatize the chemistry and the attritions of the years. In his *Modern Drama*[4] Martin Lamm makes the point that although O'Neill "has written practically nothing but plays, his gift is for narrative. The one-act plays of his youth are evocative short-stories, and his mammoth dramas are half-novels." Actually, as with most of his characteristic devices, O'Neill had a multiple motivation for use of long time-spans. It has been said of O'Casey that his dramatic nurture consisted of Shakespeare, on the one hand, and the baldest kind of nineteenth-century melodrama, on the other. O'Neill's heritage was a similarly anomalous blend: *The Count of Monte Cristo* and the other nineteenth-century Anglo-American melodramas in which his father played, and the plays of Strindberg and other nineteenth- and twentieth-century Continental tragedies. But in O'Neill's case while the influence of Strindberg is obvious, and has often been remarked upon, that of *Monte Cristo* is less so, all the more because much of it is unconscious. Yet it can be shown that on one level his elongated plays bear unmistakable analogies to the old potboiler that dominated his father's life, although it can also be shown that, upon this form, he engrafted serious meanings.

It should be emphasized first how powerfully, how inescapably, *The Count of Monte Cristo* was stamped into Eugene O'Neill's consciousness and memory. As he could never forget his family, he could never forget what can only be called the family play. That as a serious playwright O'Neill was in conscious rebellion against this old play and all it stood for: melodrama, sentiment, easy popularity, stage tricks, cardboard characters, stale rhetoric; this is all too obvious. He once said, "I suppose if one accepts the song and dance complete of the psycho-analysts, it is perfectly natural that having been brought up around the old conventional theatre, and having identi-fied it with my father, I should rebel and go in a new direction" (Gelbs, p. 451). But underneath "the song and dance" of the psychoanalysts is the deeper insight of classical psychoanalysis that there *is* no escape finally from the earliest years, or at least no easy and immediate one.

James O'Neill had been playing the role of Edmond Dantes for five years when Eugene O'Neill was born. Doris Alexander speculates that the words "Monte Cristo" must have been among the first words that young Eugene O'Neill ever heard.[5] He was to grow up on the play, seeing it rehearsed, and watching it being performed. One of his earliest acts of aggression against his father was to pour a can of green paint into a box full of metal statuettes depicting his father in his role of Edmond Dantes (Gelbs, p. 84). According to the Gelbs, he also carved a large and disfiguring "M.C." into the handsome balustrade of the family summer home in New London (*ibid.*). If the boy believed in witchcraft, which he probably did, he was destroying his father by these acts of aggression. Later on he was to participate in the play itself.

The most famous scene in the play dramatized Edmond Dantes' escape from the Château d'If. In this brief scene two gaolers toss a sack into the ocean by the prison. Sup-posedly the sack contains the body of the dead Faria, Dantes' prison companion; actually it contains the body of the living Dantes, knife in hand. The gaolers disappear and the moon breaks out on a projecting rock; Dantes rises from the sea. He is dripping (with salt and sawdust), climbs up on the rock (a stool) and exclaims: "Saved! Mine, the treasures of Monte Cristo! The world is mine!" Meanwhile the sea, a green canvas under which a couple of stagehands wriggled to simulate movement, heaved below him. In a reminiscence of O'Neill, John V. A. Weaver spoke of "how Gene's earliest delight was to make the canvas waves into which his father, the unforgettable Count of Monte Cristo, dived" (Cargill et al., p. 27).

Eugene O'Neill himself once reminisced: "I can still see my father dripping with salt and sawdust, climbing on a stool behind the swinging profile of dashing waves. It was then that the calcium lights in the gallery played on his long beard and tattered clothes, as with arms outstretched he declared the world was his" (Alexander, p. 184). When the Provincetown Players were presenting *Thirst*, William Zorach, the sculptor and painter who designed some of the settings for the Players, remembered that O'Neill's concept for staging the play, which takes place on the sea, by using a sea cloth with someone wriggling around underneath it, was suspiciously and uncomfortably like the Château d'If scene in *Monte Cristo* (Gelbs, p. 313). Even when O'Neill's first career was at its height, reviewers were still picking up echoes of the old play. In a review of *Desire Under the Elms* Heywood Broun described the play as a piece of "theatricality" eminently worthy of the son of the man who had played *The Count of Monte Cristo* so many times and, noting that *Desire* was a revenge play like *Monte Cristo*, said that it would have been possible to count " 'One, two, three' [Dantes' utterances as each of his three betrayers falls dead] as this new tale of vengeance clicked into certain well-worn grooves" (Gelbs, p. 510). And Robert Benchley's review of *Mourning Becomes Electra* conjured up an old actor with a white wig and drawn sword standing in the wings and exhorting: "That's good, son! Give 'em the old Theatre!" (Gelbs, p. 753), although, unlike Broun, Benchley meant it as a compliment.[6]

But the imprint of *Monte Cristo* on Eugene O'Neill was not superficial or nugatory, as some of these comments facetiously suggest. Doris Alexander (p. 84), for example, makes the point: "From watching rehearsals [of his father's company], Eugene learned the value of 'strong situations' as his father called them: Father and son about to fight, not knowing their relationship (*Monte Cristo*); brother against brother (*The Two Orphans, When Greek Meets Greek*); the husband whose child has been begotten by a trusted friend (*The Manx Man*). He would use such situations in his own plays—more meaningful perhaps, but just as surely for their dramatic value."

Moreover, if *Monte Cristo* was one of O'Neill's most

powerful childhood memories, its last tour in 1911 (as re-constructed by the Gelbs, pp. 175–85), in which the entire family was involved, indelibly impressed itself on his memories of his young manhood, so much so that the O'Neill familial situation of 1911 became the archetype for the Tyrones' family situation in *Long Day's Journey Into Night*. In 1911, at the age of sixty-five, James O'Neill played Dantes for the last time. The play was by now a tabloid version, condensed below the level of lucidity and merely one of the "acts" in a touring vaudeville show; it invoked only nostalgia on the part of the audience. Both of his sons, for whom the tour was a prolonged alco-holic binge, were playing small parts—no other manager would have hired them—and were given to crude jokes on the stage at their father's expense. His wife, usually in a morphine stupor, he brought to the theater every day because he was afraid to leave her alone in the hotel room. Some times she waited in the wings and would become rapt at one of the climactic moments in the play, namely, where Mercédès reveals to Dantes, by now the Count, at the end of Act IV that Albert is their son. At this point Ella O'Neill would begin to move toward the stage like a sleepwalker. She never actually arrived on the stage itself but always threatened to and always added to her husband's sense of harassment. In February 1912 *Variety* carried the news that the tour was ended and the Count was dead. *Long Day's Journey Into Night* takes place in that same year, 1912, and certainly the Tyrone relationships: the two drunken sons baiting the harassed father, with the doped mother hovering in the wings and threatening to appear, is a dramatization of what had been in fact the O'Neill family relations in the last days of *Monte Cristo*.

James O'Neill's version of *The Count of Monte Cristo* was put together by the actor-manager Charles Fechter and was therefore known as the "Fechter version." [7] Fechter divided the action into five acts and six scenes. Act I begins in 1815 and takes three scenes in order to describe how Dantes is sent to the Château d'If, torn from the arms of Mercédès just after their marriage and with her already pregnant with their child. Eighteen years pass between Act I and II, during which Albert is born and grows up and Dantes lies in prison. Acts II, III,

IV, and V describe, successively, Dantes' escape from the Château d'If, his assumption of the wealth and title of Monte Cristo, his revenge on the three villains who betrayed him, his reunion with Mercédès, and his discovery that Albert is his son. Each act ends on a melodramatic thunderclap: Dantes sent to prison (Act I); "The world is mine!" (Act II); "One!"—the first villain falls dead (Act III); Mercédès' revelation to Dantes that Albert is their son (Act IV); "Two!" "Three!" and the revelation to Albert that Dantes is his father (Act V). This ending in particular was meant to be a series of melodramatic hammer strokes. At the conclusion of the play only Danglars, the deepest-dyed villain, is still alive and although Dantes knows that Albert is his son, Albert does not know that Dantes is his father. Mercédès, of course, is also present; then come the successive hammer strokes:

DANG  Have at thee! [*lunging at him*]
EDMUND  Die! [*runs him through*]
DANG  Ha! [*dies and rolls at his feet*]
EDMUND  "Three!"
MERC  Your prayers have saved your father's life, Albert— you are his son!

*curtain*

This likable, implausible, old potboiler meant as much to O'Neill as did Strindberg although he would have been the last to admit it and was probably unaware of the depth of the impress. He was once asked to do a serious modern version of the play and for a time seriously considered doing so. But this interesting possibility was to remain only a possibility. Nevertheless, and whether he knew it or not, O'Neill throughout his early career was ringing changes on both the content and the form of the old play, whose hero, Edmond Dantes, had been, in effect, a fifth member of the O'Neill family.

There are many similarities in content between the "Fechter version" and O'Neill's plays, many of them, no doubt, only coincidental. But the over-all pattern is remarkably similar. *Monte Cristo* opens in a tavern by the sea, with the characters waiting for a ship to return, suggesting many O'Neill settings and situations. Two scenes occur in inns and there is a stage drunk, Caderouse, who espouses one of the basic philosophies of *The Iceman Cometh*: "nothing like love of the bottle"; "I drink so much as ever I like—as much as I can—and then I open the floodgates of truth and avow I love wine, hate work, and pray for widowhood!" *Monte Cristo* is, of course, an historical play, as were so many of O'Neill's. It was also a revenge play, like O'Neill's *Abortion, The Rope, The Emperor Jones, Desire Under the Elms, The Great God Brown,* and *Mourning Becomes Electra.* This is not to mention the high incidence of revenge, or contemplation of revenge, in many other of O'Neill's plays. For at least one character (a villain) in *Monte Cristo,* his own family and the past of that family are the millstone around his neck: "Great Heavens, is the hateful past of my family to haunt me ever on my aspiring path?"—a cry to be heard in many O'Neill plays. In *Monte Cristo* a young man, Albert, sees a stranger, Dantes, who is in actuality his father, and exclaims, "I experience when near you, feelings akin to those their souls must experience." A similar mystique about father and son motivates Gordon Evans in Act VII of *Strange Interlude,* when, instinctively, he feels a liking for Darrell, whom consciously he hates. Albert himself, conceived out of wedlock, is a true "love-child," like so many children in O'Neill's plays.

But the form of *Monte Cristo* is the predominant influence on O'Neill's earlier plays, the more so for probably being unconscious. First, *Monte Cristo* is full of asides, soliloquies, and disguises, all of which devices O'Neill was to employ on a much larger scale and in a much more diversified and sophisticated way. In so doing, he was often thought to be revitalizing Elizabethan techniques, but the real source was much closer to home and much more immediate to memory, namely, the "Fechter version," or any of the other melodramas in which his father played.

O'Neill's most important heritage from *The Count of Monte Cristo* was temporal, and this temporal heritage was twofold and polar: the long-term narrative movement and the brief, explosive, dramatic event. The first and most obvious temporal rhythm was long-term and involved the passage of a long period of time, like that eighteen-year gap between Acts I and II of *Monte Cristo.* The eighteen years in *Monte Cristo* pass for three reasons: so Dantes can suffer through them and hence earn his revenge; so that Albert can be born and grow up; and so that the rest of the characters can suffer and age. Most of the time O'Neill's primary motivations for time lapses were as simple as this. In some plays it is simply the period necessary for gestation and birth (*The First Man, Desire Under the Elms, Strange Interlude*), or it is the growth to maturity of a child (*The Fountain, Strange Interlude*). In *The Fountain,* O'Neill's most *Monte Cristo*-esque production, there is a "recognition" scene whereby the protagonist sees in a younger person an image of his own past. This occurs in Scene III when the aging Ponce de Leon sees the now-grown daughter of the woman who had once been his beloved. The scene could well have been written by Charles Fechter and would have been played superbly by James O'Neill:

> *The murmur of the crowd increases.* JUAN *sinks on the bench before the fountain, oblivious to it, lost in gloomy thought.* BEATRIZ DE CORDOVA *appears, attended by her duenna and a crowd of richly dressed nobles. She is a beautiful young girl of eighteen or so, the personification of youthful vitality, charm and grace. The nobles point out* JUAN *to her. She dismisses them, motioning for them to be quiet—then comes in and approaches* JUAN, *keeping the fountain between them. She holds a sealed document in her hand. Finally she calls in a trembling, eager voice.*

> BEATRIZ   Don Juan! [JUAN *whirls on his bench and stares through the fountain at her. He utters a stunned exclamation as if he saw a ghost. His eyes are held fascinated by her beauty. Then suddenly she laughs—a gay, liquid, clear note—and coming quickly around confronts him*]  It is I, Don Juan.

> JUAN   [*stares at her still fascinated—then, reminded, springs to his feet and bows low with his old mocking gallantry*]  Pardon! I am bewitched! I thought you were the spirit of the fountain.

Finally, for the long-term temporal influence from *The Count of Monte Cristo,* there is in O'Neill's plays the phenomenon of aging and suffering, of which Ponce de Leon would be only the archetype of a whole gallery of O'Neill characters. The casts of *Strange Interlude* and *The Great God Brown* are the most comprehensively and the most agonizingly detailed instances.

But O'Neill also employed these time gaps for less obvious and more serious purposes as well. O'Neill's three most powerful plays in the elongated mode are *All God's Chillun Got Wings, The Great God Brown,* and *Strange Interlude.* The long-term temporal sense conveyed in these plays is twofold: first, a sense of the steady, inexorable passage of time; and, second, within this time span, a continuous sense of smaller temporal cycles, involving the time of year and the time of day. The characteristic mode of *All God's Chillun Got Wings* and *The Great God Brown* is to begin and end each play in the same season of the year, summer in *The Great God Brown* and spring in *All God's Chillun,* and at, roughly, the same time of day, night in *The Great God Brown,* late afternoon or twilight in *All God's Chillun Got Wings.* In between there is a continuous sense of change of season in each act and a change in time of day in each scene. *Strange Interlude,* while it opens in summer, oscillates consistently between spring and fall in each act. It begins and ends in an afternoon and in between follows the clock around its ceaseless daily cycle, from morning to night. Thus the time scheme of these plays could be represented diagrammatically by one great cycle, representing the years, and, within that, a smaller epicycle, representing the seasons, and, within that, a still smaller one representing the hours. What O'Neill was striving for here was the Hardyesque sense of human life as an affair of seasons, with fall signifying decay and spring an ironic mockery of re-birth, and with time as the enemy. In a review of *Beyond the Horizon* Alexander Woolcott remarked: "O'Neill paints his canvass with what Henley called 'the exquisite chromatics of decay.' You might almost say, then, that the play is alive because it follows the inexorable processes of death. Not since Arnold Bennett's *Old Wives' Tale* has any book given us quite so persuasively a sense of the passage of time" (Cargill et al., p. 136). One of O'Neill's favorite poems was Francis Thompson's "The Hound of Heaven," and if we substitute the concept of Time for the concept of God in the poem, we have some sense of the feeling of temporal inevitability that O'Neill incorporated into these plays:

> *Still with unhurrying chase,*
> *And unperturbéd pace,*
> *Deliberate speed, majestic instancy,*
> *Came on the following Feet,*

Time then is the enemy against whom one struggles, unavailingly. Thus Nina at the beginning of Act VIII of *Strange Interlude*—"*desperately trying to conceal the obvious inroads of time by an over-emphasis on makeup that defeats its end by drawing attention to what it would conceal. Her face is thin, her cheeks taut, her mouth drawn with forced smiling.*" And the twilight atmosphere of peace at the end of the play is engendered precisely because the struggle against time has been abandoned.

Time passing and people aging are, of course, potent, moving, and inherently dramatic phenomena, as O'Neill knew (and as Alexander Dumas and Charles Fechter knew). But the exhibition of this alone does not make a good play. And O'Neill possessed the psychological insight to see that in the morphology of time, which is what the plots or fables of the elongated plays are about, change is not the only striking phenomenon, and not even the most striking phenomenon. Equally arresting and dramatic are two other happenstances of time that considerably complicate its effects and render it the less merely change, pure and simple. First, there are certain persistencies that carry on underneath the constant change and are, in a sense, subverting it or building amidst its ruins a kind of rock of permanence. Second, there is the successive unfolding of ironies that make of life a continuous surprise—not always a happy one—as the separate desires, thoughts, speeches, and actions of each individual meet, clash, modify, and coalesce with those of others with whom he or she is involved in those subtle, collective, concatenations of events that make up human life and produce a final, collective product or human situation that no single individual involved in that group would have desired or could have foreseen. As has often been remarked, time is above all the master Ironist.

In *Strange Interlude* both of these phenomena are dramatized, not by philosophical speeches on the part of any one character but by the dramatic fact that they are of the essence of the plot of the play. The rock of persistence is, of course, Marsden's devotion to Nina, his indefatigable patience, and his final triumph. This relationship is presented with some subtlety. As with most plot devices in O'Neill's plays, it has a basis in a time-honored, obvious, and archetypal human situation whose meaning can be expressed in platitude; in this instance: "All things come to him who waits." But at the end of the play Marsden does not say that at last he had received his reward. Rather he, in a sense, wipes out the whole play, all two and one-half decades of it: "So let's you and me forget the whole distressing episode, regard it as an interlude." Nina assents to the view that it has all been a strange interlude. Thus the final temporal perspective in the play is his, and from his point of view what the strange interlude has been is a victory over change and time. This victory is less a matter of what he and Nina have said or done to one another in the bulk of the play but more the result of a kind of subverbal communion that has been built up over the years, underneath the tides of passion and the cataclysms of unhappinesses that each has wallowed in. By Act VIII Marsden realizes that some kind of timeless, indefinable, yet nevertheless genuine and unshakable relationship has been achieved between them, while all the other relationships in the play are completely fluid and unstable: "Nina has turned more and more to me . . . we have built up a secret life of subtle sympathies and confidences."

Finally, and perhaps above all, it is the ironies of time that are exhibited by the plot of *Strange Interlude*. Continually, characters are standing back to contemplate and remark on the ironies that time has wrought. As Gordon Evans says, "Life is damn queer, that's all I've got to say!" (IX). For nothing ever turns out as expected, and the future, as it unfolds, often turns out to be a kind of grim joke on the past. In Act IV when Marsden enters the study of the deceased father of Nina and sees it now as the "sanctuary" of Sam Evans, the unsuccessful ad man, he ruminates on the grotesquerie of circumstances. "What a mess they've made of this study . . . poor Professor! . . . dead and forgotten . . . and his tomb desecrated . . . does Sam write his ads here of a week-end now? . . . the last touch! . . . and Nina labors with love at Gordon's biography . . . whom the Professor hated! . . . 'life is so full of a number of things!' " Indeed the "logic" of the plot demonstrates the inherent illogicality of human affairs, the essence of which is probably best summed up by Darrell in Act VII. Contemplating the ruin and unhappiness of his own life, the tortured life of Nina, the hostility to him of Gordon Evans, his natural son, and the health and happiness of Sam Evans, who at the beginning of the play was the weak person they all tried to help, Darrell thinks: "Sam is the only normal one! . . . we lunatics! . . . Nina and I! . . . have made a sane life for him out of our madness!" And, in turn, this well-meaning man, Sam Evans, is the agency for causing the suffering of other people. Even in death his well-intentioned plans cause wounds, for his will leaves money to Darrell's biological station, an act which makes Darrell feel, once more, his agonies about his own life, so promising at the start and so wasted in the living; Nina remarks: "Even in death Sam makes people suffer." The fable of *The Great God Brown* is full of even wilder ironies and metamorphoses.

Concomitant with the unfolding of the succession of events of the private lives of the characters in the elongated plays, there is a sense of the changes going on in the civilization they inhabit. In these longer plays O'Neill was not primarily a social dramatist, but there are occasions when society not only impinges upon the lives of the characters but helps to shape them as well. In the world of *Beyond the Horizon* mechanization—steam on the sea, the combustion engine on the land—gradually takes over the scene, as the small, nineteenth-century farm falls into ruin. During this same period Andy Mayo, the sturdy, honest, hard-working, nineteenth-century, would-be farmer is transformed into a twentieth-century financial speculator: *"His face seems to have grown highstrung, hardened by the look of decisiveness which comes from being constantly under a strain where judgements on the spur of the moment are compelled to be accurate. His eyes are keener and more alert. There is even a suggestion of ruthless cunning about them"* (III, 1). The modern mechanical world similarly overtakes the characters of *All God's Chillun Got Wings*, as the rich street life of the first scenes, with their songs and shouts and with the organ grinder closing each scene with a nineteenth-century sentimental song, disappears. By Act II the characters have moved indoors, into "flats," which shrink in size as the act goes on, suggesting a sense of ever increasing claustrophobia, and the modern city dweller locked in his cell.

*The Great God Brown* opens with a middle-class version of the same world that the opening of *Beyond the Horizon* exhibited on the farm and *All God's Chillun* exhibited among the urban lower class—the imagined simplicities, pieties, and sentimentalities of nineteenth-century America. The Prologue of *The Great God Brown* takes place on a pier by a casino, at which a high school dance is taking place, with "Sweet Adeline," barbershop style, in the background. As the play goes on and as Brown progresses in his career as businessman-"architect," the modern world impinges—although this is the least social of plays—suggesting bigness, confusion, and a total anarchy of values, a topsy-turvy world where fraud alone is efficacious and where the artist can only express himself by smuggling into the design of conventional creations, such as public buildings, his own unique and ironic touch, as Dion Anthony imprints the Silenus figure into a conventional cathedral designed by Brown: "It's one vivid blasphemy from sidewalk to the tips of its spires!—but so concealed that the fools will never know. They'll kneel and worship the ironic Silenus who tells them the best good is never to be born!" (II, 3). When Brown, in his turn, has donned the mask of the dead Dion Anthony and has, in a sense, become Anthony, there is an even more powerful sense of a world gone mad, as Brown chuckles over his design for the state capitol: "Here's a wondrous fair Capitol! The design would do just as well for a Home for Criminal Imbeciles! Yet to them, such is my art, it will appear to possess a pure common-sense, a fat-bellied finality, as dignified as the suspenders of an assemblyman! Only to me will that pompous façade reveal itself as the wearily ironic grin of Pan as, his ears drowsy with the crumbling hum of past and future civilizations, he half listens to the laws passed by his fleas to enslave him!" (IV, 1). *Strange Interlude* likewise passes from one time and one place to another. Beginning in New England in a university town in the house of a professor—where New Englander meets Greek—it passes on to New York and the twenties (III–VI) and the frenetic, materialistic boom of that era which was so congenial to the fortunes of Sam Evans. This gives Marsden (and O'Neill) the opportunity in Act VI to comment on the meaninglessness of this false prosperity: "What a fount of meaningless energy he's [Sam Evans] tapped! . . . always on the go . . . typical terrible child of the age . . . universal slogan . . . keep moving . . . moving where? . . . never mind that." American civilization in both *The Great God Brown* and *Strange Interlude* is Henry Adams-esque, a powerful, ever accelerating juggernaut, devoid of either coherence, design, or meaning, or, if meaningful, ironically so, as in Brown's figure of the hidden, leering blasphemies lurking behind the outwardly respectable façade of an official building. And thus there are always two kinds of temporal progressions going on in these plays, the life of the characters and the life of society; the two progressions are interrelated in that they are cross-emblematic, the ironical tragedy of the one (the personal) standing as specific instances of the colossal general meaninglessness of the other (the public).

The only design that can be seen in either the private life or the public life in these plays is a pervasive irony, which for one who has rather a macabre sense of humor, as did Karl Marx for example, can afford at times a rather macabre sense of comedy. In *The Eighteenth Brumaire* Marx quoted Hegel as saying somewhere that all great historical facts and personages recur twice, but went on to say that Hegel had forgot to add they occur "Once as tragedy, and again as farce." And it was reported of Sir Thomas Urquhart, the translator, that when he heard of the Restoration of Charles II he was taken with such a violent fit of laughter as to bring on his own demise. Of Urquhart then it could be said he literally died laughing at the ironies of history. Similarly in the later parts of *The Great God Brown* and *Strange Interlude* O'Neill's characters are given to hysterical bursts of agonized "amusement" at the ironies that life and history have wrought in their own lives and in the life of their times. But no one has the good fortune, like Urquhart, to die laughing (except Lazarus). They must live and suffer.

Counterpointing and modifying this Proustian urge to dramatize the years is an opposite impulse in these same plays toward the sudden, the dramatic *event*. This is the second heritage from *Monte Cristo*. Accordingly, these same plays of the twenties, both the elongated ones and those of a medium time span, tend to be cut up into a great number of separate acts and scenes: eight scenes in *The Hairy Ape;* two acts and seven scenes in *All God's Chillun Got Wings;* three acts and twelve scenes in *Desire Under the Elms;* nine acts in *Strange Interlude;* four acts, twelve scenes, a prologue and an epilogue in *The Great God Brown.* Many of O'Neill's best plays of his early career are based on the brief vignette form, a series of short scenes that are dramatic revelations and that end in violence, either physical or emotional or both. For example, *The Hairy Ape* has eight scenes, each of which reveals another abyss in Yank's descent from "belonging" to "not belonging," and each ends in violent action, all culminating in the final revelation of utter nothingness and self-immolation. *All God's Chillun Got Wings* has essentially the same kind of organization, with each brief scene usually ending with the characters in a cataclysmic emotional state, some times on the verge of a breakdown. This succession of near breakdowns culminates at the end of the last act where the two protagonists have broken through the barriers of adulthood and have become children once more. *The Great God Brown* follows the same pattern, one short scene after another with the central characters on or near the breaking point.

There is, finally, a third temporal impulse at work in these plays: circularity. In a discussion of the organization of *The Great God Brown* Dorothy Kauche [8] points out that the Epilogue and Prologue of the play have a basic similarity in sound patterns, verbal patterns, tone and mood, and, of course, Margaret, the eternal feminine, is present in both scenes and, in the Epilogue, announces her sameness and unchangingness. This device, as Miss Kaucher points out, is a familiar dramatic one and is known, in Hebbel's phrase, as "tying the thread." This same impulse to tie the thread, if sometimes ironically, operates in most of the other plays of this period. Thus the medley of drinking-toasts that opens *The Hairy Ape* finds its ironical equivalent at the end in the whimpering and chattering of the monkeys in the cage where Yank lies dead. *All God's Chillun* begins and ends with the communion of the white "girl" and the black "boy." *Desire Under the Elms* begins and ends on a note of admiration for the farm, the love of which or desire for which, motivates the play as a whole: "God! Purty!" (first line); "It's a jim-dandy farm, no denyin'. Wished

I owned it!" (last line). Even *Strange Interlude* ties the thread in this explicit fashion, from the first utterance, Marsden's "I'll wait in here, Mary" to the last thought (Marsden's once more) that "good old" Charlie "has all the luck at last!"

There are then three temporal impulses in many of these early plays: the long-term and the evolutionary; the abrupt and the dramatic, and the circular or the timeless; or, to put it another way, slow change, abrupt eruption, and repetitiousness or sameness.

What O'Neill seemed to have been most uncertain about at this stage of his career was how to end a play. Even the tying of the thread is, for all its neatness, finally unsatisfactory. In an early, and very astute, criticism of O'Neill's earlier plays, specifically, *The Emperor Jones, The Hairy Ape, The First Man,* and *Anna Christie,* Hugo von Hofmannsthal made the point that in the best of these earlier plays, *The Hairy Ape* and *The Emperor Jones,* the conclusion was too neat, clean, and obvious, with our expectations too fully and completely satisfied and the element of surprise gone: "The close of *The Hairy Ape,* as well as that of *The Emperor Jones,* seems to me to be too direct, too simple, too expected; it is a little disappointing to a European with his complex background, to see the arrow strike the target towards which he has watched it speeding all the while" (Cargill et al., p. 255). And, on the other hand, if O'Neill did not tie the thread, as he did not in *Anna Christie* and *The First Man,* the effect was equally unsatisfactory: "The last acts of *Anna Christie* and *The First Man* seem somewhat evasive, undecided" (*ibid.*). O'Neill hardly ever solved the problem of a satisfactory ending in the plays of his early career, although the best of these plays, *Desire Under the Elms, The Hairy Ape,* and *Strange Interlude,* have the best endings. Naturally, his worst plays have the most unskillful, unsatisfactory, and obvious endings. Particularly is this true of *Dynamo* and *Days Without End,* among the last plays of his early career. Here especially in the conclusions of these plays one can see the ghost of *Monte Cristo* hovering in the wings, as O'Neill attempts to conclude the plays with a series of melodramatic hammer strokes à la *Monte Cristo.* The effect of the ending of *Monte Cristo* depends on four of the most elementary of dramatic devices: a death, a revelation, an abrupt close, and a dialogue of brief ejaculations, each of them ending with an exclamation point. *Dynamo* has a similar conclusion: fast-moving and abrupt, with Ada's murder and Reuben's suicide and Mrs. Fife finally uttering an ambiguous and cloudy revelation about the nature of the dynamo: "You hateful old thing, you! (*Then she leaves off, having hurt her hands, and begins to cry softly.*) CURTAIN." *Days Without End* is yet another variation on the same pattern. In the Catholic Church at dawn the villain, "Loving," falls dead; John regains his faith; Father Baird hurries in with his "revelation," i.e., that Elsa will live; and John utters the final exclamations and the final revelation:

JOHN LOVING   [*exaltedly*]   I know! Love lives forever! Death is dead! Ssshh! Listen! Do you hear?
FATHER BAIRD   Hear what, Jack?
JOHN LOVING   Life laughs with God's love again! Life laughs with love!

### curtain

*Days Without End* exorcised for O'Neill many ghosts, including the ghost of Edmond Dantès. Having gotten this turgid and weak play out of his system, he went on to write *A Touch of the Poet, The Iceman Cometh, Long Day's Journey Into Night, Hughie,* and *A Moon for the Misbegotten,* whose observances of the unities of time, place, and action, whose firmly developed characters, whose plausible dialogues, whose unmelodramatic plots, and whose quiet and sad endings are at the opposite pole, dramatically speaking, from the "Fechter version." Among other things, these plays constitute a triumph for Eugene O'Neill that was denied to his father: a final escape from the dungeon of the Château d'If. Still almost the whole story of Eugene O'Neill was somehow prefigured by that central biographical image: the youth wriggling under the green "waves" while, above him, under the calcium lights, his father triumphantly shouts: "The world is mine!"

IN 1923 in the *Dublin Magazine* Andrew Malone said of O'Neill: "He may decide as he grows older that the rules of Aristotle are good rules and still useful to the dramatist" (Cargill et al., p. 263). This was a perceptive guess at the future, and time has proved it a prophecy of things to come in O'Neill's plays. Throughout his first career he was a narrative dramatist, notable for his strong plots; in his second career the dramas tend to be without much narrative interest and to be retrospective meditations or agonizings. Dramatic exposition, which had formerly been the necessary machinery at the beginning of the play or at the resumption of the dramatic action after a time lapse, finally became in effect the entire substance of the play itself. This switch from a temporal perspective that goes from the present into the future and often occupies years in the telling to one which goes from the present into the past and takes only a day or so in present time coincides precisely with the dramatist's declaration (quoted in Chapter 2, Introduction above) at the time of the production of *The Iceman Cometh* that he felt that the writer could not write about the present but only about a past that was far enough back in time to be seen with some degree of wholeness and coherence. From now on his dramas tend to be retrospective expositions rather than narratives.

O'Neill did not, however, arrive at the final form in an instantaneous fashion, and one can see some of its lineaments in at least two of his earlier plays, *The Emperor Jones* and *Homecoming*, the first play of *Mourning Becomes Electra*. In *The Emperor Jones*, as Brutus Jones stumbles through the jungle, his personality disintegrating, the fantasy interludes of each scene carry us back through Jones's life; by Scene V this retrospective account has passed over into a history of Jones's race. Just before Jones is killed, we arrive back to his ultimate origin, the savagery of Africa. The form of *Homecoming* brings us even closer to the form of the late plays. When *Mourning Becomes Electra* was first performed, John Hutchens, who reviewed it for *Theatre Arts* in 1932 remarked: "Mr. O'Neill's writing in this trilogy is admirably straightforward and full of fine splendor, particularly in the soliloquies, which are beautifully written and, by no accident, shrewdly expository" (Cargill et al., p. 192). What he meant was that exposition in this play was less what it often tended to be in the earlier plays, a "seated lump of information" in Henry James's phrase, and more a matter of subtle distribution throughout the play as a whole.

The dramatic action, the movement from the opening

to the close, of *Homecoming* consists of the build-up to, and finally, the consummation of, the murder of Ezra Mannon by his wife Christine. Simultaneously, there is going on a sustained unveiling of the secrets of the past. This series of unveilings becomes progressively more intimate, revealing more and more hidden elements, and its ultimate discovery coincides directly with the murder itself. This movement back into the past and into the private is very skillfully distributed over the play as a whole, and, over the play as a whole, moves from the public to the private, from the collective to the individual, and from general gossip about a family to the private relationship between the central male and female of this same family. Act I of *Homecoming* opens with neighbors gossiping about the Mannons, their wealth, their long-standing eminence, their pride, their aloofness, their abilities, the masklike faces that they have and those that they develop on their wives, the breath of scandal in the family and the hint of skeletons in the closet, the "furrin" look of Christine, and the queerness of Lavinia. After this prologue-chorus, the private action begins: the tension between Christine and Lavinia; the existence of the lover, Adam Brant; the plot to kill Ezra Mannon. With Mannon's return the plot moves closer to the private malaise which is at the root of the impending tragedy, and which is lodged in the relationship between Christine and Ezra. We move finally in the last act to the marital bed and the marital relation, Christine's ultimate accusation: "You've guessed it! You've used me, you've given me children, but I've never been yours! I never could be! And whose fault is it? I loved you when I married you! I wanted to give myself! But you made me so I couldn't give! You filled me with disgust!" Then comes the murder, and the end of the play. The action of the play has consumed a late afternoon of one day, the evening of another, and the dawn of a third, with a one-week lapse between the late-afternoon and the evening, but, by the exposition, several lives have been presented in their totality.

While the late plays follow the form of *The Emperor Jones* and *Homecoming*, they do not usually culminate in a violent event, like Jones's death and Ezra Mannon's murder. (In O'Neill's late plays there are only two deaths, both off stage, Parritt's and that of Melody's mare.) In these plays there are two intertwined and correlated lines of action, one the usually desultory events that happen in the day or so that passes in the present, the other the backward journey into the past which is not fully accomplished and done with at the beginning of the first act or even with the conclusion of that act. In fact, in the most moving and skillful of these plays, the ultimate disclosures are not made until the end, or near the end, of the play. These final disclosures by the main characters, usually uttered in Act IV (Act III for Jamie Tyrone in *A Moon for the Misbegotten*) are either confessionals or justifications, that is, characters either confess their sins, what they have done, or they explain themselves, why they are what they are. More often than not there is a combination of the two modes, as, for example, Hickey begins in justification and ends in an inadvertent confessional. In whatever guise this verbal coda appears it is usually an agonized attempt on the part of the character to tell "the truth" about himself or herself. But it is a tribute to the complexity of these plays that it is not *the* truth, or at least the whole truth, for the audience and the reader, for more often than not the backward journey leads to an ambiguity either about a character, or about the relationship between two characters, or about the relationship between a character and his own past or the activities he pursued.

Sometimes two, or even three, of these ambiguities are involved for a single character, as they are in *A Touch of the Poet* for Con Melody who is ambiguous in himself, ambiguous in his relationship with his wife and daughter, and ambiguous in relation to his two pasts. None of these ambiguities in his character and the play are ever finally and neatly resolved. There is, however, an ultimate revelation in Act IV when Nora who, to our knowledge anyway, has never questioned his role as the grand Major bursts out: "Sure, he'd never stoop to think of me, the grand gentleman in his red livery av bloody England! His pride, indade! What is it but a lie? What's in his veins, God pity him, but the blood of theivin' auld Ned Melody who kept a dirty shebeen?" She is immediately horrified by her own blasphemy and quickly exclaims: "I'm the only one in the world he knows navir sneers at his dreams." Under the layers of the years, stretching all the way back to Melody's birth and heritage, this is the final fact: that Melody, splendid uniform, gallant conduct in war, and all the rest, is still the son of Ned Melody and that his wife, while having no illusions herself about him and his past, yet shares his illusion with him and in a sense believes in it for him since he cannot sustain his illusions by himself alone. Yet, as in most of O'Neill's late plays, there is no sharp distinction drawn between reality and illusion for either Melody or his wife. His glorious past was not all illusory, as Creegan attests. Thus when he does finally in Act IV turn into a peasant, Nora assumes that this is another piece of play-acting that she will have to help sustain and help him in. He has then finally substituted one past for another, and his ambiguity remains. This is about the only freedom permitted the characters in the late plays: the freedom to choose one of your own pasts, which is tantamount to choosing the lesser of two evils.

The Iceman Cometh contains a number of backward journeys, often to an ambiguous relationship: Harry Hope and Bessie, Oban and his father, Jimmy Tomorrow and his wife, Larry Slade and Mrs. Parritt, Parritt himself and this same woman, and, climactically, Hickey and Evelyn. Again the trail may lead back to a failure in a profession or activity: military, political, or what have you. The exposition of The Iceman Cometh then is a series of interspersed vignettes of the past of the various characters, all of which are complete before the monologue by Hickey that leads to the conclusion. Hickey's story requires the most terrible exercise of memory and discloses the most ambiguous relationship of all, that between Hickey and Evelyn. Coincident with this is the final unveiling of the other ambiguous relationship, that between Parritt and his mother. In both cases there is revealed finally—back behind the years and the endless verbiage—hate, which thought it was love. In Long Day's Journey Into Night each of the Tyrones travels back, throughout the day of the play, but the big revelations are saved for Act IV, as each character finally explains himself, what he was, what life has done to him, and why he is what he is: the father's penury; Edmund's chronic nervousness and yearning for oblivion, Jamie's love-hate relationship to his brother. The mother, in her dreamlike state, does travel back to become what she had been. *A Moon for the Misbegotten* has its shattering backward journey in Act III when Jamie Tyrone finally manages to tell Josie Hogan of his execrable conduct during the final illness and the death of his mother.

At the same time these disclosures are hinted at, almost from the beginning of the play, as they are in *A Touch of the Poet* and *Long Day's Journey Into Night*. As a result there is set up almost immediately a continuous tension between the present and the past, and, since the ominous hints about the past usually refer to deep-set habits or unredeemable guilts or habitual attitudes, their bearing on the future is ominous as well. The opening lines of *Long Day's Journey Into Night* are the best example of O'Neill's final and climactic way of handling action and exposition as a continuous tension between the present and the past. The first thirteen speeches in the play, all rather brief, are between James and Mary Tyrone. The morning is sunny and, presumably, both are happy. Yet there is established immediately an ominous undercurrent that points to a less felicitous past: that Mary Tyrone has gained twenty pounds (something wrong in the past?) but that she had eaten little on this particular morning (the past returning?); that the two young male Tyrones, both off stage at this point, are probably concocting some scheme "to touch the Old Man"; that James Tyrone has a fabulously durable physical constitution and that he is an inveterate and unsuccessful speculator in land and is easily fleeced; and that Mary Tyrone worries about the cough of one of her sons. Here there is a brief abstract of some of the major forces in the family tragedy and the grim hint that the Tyrones on this sunny morning in August 1912 are poised on the knife-edge of the insubstantial happiness of a tenuous present, with a darker past behind them and a darker future to come.

In his discussion of O'Neill's early plays, which had contained so much action, Hugh von Hofmannsthal said (Cargill et al., p. 252):

The essence of drama is movement, but that movement must be held in check, firmly controlled.

I shall not venture to decide which is the more important

in drama, the driving motive-element of action, or the retarding or "static" element; at any rate, it is the combination, the interpenetration of the two that makes great drama. In Shakespeare's plays there is not a line that does not serve the ultimate end, but when one goes through the text to discover this for oneself, one perceives that the relation between means and end is by no means evident: the means seem tortuously indirect, often diametrically opposed to the end. Nineteen lines out of twenty in a comedy or tragedy of Shakespeare are (seemingly) a digression, an interpolative obstruction thrown across the path of the direct rays; retarding motives of every sort impede the onward march of events. But it is precisely these obstacles that reveal the plasticity, the vitality, of the story and character; it is these that cast the necessary atmosphere about the central idea of the work. As a matter of fact, the unity of the play lies in these diversified and apparently aimless "digressions."

If we apply this same dichotomy, between static and active, to O'Neill's late plays we find that the static element is action in the present and the dynamic element is the unfolding of the past. In each of these plays excruciating feelings and passions are aroused, and sometimes human relationships are rearranged; but nothing decisive happens to anyone except Parritt. What *happens* is that some one gets drunk, or several do, and they all talk; and a day or so passes. The driving and dramatic action is the backward journey down into the well of the past, the reluctant search down the long, dim avenues of the years, the unwilling but inescapable necessity to refind the fatal cross road where the wrong turn was taken or the wrong relationship begun or where necessity replaced freedom or the true self was lost or reality and illusion merged and blurred. The metaphysics of a dramatic fable or plot is, as von Hofmannsthal has indicated, as mysterious as life itself and, like the peace of God, passes all understanding. If a psychological principle could be inferred from O'Neill's late plays it would be that behind the frustration and stasis of the present is a protean past that continues to well up and spill out into the present. For this reason the past is never done or finished or put away. Its passions never lose their potency; its tears never cease to flow. Like mankind itself, these characters are condemned forever to sorrow over their lost innocence, and to contemplate their "might-have-beens": "Look in my face. My name is Might-Have-Been; I am called No More, Too Late, Farewell."

These plays then are about the ways of memory, and a great deal of their power and complexity arises from the powers and complexities of memory itself. In the first place memory is omnipotent and implacable. In Freud's words in *Civilization and Its Discontents*: "nothing once formed in the mind [can] perish, . . . everything survives in some way or other, and is capable under certain conditions of being brought to light again, as, for instance, when regression extends back far enough" (p. 7). And memory is the conveyor of guilt, *the* great problem of civilized man. To quote Freud once more, "the sense of guilt [is] the most important problem in the evolution of culture" (p. 90). Thus O'Neill's characters, standing by proxy for mankind itself, are haunted by their sins, mistakes, wrongdoings, betrayals. This sense of guilt forges a chain, link by link, that binds them forever to the terrible things they have done or, equally terrible, what they have not done. An inescapable determinism prevails, and the past, "sleepless with pale commemorative eyes," stands watch on the present. Since it is a fact of human life that it is often more harrowing to relive by memory a painful experience than it was to have actually undergone that experience itself in the first place, memory becomes a kind of avenging Fate or a Force that drives the characters back on themselves by its insatiable, never satisfied demands to make them continually relive the agonies of their experiences. And the play itself cannot end until the agony is complete and total.

Historically considered, the characters are in the position of mankind itself, as described by Hannah Arendt.[9] After citing a parable by Kafka about the relationship between the past and the future, Miss Arendt explains: "The first thing to be noticed is that not only the future—'the wave of the future'—but also the past is seen as a force, and not, as in nearly all our metaphors, as a burden man has to shoulder and of whose dead weight the living can or even must get rid in their march into the future. In the words of Faulkner, 'the past is never dead, it is not even past.' This past, moreover, reaching all the way back into the origin, does not pull back but presses forward, and it is, contrary to what one would expect, the future which drives us back into the past."

Human memory, however, also splits. Melody's inability to tell which of his two pasts is the real one is an extreme manifestation of the tendency of memory to split in two, usually into guilt and into nostalgia or sentiment. Thus the evocations of the past in A Touch of the Poet, The Iceman Cometh, and Long Day's Journey Into Night are not always sad and guilt-ridden. There are also memories of happy moments, and despite the fact that these moments are only memories and, unlike the guilt memories, are entirely cut off from what is happening in the present, they yet provide a little warmth, a little flame in the cold and hopeless present: "I had a little talk with Mother Elizabeth. She is so sweet and good. A saint on earth. I love her dearly." Or, "I was wild with ambition. I read all the plays ever written." Or, "I belonged, without past or future, within place and unity and wild joy, within something greater than my own life, or the life of man, to life itself!" And these "islands in time," as Wordsworth called them, were real enough too and sound a faint, light counterpoint, in the orchestrations of memory, to the large dark chords of grief. Thus the late plays, besides being a blend of tragedy and comedy are also a blend of guilt and nostalgia.

And memory not only splits; it is both complex and deceptive in its workings: it forgets, evades, distorts, minimizes, enlarges, simplifies, exonerates, exaggerates, accuses, invents. It hardly ever simply "remembers," and when it is vitally alive, as it is in O'Neill's late plays, it immeasurably complicates both the individual characters and the meaning of the plays. Thus the form that O'Neill finally came to—action as remembering the past—gave to his characters a complexity, without confusion, as in The Great God Brown, that had been lacking in his earlier plays.

There is, of course, an enormous difference, whatever the form of the play, between the sticklike bundles of clichés that pass for representations of human character in some of the early plays, like Abortion or Servitude or The First Man and the excruciatingly "real" people of Long Day's Journey and A Moon for the Misbegotten. This difference is in great part just the result of plain experience, dramatically speaking, on the part of the playwright. While there are convincing characters in the early plays, like the sailors on the "S. S. Glencairn," they tend to be rather simple characters as well. When O'Neill began to break out of what he regarded as the limitations of the straight, naturalistic dramatic form—the heritage of Ibsen—in *The Emperor Jones* and *The Hairy Ape*, with their symbolic settings and other nonnaturalistic devices, he was attempting, among other things, to create depth and complexity of human character. This kind of experimentation reached its climax with the various experiments with masks, asides, and soliloquies that dominated his work in the middle and late twenties and early thirties, especially in *The Great God Brown, Lazarus Laughed, Strange Interlude, Dynamo,* and *Days Without End.*

What O'Neill came to learn finally was that the naturalistic form was perfectly capable of expressing human depth and complexity, and thus the late plays are a happy conjunction of the spare and unadorned form of the early period coupled to a sense of the complications of human character that the plays of the middle period used soliloquies, asides, masks, and symbolic settings to convey. For the drama is best when, as in Greek and Elizabethan drama, the dialogue does all, or most, of the work. In *Lazarus Laughed* and *The Great God Brown,* for example, masks are used to express two things: internal splits torturing characters and external forces driving them. But similar splits and forces are also presented in completely realistic, and convincing, terms in the characters of the late plays.

In *The Iceman Cometh, A Touch of the Poet, Long Day's Journey,* and *A Moon for the Misbegotten* one might say that alcohol and dope take the place of the earlier masks and soliloquies. Through the use of depressants the characters travel back in time, reveal obscure facts about themselves, give vent to suppressed feelings, say exactly what they think, and reveal all their splits and cracks.

But memory is unique for each individual, and the quirks of individual memories put a different stamp on the same remembered event. In *The Great God Brown* or *Strange Interlude* we witness the lives of the characters unfolding as the years pass by. Thus there are certain indubitable, unequivocal facts presented, as that, for example, Darrell was once an extremely capable and promising doctor or that he is in fact the real father of Nina's child. But in the late plays the same set of facts is refracted through disparate and distorting memories, e.g., Mary Tyrone's version of her past and Tyrone's summary of that same past; or, in *A Moon for the Misbegotten* Jamie Tyrone's memory of his father and Josie Hogan's memory of the same man. One of the great sources of power of *Long Day's Journey* arises from the fact that four passionate but disparate imaginations are all focused on essentially the same set of past facts. But how differently this identical past comes out of each of the four wells of memory!

Again in the earlier plays people change before our eyes. But in the late plays the essential changes have long since taken place, before the play opens, and the fall from innocence to experience has been completed long ago. We are asked to take nothing on faith in these late plays. The present is all there and, finally, the past is all there. Between the beginning of Act I and the conclusion of Act IV all the necessary connections, ambiguous as some of them are, are made and the lines are drawn between that past and this present.

ARE THERE some quintessential aspects to the form of the late plays over and above those that have been discussed, such as the observation of the unities, the tendency to begin in comedy and end in tragedy, and the dramatization of the ways of guilt and memory? The answer is that there are other resemblances as well; in fact these plays bear a remarkable generic likeness to each other, disparate as they may appear to be at a hasty glance.

In the first place they always take place on, or begin on, excessively hot days. (In an ideal production O'Neill, with his desire to involve the audience directly in the play, would probably have wished to heat up the theater to the appropriate temperature.) Primordially, in the workings of the human imagination, hell is the place of fire and heat and thus the suffering caused by heat is the ultimate torment that man can invent for himself. In "Fire and Ice" Frost speculates that cold would do as well and would suffice, but O'Neill's imagination was traditional in this respect; he thought of human suffering as being heightened by heat. Not only in the late plays but in all his plays, from first to last, the frayed nerves of his characters are further exacerbated by the heat and humidity of an oppressive summer day. Thus his characters tend to suffer not only morally and emotionally but physiologically as well. Significantly, the rather limp and vague stage directions of his early plays came to life only when some extreme of heat or cold is suggested. In *Fog* a looming iceberg is described as "*Something huge and white . . . looming up through the fog directly beside the boat . . . its whiteness vivid above the blue-gray water, seems like the façade of some huge Viking temple.*" *Thirst* opens and closes with a vivid and concrete image of the horrors of a blazing sun: "*The sun glares down from straight overhead like a great angry eye of God.*" In *Beyond the Horizon* the tragedy begins in Act II, Scene 1, which takes place inside the now decaying farmhouse on a "*hot, sun-baked day*" when there is "*no breeze*" to stir "*the soiled white curtains.*" When Ruth Atkins enters, she is perspiring from the heat:

RUTH  Land sakes, if this isn't a scorcher! That kitchen's like a furnace. Phew! [*She pushes the damp hair back from her forehead.*]
MRS. MAYO  Why didn't you call me to help with the dishes?
RUTH  [*shortly*]  No. The heat in there'd kill you.

Similarly, Robert Mayo enters from the outside, streaked with dirt and sweat. Time after time in the plays that follow, the depressing and nervewracking effect of excessive heat is suggested. Act I of *Strange Interlude*, for example, takes place in "the hottest part of August" and Marsden remarks on "the depressing heat and humidity." Part of Mildred Douglas' horror in Scene III of *The Hairy Ape* arises from the hell-like heat of the stoke-hole. The peculiar cruelty of Hickey's plan for salvation for the derelicts in *The Iceman Cometh* arises from the fact that he is sending these shaky, shaking alcoholics out into the furnace of the streets of New York on a blinding hot summer day. As Harry Hope says before he embarks on his abortive expedition into reality in Act III: "Too damned hot for a walk, though, if you ask me. Well, do me good to sweat the booze of me." In *Hughie* Erie Smith is described as *"drying out"* after a *"bat"* as he mops his face in the humid and fetid atmosphere of the shabby hotel. In *A Touch of the Poet* the rankness of Nora Melodys' hair, which the Major cannot abide but which "Auld Ned" Melody's son finally kisses at the end of the play, has been created by her labors with producing food in the steaming kitchen of Melody's tavern on a hot July day. In Act I of *Long Day's Journey* Jamie Tyrone is condemned to labor with his father in the hot sun; as his father says to him, "The hot sun will sweat some of that booze fat off your middle." *A Moon for the Misbegotten* opens on *"a blazing hot day."* In short, in all these plays a secular, naturalistic version of hell is suggested as being the background and environment.

Like Henry James in his late works, O'Neill in his final phase tended to limit radically the number of characters: four central ones in *Long Day's Journey*, two in *Hughie*, and three in *A Moon*. In *The Iceman Cometh* and *A Touch of the Poet* the cast is larger, but it is bound together by unifying preoccupations and themes. In a sense all stories in *The Iceman Cometh* are individual variations on one story: the enticements, deceptions, complexities, and ambiguities of "the pipe dream." *A Touch of the Poet* is shot through with correspondences, many of them unexpected: Con seduced Nora, and Sara seduces Simon Harford; Mrs. Harford has a delicate, finely drawn, and "aristocratic" frame and physiognomy which equates her to Con's mare; and the delicate ankles and feet of the woman and the delicate ankles and feet of the horse are both set off against the thick ankles and "peasant" feet of Sara Melody; Simon Harford's poetry turns out to be bad, imitation Byron, which Con recites; Simon himself has "a touch av the poet" as does Con; the Harford family, like the Melody family, has a great dream or ambition that it never can realize.

There is a tendency to create in all these plays, sometimes rather completely, off-stage characters, who never actually appear but who nevertheless are felt presences: Mrs. Parritt and Evelyn Hickman in *The Iceman Cometh*; Hughie and his wife in *Hughie*; Simon Harford and his father in *A Touch of the Poet*; more briefly, Shaunnessy, Harkness, McGuire, and "Doc" Hardy in *Long Day's Journey*. There is also a tendency to refer to, and sometimes characterize, if slightly, personages who were actual living people at or around the historical time of the play: Napoleon in *A Touch of the Poet*; "Big Tim" Sullivan in *The Iceman Cometh*; Arnold Rothstein in *Hughie*; Edward Harkness, the Standard Oil eminence, whose son and heir, as Harder-Harker comes into *Long Day's Journey* and *A Moon for the Misbegotten*.

Among the characters there are two cravings: one for beauty and the other for reconciliation, with themselves and with their mates or fellows. Since all the plays take place in rather oppressive settings on oppressive days, the characters can see no beauty in their own lives and physical surroundings nor in human life itself. Accordingly, there crops up in these plays the image of one of the most beautiful of animals, the horse. Jamie Tyrone, Erie Smith, and Con Melody have at the root of their imagination the image of the sleekness and symmetry of a horse as representing some kind of physical beauty that human life cannot approximate. Erie would prefer Man O'War to the whole cast of the Follies; Con declares: "Give me a horse to love and I'll cry quits to men." Even Jamie Tyrone can imagine that perhaps in "following the horses" he would find a kind of existence that will be bearable. Of the two deaths that occur in the late plays, the human one, that of Parritt, is seen as necessary and just, but the animal one, Con's mare, is seen as unnecessary and tragic: "Blessed Christ, the look in her eyes by the lantern light with life ebbing out of them—wondering and sad, but still trustful, not reproaching me—with no fear in them—proud, understanding pride—loving me—she saw I was dying with her. She understood! She forgave me!" (IV).

Still, if beauty cannot be found in human existence, some kind of reconciliation is possible for some people. Despite the various tragedies, these same late plays tend to have also an element of reconciliation, of people coming together to understand and to forgive and, sometimes, to love: Erie and Charlie Hughes in *Hughie*; Edmund Tyrone and his father and the two Tyrone brothers in *Long Day's Journey Into Night*; Con and Nora Melody in *A Touch of the Poet*; Jamie Tyrone and Josie Hogan and, at the end, Josie and Phil Hogan in *A Moon for the Misbegotten*. There are no happy endings, except for Sara Melody, but at least everyone is given a chance to attempt to explain himself or herself. The final implication of the form of these plays would seem to be that the highest act of human charity is simply to try to understand, although this is not always to be understood as equivalent to forgiving.

How long do these plays last? It is an interesting question, for while in actuality they last but a day or sometimes a bit more, they *seem* to last forever. As Nicola Chiarmonte [10] said: "The action lasts for one day, but it might have lasted for a century: it lasts in fact as long as the torments of hell." Thus if the early plays tend to be narratives about the agonies of the years and their essence is temporality, the late plays are disquisitions upon the infinity of human guilt and the endlessness of human suffering. They all thus give the impression of that suspension of time that brooding breeds. The distinction between the present and the past has been obliterated, and the characters are suspended in a seemingly nontemporal continuum, whose only moving part is the mechanism of repetition. Another way of expressing the paradoxes of time and timelessness in these plays would be to say that they are dramatizations of the paradox that philosophers find when they try to formulate notions about the nature of time itself. In the words of Hans Reichenbach [11] what time means psychologically is the "crystallizations of some fluid entity that was future and now is unalterable past. We are placed in the center of the flow, called the present; but what now is present slides into the past, while we move along to a new present, *forever remaining in the eternal now*" (italics mine).

The plays tend to end, *The Iceman* and *Hughie* excepted, quietly and elegiacally, having neither the neatness of those that "tie the thread" nor the "question mark" atmosphere of *Anna Christie*, nor the apocalyptical thunder of *Dynamo* or *Days Without End*, nor the tormented resolutions of *Welded* and *All God's Chillun Got Wings*. They end simply because the long day's journey into night is complete.


## II *Language*

O'Neill and words are a curious phenomenon. That he had only a touch of the poet he was the first to recognize and lament. At times he doubted that even the "touch" was there. When James Tyrone (James O'Neill) tells Edmund (Eugene O'Neill) in *Long Day's Journey Into Night* that he has the makings of a poet, Edmund replies: "The *makings* of a poet. No, I'm afraid I'm like the guy who is always panhandling for a smoke. He hasn't even got the makings. He's got only the habit. I couldn't touch what I tried to tell you just now [he has been trying to tell his father, not very convincingly, of the mystic rapture he felt aboard a sailing ship]. I just stammered. That's the best I'll ever do. I mean, if I live. Well, it will be faithful realism, at least. Stammering is the native eloquence of us fog people" (IV). And when he was writing *Long Day's Journey* he read aloud in the evenings the poetry of Yeats, as if, besides enjoyment, he wished always to have running through his head the sacred words of a real poet. In some strange, deep way, and for reasons beyond his lack of a consistent poetic talent, he sometimes did not believe in language, or at least in meaningful language. Like Dreiser, he was a kind of giant in chains, a great writer who could not write, a volcanic genius who did not think what he had to express could be verbalized or that if it could, he had not the powers to do so. Like a stranded whale, he blows and spouts and heaves and pants and manages to suggest great agonies and mighty struggles, but only seldom does he hit it off in an image or a phrase or a line or a poem or a passage, as could Yeats. At times he seemed genuinely to believe that the "rest is silence." One of his many spokesmen, Nina Leeds of *Strange Interlude*, exclaims, "How we poor monkeys hide from ourselves behind the sounds called words!" (II). In *Welded*, one of his most autobiographical works, the two protagonists are described as *"deeply in love but separated by a barrier of language"* (III). On at least one occasion he threw up his hands in a gesture of verbal despair such as probably no other major dramatist ever made when he suggested that the part of Lazarus in *Lazarus Laughed* be translated into Russian and the Chaliapin be engaged for the role, while the rest of the cast would continue to speak English: "It would be a wonderful, strange effect. And as far as most of an average audience understanding what Lazarus means, why it would probably be a lot clearer to them in Russian!" (Gelbs, p. 603). Even when he was successful, verbally, as with the simple and functional prose of *Mourning Becomes Electra,* he still regretted his lack of verbal talent, and he wrote to Arthur Hobson Quinn that he was "deeply dissatisfied" with the play because it needed "great language," which he did not have (Cargill et al., p. 463).

At best, writing for him seemed to be a kind of torture or agony, a process that he sometimes dramatized in the plays. In *Marco Millions* O'Neill describes his young hero trying to write a poem: *"scratching himself, twisting and turning his legs and feet, tearing his hair in a perfect frenzy of baulked inspiration* (I, 2). He produces finally, like O'Neill himself, a bad poem, and Tedaldo, the papal legate, tells him that he will be better as a Polo than as a poet. One of the many torments of Michael Cape, the O'Neill *persona* of *Welded,* is the intractability of words, and when he tries to tell his wife of his ecstatic ideal of their union, he suddenly breaks off in furious anger and exclaims: "God, what I feel of the truth of this—the beauty!—but how can I express it?" (I). Richard Miller of *Ah, Wilderness!,* another O'Neill *persona,* suffers from the same disability. Pacing the moonlit beach, he says to himself, "I wish I could write poetry . . . about her and me" (IV, 2). But he must always quote the verse of others.

Nevertheless, and with due recognition of all the foregoing, O'Neill's verbal powers, as I hope to show, were more considerable than either he or his critics would allow and, as with all other aspects of his art, improved considerably over his career as a whole.

As a playwright who, like Shaw, set great store by stage directions and by the published version of his plays, O'Neill as a writer is best considered first as a creator of stage directions and then, and more important, as a creator of dialogue. In writing stage directions O'Neill was consistently effective, from first to last. Not that he was incapable of writing embarrassing or unconsciously ludicrous stage directions. He never achieved anything so horrific as "enter Lavinia, ravished; her hands cut off, and her tongue cut out." Be he came close, as in *Lazarus Laughed* when Lazarus sees the crucified lion outside Tiberius' palace: "LAZARUS. (*walks up the steps to the cross and, stretching to his full height, gently pushes the lion's hair out of its eyes—tenderly*) Poor brother!" (III, 1). Or, to go to the other extreme, he could sorely try the sense of humor of the audience and that of a player in the cast, as, for example, in Act II of *Strange Interlude* it is indicated that the actress playing the role of Nina—seated in Marsden's lap—is directed to fall asleep and give "*a soft little snore.*" Equally trying must be the "coltish caper" that Brown in *The Great God Brown*, Evans in *Strange Interlude*, and Caligula in *Lazarus Laughed* are all called upon to perform. But these lapses are rare, and, generally speaking, O'Neill's stage directions are accurate, convincing, and suggestive. The setting of *Where the Cross Is Made*, for example, is described in such a manner as to make any imaginative stage designer see exactly and concretely the scene and mood the playwright desires: "*The time is an early hour of a clear windy night in the fall of the year 1900. Moonlight, winnowed by the wind which moans in the stubborn angles of the old house, creeps wearily in through the portholes and rests like tired dust in circular patches upon the floor and table.*" Throughout his career O'Neill had no difficulty in describing natural objects, i.e., his settings, with great accuracy and vividness; not only what they looked like but what symbolic value or feeling was to be attached to them: the Mannon house in *Mourning Becomes Electra*, Harry Hope's saloon in *The Iceman Cometh*, Con Melody's decaying tavern in *A Touch of the Poet*, the dynamo in *Dynamo*, Hogan's shack in *A Moon for the Misbegotten*, and so on. Probably the most famous, and symbolically potent, of these descriptions is that of the "elums" in *Desire Under the Elms*: "*There is a sinister maternity in their aspect, a crushing, jealous absorption. They have developed from their intimate contact with the life of man in the house an appalling humaneness. They brood oppressively over the house. They are like exhausted women resting their sagging breasts and hands and hair on its roof, and when it rains their tears trickle down monotonously and rot on the shingles.*"

Similarly, his stage directions describing human beings are acute, detailed, and psychologically convincing. In fact in some of his late plays he was putting almost insuperable burdens on directors and actors, such as in finding an actress who could play the role of Josie Hogan in *A Moon for the Misbegotten* or in finding some way of expressing the interior monologues of the night clerk in

*Hughie*. He was setting down on the printed page what could not be transferred successfully to the stage. He himself said that *Hughie*, which is really a short story, could not be given a conventional stage production. According to the Gelbs (p. 844), he told Mrs. O'Neill that *Hughie,* and the rest of the planned one-act plays that were to make up his series, "By Way of Obit," would have to be produced by some new techniques involving possibly a filmed background and sound track. Whatever the method it would require "tremendous imagination."

Generally speaking, O'Neill's stage directions over his career as a whole become more detailed and elaborate, more "novelistic," in his late plays. For example, John Loving of *Days Without End* is described in conventional, almost generalized terms: *"handsome, with the rather heavy, conventional American type of good looks— a straight nose and a square jaw, a wide mouth that has an incongruous feminine sensitiveness, a broad forehead, blue eyes"* (I). But in *The Iceman Cometh* the lengthy and elaborate stage directions of the opening act, which occupy approximately six pages of the printed text, exactly identify each character with a Chaucerian flair for the idiosyncratic and telling detail, as, for example, in the description of Hugo:

> HUGO *is a small man in his late fifties. He has a head much too big for his body, a high forehead, crinkly long black hair streaked with gray, a square face with a pug nose, a walrus mustache, black eyes which peer near-sightedly from behind thick-lensed spectacles, tiny hands and feet. He is dressed in threadbare black clothes and his white shirt is frayed at collar and cuffs, but everything about him is fastidiously clean. Even his flowing Windsor tie is neatly tied. There is a foreign atmosphere about him, the stamp of an alien radical, a strong resemblance to the type Anarchist as portrayed, bomb in hand, in newspaper cartoons.*

It is not that O'Neill did not give the details and idiosyncracies of his characters in his earlier plays, but that the descriptions in these plays do not have the programmatic and systematic concreteness of those of the late plays.

Beyond that in *Hughie* the stage directions throughout the play describing states of mind and appearances of the characters possess a genuine literary distinction and demonstrate that in his final, agonizing days O'Neill had achieved almost perfect control over what had always baulked him: words. (See Chapter 1, iv, for examples of the prose of *Hughie*.) Through concreteness and irony he achieved an exactness in language that was impossible in the hyperbolical phase of his career. For example, Erie at his nadir in the play: *"his false poker face as nakedly forlorn as an organ grinder's monkey's."* Or the night clerk dreaming of beating Arnold Rothstein: *"Beatific vision swoons on the empty pools of the Night Clerk's eyes. He resembles a holy saint, recently elected to Paradise."*

A playwright, however, must stand or fall by his dialogue, and here again O'Neill is more complex and able than he is usually given credit for. Over all, O'Neill's dialogue has both a monolithic aspect and a developmental aspect. The monolithic aspect is given, once more, by his key concept, "rhythm," which in this context means simply verbal repetition and which remained a fundamental device throughout his plays. When *The Iceman Cometh* was being rehearsed, someone pointed out to O'Neill that an assertion by Parritt was repeated eighteen times; the playwright replied that he had *intended* it to be repeated eighteen times.[12] In *Diff'rent* the key word is the title itself. In Act I the word "diff'rent" is repeated, in various and separate contexts, twenty-five times, with a couple of "diff'rences" thrown in for good measure. O'Neill actually wanted the actors to "freeze" every time they repeated the word and to say the word itself in a kind of expressionless monotone, so that it would become like the tom-tom beat of *The Emperor Jones*. It was pointed out to him that by the third repetition the audience would be tittering, so he wisely abandoned the idea (Gelbs, p. 453).

These repetitions vary in range from the repeated use of a sound that may have no meaning in itself, such as the tom-tom beat of *The Emperor Jones* or the whistle in *Bound East for Cardiff*, but that acquires a portentous meaning because of its repeated use in a certain context (doom in both of these plays), to the repetitious insistence on some idea or concept, always expressed in the same word of phrase, which is an explicit statement of the central idea of the play, as, for example, "death" in *Mourning Becomes Electra*, "pipe dream" in *The Ice-*

*man Cometh,* "the poison" in *Long Day's Journey Into Night,* "ghost" in *Long Day's Journey* and *A Moon for the Misbegotten.* Or the repeated word may bridge the realms of sound and meaning, as does "aye-eh" in *Desire Under the Elms.* "Aye-eh" is a New Englandism, still extant, and signifies "yeah" or "yes" and is used as a kind of assentual grunt delivered in a slurred drawl. O'Neill's typist told him that this was an odd way of spelling "yeah," but the playwright assured him that "aye-eh" was just what he wanted. He evidently meant to convey by it not only the historical flavor of New England but also to suggest some of the qualities of its life, namely a kind of inarticulate and unlovely monotony, under which raged the lust and greed of the individual characters. Again the repetition could be musical, "Shenandoah" in *Mourning Becomes Electra,* or literary, Hugo's phrase from Carlyle in *The Iceman Cometh,* or a fragment of O'Neill's own bad "poetry" as in *Lazarus Laughed* or *The Fountain.*

It is practically inescapable to think that this practice of insistent, high-lighted repetitions was, in part, one of the many legacies from *The Count of Monte Cristo,* in which one of the dramatic high points was the "One!" "Two!" "Three!" that James O'Neill sang out in stylized fashion as each of the three villains fell dead. O'Neill's rhetoric generally is at its worst when he was, perhaps once more unconsciously, echoing the dialogue of the old melodrama. The examples of the endings of *Dynamo* and *Days Without End* have already been cited above (see section i). But the influence of Fechter's rhetoric on O'Neill's during his first career was even more pervasive than this. The "art" of Fechter's dialogue consisted of stringing together in a fragmentary manner a series of fairly neutral and abstract nouns and/or adjectives and indicating their desired intensity by repeated exclamation points. It is virtually impossible then not to think that Fechter's "Saved! The world is mine!" or "Ha! Have at thee!" or "One!" is not the unwitting parent of Lazarus' "Laugh! Laugh with me! Death is dead! Fear no more!" or of John Loving's "I know! Love lives forever!" or so many other ejaculations in O'Neill's plays.

What is often forgotten, however, is that O'Neill did not write in one mode of speech but in several, and in this, as in all other matters, he was constantly experimenting and turning in new directions. Basically, O'Neill wrote four kinds of dialogue: middle-class American speech; American slang; racial and other kinds of dialects based on American speech; and what I shall call "historical prose," that is, the kind of timeless English that he employed in writing such plays as *Lazarus Laughed, Marco Millions, Mourning Becomes Electra*, and the dialogue for the non-Irish speakers of *A Touch of the Poet*. (Mode one, American middle-class speech, and mode four, "historical prose," are not sharply distinct.)

To discuss the four in reverse order, the "historical prose" gravitates between two poles: the "poetic" style or the *Monte Cristo* style, and the plain style. *The Fountain* and *Lazarus Laughed* are examples of the poetic style, romantic in *The Fountain*, religious in *Lazarus Laughed*. Both plays strain toward some kind of mystic insight that is expressed in plain words, but words put together in such a way as to strive after a hyperbolic effect. In Scene X of *The Fountain* Juan sees the visions in the fountain and draws from them the moral or the meaning of life: "All is within! All things dissolve, flow on eternally!" In *Lazarus Laughed* a kind of D. H. Lawrencean affirmation is sought after by the same methods: "Yes! Yes! Yes! Men die! Even a Son of Man must die to show men that Man may live! But there is no death!" (I, 2). Both plays fail, *The Fountain* almost totally, *Lazarus* partially, because, among other things, the repetition of simple and abstract words—"yes," "no," "man," "death," "life," "all," "eternally," "within," and so on—accompanied by repeated exclamation points do not a poem make. Poetry is complex, concrete, and metaphorical, three qualities that were, by and large, denied to O'Neill's invention.

*Mourning Becomes Electra* is less flawed precisely because the words do not pretend to any other effect than to convey, simply and elementally, the emotions of the characters. There is no differentiation in the speech of all the main characters (although some minor characters speak New England dialects). At the end of *The Haunted* Lavinia, about to incarcerate herself in the mansion permanently, has a final dialogue with Seth, the caretaker:

LAVINIA  [*turns to him sharply*]  You go now and close the shutters and nail them tight.
SETH  Ayeh.

LAVINIA    And tell Hannah to throw out all the flowers.
SETH    Ayeh.

This simplicity and directness of language is characteristic
of the play as a whole, and while we cannot say that the
language of the play is grand or moving or memorable or
quotable, at least it cannot be said either that it is strained
and hyperbolical, as it often is in *The Fountain* and *Lazarus Laughed*. Indeed the only way in which the dialogue
of *Mourning Becomes Electra* attempts to indicate intensity is by fragmenting speech, that is, by having the characters speak, under stress, in fragmented ejaculations rather
than in sentences or phrases, although the inevitable and
ubiquitous exclamation points are usually there. Thus
when in Act V of *The Hunted* Christine shoots herself
Orin cries out: "Vinnie! (*He grabs her arm and stam-
mers distractedly*) Mother—shot herself—Father's pistol
—get a doctor—(*Then with hopeless anguish*) No—it's
too late—she's dead! (*Then wildly*) Why—why did she,
Vinnie (*With tortured self-accusation*) I drove her to it!
I wanted to torture her! She couldn't forgive me! Why
did I have to boast killing him? Why—?" Mrs. Harford,
the Harford lawyer, and Major Melody in *A Touch of the
Poet* speak essentially this normative American speech,
straightforward, simple, slangless, and not related directly
to any particular period in American history. In *Marco
Millions* the two poles of O'Neill's historical prose, the
poetic and the plain, come together and exist in the same
play. Marco's speech is in the plain style, but the speech
of the Kaan and Kukachin is more in the poetic vein.

There is no sharp distinction, of course, between what
I have called O'Neill's "historical prose" and the ordinary
middle-class speech of such plays as *The Great God Brown*
and *Strange Interlude*, save that in the latter there is an
infusion of contemporary slang. When critics claim that
O'Neill could not write, it is this dialogue, that of many
of the plays of his early career, that they are referring to.
But this criticism, too, is a generalization that, while often
true, is not always so, and even in this area some distinctions should be made.

It must first be freely admitted that no great playwright,
at least in English, has ever been guilty of such embar-
rassingly elephantine lines as has O'Neill. Of this ineptitude, the examples of attempts at wit are even more

revealing than the attempts at tragic statement. For instance, in *The First Man* Lily Jason is supposed to be a
picture of the modern young woman, educated, emancipated, high-strung, and intellectually alive. To suggest
this O'Neill gives her such lines (to her detested sister-
in-law Emily) as: "Twinkle, twinkle, little bat!" (I).
Other gambols in the realms of wit are equally obtunded.
In Act III of *Strange Interlude* some light-hearted badinage is meant to take place between Nina and Marsden:

NINA   [*immediately gaily mocking*]   Oh, very well, old
     thing! "God's in his heaven, all's right with the world!"
     And Pippa's cured of the pip! [*She dances up to him.*]
MARSDEN   [*gallantly*]   Pippa is certainly a pippin this
     morning!

Again in *The Great God Brown* in Scene 1 of Act II when
Dion Anthony is leaving Cybel for the last time Dion
attempts some bravado-like gaiety by calling her a "sentimental old pig."

The many awkwardnesses admitted, O'Neill's historical
prose and his middle-class prose still have their moments
of authenticity. Oliver Elton once remarked of Thackeray's
style that it was like a Roman villa, orderly and prosaic,
but with an effluvium, a pool of poetry, at its center. So
it could be said of O'Neill's style, early and late, that
there is an effluvium, a pool of poetry, at its center, showing itself intermittently and unexpectedly, coming sometimes it would seem as a kind of surprise to the playwright
himself. At the end of Act III of *A Moon for the Misbegotten* the prosaic Josie Hogan rises to poetry as she sits
in the moonlight hugging Jamie Tyrone to her bosom:
"You're a fine one, wanting to leave me when the night
I promised I'd give you has just begun, our night that'll
be different from all the others, with a dawn that won't
creep over dirty windowpanes but will wake in the sky
like a promise of God's peace in the soul's dark sadness.
(*She smiles a little amused smile*) Will you listen to me,
Jim! I must be a poet. Who would have guessed it?"
"Who would have guessed it?" can be said of O'Neill as
well. *The Great God Brown* is a case in point. The most
famous set-piece, or speech, in the play is Cybel's repetitious declamation or "chalice" speech at the end of the
play (see Chapter 1, Sec. i). This verbal set-piece is not

without its merits, but it goes on too long, is too consciously and designedly "lyrical" and "rhetorical," and it
is repetitious. Its meaning is of the most general order,
saying simply and only—what it needs no Cybel to tell
us—that life repeats itself. There are, however, at least
two other monologues in the play, both by Dion Anthony
—his "Why am I afraid?" speech (see Chapter 5, section
ii) and his speech about himself and his parents:

> What aliens we were to each other! When he lay dead,
> his face looked so familiar that I wondered where I had
> met the man before. Only at the second of my concep-
> tion. After that, we grew hostile with concealed shame.
> And my mother? I remember a sweet, shy girl, with affec-
> tionate, bewildered eyes as if God had locked her in a dark
> closet without any explanation. I was the sole doll our
> ogre, her husband, allowed her and she played mother and
> child with me for many years in that house until at last
> through two years I watched her die with the shy pride
> of one who has lengthened her dress and put up her
> hair. And I felt like a forsaken toy and cried to be buried
> with her, because her hands alone had caressed without
> clawing [I, 3].

These speeches are striking, original, and powerful; and
powerful precisely because they do not embody a platitude,
as does Cybel's musings about life's repetitions, but constitute an original statement about a complex and unique
human situation. Similarly, the Kaan in *Marco Millions*,
Tiberius in *Lazarus Laughed*, and Nina in *Strange Interlude*, among others, are given lines of force and originality.
One can almost generalize to the point of saying that
whenever O'Neill attempts an affirmative and unifying
statement about the meaning of life—Cybel's "chalice"
speech, Lazarus' affirmations, the unificatory statements
of Ponce de Leon and the Great Kaan at the end of their
respective plays, he invariably fails, falling into verbosity
and vagueness. But on the stark terror and the irreducible
ambiguities of individual concrete human experience he
is assured, complex, felicitous and "true." This split can
sometimes be seen in the speeches of one character, as it
can in that of the Kaan in *Marco Millions*. Affirmatively,
the Kaan sounds like Cybel: "Know in your heart that the
living of life can be noble! Know that the dying of death
can be noble! Be exalted by life! Be inspired by death!

Be humbly proud! Be proudly grateful! Be immortal because life is immortal" (III, 2). But he can also sound like Melville, when discoursing on the sadness of life: "My hideous suspicion is that God is only an infinite, insane energy which creates and destroys without other purpose than to pass eternity in avoiding thought. Then the stupid man becomes the Perfect Incarnation of Omnipotence and the Polos are the true children of God!" (III, 1). For O'Neill could not write of what he did not know—harmony, unity, affirmation—but he was eloquent, like a good American, about darkness, meaninglessness, loneliness, and despair, and it was at these moments that his language in the middle-class American mode or in the "historical prose" was equal to the occasion, nearly always in his first career and almost always in his second and last career.

Racial dialects were always handled by O'Neill competently, if not brilliantly. He employed dialects for various reasons: first, his subject matter often dictated it; second, it offered a relatively easy way of achieving colorful effects; third, it offered an escape from the banalities of twentieth-century, middle-class American slang, whose repertoire contains as many flat and stale phrases as any language in history ever generated; e.g., "This rotten headache has my nerves shot to pieces" (*Beyond the Horizon*, II, 2); "I love those rotten old sob tunes" (*The Great God Brown*, II, 1).

In the early sea plays the various dialects give color to the dialogue and underline the fact that a Melvillean "melting-pot" is being evoked. In all the "S. S. Glencairn" plays, considered as a group, there is, more or less, the same medley of dialects: Driscoll (Irish brogue); Cocky (Cockney); Smitty (English upper class); Big Frank (Swedish); Yank (American lower class); Davis (American lower class); Max (Swedish); Lamps (Swedish); Chips (Swedish); Olson (Swedish); Paddy (Liverpool Irish); Ivan (Russian); Swanson (Swedish); Scotty (Scots); Jack (Lower-class American). This same cast, with variations, reappears in *The Hairy Ape* which opens with a medley of drinking toasts:

Gif me trink dere, you!
'Ave a wet!
Salute!
Gesundheit!

Skoal!
Drunk as a lord, God stiffen you!
Here's how!
Luck!

Thus the language of each speaker is both colorful and distinct. It is, to be sure, very simple and limited, but these characters are simple and limited and their speech fits them perfectly. As in the case of Wordsworth's peasants, their feelings are elemental and deeply, simply, felt, and their rhetoric is, in Wordsworth's phrase in the Preface to "The Lyrical Ballads" "plainer and more emphatic ..." than educated speech. Wordsworth continues: "... from their rank in society and the sameness and narrow circle of their intercourse, being less under the influence of social vanity, they convey their feelings and notions in simple and unelaborated expressions." All verbal rebellions or turnings in new directions of the written English language, from Dryden, through Wordsworth and Coleridge, to Eliot and Pound, tend to be away from formality and artificiality and toward the rhythm and diction of common speech. In the history of the American drama in the twentieth century O'Neill played the same role as Pound, Eliot, Frost, and others did in poetry. He detached dramatic dialogue from the stilted conventionality of the average American play of the early twentieth century and attached it to the living, spoken language.

The principal racial or cultural dialects that O'Neill employed throughout his career were: Negro (*The Dreamy Kid, The Emperor Jones, All God's Chillun Got Wings*), Swedish (*Anna Christie*), New England-biblical (*Ile, The Rope, Where the Cross Is Made, Gold, Desire Under the Elms*), and, of course, the Irish brogue (*The Straw, Anna Christie, A Touch of the Poet, A Moon for the Misbegotten,* and *Long Day's Journey Into Night*). The best example of each type would be *The Emperor Jones* for the Negro; *Anna Christie* for the Swedish; *Desire Under the Elms* for the New England-biblical; and *A Touch of the Poet* and *A Moon for the Misbegotten* for the Irish brogue.

Actually each of these dialects is fairly easy to do, involving only an elementary kind of translation. For example: "It's no use in your raking up old times. What I was then is one thing. What I am now is another. You did not let me in on your crooked work out of any kind feelings at that time. I did the dirty work for you—and most of the brain work, too, for that matter—and I was worth money to you. That's the reason." Translated into the dialect of Brutus Jones, which involves running sentences together, speaking in fragments, slurring pronunciation, mixing up parts of speech, mispronouncing both vowels and consonants, mixing up tenses, and suppressing the last letter, or letters, of words, this same speech comes out this way: "No use'n you rakin' up ole times. What I was den is one thing. What I is now's another. You didn't let me in on yo' crooked work out o' no kind feelin's dat time. I done de dirty work fo' you—and most o' de brain work, too, fo' dat matter—and I was wu'th money to you, dat's de reason" (*The Emperor Jones*, I). Swedish dialect offers even less difficulties. In the accent of Chris in *Anna Christie* the song "Josephine" comes out thus (I):

> "My Yosephine, come board de ship. Long time Ay
>     vait for you.
> De moon, she shi-i-i-ne. She looka yust like you. . . ."

Similarly, "that old devil, sea," becomes "dat ole davil, sea." New England-biblical involves truncations, transposing tenses, a special pronunciation of vowels, using nouns as verbs, dropping final consonants and vowels, and adding an infusion of biblical phrases. Thus Ephraim Cabot of *Desire Under the Elms*, after he has found out that "his" baby is, or was, really Eben's and that it has been murdered by Abbie: "If he was Eben's, I be glad he air gone! An' mebbe I suspicioned it all along. I felt they was somethin' onnateral—somewhars—the house got so lonesome—an' cold—drivin' me down t' the barn—t' the beasts o' the field. . . . Ay-eh. I must've suspicioned—somethin'. Ye didn't fool me—not altogether, leastways—I'm too old a bird—growin' ripe on the bough" (III, 4).

As Synge first proved, an Irish brogue comes as ready-made prose-poetry. O'Neill's use of the brogue breaks down into two categories. First—and only once—there is the transparently stagey and stage-Irish effusions of Matt Burke in *Anna Christie*. O'Neill admitted this play was not fully serious, and this is apparent nowhere more than in the high-pitched verbalizings of his hero. Thus when Burke finds out that his betrothed, Anna, had once been a whore, he breaks into a keen: "(*His voice high pitched*

*in a lamentation that is like a keen*) Yerra, God help me!
I'm destroyed entirely and my heart is broken in bits!"

But most of the rest of the time O'Neill employed the
brogue in a fairly honest fashion; as with the other dialects,
the principles of translation were fairly simple. Here, for
example, is a middle-class American translation (mine)
of a speech by brogue-speaking Bill Carmody, the brutal
father of *The Straw*. He is upbraiding Eileen's spineless
fiance for deserting his daughter: "You are engaged to
marry her and yet you are anxious to get out of her sight.
. . . You have no heart at all, that's for sure. She was your
sweetheart for years and now she's sick with consumption.
And you are wild to run away and leave her alone." In
Carmody's brogue the speech comes out like this: "Is it
anxious to get out of her sight you are, and you engaged
to marry her? . . . Sure, it's no heart at all you have—and
her your sweetheart for years—and her sick with consumption—and you wild to run away and leave her alone" (I,
2). The principles of translation here are obvious enough.

The most complex and powerful use of the Irish brogue
occurs in the late plays, specifically in A *Touch of the
Poet*, A *Moon for the Misbegotten*, and *Long Day's Journey Into Night*.

A *Touch of the Poet* is O'Neill's most "Irish" play.
The majority of the characters, Nora, Cregan, Maloy,
Roche, O'Dowd, and Riley, speak in a brogue. With the
two key characters, Sara and Con, who are at once the
most complex and the most susceptible to change of all
the characters in the play, the use or nonuse of the brogue
is the veritable key to their respective personalities and
their relationship. With them the brogue represents Ireland, the peasantry, the past, the mud hovel with the pigs
on the floor, in short, all that is coarse and brutal and
common. Nonbrogue represents all that is civilized, proud,
aristocratic, courtly: for Con his glorious past, both as an
Irish landowner and a major in Wellington's army in the
Peninsular War; for Sara her aspirations to wed Simon
Harford and join the New England native aristocracy.
In a way it could be said that the brogue represents
reality, while nonbrogue signifies illusion or dream. But
it is not that simple either, for part of Con's past *was*
glorious, and Sara's future is to be aristocratic. More precisely, the antithesis between brogue and nonbrogue, as

it is manifested in the mercurial characters of Con Melody and his daughter, is yet another dramatization of the past-future obsession that is endemic in all of O'Neill's plays. Con has no future and two pasts: one ignoble (brogue) and the other glorious (nonbrogue); Sara has a future (nonbrogue) and an ambiguous past-present (brogue and nonbrogue). The play in a sense is a contest between them as to who will use the brogue and who will not. Throughout their long struggle with one another the weapon that they use against one another is the brogue. For the first three acts of the play the use of the brogue is Sara's ultimate taunt against her father, reminding him of his own real background, of his dismal present, and of what he most hates in her, that is, her peasant element which is signified physically by her thick ankles and her stubby, blunt fingers. Thus in Act I when Con pays her a compliment:

S A R A   [*With a mocking, awkward, servant's curtsy—in broad brogue.*]   Oh, thank ye, yer Honor.

M E L O D Y   Every day you resemble your mother more, as she looked when I first knew her.

S A R A   Musha, but it's you have the blarneyin' tongue, God forgive you!

M E L O D Y   [*In spite of himself, this gets under his skin—angrily.*]   Be quiet! How dare you talk to me like a common, ignorant—You're my daughter, damn you. [*He controls himself and forces a laugh.*]

By Act IV, however, she has fallen in love with, has seduced, and is to marry Simon Harford; thus from her the brogue is heard no more. But ironically, Con's spirit has finally been broken by his beating at the hands of the Harford servants; in his own words: "Cursing like a drunken, foulmouthed son of a thieving shebeen keeper who sprang from the filth of a peasant hovel, with pigs on the floor—with that pale Yankee bitch [Mrs. Harford] watching from a window, sneering with disgust!"

After his symbolic suicide—the shooting of his beloved mare who represents the character of the major—he has one final struggle with his nonbrogue-speaking daughter, who now wants him to become the nonbrogue-speaking major once more. Now the father and daughter, their original positions reversed, struggle for the identity of Melody. At one point in the verbal struggle Con is reduced to no character at all and in his agony shouts at his daughter: "Sara! For the love of God, stop—let me go—!" And it is Nora's words, in brogue, that decide the issue in favor of the Irish peasant:

DULLY    Lave your poor father be. It's best. [*In a flash Melody recovers and is the leering peasant again.*]

SARA    [*With bitter hopelessness.*]   Oh, Mother! Why couldn't you be still!

In this play then the Irish brogue, which in the early plays was employed for humor, e.g., "If he owned the ocean he wouldn't give a fish a drink" (*The Rope*), becomes a pervasive and powerful cultural and psychological index, expressive of the character and fate of the principals.

In *A Long Day's Journey Into Night* and *A Moon for the Misbegotten* the brogue is less meaningful, but, if anything, more pervasive. In both plays there is on stage an authentic brogue-speaking Irish peasant, Hogan in *A Moon* and Cathleen in *A Long Day's Journey*, who are there for comic relief. With Hogan, especially, the Irish penchant for rapidity of speech and wild exaggeration is used for the comedy of Act I, especially in his encounter with Harder, the scion of Standard Oil Money. He is assisted by Josie, who likewise has a brogue although to a lesser extent. Harder, dressed in riding clothes, has come to the Hogan shack to protest the fact that Hogan's pigs wallow in his ice pond: "*The experienced strategy of the* HOGANS *in verbal battle is to take the offensive at once and never let an opponent get set to hit back. Also, they use a beautifully co-ordinated, bewildering change of pace, switching suddenly from jarring shouts to low, confidential vituperation. And they exaggerate their Irish brogues to confuse an enemy still further.*" They immediately launch a verbal assault on Harder, naming him a "jockey," bringing into question his masculinity, and thoroughly confounding him.

HOGAN    I don't think he's a jockey. It's only the funny pants he's wearing. I'll bet if you asked his horse, you'd find he's no cowboy either. [*To* HARDER, *jeeringly.*] Come, tell us the truth, me honey. Don't you kiss your horse each time you mount and beg him, please don't throw me today, darlin', and I'll give you an extra bucket of oats. [*He bursts into an extravagant roar of laughter, slapping his thigh, and* JOSIE *guffaws with him, while they watch the disconcerting effect of this theatrical mirth on* HARDER.]

HARDER [*Beginning to lose his temper*] Listen to me, Hogan! I didn't come here—[*He is going to add "to listen to your damned jokes" or something like that, but* HOGAN *silences him.*]

HOGAN [*Shouts*] What! What's that you said? [*He stares at the dumbfounded* HARDER *with droll amazement as if he couldn't believe his ears*] You didn't come here? [*He turns to* JOSIE—*in a whisper*] Did you hear that, Josie? [*He takes off his hat and scratches his head in comic bewilderment*] Well, that's a puzzle, surely. How d'you suppose he got here?

JOSIE Maybe the stork brought him, bad luck to it for a dirty bird. [*Again* TYRONE's *laughter is heard from the bedroom.*]

HARDER [*So off balance now he can only repeat angrily*] I said I didn't come here—

HOGAN [*Shouts*] Wait! Wait, now! [*Threateningly*] We've had enough of that. Say it a third time and I'll send my daughter to telephone the asylum.

This goes on until the unfortunate Harder is thoroughly humiliated and finally ignominiously routed.

In *Long Day's Journey Into Night*, while the brogue proper is confined to Cathleen, the Irish "lilt" is all-pervasive, especially in the speech of the father and, to a lesser degree, that of the mother. As Tyrone explains to Edmund in Act IV, he had been successful as a young actor because he had gotten rid of a brogue that, "you could cut with a knife." But Irish locutions and phrases remain a faint but definable part and parcel of his speech: "I got them dead cheap. It was McGuire put me on to them"; "For the love of God, why couldn't you have the strength to keep on?"; "I'll kick you out in the gutter tomorrow, so help me God."

O'Neill's use of American slang follows the same pattern of everything else he did: early experiments, self-conscious and only partially successful, with final mastery in the late plays, specifically, *The Iceman Cometh* and, especially, *Hughie*. The two most illustrative examples of O'Neill's early use of American slang are *The Straw* and *Diff'rent*. In Act II, Scene 1, of *The Straw* there is a weighing-in scene for all the inhabitants of the sanitarium. Here is introduced one Flynn who speaks, as a Hemingway character, in the metaphor of American baseball. When he is called to the scales, he says, "Me to the plate!" When he finds that he has gained two pounds, he exclaims to Murray: "I hit 'er for a two-bagger, Steve. Come on now, Bo, and bring me home! 'Atta boy!" Unfortunately, this rhetoric is as stale and flat as is the original upon which it is based. In Act II of *Diff'rent* there is a torrent of 1920's slang uttered by Benny, the young wastrel who had been to France with the A.E.F. Benny seems also to be O'Neill's embodiment of the amoral, frivolous, greedy, meaninglessness of the American 1920's. His speech then is meant to express the hectic, feverish, ceaseless search for new and easy excitements, coupled to a basic, inner emptiness. Benny is engaged in playing upon the affections of the frustrated spinster, Emma Crosby, in order to get her money. Benny's dialogue is filled with thin, excited interjections: "Oh, baby! Some jazz, I'll tell the world!" Various other elements of the patois of the twenties are gradually and successively woven in: "That's all bunk"; "this dead dump"; "We'll have a circus"; "give me some kale"; "I wasn't born yesterday"; "They're some pippins"; "Oui, tooty sweet"; "I'll spill the beans for both of you, if you try to gum me!" And so on. And again only flatness is achieved.

O'Neill's various kinds of language have been discussed here separately, but, of course, in the individual plays several different kinds are often employed, forming a medley and creating a "rhythm of language," always accompanying the various other rhythms. In the sea plays this is quite obvious, but the same medley effect is achieved in less obvious ways in other plays. In *Beyond the Horizon* there are four kinds of American speech: the normative, middle-class American (Andrew and Robert Mayo, and Ruth Mayo, *nee* Atkins); the sea lingo of the sailing era (Captain Scott); New England farmer dialect (Mayo, Sr.), New England farm, *cum* biblical-Calvinistic flavor (Mrs. Atkins). Many other plays have similar medley-like effects.

The greatest and most comprehensive linguistic symphony that O'Neill composed was *The Iceman Cometh*, which was in a sense a return to the "melting-pot" cast of the "S. S. Glencairn" plays, but with many additions: Rocky and Chuck (lower-class New Yorkese); Larry (middle-class American); Hugo (Hungarian-American); Willie (middle-class American); Harry (New York-Irish); Joe (Negro-American); Parritt (middle-class American); Lewis (English); Wetjoen (Dutch); Jimmy (middle-class American with a Scots flavor); McGloin and Mosher (New York-Irish); Margie, Pearl, and Cora (New York lower class); and Hickey (Mid-Western American salesman lingo.) Of this collection of accents O'Neill is in complete control, especially the resources for humor, and Act I of the play is, as he thought, one of the funniest acts that he ever wrote. For example, there is Rocky's speculations about Chuck and Cora settling down, bucolically, to wedded bliss on the farm:

> What would gettin' married get dem? But de farm stuff is de sappiest part. When bot' of 'em was dragged up in dis ward and ain't never been nearer a farm dan Coney Island! Jees, dey'd tink dey'd gone deef if dey didn't hear de El rattle! Dey'd get D.T.'s if dey ever hoid a cricket choip! I hoid crickets once on my cousin's place in Joisey. I couldn't sleep a wink. Dey give me de heebic-jccbies. [*With deeper disgust*] Jees, can yuh picture a good barkeep like Chuck diggin' spuds? And imagine a whore hustlin' de cows home! For Christ sake! Ain't dat a sweet picture!
>
> MARGIE [*rebukingly*]  Yuh oughtn't to call Cora dat, Rocky. She's a good kid. She may be a tart, but—
> ROCKY [*considerately*]  Sure, dat's all I meant, a tart.
> PEARL [*giggling*]  But he's right about de damned cows, Margie. Jees, I bet Cora don't know which end of de cow has de horns! I'm goin' to ask her.

Or McGloin to his patron, Harry Hope: "It's not like you to be so hard-hearted, Harry. Sure, it's hot, parching work laughing at your jokes so early in the morning on an empty stomach!" Generally, the various dialects and slang levels of *The Iceman Cometh* are functional in the same sense as is the plain prose of *Mourning Becomes Electra:* the language is not memorable nor does it call attention to itself; it exists as an efficient medium to convey the emotions of the characters. Hickey's monologue uses slang— "Why, you bonehead, I haven't got a single damned lying hope or pipe dream left!"—every bit as monotonous and colorless as that of Benny in *Diff'rent.* But the speech generates its great force from the terrible story it tells and the genuine agony of its teller.

The real O'Neill tour de force in the use of American slang is Erie Smith's monologue in *Hughie*, at once the most complex and colorful as well as the most convincing of O'Neill's uses of the vernacular. The complexity is given first by the range of the vocabulary. As the Gelbs point out, it is an amazing collection of Broadway-gambler argot: sap, noggin, sucker, puss, moniker, hooked, bangtail, finn, babe, scratch, sawbuck, croaked, bum dope, old bones, in spades, raw babies, rubbed out, real jack, old turtle, round-heeled, in my book, the sticks, the Big Stem, run-out powder, fall guy, clam shut, hit the hay, crummy dump, the once-over, het up, beat the racket, poor boob, square shake, lap it up, put the bite on, wrong G's, take it on the lam, C note, and so on. This is a considerable advance, in concreteness, complexity, and color, over the simple ejaculations of Benny or even the rather normative vocabulary of *The Iceman Cometh*. But Erie is not an illiterate either, and uses such words as "resigned," "impediment," "paralyzed," "romantic." His pronunciation and rhetoric are equally complex and varied: mixing up of tenses, suppression of final consonants, consistent use of the double negative: "Dolls didn't call him no riot"; "Not that I'd ever ring in no phonies on a pal. I'm no heel." Another device is to use "except" for "unless." In its content Erie's statements run to hyperbole, on the one hand, and, on the other, elaborately hyperbolical understatement. As for hyperbole: "Christ, I wish Hughie was alive and kickin'. I'd tell him I win ten grand from the bookies, and ten grand at stud, and ten grand in a crap game! I'd tell him I bought one of those Mercedes sport roadsters with nickel pipes sticking out of the hood! I'd tell him I lay three babes from the Follies—two blondes and one brunette!" For elaborate understatement, using the "except" formation, there is Erie's description of Hughie's wife: "Well, I suppose marriage ain't such a bum racket, if you're made for it. Hughie didn't seem to mind it much, although if you want my low-down, his wife is a bum—in spades! Oh, I don't mean cheatin'. With her puss and figure, she'd never make no one except she raided a blind asylum." Again he says of her, in Anglo-Saxon understatement: "When you call her plain, you give her all the breaks." The authenticity, concreteness, and ease with which O'Neill handled Broadway-ese in

*Hughie* made him finally one of the masters of the literary use of the American vernacular. Compared to *Hughie* or even *The Iceman Cometh,* the language of Runyon seems even more artificial and coy, that of Lardner formally conscious and stilted, that of Lewis a suggestive notation rather than an authentic representation. As in all other respects, O'Neill was just coming into his own —at the end.

Broadway lingo, however, in the two other late plays, *Long Day's Journey Into Night* and *A Moon for the Misbegotten* is employed in quite a different manner. While in *Hughie* it is the language of hope and courage, in the other two plays it is the language of hatred, cynicism and nihilism, for it is the accent that Jamie Tyrone affects when he is being his most cynical. And it has none of the concreteness, humor, understatement, and complexity of Erie's monologue; rather it is flat, stale, empty, and colorless, the vehicle for the most elementary and bald kind of cynicism. In the words of Edmund's scornful parody of Jamie's outlook and language in Act II, Scene 2, of *Long Day's Journey:* "They never come back! Everything is in the bag! It's all a frame-up! We're all fall guys and suckers and we can't beat the game! *Disdainfully.* Christ, if I felt the way you do—!" For this is the language of hatred, and it is stigmatized by James Tyrone in *Long Day's Journey* as "your rotten Broadway loafer's lingo!" (II, 2), and by Josie Hogan in *A Moon* as "your rotten Broadway blather!" (I). It is the language of Jamie Tyrone's "dead" side, which perverts everything, from his love of Josie Hogan to his love of his brother Edmund. When in Act III of *A Moon for the Misbegotten* Josie admits to Tyrone that she is a virgin and then offers herself to him, out of love, he falls into the role of a Broadway "sport" with his doxie: "Come on, Baby Doll, let's hit the hay"; she, stricken and horrified, pulls away from him and exclaims, "Jim! I'm not a whore." And the last chance of their love being genuinely and lovingly consummated is forever lost. And when Jamie is being honest, in his "confession" to his brother near the end of *Long Day's Journey,* he admits that both the Broadway attitude and the Broadway language are fake and the vehicles of destruction: "Made my mistakes look good. Made getting drunk romantic. . . . Made fun of work as sucker's game."

Actually, although in a less obvious fashion than in *The Iceman Cometh*, both *A Long Day's Journey Into Night* and *A Moon for the Misbegotten* are, from the point of view of language, medley plays, with a variety of accents and vocabulary being heard. What sets them both off from the rest of the plays is the fact that here O'Neill employed one of the characteristic devices of modern literature— Joyce and Eliot would be the great exemplars in the English language—of using literary quotations both to create a cultural continuum for the plays, that is, to put them into a meaningful relationship with their cultural past, and to characterize individuals in the play. More than any other of O'Neill's plays, the central male characters in these two plays tend to be bookish and not bookish in a dilettantish way but crucially, with books affecting their characters and fate. The quotations that rise from their memories are an index to the deepest levels of their characters. As usual, O'Neill had attempted something like this in an earlier play and had not succeeded in making it convincing. In *The First Man* Curtis Jayson is described as a natural romantic whose life has been dominated by ideas derived from books. The background of this phenomenon is given in a rather obvious and bald piece of exposition—somewhat like Father Baird's lengthy explanation of John Loving's intellectual evolution in *Days Without End*—in the first part of Act I by Curtis' old friend Edward Bigelow. Thus we are told by Bigelow that Curtis broke with the family tradition of getting a classical degree at Yale and went in, instead, for mining engineering at Cornell. The reason for this was that he had read Bret Harte in prep school, took him seriously, and decided he would go West, which he had accordingly romanticized. Disillusioned by the drab reality, he goes in for prospecting. Disappointed with finding nothing but pebbles, he goes in for geology, "the Romance of the Rocks" and from that to anthropology, "the last romance of all." But neither Curtis nor his story, nor the play, are very convincing. A much more successful picture of a romantic young imagination wedding life and literature, and living by quotations, so to speak, is that of Richard Miller in *Ah, Wilderness!* But this is a comedy and Richard is an adolescent, who, presumably, will recover from his infatuation with words. For the conjunction of life and literature at a mature and tragic level, it is to *A Long Day's Journey Into Night* and *A Moon for the Misbegotten* that we must turn.

O'Neill's most "literary" play is *Long Day's Journey Into Night*, in which the three male characters are steeped in literature, each in his own way. The most simple relationship between literature and life is demonstrated by the father. As he explains to Edmund in Act IV, his early urge to become an actor intoxicated him with the drama. He read every play that was ever written and studied Shakespeare as one might study the Bible. Accordingly, he has at the tip of his tongue a Shakespearean quotation for any occasion. But there are many Shakespeares, and Tyrone's version is of a rather benign, and, on the whole, optimistic, moralizer, with a common-sense aphorism for every human dilemma. In Tyrone's mind Shakespeare represents the saner, wiser, simpler outlook on life which he sets up against Nietzsche, Swinburne, Baudelaire, and so on, the degenerate, alcoholic, homosexual, atheistic, morbid nineteenth-century European writers in whom his sons are steeped. In his dialogue with Edmund in Act IV, he says wistfully: "Why can't you remember your Shakespeare and forget the third-raters. You'll find what you're trying to say in him—as you'll find everything else worth saying. *He quotes, using his fine voice.* 'We are such stuff as dreams are made on, and our little life is rounded with a sleep.' " At which Edmund laughs ironically and declares that we are such "stuff" as "manure" is made on. For the sons think that the baleful forces of life are overwhelmingly powerful and that only in irony, bitterness, and drink can the hapless and helpless individual find any refuge, while the father believes in individual will, effort, and responsibility. Thus when his son tells him that life is crazy, he returns with a quotation from *Julius Caesar:* " 'The fault, dear Brutus, is not in our stars, but in ourselves that we are underlings.' " It is true that he can also use Shakespeare for darker moods and moments. His troublesome sons are so familiar with King Lear's lament, "How sharper than a serpent's tooth it is, / To have a thankless child," that they finish the lines for him, once he has enunciated the first part. He can also use Shakespeare ironically and humorously, as when he tells Edmund that, as a son, Edmund has been a "case of 'A poor thing but mine own.' "

Jamie, on his part, turns Shakespeare upside down and

uses Shakespearian lines as one of his many weapons in his endless verbal war with his father, often taking a neutral Shakespearian line, even a stage direction, and using it to make some grim or ironical remark about the troubled Tyrones. (Significantly, he twice quotes Iago.) The only wholly humorous use of Shakespeare made by Jamie occurs in Act I—before the tragedy proper begins—when there is a discussion of the power of James Tyrone's snoring and Jamie quotes Iago, "The Moor, I know his trumpet." But his other uses of Shakespeare are devastatingly mordant. When in Act IV Edmund and Jamie discuss Jamie's bottomless cynicism, they conclude that he (Jamie) probably thinks that you can bribe your way into heaven and, if penniless, would inevitably go to hell. Jamie concurs and once more quotes Iago, the most cynical of Shakespearian villains, "Therefore put money in thy purse." But Jamies puts to the most terrible use a version of a perfectly neutral Shakespearian stage direction, and that at the climax of the play when his mother wanders onto the stage, murmuring of her past, at which Jamie exclaims, "The Mad Scene. Enter Ophelia!" (After which Edmund hits him.) And if his mother is the mad Ophelia, his father is Clarence of *Richard III*. When they confront one another in Act IV, Jamie exclaims, quoting from the grisly dream that the doomed Clarence has had of his own death in the prison scene of *Richard III*:

> "Clarence is come, false, fleeting, perjured Clarence,
>     That stabbed me in the field by Tewksbury.
>     Seize on him, Furies, take him into torment."

Jamie Tyrone's character is outlined by the different kinds of language he uses; there are actually four aspects to Jamie: the hateful, the boisterous, the lyrical or romantic, and the elegiac. In *Long Day's Journey*, throughout the bulk of the play and except for isolated moments, he is either hateful or boisterous. But in Act IV, where the greatest number of literary quotations are uttered, he is at first boisterous (Kipling), but finally elegiac as he ends by quoting three stanzas of Swinburne's "A Leavetaking." And throughout the play as a whole there is a design to his literary quotations: hate is Shakespeare; boisterousness is Kipling; elegy is Wilde, Rossetti, and, above all, Swinburne. His last words in the play are to recite, sadly, bitterly, sincerely, elegiacally, three stanzas from Swinburne's "A Leave-taking"; thus the last literary quotation in the play is:

"Let us go hence, go hence; she will not see.
Sing all once more together; surely she,
She too, remembering days and words that were,
Will turn a little toward us, sighing; but we,
We are hence, we are gone, as though we had not been
    there.
Nay, and though all men seeing had pity on me,
She would not see."

*A Moon for the Misbegotten* is the play devoted to understanding and forgiving Jamie, as *A Long Day's Journey Into Night* understands and forgives James and Mary Tyrone. As Jamie is aggressive and cynical in *Long Day's Journey*, he is only briefly and intermittently so in *A Moon*, in which he has become, like Mary Tyrone of *Long Day's Journey*, one of the walking wounded, lost, lonely, afraid, and separated irrevocably from what he should have become. Thus in this play he is, by and large, romantic and elegiac. All reports on the early years of the real James O'Neill, Jr., the years before he went wrong, indicate that he was talented. In Act IV of *Long Day's Journey Into Night* his father contemplates the drunken, visibly deteriorating wreck that is his first son and remarks with a *"bitter sadness"*: "A sweet spectacle for me! My first-born, who I hoped would bear my name in honor and dignity, who showed such brilliant promise!" In this same act, before he had passed out, Jamie reminds Edmund that he (Jamie) had once aspired to be a writer, that he had first introduced Edmund to Swinburne, and that it was he who had really led Edmund on to become a writer. Thus when he first comes on stage in *A Moon for the Misbegotten* we are reminded that he is a man of education and talent by O'Neill having him speak his first words in Latin:

"Fortunate senex, ergo tua rura manebunt,
    et tibi magna satis, quamvis lapis omnia nudus."

He almost immediately reverts to the hail-fellow-well-met guise under which he is a bosom friend of the cunning and crude peasant farmer, Phil Hogan, by translating his own Latin tag: "Translated very freely into Irish English, something like this. (*He imitates* HOGAN's *brogue*) 'Ain't you the lucky old bastard to have this beautiful farm, if it is full of nude rocks.'" (Hogan replies that it is easy to see that Tyrone has had a fine education and goes on to observe acidly that he, Tyrone, must find this education a great help to him in conversing with whores and barkeeps.) In Act III when Josie tries to boast of her many nonexistent lovers, Jamie refers to her, affectionately and jokingly, as "Messalina," who was, historically, the notoriously profligate wife of Claudius.

Within this frame of a reminder of Tyrone's classical education, there is gradually revealed, as the play goes on, that he does in fact have a "soul" buried under the load of guilt and cynicism that he bears although this soul can only and uncertainly and forlornly venture forth in the presence of Josie. To her he quotes from what is perhaps the most desolately beautiful poem in the English language, Keats's "Ode to a Nightingale." Thus when Hogan goes off in Act II, singing, "Oh, the parties they grow small," Tyrone says sardonically, "Hark, Hark, the Donegal lark!" and adds, "Thou wast not born for death, immortal bird." Ashamed of himself, he drops Keats and complains about Hogan's "dirge." But, in the moonlight and in the presence of Josie and in his present mood, Keats seems appropriate, and he goes on:

> 'Now more than ever seems it rich to die,
> To cease upon the midnight with no pain,
> In such an ecstasy!'

(*He has recited this with deep feeling. Now he sneers*) Good God! Ode to Phil the Irish Nightingale! I must have the D.T.'s." In the great third act when, writing his last complete play, O'Neill tells for the last time his recurrent story of the impossibility of genuine communication between two human beings, especially a man and a woman, he gives to Jamie two literary fragments, carefully chosen to convey two of his persistent themes throughout his career: the ill consequences of pretense: "Pride is the sin by which the angels fell" and the precariousness of human reason:

> "It is the very error of the moon:
> She comes more nearer earth than she was wont,
> And makes men mad."

This last is *Othello* once more, but, significantly, it is not Iago speaking, as in *Long Day's Journey Into Night*, but Othello himself. However—further irony—it is spoken by Othello to Emilia after he has killed Desdemona.

In *Long Day's Journey* Edmund is similarly characterized by his literary allusions. He is also obsessed with death and with the meaninglessness of modern life: Nietzsche ("God is dead: of His pity for man hath God died"); Dowson ("They are not long, the days of wine and roses"); and, above all, Baudelaire ("Be always drunken. Nothing else matters"). And he will not even allow his authors to romanticize anything in life. Thus after quoting some lines from Dowson's "Non Sum Qualis Eram Bonae Sub Regno Cynarae," with its Latin title and its romanticization of a prostitute, he goes on to remark that, in reality, Dowson, in composing the poem, was inspired by an absinthe hangover and was writing it for a stupid barmaid who thought he was only a "crazy souse," and "gave him the gate to marry a waiter!"

By and large the dialogue of the main characters in *Long Day's Journey Into Night* is plain, unadorned middle-class American speech, leavened by early twentieth-century slang in the utterances of the sons and the Irish "lilt" in those of the parents. Only Edmund, of them all, is capable, sporadically, of a certain eloquence, but he is given some of the best lines O'Neill ever wrote, despite his own deprecatory attitude toward his own verbal gifts. Thus some of the speeches of Edmund show that in writing normal American "talk" O'Neill had, at the end of his career, finally achieved some dominance over his medium. As Josie Hogan surprises herself with her unknown and unexpected vein of poetry, so Edmund, to his own delight, can occasionally hit things off verbally although never to perfection. An example of this would be his description of his mother in Act IV: "Yes, she moves above and beyond us, a ghost haunting the past, and here we sit pretending to forget, but straining our ears listening for the slightest sound, hearing the fog drip from the eaves like the uneven tick of a rundown, crazy clock—or like the dreary tears of a trollop spattering in a puddle of stale beer on a honky-tonk table top!" That characteristic deflation, in the trollop simile, of the opening elegy is too abrupt, brutal, and obvious. Nevertheless the lines are a perfect index to the two sides of his character, and are not without their merits as English prose. And he himself is so infatuated with words that he can momentarily stand back from or step out of the mutual tragedy of the Tyrones to take a more or less objective look at his own rhetoric. Thus after he makes the above-quoted speech he laughs with "maudlin appreciation" and goes on to say, "Not so bad, that last, eh? Original, not Baudelaire. Give me credit!" But, as if to remind himself that his mastery of English prose was fitful, O'Neill then has Edmund continue on to try to tell his father about the "ecstatic moment" on the sailing vessel, a speech which he admits is a failure, and he finally concludes his lengthy exercises in rhetoric by concluding: "Stammering is the native eloquence of us fog people."

Still we may wonder, if great verbal talent and gifts are lacking, at the power and the catastrophic conclusiveness of O'Neill's late plays. In the last analysis the plays are but words on pages, as is all literature finally, and the words themselves very often have little about them that can be called distinctive. Surely, future editions of Bartlett's *Familiar Quotations* will not be enlarged by copious quotations from O'Neill. Nor does it help to say that, of course, these characters do not speak in eternal phrases and for posterity because they are just people, speaking normally, if under great stress, and trying, sometimes succeeding, more often failing, to achieve the two most difficult of verbal aspirations: to express oneself and to communicate to others. To say this would be to say that *Long Day's Journey Into Night* and the other late plays are photographic or photographic representations of life itself, which they are not, although they certainly give the appearance of it. But in life itself the stammering of the fog people is more sustained and is certainly without meaning and utterly devoid of dramatic continuity.

The clue to O'Neill's mastery over dramatic language, and over the medium itself, is given by Hugo von Hofmannsthal in his analysis of O'Neill's early plays. Effective dramatic dialogue, said von Hofmannsthal, is not dependent on "lyrical quality or rhetorical power" (Cargill et al., pp. 250–51):

The best dramatic dialogue reveals not only the motives that determine what a character is to do—as well as what he tries to conceal—but suggests his very appearance, his metaphysical being as well as the grosser material figure. How this is done remains one of the unanswerable riddles of artistic creation. This suggestion of the 'metaphysical' enables us to determine in an instant, the moment a person enters the room whether he is sympathetic or abhorrent, whether he brings agitation or peace; he affects the atmosphere about us, making it solemn or trivial, as the case may be.

Hofmannsthal went on to criticize O'Neill's early plays on the grounds that the characters are not "sufficiently drenched in the atmosphere of their own individual past." And, further, that they always said what was expected of them and thus seldom evoked in the spectator or the reader the faculty of wonder or surprise: "Much of what they say seems too openly and frankly sincere, and consequently lacking in the element of wonder or surprise; for the ultimate sincerity that comes from the lips of man is always surprising" (*ibid.*). For, as Hofmannsthal says: "Masterly dialogue resembles the movements of a high-spirited horse; there is not a single unnecessary movement, everything tends towards a predetermined goal; but at the same time each movement unconsciously betrays a richness and variety of vital energy that seems directed to no special end; it appears rather like the prodigality of an inexhaustible abundance" (*ibid.*). These words of von Hofmannsthal are an unconscious prophecy of what O'Neill's dialogue was to be in his late plays: each character speaking so as to reveal both his or her gross body and his or her metaphysical essence; each bearing with him his special atmosphere; each character drenched in his or her past; each speaking those ultimate sincerities that startle and surprise; the whole chorus moving toward a predetermined goal but, along the way, giving no hint of a special end in sight or in view. We know, well in advance, just what the ending is to be of *The Emperor Jones* or *The Hairy Ape*, but we could not even guess what is to be the conclusion of *A Long Day's Journey* or *A Moon for the Misbegotten* although when these endings come they are perfectly appropriate and dictated by the inner logic of the play as a whole.

In a general way what O'Neill finally learned about words and their uses was three things: the necessity for

restraint, the tonic value of irony, and, the *sine qua non*
for the drama, propriety of speech to speaker. Throughout much of his career O'Neill was striving to capture
the Sadness, the Beauty, the Terror, the Humor of Life
through hyperbole. But in the late plays he arrived at the
final summit of art, the writer's Valhalla, Irony, whereby
he himself says, or affirms, nothing and whereby what his
characters say or affirm is ringed with ambiguities and
qualifications, each character saying what is true or untrue
for him or her alone. No one can speak for the universe,
as could Cybel or Lazarus. Thus there is in the late plays
a kind of ultimate individuality: each of the characters
in *Long Day's Journey* says only what he or she *could* say.

One of the most devastating remarks ever made about
O'Neill's early tendency toward verbal hyperbole and toward the literal, unadorned translation of his own emotions and ideals into the words of his dramatic protagonists
was made by Stark Young about the production of
*Welded*, O'Neill's play about himself and Agnes Bolton:
" 'Gene and Agnes would sit there, like two little birds,
... They believed every word of the play. Those vulgar
speeches. God!' " (Gelbs, p. 544). But when Harold Clur-
man reviewed *Long Day's Journey Into Night* he concluded his review by remarking: "O'Neill's work is more
than realism. And if it is stammering—it is still the most
eloquent and significant stammer of the American theatre.
We have not yet developed a cultivated speech that is
either superior to it or as good" (Cargill et al., p. 216).
When the drugged Mary Tyrone moves to the center
of the stage at the end of *Long Day's Journey Into Night*
we are witnessing the soul-chilling climax of the greatest
tragedy in the history of the American theater and one of
the great tragedies of the Western theater, not the least
of the reasons for its power being that the characters speak
with almost perfect propriety, for their time, their place,
their culture, their respective characters. Only the pro-
scenium arch is a mute reminder that it is "art," not
"life," that we are observing.

O'NEILL AS AN
AMERICAN WRITER

O'NEILL IS OFTEN viewed in histories of the American drama
as a kind of inexplicable and unexplainable upthrust in that
history, a huge alp looming up between William Vaughn
Moody or Percy McKaye and Arthur Miller or Tennessee
Williams and not appearing to have solid connections with
either his predecessors or his successors. While it is true
that O'Neill has strong roots in the popular stage of nineteenth-century America, as has been shown above (see
Chap. 4, Sec. i), and while it is true that subsequent American playwrights after him have tried to remain in his tradition and have attempted to recapture some of his complexity and power, still he seems either out of place in,
or disconnected to, the history of American drama. It is
revealing and enlightening then to place him in, and view
him in, the context and tradition to which he belongs,
the tradition of serious American writing of both the nineteenth and twentieth centuries.[1] Once this readjustment
is made, it becomes apparent that O'Neill is a major
American writer and that his work constitutes one of the
quintessential expressions of American culture. In fact few
other American writers have explored so thoroughly the
ranges and the depths of the national experience.

## I *Twentieth-Century American Literature*

It is easy, first, to forget or overlook the simul-
taneity of O'Neill's work with that of such writers as Eliot,
Pound, Hemingway, Fitzgerald, Lewis, Faulkner, Stevens,
and the other eminences of American literature of the first

part of the twentieth century: that, for example, *Fog*, *The Sniper*, *Ile*, *In the Zone*, and *The Long Voyage Home* were all produced in the year of *Prufrock and Other Observations* (1917); or that *Beyond the Horizon*, *The Emperor Jones*, and *Diff'rent* are contemporaneous with Wharton's *Age of Innocence*, Lewis's *Main Street*, Fitzgerald's *This Side of Paradise*, and Pound's "Hugh Selwyn Mauberley" (1920); *The Hairy Ape* with Eliot's *The Waste Land* and Lewis's *Babbitt* (1922); *Desire Under the Elms* and *All God's Chillun Got Wings* with Hemingway's *In Our Time* and Faulkner's *The Marble Faun* (1924); *The Great God Brown* with Hemingway's *The Sun Also Rises* (1926); *Dynamo* with Wolfe's *Look Homeward Angel* (1929); *Mourning Becomes Electra* with Stevens' *Harmonium* (2nd edition) (1931).

This is the company to which O'Neill belongs, and in some respects he is the central figure in it. In *The Confident Years* Van Wyck Brooks [2] observed about O'Neill that there was scarcely a literary current of the time that had not flowed through his mind. One after another he had taken up the themes that had filled the lives of other writers and had often developed them better than anyone else. Brooks went on to enumerate some: Henry Adams' dynamo in *Dynamo*; hatred of bourgeois family life in *The First Man*; the attack upon commercialism in *Marco Millions* and *The Great God Brown*; the treatment of the dead end of Puritanism in which "no one equalled O'Neill" in *Desire Under the Elms*, *The Rope*, and *Mourning Becomes Electra*; the feeling for the saloon and its habitués (the equivalent to the drawing room of the traditional novel or play) that filled the imagination of a multitude of American writers from Jack London on; the sympathy for primitive types as in the work of Lardner, Hemingway, Steinbeck, and Faulkner; and, of course, the feeling for the Negro. But Francis Fergusson, looking at O'Neill from another angle, placed him in the 1912 Renaissance group, along with Mencken, Anderson, and Dreiser.[3] Irrespective of where the individual critic or historian places O'Neill, one can see his cultural importance merely by enumerating his institutional connections, few as they are: the Provincetown Players, Mencken and Nathan's *The Smart Set*, and the Theatre Guild.

When one considers the concerns, themes, characters,

and techniques of O'Neill, the circle of receptivity and achievement extends its circumference. Psychoanalytic ideas, or a version of them, appear in *Strange Interlude* and *Mourning Becomes Electra*; Marxism, or a version of it, in *The Hairy Ape*; Frazer, or a version of Frazer, in *Lazarus Laughed*; all the plays are, if nothing else, Darwinian. Babbitt, the crass but decent American business-man, appears in *Marco Millions*; Prufrock (Marsden) in *Strange Interlude*; "The Outsider," the Negro rebel, in *The Dreamy Kid* and *The Emperor Jones*; "the aged eagle" persona, tortured by belief and unbelief, of *Ash Wednesday* in *Days Without End*; Meyer Wolfsheim of *The Great Gatsby* is mentioned in *Hughie* by his real name, Arnold Rothstein; Dick Diver, the doctor who fails because of a woman, of *Tender Is the Night* appears as Ned Darrell in *Strange Interlude*; the cast and setting of *Time of Your Life* appear in *The Iceman Cometh*; the cast and setting of *Ethan Frome* in *Beyond the Horizon*; "modern woman" in *Strange Interlude*; "modern man" in *The Great God Brown*.

The continuous fight that serious twentieth-century writers have had to wage against a puritanical censorship, O'Neill fought too, and at least four of his plays were involved in either threatened or actual suppression: *The Hairy Ape*, *All God's Chillun Got Wings*, *Desire Under the Elms* (tried in court in Los Angeles), and *A Moon for the Misbegotten* (closed by the Detroit police). On the other hand, O'Neill's work had stronger popular ap-peal for middle-class American audiences than that of al-most any other serious writer of his time. Many of his plays were Broadway successes, and on several occasions were made into moderately popular movies. Norman Rockwell could well have used the physiognomies and the interiors of *Ah, Wilderness!* as a cover for *The Saturday Evening Post* to illustrate the American middle-class family at its best. In more recent memory both *Anna Christie* and *Ah, Wilderness!* have been canonized by the Broadway stage and made into "musical plays": *New Girl in Town* (*Anna*) and *Take Me Along* (*Ah, Wilderness!*). *Long Day's Journey Into Night* has been filmed in its entirety, there is a television tape of *The Iceman Cometh*, and a phono-graph recording has been made of a full-length production of *Strange Interlude*. The list will continue to extend itself.

The rebellion against the artifices, artificialities, and euphemisms of Victorian language that Eliot and Pound led in the domain of poetry, O'Neill led, and prevailed with, in the drama. The modern practice of using a Greek myth as the frame for a story of the present, employed by Joyce, Eliot, Jeffers, and others, appears in *Mourning Becomes Electra*. On the other hand, the whole experimental tendency of twentieth-century literature has O'Neill as one of its chief exponents, and the wild, hallucinatory, dreamlike, nightmare-like quality of human experience that so much of modern literature has tried to convey is dramatized in *The Great God Brown* and *Dynamo*, among others. But, to put the opposite once more, the modern reaction away from this kind of subjectivity, toward a kind of classical objectivity, as in the admonitions of T. S. Eliot, is embodied in *Lazarus Laughed* or *Desire Under the Elms*. On the other hand, the autobiographical tendency of art in the twentieth century has as two of its finest fruits *Long Day's Journey Into Night* and *A Moon for the Misbegotten*. Considered from almost any angle, either that of subject matter, or theme, or form, or language, O'Neill is one of the key figures in the second great efflorescence of American literature that occurred in the first part of the twentieth century.

## II  *Nineteenth-Century American Literature*

But O'Neill's deepest affinities are back in the first flowering of American literary culture, the so-called American Renaissance; in fact O'Neill represents the belated explosion in the American drama of themes and concerns that had first appeared in other literary genres in the nineteenth century. In her introduction to *Six Plays of Strindberg*, Elizabeth Sprigge [4] remarks that the "drama had, as usual, lagged behind the times," asserting as a fact of literary history that new ideas and concerns that first appear in the other genres, in the novel, for instance, have a tendency to show up last in the drama. Thus Shaw injected into the English drama preoccupations and concerns that had been agitating Victorian culture in the novel and poetry for decades: feminism, the nature of the relation between the sexes, marriage, the "new morality," social injustice, the workings of modern capital, socialism, the implications of modern science, the consequences of "the death of God," the meaning of history, the nature of the great man, teleology, and so on.

The analogy holds for O'Neill, but with the important difference that while there are many ideas, and discussions of ideas, in his plays, the ideas keep changing from play to play, and there is not, as in Shaw's plays, a consistent ideological pattern, nor is there the implication that ideas finally are of great or determining importance in human affairs. Rather, in considering O'Neill's plays in their totality and attempting to ascertain what they mean or signify, one feels that they contain an over-all quality, indefinable but unmistakable, that is not ideological at all. Profound, obscure, dark, tortuous, and powerful emotions are brooded over; no conclusions are reached; and we are finally presented with an ambiguity. In short, the O'Neill corpus suggests nothing so much as the complex tortuousness of classical American literature of the nineteenth century. Almost everything is there in O'Neill: Henry Adams' dynamo; Hawthorne's scenes in the spiritualizing moonlight and his New England family, ancestrally cursed and inhabiting a gloomy mansion from whose walls glare down the grim visages of the Puritan, witch-burning ancestors; Dana's folk material of sea life; Melville's "melting pot" crews and mystique of the sea; Whitman's "roughs"; Henry James, Sr.'s "Mother God"; and Poe's tubercular heroines, dope addiction, incest, alcoholism, icebergs, fog, and orangoutangs, all presided over by "the imp of the perverse" (Poe's *The Imp of the Perverse* was one of O'Neill's favorite stories, Gelbs, p. 613). That O'Neill himself was aware of his tradition is evidenced by the fact that one of his favorite quotations was Whitman's "Do I contradict myself? Very well, I contradict myself."

The basic resemblances were noted by some reviewers and critics virtually from the start, and some of the resemblances extended even to O'Neill's appearance and way of life. For example, the writer-artist, S. J. Woolf, who drew a portrait of O'Neill for the *New York Times Magazine*, described him as looking like Poe, "as if he were surrounded by an aura of mysterious sorrow" (Gelbs,

p. 871). On the other hand, and in a consideration of O'Neill's manner of life, Walter Pritchard Eaton saw him as a kind of Thoreau figure, the solitary who wrestled with his soul in the wilderness.[5]

In fact, O'Neill's life was veritably mythic in that over his long and varied travail he recapitulated in brief the lives of many other American writers of both the nineteenth and twentieth centuries. Not only did he look like Poe, he also at one time in his life *was* Poe: tubercular, down-and-out, alcoholic, and suicidal at "Jimmy-the-Priest's" saloon in 1912. During the whole early period of his life he was the friend and companion of the low and the lost and could have said with Whitman:

> I take for my love some prostitute—I pick out some
>     low person for my dearest friend
> He shall be lawless, rude, illiterate—he shall be one
>     condemned by others for deeds done.

Or with Emerson, "I embrace the common, I explore and sit at the feet of the familiar, the low." Like Fitzgerald, and so many American writers, he fought, and, unlike so many of them, won the battle of alcoholism. Like Parkman, he was for many years a seriously ill man who composed some of his greatest work under great stress and pain. Like Melville, he had a son who died by his own hand.

But, to put the other side, he had sailed before the mast, like Cooper, Melville, and Dana, and like them he later wrote about the sea. Like Thoreau (although O'Neill was married at the time), he had once lived a Thoreau-like existence in utter isolation in a remodeled Coast Guard Station on Cape Cod amidst trackless sand dunes that were bounded on the east, west, and south by "land unknown" and on the north by the Atlantic Ocean. For great periods of his life, no matter where he happened to be living at the time, he *was* the twentieth-century Thoreau, almost completely isolated from normal human society.

On the other hand, he was, like Mark Twain, a considerable financial success and, like Twain, a nationally and internationally known "personality," whose comings and goings were deemed worthy of the attention of the newspaper press. He had in fact once contemplated buying the Florentine-style villa in Stormfield, Connecticut, where Mark Twain had died in 1910. And he did buy a country estate at Ridgefield, Connecticut, and lived for a time as a country squire in the tradition of Cooper and Washington Irving, although we may assume that O'Neill's squire-archy was a much less placid one than that of either of his predecessors in this role. Later on he was to live an Edith Wharton-like existence in a château in France. Like Henry James, he lived for some years as an expatriate in Europe, but, like Henry James, Sr., he was incurably, although not uncritically, American and had finally to return to his native land.

He had been at one time or another a New Englander, a New Yorker, a Georgian (Sea Island), and a Californian: he died in Boston. Like so many American writers, he was an incurable wanderer, an Ishmael, but like Melville's Ishmael, he survived the wreck that was the final fate of many American writers in both the nineteenth and the twentieth centuries. When one thinks of the literary talent in America that has gone aground or been torpedoed or sunk in a tempest, or the promise that has petered out or failed, it is irresistible not to think that O'Neill was one of the very few who could have finally said, with Melville's Ishmael, "And I only am escaped alone to tell thee." (What O'Neill actually said—his dying words—was, "Born in a hotel room and, God damn it, died in a hotel room.") Perhaps only Henry James, of all other American writers, could have said the same.

The work is like the man, full of echoes of the American nineteenth century. Foreign critics were quick to see this. By the Germans especially he was thought to be, along with Poe and Whitman, a third authentic American genius and a third great artistic gift bestowed by America on Europe. American critics too could discern historical reverberations. Gilbert W. Gabriel, for instance, in his review of *The Great God Brown* in the New York *Sun* on January 25, 1926, remarked of the play: "Poesque in its impossibilities, violent under the strait jacket of theatrical restrictions" (Cargill et al., p. 176).

It is only, however, by detailed comparison with specific American writers of the nineteenth century that one can realize the startling resemblances between them and O'Neill, not only in the content but in the form. It is not my intention here, and it would require another book in itself, to enumerate every correspondence between O'Neill and the American writers of the nineteenth century. Rather I shall first present a detailed correlation between O'Neill and three of his predecessors, Henry Adams (in the *Education*), Melville, and Emerson, the hope being that these three writers are both distinctive enough in themselves and representative enough as a group to make my general points about O'Neill and the American nineteenth century; after each of the three comparisons, I shall try to show how the common themes discussed run through American literature at large.

Henry Adams and O'Neill coincide on the themes of the "doubleness" of life, on—a correlary of "doubleness" —New England as the home of the war between opposites, and, of course, on the dynamo. The sense of contrasts, of doubleness, that O'Neill saw in New England was one of the ground themes of *The Education of Henry Adams* whose author, if he regretted the barren sameness of the American scene at large and its consequent sterility for the writer (see Chapt. 2, Sec. ii above), attributed both the formation of his character and his mature intellectual interests to his New England boyhood: "The chief charm of New England was harshness of contrasts and extremes of sensibility—a cold that froze the blood, and a heat that boiled it—so that the pleasure of hating—one's self if no better victim offered—was not its rarest amusement" ("Quincy"). This sense of contrast and dualism, whose cosmic embodiment was the climate itself, ramified out into other pairs: winter was to summer, as cold was to heat, as town to country, and as force to freedom: "The double exterior nature gave life its relative values." The summer meant country, liberty, diversity, outlawry, and the endless delight of mere sense impressions, especially those of smell and taste. The town meant winter, confinement, school, rule, discipline, streets that were narrow, gloomy, and snow-packed, rigid relatives, restraint, law, and unity. Over it all presided a harsh presence that seemed to permeate the very atmosphere: "The New England light is glare, and the atmosphere harshens color." Bostonians could not help but develop a double sense, for life was "a double thing": "The bearing of the two seasons on the education of Henry Adams was no fancy;

it was the most decisive force he ever knew; it ran through life, and made the division between itself perplexing, the warring, irreconcilable problems, irreducible opposites, with growing emphasis to the last year of study. From earliest childhood the boy was accustomed to feel that, for him, life was double" (*ibid.*). Thus too O'Neill's New England play, *Beyond the Horizon,* was constructed on the principle of doubleness, in both its form and content, and has scenes occurring in both the extreme heat and the biting cold, with the appropriate emotions thereto, that Adams has indicated as being the polar extremes of the New England scene.

Similarly, Adams had, from childhood, a preoccupation with electrical force, the double power. As a child, magnets fascinated him and were his oldest and favorite toys. Later he covered his desk with magnets and read books on the subject of electricity. But the books "confounded" him although he was to remain all his life a kind of superstitious devotee or amateur adept of electrical power, especially of the dynamo, whose invention, he said, "passed belief." At the exhibition of the dynamos in Chicago in 1900 Adams experienced feelings and sensations that O'Neill attributed to Reuben Light in *Dynamo:* the dynamo as the symbol of infinity; the dynamo as a strange kind of moral force about which one felt as did the early Christians about the Cross; electricity as an absolute *fiat,* as in religious faith. As with O'Neill, it was the seemingly boundless and endless power of electricity that fascinated Adams. In the chapter entitled "Chicago" in his speculations about the development of power, Adams said that in most of the previous advances in man's dominion over natural forces one could calculate the future growth of the power, as with Cunard steamers or railroads. One could tell most about the course of power in the development of explosives, but it needed an army of chemists, physicists, and mathematicians to do the explaining. The dynamo, however, was the Mona Lisa of the powers. It had barely reached infancy but promised steady and constant growth of power up to the point where that power would be, literally, "infinite." At the same time the nature of electrical power was incomprehensible to the layman who could only understand things in terms of common-sense functions, such as pull or push, screw or thrust, flow or vibration, wire or mathematical line, but the phenomenon of electricity was not precisely explainable in any of these antithetical terms.

If electricity were power and mystery in the modern world for both Henry Adams and O'Neill, it was also paradox. One of the great dramatic contrasts in *Dynamo* is that between the soft, gentle hum of the dynamo and the terrifying power that this same gentle hum is generating. Similarly, at the Chicago exhibition Adams was moved to note that a baby could sleep by the dynamo which was "scarcely humming an audible warning to stand a hair's-breadth further for respect of its power—." Adams, intellectually, and O'Neill, dramatically, were searching for the center, the nexus, of the modern world. In America in particular this nexus would seem to reside in one of the many giant forces or powers that modern science had deciphered and harnessed. As artists, both writers were imaginatively archaic, and it was to a modern version of the ancient Promethean myth, the taming of fire, that each unerringly gravitated.

In many ways the Promethean figure is the tutelary god of American literary culture. Emerson calls Prometheus the Jesus of the old mythology and exclaims, concerning the myth itself, on its range of meanings and its perpetual pertinence ("History," the first essay of the First Series). And, as with so many other things that were to happen in American culture, the primitive genesis of this preoccupation can be glimpsed in Tocqueville's account of his American experiences.

In July of 1831 Tocqueville and Beaumont visited the wilderness, the authentic, untouched West in what is now the state of Michigan. July 26 had been a terrible day, with burning heat to endure and swarms of mosquitoes to fight off. The night that came on, with the mosquitoes still ubiquitous, was one of the "most painful" of Tocqueville's life, and fatigued as he was, he was unable to sleep. Toward midnight a storm that had long been threatening finally broke, and Tocqueville stepped outside his cabin into the now fresh air. The rain had not yet begun, but the forest was tossing and from it issued deep moans and long clamours. Periodically, the lightning illuminated the sky: "The quiet course of the Saginaw, the small clearing on its banks, the roofs of the five or six cabins, and the belt of enveloping foliage appeared then for an instant like a sublime evocation of the future. Then everything was lost in the most profound obscurity, and the formidable voice of the wilderness made itself heard again." [6] Tocqueville, moved by the tremendous spectacle, stood watching until he heard a sigh at his side and realized that an Indian was standing there and that the man, staring fixedly at the storm, was troubled. Tocqueville tried to reconstruct imaginatively the portentous message that the great voice of the wilderness was enunciating to the savage (p. 280):

> Was this man afraid of thunder? or did he see in the shock of the elements anything but a passing convulsion of nature? Did these fugitive images of civilization, which surged up of themselves in the tumult of the wilderness, have for him a prophetic meaning? Did these groans of the forest which seemed to be fighting an uneven battle, reach his ear like the secret warning of God, a solemn revelation of the final fate reserved to the savage races? I could not say. But his agitated lips seemed to be murmuring some prayers, and all his lineaments seemed graven with superstitious terror.

But the conquering white man was also to find majestic meanings in these displays of the power of God or Nature. In his chapter on Dana's *Two Years Before the Mast* in *Studies in Classic American Literature*, D. H. Lawrence remarked that electricity was the first, intrinsic principle among the Forces. For it seemed to have a mystic power of readjustment and was the overlord of the two naked elements, fire and water, capable of mysteriously putting the two together and, as easily and quickly, sundering them:

> When the two great elements become hopelessly clogged, entangled, the sword of lightning can separate them. The crash of thunder is really not the clapping together of waves of air. Thunder is the noise of the explosion which takes place when the waters are loosed from the elemental fire, when the old vapours are suddenly decomposed in the upper air by the electric force. Then fire flies fluid, and the waters roll off in purity. It is the liberation of the elements from hopeless conjunction. Thunder, the electric force, is the counterpart in the material-dynamic world of life-force, the creative mystery itself, in the creative world.

Lawrence then notes that Dana is "wonderful" at describing a tropical thunderstorm, giving a long quotation from Dana to prove the assertion, which it does. Lawrence concludes: "Dana is wonderful at relating these mechanical, or dynamic-physical events. He could not talk about the being of men: only about forces."

This is one of the central mystiques and one of the central scenes in the American fable: man involved in the furious display of God the Father with the voice of thunder announcing some powerful, although obscure, meaning: fearful, awesome, sublime, ecstatic. In this mighty grip man is both a Job and a Prometheus; he is simultaneously a tiny speck amidst the giant forces of the tumult in the skies and, in a sense, that universe itself, a participant in the sublime display, almost an orchestrator of the divine dissonances.

Almost everything ultimately appears in *Moby Dick*, and in *Moby Dick* especially is nature's most awesome display an actor in the drama with the protangonist, Ahab, the Promethean who steals the fire from the skies and subdues it to his will. In the great chapter "The Candles" Ahab, who calls himself here "Old Thunder," identifies himself, like Reuben in *Dynamo*, with the nocturnal clamor of the thunder and lightning. As the corposants light the mastheads and the compasses are reversed, Starbuck makes a desperate appeal to his mad captain to turn back and almost succeeds in rousing the crew who raise a "half mutinous cry." But Ahab transfixes them with his burning harpoon, and the fiery hunt rushes on to its fated consummation. As Lawrence says, "It is storm, the electric storm of the *Pequod*, when the corposants burn in high, tapering flames of supernatural pallor upon the masthead, and when the compass is reversed. After this all is fatality. Life itself is mystically reversed."

Climactic thunder and lightning—over the sea, over the prairie, over the forest, over the river, over the mountains —are a recurring phenomena in American literature, as in no other literature. From the thunder of God apostrophized by Cotton Mather in the *Magnalia*, to the rumbles in the Catskills immortalized by Washington Irving, to the flash of lightning that ends the sailors' brawl in the forecastle in *Moby Dick*, to the storm that reverberates through the Berkshires in "The Lightning Rod Man," to the lovely storm that is enjoyed by Huck and Jim in Chapter IV of *Huckleberry Finn*, to the thundercap at the end of *The Waste Land*, to the "thunder and lightning" of the guns in the mountains at the opening of *Farewell to Arms*, to the "faint flow of thunder" over Long Island Sound when Gatsby has lured Daisy to his mansion in *The Great Gatsby*, to Reuben Light of *Dynamo* standing on the open hillside at night during a thunderstorm, the displays of God the Father have been a constant chorus in the American drama, if reduced only to a faint hum in *The Education of Henry Adams*. What O'Neill did then in *Dynamo* was to repeat in miniature the evolution from Cotton Mather to Henry Adams: from thunder as the rumblings of God and lightnings as His flashings (Act I) to the crooning, awesome dynamo, with the power of the storm captured and subdued but still emblematic of supernatural power and significatory of mysterious moral or religious meanings (Act III). For in America the myth of Prometheus had finally found its natural habitat.

Of all other American writers it is Melville, as might be expected, to whom O'Neill has the most affinities, in the content, in the form, in the very language that he wrote. Appropriately, it is only Melville, of previous American writers, who is discussed at any length in an O'Neill play, specifically, in *Mourning Becomes Electra*. In *The Hunted*, the second play of the O'Neill trilogy, Orin Mannon tells his mother of having been lent a copy of *Typee* while in the Army and having read and reread the book until Melville's islands came to mean everything that was not war, everything that was peace, warmth, and security (II). Both *Diff'rent* and *Mourning Becomes Electra* employ the Melvillean contrast between the warm lure of the South Seas, its freedom, and uninhibited sexuality and the bleakness of New England with its rigid Puritanism (see above, Chap. 1, Sec. iii). Other Melville themes and preoccupations resound throughout the O'Neill corpus: the ship as a microcosm of human life (the early sea plays); the obsessed whaling captain with the younger wife (*Ile*), as well as other variations on the Ahab-figure (*Gold*, *Where the Cross Is Made*, and *Diff'rent*). The sea itself in O'Neill's plays has the same enormous and contradictory range of meanings that it does in Melville's works.

The central, mystical experience in life for each writer, which he put into his works again and again, was the inexpressible feeling of wonder and rapture of the experience of sailing, the feeling of One-ness and of being at the center of the All. In Redburn's words: "... [I] was lost in one delirious throb at the center of the All. A wild bubbling and bursting was at my heart; and my blood ran tingling along my frame, like mountain brooks in spring freshets" (*Redburn*, chap. 13). It is this same feeling that Paddy of *The Hairy Ape*, Adam Brant of *Mourning Becomes Electra*, and Edmund Tyrone of *Long Day's Journey Into Night* attempt to convey. Both writers apotheosized the age of sail and lamented the coming of steam (see above, Chap. I, Sec. iii). *Billy Budd* begins its idyllic prelude with the words "In the time before steamships, ..." As two of Melville's biographers remark: "In his last years, 'thrown more and more upon retrospective musings,' like his John Marr, Melville had become increasingly preoccupied with memories of his own earlier years and with reflections of that historic Past, 'in the time before steamships' that had come to seem infinitely grander and nobler than the prosaic Present." [7] And for both writers this stirring past was the era of the French Revolution.

The "melting pot" crew of *White Jacket, Redburn*, and *Moby Dick* reappears in all of the early O'Neill plays, as it does, becalmed, in *The Iceman Cometh*. Its concomitant, the attack on racial intolerance, best succinctly expressed in Melville's famous Anacharsis Cloots' metaphor, is a constant theme of both writers. Their respective noble savages, Queequeg in *Moby Dick* and Nano in *The Fountain*, have alike the same feeling that it is the mission of "savages" to Christianize the "Christians." The beauty and the power of the noble black man is evoked in both *The Emperor Jones* and the beginning of *Billy Budd*, wherein is glimpsed a magnificent African of "the unadulterate blood of Ham——."

The dying sailor of *White Jacket* reappears, in all his pathos, in *Bound East for Cardiff*. The lonely, bottom-dog, outsider, city-dweller is the protagonist of both *Bartleby* and *Hughie*. The terror of the city's infrequent silences that plays so crucial a role in *Hughie* is "heard" also in *Pierre:* When Isabel and Pierre arrive in the city, she exclaims, "Pierre, this silence is unnatural, is fearful. The forests are never so still" (XVI, 1).

Each author wrote his "Fourth of July story," *Israel Potter* and *Ah, Wilderness!* Both wrote autobiographical works with heroes who have fallen from innocence and are writing autobiographical novels about the experience (*Pierre* and *Days Without End*). Both wrote wild laments about the impossibilities of the male-female relationship (*Pierre* and *The Great God Brown*). Both wrote powerful and confusing works about disguised or masked characters who interchange psyches (*The Confidence Man* and *The Great God Brown*). Both wrote works in which the title is the key word and is reiterated, both straightforwardly and ironically, throughout the work as a whole (*The Confidence Man* and *Diff'rent*).

Considered as artists, as shapers, the two writers bear an unmistakable resemblance: the basic and primary symbols of black and white; the preoccupation with metaphors of flight—into the silence of interstellar spaces—and descent—into the infinite recesses of the psyche or down to the bottom of the ocean or immersion in the fog. Michael Cape of *Welded* and Melville's Ishmael shudder at the blank silence of space, while Melville's Pip and O'Neill's Edmund Tyrone find the inexpressible on the floor of the sea and in the bosom of the fog. For both writers, and men, the most terrible descent of all was that into the self. As Melville put it in *Pierre*: "Deep, deep, and still deep and deeper must we go, if we would find out the heart of man; descending into which is as descending a spiral stair in a shaft, without any end, and where that endlessness is only concealed by the spiralness of the stair, and the blackness of the shaft" (XXI, 2). Both men were preoccupied with the Lazarus-figure: O'Neill wrote a play about him and he crops up as simile and metaphor in *The Confidence Man* and other Melville novels. The Promethean myth and the fire from the skies, as noted above, fascinated both writers. When at the climax of *Pierre*, Pierre picks up the murderous pistols, he exclaims, "Ha! What wondrous tools Prometheus used, who knows? but more wondrous these, that in an instant, can unmake the topmost three-score-years-and-ten of all Prometheus' makings" (XXVI, 5).

As writers of prose, Melville and O'Neill had three, sometimes contradictory, impulses. First, they believed that somehow words alone could never fully express the true tumult of the soul and the inexhaustible variousness and contradictions of life. But, second, they tended to fly at the mark furiously, and hyperbole is the note of their work of their respective middle periods, as in *Moby Dick* or *The Great God Brown*, although each finally quieted down, with restraint being the keynote to the prose of both *Billy Budd* and *A Moon for the Misbegotten*, each, in its own way, a "resolution" for each writer. But, third, neither writer had one "style": O'Neill used a variety of speech levels, and Melville, particularly in *Moby Dick*, operated on a great range of literary levels. From work to work their respective styles varied enormously.

In larger outline, their generic resemblances to each other still prevail. Melville was a novelist with a strong dramatic impulse who frequently cast sections of his novels in dramatic form; O'Neill was a dramatist with a powerful narrative impulse who frequently in his plays "told stories." Both had a strong melodramatic urge. Both were restless and indefatigable experimenters, with the language itself and with their respective forms, although, again, each ended in convention: Melville in the *nouvelle*, O'Neill in the Aristotelian or Ibsenesque dramatic form. Both in mid-career were incredibly fecund and inventive, with each separate work bursting with the seed or the seedling of the work to come. A casual reference in one work becomes later a full-scale work on its own.

Their separate works often, although not always, tend to be "unfinished," neither perfect nor self-contained, but are rather like great chunks of reality, full of great beauties and often great flaws, that have been torn out of the chaos of existence, and given a life of their own but with the stigmata of the agony and toil of their birth still clinging to them, all visible on the printed page. In reading them, one almost participates in the writing of them, for the mistakes never quite disappear and the happy discoveries are always visible. Such writings as these are not, in Wordsworth's phrase, emotion recollected in tranquility but are the emotion itself, raw, at times formless, almost inarticulate, sometimes inchoate; they are the expressions of powerful imaginations that know no limit and raging emotions that know no stay. Banalities and profundities, ineptitude and brilliance, exist side by side. Both men could be tedious, repetitious, irritating, but seldom dull or vacuous. Melville's preoccupation at the end of *Pierre* with Enceladus, the giant who attempted the impossible, i.e., stormed heaven, and was defeated, is equally applicable to both writers as a mythic equivalent to their strivings.

When we come in the works of Melville and O'Neill to the heart of the matter, human character and the human relation, we find ambiguity in human nature, loneliness in the human situation, and, when human relations are formed, a constant diastole and systole between people, with love and indifference, attraction and repulsion going on and off like an electrical current.

Characterization in both O'Neill and Melville tends to run to two extremes (which often blend): either abstractions, types, practically allegorical figures, or, at the other extreme, insuperably complex multicharacters that all reside in one human psyche. Ahab himself is a good example of both tendencies. Considered from one angle, he is severe, stark, classical in outline: the Promethean figure, the whaling captain, and the mad old man whose fury constitutes a monomania so all-consuming as to devour his character. Yet like O'Neill's Ephraim Cabot, similarly stark and simple in outline, his character is also Dostoevskian in its complexity and contradictions. A mystic, a father (to Pip), a husband, a leader of men, a Moses, a Pyrrhonist, as tender as he is fierce, as full of self-doubt as he is of self-confidence, he is almost impossible to type. Like Con Melody, he has at least three characters, or so it seems to him. Looking at the doubloon, he exclaims: " '—three peaks as proud as Lucifer. The firm tower, that is Ahab; the volcano, that is Ahab; the courageous, the undaunted, the victorious fowl, that, too, is Ahab; all are Ahab; and this round gold is but the image of the rounder globe, which, like a magician's glass, to each and every man in turn but mirrors back his own mysterious self' " (XCIX). In short, in Melville, as in O'Neill, character is like the globe itself, simple and elemental when looked at in the large but infinitely complex upon closer examination.

At the same time this simple-complex character exists in a kind of cosmic aloneness which is his natural state. In all of *Moby Dick* only three characters even faintly enter into human contact with Ahab, principally Starbuck and Pip and, to an even lesser degree, Stubb. But at the climax of the book Pip has gone mad, and Ahab rejects the others, and mankind: " '—Begone! Ye are the opposite poles of one thing; Starbuck is Stubb reversed, and Stubb is Starbuck; and ye two are mankind; and Ahab stands alone among the millions of the peopled earth; nor Gods nor men his neighbors! Cold, cold—I shiver!' " So Dion Anthony in *The Great God Brown* or Con Melody in *A Touch of the Poet* or Mary and Edmund Tyrone in *Long Day's Journey Into Night*. At the end of Act II, Scene 2, of *Long Day's Journey* Mary Tyrone, alone, says of her departed men, "You're glad they're gone. *She gives a little despairing laugh.* Then Mother of God, why do I feel so lonely?"

When these characters do enter into human contact, the relationship is never stable but fluctuates constantly between withdrawal into a solitary state and the equally real, if less powerful, desire to enter into communion and love with another human being. The perfectly analogous situations in Melville and O'Neill, *Moby Dick* and *Ile*, have this ambiguity at their center: the monomaniac captains momentarily torn between their psyche's grim and lonely drive and the communism of their softer feelings for a fellow being.

[KEENEY.] (*holds her [his wife] out at arms length, his expression softening. For a moment his shoulders sag, he becomes old, his iron spirit weakens as he looks at her tear-stained face.*)

K E E N E Y    [*dragging out the words with an effort*]    I'll do it, Annie—for your sake—if you say it's needful for ye.

But the ice breaks up, and Keeney drives on after the whales, as his wife, hitherto teetering on the verge, goes insane.

The emotional constellation is almost identical in "The Symphony" chapter of *Moby Dick*, as Ahab speaks:

"Oh Starbuck! it is a mild, mild wind and a mild looking sky. On such a day—very much such a sweetness as this—I struck my first whale.... whole oceans away, from that young girl-wife I wedded past fifty, and sailed for Cape Horn the next day, leaving but one dent in my marriage pillow—wife? wife?—rather a widow with her husband alive! Aye, I widowed that poor girl when I married her, ..."

"What is it, what nameless, inscrutable, unearthly thing is it; what cozzening, hidden lord and master, and cruel remorseless emperor commands me; that against all natural lovings and longings, I do keep pushing, and crowding, and jamming myself all the time; . . ."

But he concludes:

"Sleep? Aye, and rest amid greenness; as last years scyths flung down, and left in the half-cut swaths—Starbuck!"
But blanched to a corpse's hue with despair, the Mate has stolen away.

Ringed with incertitude, human life becomes in both Melville's and O'Neill's respective worlds a highly problematical affair, seen variously as a dream, or a mystery, or an ambiguity: " 'It is all a dream—we dreamed that we dreamed a dream' " (*Pierre*, XIX, 2). "Now Pierre began to see mysteries interpierced with mysteries, and mysteries eluding mysteries" (VII, 8). Attracted to the mysterious Isabel, Pierre feels a range of impalpable emotions: "For over all these things, and interfusing itself with the sparkling electricity in which she seemed to swim, was an ever-creeping and condensing haze of ambiguities" (VIII, 3).

Identity itself disappears: "What are you? What am I? Nobody knows who anybody is" (*The Confidence Man*, chap. 36). And it must all end, the whole story, on a question mark: "Something further may follow of this Masquerade" (*The Confidence Man*, last sentence).

This "doubt of identity" that occurs in the work of O'Neill and Melville runs like a skein through American literature. It was Mark Twain's obsessive theme and appears throughout his work in the constant preoccupation with doubles or twins who often exchange roles and, in a sense, psyches. Twain's concern with the ambiguities of the Southern classifications of the white man and the black man is an analogous preoccupation. These two preoccupations coalesce in *Pudd'nhead Wilson*, Twain's darkest and most ambiguous novel, built on the principle of Chinese boxes, twin and twin and white and black being so thoroughly confused and confounded that finally the only reliable index of individual identity is the tiny whorl marks at the tips of the human fingers. To go to the other end of the scale—from Mark Twain—Henry James's John Marcher in *The Beast in the Jungle* (James's *Bartleby* or *Hughie*) is always "lost" in the crowd. He is "*the*" man of his time to whom nothing has ever happened, and he longs for a disaster to give him an identity; for it is a "failure not to be anything." The *Beast in the Jungle* is in many respects the great *nouvelle* on American somnambulism. As in *Hughie*, only two, infinitely lonely, infinitely sad, people inhabit this eerie world where nothing ever happens and no one is ever clearly defined. The guiding scenic metaphor is of a stream (life) on which drift a few, vaguely discernable boats (humans). They may occasionally touch the shore and one another but only tangentially in space and fitfully in time. In Wallace Stevens' words:

> "Let the place of the solitaires
> Be a place of perpetual undulation."

A correlative theme of the doubt of identity is that of the interchange of energy between individuals—one of O'Neill's persistent concerns (see Chap. III, Sec. iii)—as one borrows the strength and, in a sense, the persona of another. It is a theme common to both James's *The Sacred Fount* and Fitzgerald's *Tender Is the Night*. The phenomenon is dramatized with great power, and confusion, in *The Great God Brown*, wherein is also given, by Dion Anthony, one of the most powerful utterances in the language on this persistent "doubt of identity" (Prologue):

> Why am I afraid to dance, I who love music and rhythm and grace and song and laughter? Why am I afraid to live, I who love life and the beauty of the flesh and the living colors of earth and sky and sea? Why am I afraid of love, I who love? Why am I afraid, I who am not afraid? Why must I pretend to scorn in order to pity? Why must I be so ashamed of my strength, so proud of my weakness? Why must I live in a cage like a criminal, defying and hating, I who love peace and friendship? Why was I born without a skin, O God, that I must wear armor in order to touch or to be touched?

For the American man was both Everything and Nothing and was therefore a walking contradiction. In Whitman's famous words:

> One's-self I sing, a single separate person,
> Yet utter the word Democratic, the word En-masse.

If we translate all this duality and doubt, in Melville,

Henry Adams, and O'Neill, into philosophical terms, out comes the darker, more solipsistic, pessimistic, skeptical side of Emerson.[8] To wit:

"There is a crack in every thing God has made."
EMERSON, "Compensation"
"Man is born broken. He lives by mending. The Grace of God is glue."
BROWN, *The Great God Brown* (IV, 1)
"Nothing is left to us now but death. We look to that with a grim satisfaction, saying, there at least is reality that will not dodge us."
EMERSON, "Experience"
"Life is too much for me! I'll be a weak fool looking with pity at the two sides of everything till the day I die! (*With an intense bitter sincerity*) May that day come soon! (*He pauses startledly, surprised at himself—then with a sardonic grin*) Be God, I'm the only real convert to death Hickey made here. From the bottom of my coward's heart I mean that now!"
LARRY SLADE, *The Iceman Cometh* (IV)
"Where do we find ourselves? In a series of which we do not know the extremes, and believe that it has none."
EMERSON, *"Experience"*
"I ain't on oith and I ain't in heaven, get me? I'm in de middle tryin' to separate 'em, takin' all de woist punches from bot' of 'em."
YANK, *The Hairy Ape* (VIII)

Most American writers have several faces, and Emerson is no exception. There is the benign, sagacious, shrewd, self-reliant Yankee; there is the mystic, the prophet, the seer; there is the great individualist and the spokesman for his nation; and so on. But there is still another Emerson who is often overlooked by both friends and detractors, and with this Emerson we go echoing down, in John Lydenberg's words,[9] "the echoing corridors of American horror," hearing, among other voices, "the despair in O'Neill . . ."; in fact we are in the world of *The Great God Brown* or *The Iceman Cometh* or *Long Day's Journey Into Night*. But to demonstrate this, it will be necessary to stop referring to O'Neill for a while and reconstruct Emerson from this point of view.

Emerson is virtually impossible, in my estimation, to summarize or synthesize although many valiant attempts have been made.[10] And this difficulty does not arise from the fact that he did not organize his essays logically. The real causes lie deeper. First, his thought is full of undefined abstractions or generic terms. Did Emerson know, asked Santayana rhetorically, what he meant by those terms, so constantly on his lips, Nature, Law, God, Benefit, or Beauty? [11] But, second, Emerson continually swooped down from these vaguenesses to the most prosaic of material facts. Thus his argument is fundamentally and initially split by his choice of words. Third, as a seer or mystic, he often casts his utterances in plain paradox, e.g., "Nature is a mutable cloud which is always and never the same" ("History"). Fourth, the argument itself is usually a series of assertions and counterassertions, generally a negative and a positive. In short, insofar as it is possible to ascertain a clear-cut movement in Emerson's imagination, this movement is indisputably polar, as he himself kept insisting: "*POLARITY*, or action and reaction, we meet in every part of nature"; "Whilst the world is thus dual, so is every one of its parts." "All things are double, are against the other.—Tit for tat; an eye for an eye, a tooth for a tooth; blood for blood; measure for measure; love for love—" ("Compensation"). "Motion or change, and identity or rest, are first and second secrets of nature: Motion and Rest" ("Nature"). No matter how often he affirmed, ecstatically and wishfully, the existence of "The Over-Soul," "the eternal *ONE*," "the ever-blessed *ONE*," he is always thrown back on these inescapable dualities, which he often images, as did Henry Adams, Melville, and O'Neill, as electricity: "The law of nature is alternation forevermore. Each electrical state superinduces its opposite" ("Friendship"). Other analogies for this basic movement are the systole-diastole of the heart and the inhalation and exhalation of the breath.

As Sherman Paul points out in *Emerson's Angle of Vision*, Emerson tried to bridge this perpetual gap with his doctrine of correspondences,[12] yet, so it appears to me, his thought always remained in the same basic form: two extremes with a blank or void in the middle. So Emerson could never get around this last, irreducible, unyielding antinomy which was carried to him by the very action of his heart and breath. And whenever he affirmed this bedrock polarity, he did sound, as contrasted to his misty assertions about the One, convincing: "All things are in contact; every atom has a sphere of repulsion;—Things are, and are not, at the same time; and the like. All the universe over, there is *but one thing* [italics added],—this old Two-Face, creator-creature, mind-matter, right-wrong, of which any proposition may be affirmed or denied" ("Nominalist and Realist"). He did not, of course, always regard this dualism as the human predicament. Sometimes it is only his dispassionate way of scientifically describing the true nature of things. Or it could be a beneficent force for the reason that the perpetual contest called forth their best efforts from the contestants, who are conceived of not as opposites but as complements, like male and female or spirit and act: "The fact of two poles, of two forces, centripetal and centrifugal, is universal, and each force by its own activity develops the other" ("Politics").

Some of the time, however, the perpetual systole-diastole is between human goods and evils, which are seen to be exactly equal, as in "Compensation" or sadly disequal, as in "Experience." But even in the more generally benign sounding essays, the eternal note of sadness always enters in. Thus it is in "Friendship" that he remarks, "We walk alone in the world"; in "Love," "It is strange how painful is the actual world—the painful kingdom of time and place. There dwells care and canker and fear"; in "Spiritual Laws," " 'My children,' said an old man to his boys scared by a figure in the dark entry, 'my children, you will never see anything worse than yourselves' "; in "The Poet," "The fate of the poor shepherd, who, blinded and lost in the snow-storm, perishes in a drift within a few feet of the cottage door, is an emblem of the state of man. On the brink of the waters of life and truth, we are miserably dying."

Accordingly, by tracing out the pessimistic counterpoint in Emerson's essays, it is possible to reconstruct a world remarkably similar to that of Melville and O'Neill. It is a universe something like this: [13] Nature is either despotic or fluid, and in his relationship to it man suffers from a fatal dislocation. Man's own source is hidden and he knows not whence he comes. He inherits, however, a frightening biological destiny by which the sins of the fathers are visited on the sons, generation after generation. Every violation of nature by one generation means expiation by the next. This necessity girds the human race: "A lockjaw that bends a man's head back to his heels; hydrophobia that makes him bark at his wife and babes; insanity that makes him eat grass; war, plague, cholera, famine, indicate a certain ferocity in nature, which, as it had its inlet by human crime, must have its outlet by human suffering. Unhappily almost no man exists who has not in his own person become to some amount a stockholder in the sin, and so made himself liable to a share in the expiation" ("Heroism").

Man is thus born into a state of war and should come armed, but unfortunately he does not. Fate and history alike have him at their mercies, and men are like ships, "battered by the waves, . . ." ("Intellect"). In himself he is superficial, weak, wasteful, and never wholly sane. He learns nothing, even from sorrow: "The only thing grief has taught me, is to know how shallow it is" ("Experience"). He is completely victimized by his capricious moods. By virtue of existing he is faced with and must choose between conditions of mind by which he can either enjoy repose but not thought or struggle with restless thought without repose. When he looks back on his own past, he sees it covered with "a slime of error" ("Love"). When he observes his fellow man, he sees the fellow as stronger, more powerful and virtuous than he, but, if he only knew it, the other man is thinking precisely the same of him. Both are fearful of one another. At best his relations to his fellows are oblique and casual, and human beings are like "globes which touch only in a point, . . ." ("Experience").

When he looks out to society at large, he sees one vast conspiracy against the individual and a gigantic game of convention which is like blindman's buff. "They" are hardly identifiable, individually anyway, but "melt so fast into each other that they are like grass and trees, and it needs an effort to treat them as individuals" ("Nominalist and Realist"). In America in particular society is threatened with actual granulation. Society means the city, which deadens the senses and breeds faintheartedness, corruption, and effeminacy; still if the city is fatal, "Solitude is impracticable, . . ." ("Society and Solitude").

Over both government and property bodes the carrion crow, Fear, that obscene bird. Americans generally are a puny and a fickle folk, lacking Faith and Hope and diseased by avarice, hesitation, and following; "Democracy is morose, and runs to anarchy, . . ." ("Nominalist and Realist"). It is run by the majority, and "the majority are wicked . . ." ("Considerations by the Way"). In American life private opinion is virtually lacking and public opinion tyrannical (when Emerson came to name the things men quake in fear at, he named first "public opinion," and after that, threat of assault, contumely, bad neighbors, poverty, mutilation, rumor of murder, and murder ["Character"]).

The State or government offers no hope, for every actual State is, almost by definition, "corrupt" ("Politics"). In America in particular *"politics"* is a synonym for *"cunning."* In the leading men there is no sincerity, and in the respective major parties no decent alternative: "The spirit of our American radicalism is destructive and aimless; it is not loving, it has no ulterior and divine ends; but is destructive only out of hatred and selfishness. On the other side, the conservative party, composed of the most moderate, able, and cultivated part of the population, is timid, and merely defensive of property" ("Politics"). Thus the one party has the better principles and the worser men, while the other has the better men and the worser principles. Neither will do anything to promote the common good in any way, nothing to foster freedom, science, art, or humanity. The poet and the lawgiver are forever separate, and the promises of both parties are like western roads which open in a stately fashion with planted trees on either side: they tempt the traveler, but they soon become narrower and narrower and end in a squirrel track and finally run up a tree. Washington, the first president, is to be envied for lying forever safe, wrapped in his shroud, where he can never observe "the meanness of our politics" ("Heroism"). Surveying America (in the year 1877), one wonders if "our corruption in this country has not gone a little over the mark of safety, . . . The divine knowledge has ebbed out of us and we do not know enough to be free" ("Perpetual Forces").

Thrown back on himself, the individual searches within for some stability and system of values. But he finds that all values are relative. One man's justice is another man's injustice; one man's beauty, another's ugliness; and so on: "There is no virtue which is final; all are initial. The virtues of society are the vices of the saint" ("Circles"). Neither are there any ultimate facts, for every fact that appears final is only the first of a new series, and every general law only a particular fact of some more general law which will presently disclose itself. Perhaps culture is the answer? But culture ends in "headache" ("Experience"). Dedication to thought is quickly "odious," for we need "change of objects" (*ibid.*). Man longs to escape into some great, strong, central tendency, the substance of things hoped for and the promise of things unseen. But he cannot find it, and this is why his "bards love wine, mead, narcotics, coffee, tea, opium, the fumes of sandalwood and tobacco, or whatever other species of animal exhilaration" ("The Poet"). "Dreams and drunkenness, the use of opium and alcohol are the semblance and counterfeit of ... oracular genius and hence their dangerous attraction for men" ("Circles").

What finally emerges down in the depths of Emersonian diastole is the Dion Anthony-Pierre figure, for whom life, at once so complex and so insubstantial, has become phantasmagoric; as "Experience" puts it: "Dreams deliver us to dream, and there is no end to illusion." "Life itself is a bubble and a scepticism, and a sleep within a sleep." It is a drama in which, as in *Pierre* or *The Iceman Cometh*, humanity has passed beyond good and evil. Looked at in the long view men dwindle into little manikens of whom one does not know what to make. In the Emersonian parable (Minerva is speaking): "they were only ridiculous little creatures, with this odd circumstance, that they had a blur or indeterminate aspect, seen far or seen near; if you called them bad, they would appear so; if you called them good they would appear so; and there was no one person or action among them, which would not puzzle her owl, much all Olympus, to know whether it was fundamentally bad or good" ("Manners").

As mankind itself is, in his own fable of Minerva, so many of Emerson's essays are frankly ambiguous. The form of "Experience," and to a lesser degree the form of the other essays, such as "Circles," is that of a tragi-comedy, so bleak in so much of the implications of the body of the thought as a whole, so bland in the conclusion: "Never mind the ridicule, never mind the defeat: up again, old heart!" ("Experience"). But the two opposing strains of thought are not dialectical or complementary: they just contradict one another.

The ambiguous document is yet another distinctive mark of American culture, and along with the "Who am I?" that characters in an American novel ask themselves, there is an analogous, "What does it all mean?" which is asked by the reader. Every major American author has written at least one document that is either frankly ambiguous in its entirety, like *The Sacred Fount* or *The Marble Faun* or *The Confidence Man* or *The Great God Brown*, or ones that have ambiguous elements, or ones that have an ambiguous ending, like *The Portrait of a Lady* or *The Wings of the Dove* or *The Mysterious Stranger* or *Dynamo*. Very often these ambiguities are caused by an habitual movement from one extreme to another, as in Emerson. Thus Henry L. Mencken: "It may be, as they say, we Americans lie in the gutter of civilization, but all the while our eyes steal cautious glances at the stars." [14] Or Sinclair Lewis: "Such magnificence of self-consciousness and duty-mongering and hysterical bounding to extremes may be in all its richness to be found only in our sturdy land." [15]

For most American phenomena present the ambiguous form of two extremes without a "middle term," as has often been remarked. The most acute observer of the whole process is still Tocqueville, and one of the ground themes of *Democracy in America* is the American "split" which Tocqueville saw even in the most unlikely places. For example, about public monuments Tocqueville wrote, "Thus democracy not only leads men to a vast number of inconsiderable productions; it also leads them to raise some monuments on the largest scale; but between these two extremes there is a blank." [16] In industrial activities American efforts called forth an innumerable multitude of small undertakings and a few things of marvelous "grandeur" (II, ii, 19). Political oratory flew to two rhetorical extremes, either the extremely minute and clear, or the extremely general and vague: "what lies between is a void" (II, i, 18). This was to be the fate—two extremes with a blank in the middle—of all things in America, from its public monuments to its literature, right from the start, and was to continue, irrespective of century. But to see the full impli-

cation for O'Neill of this generalization, we must turn to
Tocqueville's full analysis.

## iii  *American Culture*

In the epic of American culture, Tocqueville is
like Michael in Book XII of *Paradise Lost:* he foretells the
whole story in advance. In fact, not Emerson but Tocqueville seems to have invented Whitman, as well as most
other American writers. Many of the most distinctive
characters and themes of American literature make their
first appearance in print in the pages of *Democracy in
America* and very often in sections where Tocqueville is
not discussing literature itself.

For example, of the American girl Tocqueville observed
(II, iii, 9):

> Long before an American girl arrives at the marriageable
> age, her emancipation from maternal control begins; she
> has scarcely ceased to be a child when she already thinks
> for herself, speaks with freedom, and acts on her own im-
> pulse. The great scene of the world is constantly open to
> her view; far from seeking to conceal it from her, it is every
> day disclosed more completely and she is taught to survey
> it with a firm and calm gaze. Thus the vices and dangers
> of society are early revealed to her; as she sees them clearly,
> she views them without illusion and braves them without
> fear, for she is full of reliance on her own strength, and her
> confidence seems to be shared by all around her.

Here then is an abstract picture of Daisy Miller, Isabel
Archer, and a whole gallery of Jamesian heroines, as well
as the subject or theme of *The Awkward Age.*

Or, again, Tocqueville on the ever-receding promise of
American life (II, ii, 13):

> Among democratic nations, men easily attain a certain
> equality of condition, but they can never attain as much
> as they desire. It perpetually retires from before them, yet
> without hiding itself from their sight, and in retiring draws
> them on. At every moment they think they are about to
> grasp it; it escapes at every moment from their hold. They
> are near enough to see its charms, but too far off to enjoy
> them; and before they have fully tasted its delights, they die.

Here is the story and the fate of the Great Gatsby, *and*
the last paragraph of Fitzgerald's novel:

Gatsby believed in the green light, the orgiastic future that year by year recedes before us. It eluded us then, but that's no matter—tomorrow we will run faster, stretch our arms further.... And one fine morning—
So we beat on, boats against the current, borne back ceaselessly into the past.

I propose here to look at the Tocquevillean forecasts and the dramas of O'Neill from three, ever-broadening aspects: first, from the perspective of Tocqueville's specific remarks on the drama in America; second, from that of his general remarks on literature; and, third, from the general point of view of his analysis of the nature of man in America.

In his specific observations on the drama among democratic nations Tocqueville ran up against one of the continuing ambiguities of his subject matter, namely, that he was simultaneously making broad observations about the nature of democracies in general and specific, empirical remarks about a particular, historical democracy, the American. Thus he had a theoretical conception that the drama would be the foremost or at least the most popular art in a democracy. But in America it was not, the reason being that the Puritan founders had frowned, especially, on the stage, and this cultural prohibition still hung on. Thus while American laws allowed, in Tocqueville's eyes, the utmost freedom, American dramatic authors were singled out for censorship, and theatrical performances could only take place by permission of municipal authorities. In a quite precise way O'Neill experienced both sides of Tocqueville's antinomy: he was both extraordinarily popular and on several occasions was either banned or threatened with banning by municipal authorities.

More specifically, Tocqueville prophesied that the condition of the drama in a democracy would exhibit the following characteristics (their relevance to O'Neill should be obvious): that in the drama would be seen most of the good qualities and all the defects of a democratic culture; that the audience would wish to see a medley of conditions, feelings, and opinions enacted before their eyes and that as a consequence the democratic drama, as contrasted to the more lofty, regulated, and austere aristocratic drama, would be "more striking, more vulgar, and more true" (II, i, 19); that there would be anarchic license in choice of subject as well as in treatment of subject; that not the subtle pleasures of the mind but the keen emotions of the heart would be most prized; that purely literary merits or distinction of language would be completely set aside and all that would be asked of dramatic language is that it be written correctly enough to be understood; and that in the making of the dramatic plot it would not be regularity or symmetry that would be desired but rather perpetual novelty, surprise, and rapidity of invention.

Tocqueville's more general and more well-known remarks on the nature of democratic literature and language are equally applicable to O'Neill: no rules for art, or at least no permanent ones; no learned researches; no subtle beauties; the conjuring up of strong and rapid emotions; startling passages; the constant parade of truths or errors brilliant enough always to rouse the audience; the tendency to plunge the audience at once—as if by "violence" —into the midst of the subject; all this in a language that would be fantastic, incorrect, overburdened, loose, bold, and vehement. The language itself would have a partiality for generic terms and abstract expressions.

The subject matter of democratic literature, said Tocqueville, would be driven in two contrary directions: up and out: up into the clouds of metaphysical fancy and out into terrestrial universality, that is, a concern with the destinies of mankind; and down and in: into the recesses of the individual soul, in order "to throw light on some of the obscurer recesses of the human heart" (II, i, 17). These twin tendencies would be both its glory and its bane. The authors would constantly have to be reaching outward and upward, forced by their ambition to abandon the great in order to reach the gigantic. Their creations would be surcharged with "immense and incoherent energy, with exaggerated descriptions and strange creations; . . . the fantastic beings of their brain may sometimes make us regret the world of reality" (II, i, 18). This predicted flight to the stars and plunge into the psyche is, of course, the characteristic movement of American literature generally. What Tocqueville meant by saying that at times this inward obsession would breed monsters can be illustrated, at random, by a metaphor from James's *The Middle Years:* "He dived once more into his story and was drawn down, as by a siren's hand, to where, in the dim underground of fiction, the great glazed tank of art, strange, silent subjects float."

But *Democracy in America* in many ways tells more about American literature and O'Neill when considered in its entirety and as a psychological document, that is, as a vast assemblage of empirical observations on the nature of man in America. To see this one must bypass both Tocqueville's generalizations about American politics and society and his ubiquitous and ambiguous "égalité" and "démocratie," which are used so variously and in such varying contexts as to make most existing English translations of Tocqueville into problematical documents in important respects. If *Democracy in America* is considered as a prolonged psychognosis, many types of Americans emerge, but most prominent are two polar types: the happy bourgeoise and the skeptical doubter, or, to put it in terms of O'Neill's plays, the characters and the mood of *Ah, Wilderness!* and the characters and mood of *The Iceman Cometh* or *Long Day's Journey Into Night*. (It should be added that these two types are not a conscious creation on Tocqueville's part, as he generally speaks of Americans as a generic species. Rather it is my conscious reconstruction from *Democracy* and from the Notebooks of his various empirical observations, which like almost everything else in the subject under consideration tend to split in two.)

What was most striking to foreign eyes and ears about the America of 1831 was the bustle, cheer, optimism, and energy that paraded before the eyes of the observer, for here was a nation that was futuristic in its fundamental orientation, full of good sense, good will, and great expectations, racing along, ahead of history, creating the future and transforming nature. Fate and the past had been banished, and Destiny had been taken by the scruff of the neck. Howsoever powerful and impetuous the course of time or history was in the United States, the human imagination always went well in advance of it, and the picture ("tableau") was never large enough. No country in the world had ever so confidently taken charge of the future or felt such pride that it could fashion the universe to please itself. For the first time in history, Tocqueville said, "it is nature that changes, while man is unchanging." [17]

Fortune's wheel, Fortuna, Chance, Change, all the terrible instabilities of human existence that man had feared and had tried to propitiate from the time that he had first advanced to the threshold of thought were in America embraced, even enshrined, for the American was accustomed only to chance and ended by looking on it as the natural state of man. Instability instead of causing him disasters seemed only to bring forth wonders. Human fate then became a great lottery in which the American entered in the spirit of a gambler who had nothing to lose but his winnings. Passivity, which had been the traditional human stance in the face of Destiny, had given way to a cosmic restlessness which had been set off first three centuries ago in Europe during the age of exploration and which had been mightily reinforced in early nineteenth-century America by the awakening awareness of the vast, rich continent to the West that awaited the dominion of the white man. Out into this immense, silent wilderness went the new men, the pioneers, the supreme individualists, members of a restless, reasoning, adventurous race, at once cold and passionate "who shut themselves in the American solitudes with an axe and some newspapers" (Pierson, p. 244).

This was the macrocosm, but even in the microcosm of daily existence one could perceive the same ferment at work. As the western spaces were silent with a profundity that startled the European, the eastern cities were alive with a human hum that the European had never heard. The political activity that pervaded America had to be seen to be understood: it was a kind of perpetual tumult with thousands of simultaneous voices demanding the satisfaction of their social wants. Moreover, Tocqueville genuinely liked these people: "I have lived much with the people of the United States, and I cannot express how much I admire their experience and good sense" (I, 17). They loved God, order, sobriety, education (universal and state-supported), regularity in conduct, and marriage. In no country in the world was the conjugal tie more respected or marital joys so highly and worthily appreciated. Their women were superb, and Tocqueville said that if he were to answer the question as to what power in society gave Americans their singular prosperity and growing strength, he would attribute it, as later on would Emerson and

Henry James, to the superiority of their women. The world that passed before American eyes was a steady march of public order and public prosperity, and the individual American could not imagine that the one could exist without the other. Most Europeans have to unlearn their early education, since it does not tell them the truth about public matters, but the American had nothing to unlearn.

In short, here is the world, both the characters and the social background, of O'Neill's *Ah, Wilderness!*, which when it was first produced almost completely bemused O'Neill's critics who could not reconcile the dark genius of the American drama with this gentle comedy and thought O'Neill had turned into Booth Tarkington. But O'Neill was serious about the play, that is, he did not think he was idealizing and glorifying the Millers and their America; in fact he said, in a famous statement about the play (see Chapter 2, Sec. iii) that theirs was "the real America" of the turn of the century. It is true that the bourgeois world is one that is seldom, if ever, portrayed in serious American literature, which, in effect, either denies its existence or, if admitting its existence, denounces it in the fashion of O'Neill in his other surburban play, *The First Man*. Even O'Neill himself came to feel finally that *perhaps* he was not dealing with anything serious in the play, and in a letter to Lawrence Langner expressed some doubts: ". . . [*Ah, Wilderness!*] is out of my previous line. Has it got something finer to it than its obvious surface value—a depth of mood and atmosphere, so to speak, that would distinguish it from another play of the same genre, the usual type? I felt it had when I wrote it. (Nathan, for example, says most emphatically yes.) But now, frankly, . . ." (Gelbs, p. 769). But it was real, this world, as Tocqueville, the least superficial of observers, had attested in the 1830's and O'Neill, the least superficial of writers, attested in the 1930's. Of all great American writers in the dramatic (or novelistic) mode only O'Neill has taken this world seriously and immortalized it in an enduring literary document. As such, O'Neill was in part, as he himself admitted, like Thomas Mann: the *bourgeoise manqué*, and could have said of himself what Tonio Kröger does say of himself in the letter to Lisabeta in the last pages of Mann's story (H. T. Lowe-Porter, trans.):

As I write, the sea whispers to me and I close my eyes. I am looking into a world unborn and formless, that needs to be ordered and shaped; I see into a whirl of shadows of human figures who beckon to me to weave spells to redeem them: tragic and laughable figures and some that are both together—and to these I am drawn. But my deepest and secretest love belongs to the blond and blue-eyed, the fair and living, the happy, lovely, and commonplace.

Do not chide this love, Lisabeta; it is good and fruitful. There is longing in it, and a gentle envy; a touch of contempt and no little innocent bliss.

And thus if the American "dream" bred nightmares, it also bred, literally—for O'Neill claimed to have dreamed the play in one night [18]—an idyll in *Ah, Wilderness!*

But, in D. H. Lawrence's phrase, the American soul was a "torn, divided monster," sometimes happy, sometimes sick. Thus the benign, avuncular O'Neill who dashed off in a few weeks *Ah, Wilderness!*, the story of the youth he would have liked to have had, was also the tortured O'Neill who at this same period in his life, in the early 1930's, was struggling with the torments and unanswerable questions of *Days Without End*, whose very essence, up to its lamented conclusion, so agonizingly arrived at after attempts at so many other equally unsatisfactory conclusions, is doubt and incertitude.

So, too, when Tocqueville looked at the American from another angle, he saw the other half of Lawrence's "divided monster." For if the American circumstance had given birth to a new kind of happiness and certitude, it had also given birth to a new kind of unhappiness and incertitude. America had bred both an unprecedented number of "yes's" and an unprecedented number of "but's." Not that—it should be said (although Tocqueville does not expressly say it)—other nations or cultures were without their paradoxes and ambiguities. On the contrary, they had usually been founded on an ambiguity and consecrated, if consecrated at all, in doubt. But the ambiguities tended to become buried under masses of history or blended into the richness of customs or blurred by the infinite variety of an aristocratic society, which, of course, made no pretense of being logical anyway. But in America, under Tocqueville's acute gaze, the national ambiguities seemed naked, open, and on the surface, showing in the very faces of the Americans themselves: "In America I saw the freest and most enlightened men placed in the happiest circumstances that the world affords; it seemed to me as if a cloud habitually hung upon their brow, and I thought them serious and almost sad, even in their pleasures" (II, ii, 13). Thus if the American could always find his fortune, he could seldom find happiness. It was the most crassly materialistic of civilizations, yet there was always the sudden, surprising impulse to "soar impetuously towards heaven" (II, ii, 12), and there was an unusually high incidence of religious insanity. Again, "The Americans, who almost always preserve a staid demeanor and a frigid air, nevertheless frequently allow themselves to be borne away, far beyond the bounds of reason, by a sudden passion or a hasty opinion and sometimes *gravely commit strange absurdities* (II, iii, 15; italics added). Prosaic common sense disrupted by fitful, inexplicable outbursts of irrationality is exactly the same blend that Lawrence described repeatedly in *Studies in Classic American Literature*, the literary equivalent to *Democracy in America*, and which though primarily a work of literary analysis is also, like *Democracy in America*, an essay on the nature of man in America. Thus Lawrence on the Tocquevillean paradox: "America is tense with latent violence and resistance. The very common sense of white Americans has a tinge of helplessness in it, and deep fear of what might be if they were not common-sensical" ("Fenimore Cooper's Leatherstocking Novels").

In Tocqueville's somber analysis, especially in the more philosophical and reflective second volume of *Democracy in America*, a series of disjunctions are usually the rule. Sexual morals of the Americans were rigorous, while economic and political "morals" were nonexistent. There was freedom of the body but enslavement of the soul. Action was fluid and free, while thought was constrained and contained, or, to go to the other extreme, it ran wild. In fact body and soul seemed separate. There was much ambition, but none of it lofty; much labor but no sustained, long-range labor. It was a nation in which the people wished for peace and the army wanted war. Americans were simultaneously servile and arrogant with Europeans, as they were with their own servants. No one, master or servant, seemed to know his exact "place." It was a society that was always changing but was at the same time unfailingly monotonous because all the changes were the same. The citizenry was an inextricable blend of self-regarding selfishness and public-spirited generosity. For here—the greatest paradox of all—was a nation composed of proud, self-reliant individuals, each of whom feared for his own weakness and insignificance, and a national imagination that was fixed on individualism or egoism (Tocqueville in composing Volume II wavered between *égoisme* and *individualisme*, finally settling for the latter).[19]

What emerges at the social level, in the interactions of Americans as social beings, in Tocqueville's vast, multifarious analysis is a feeling of fluidity and fragility, as if the intramural relations of the nation—so monolithic and powerful in the mass—were hung on individual, gossamer, practically Jamesian threads. For while Americans mingled readily and freely in their political assemblies and courts of justice, they were wont carefully to separate into small distinct circles in order to enjoy by themselves the amenities of private life, which, in its turn, was divided by "many small and almost invisible threads, which are constantly broken or moved from place to place" (II, iii, 13). Habitual social intercourse is on a free and easy footing, but Americans did not seem to be strongly attached to one another. As Mill said in his famous review of the *Democracy*, members of democracies are like the sands on the seashore, each very minute and no one adhering to any other.

This social isolation or tenuousness was reinforced by a temporal isolation, for, like Yank in *The Hairy Ape*, American man tended to be cut off from both the past and the future. (Thus in a sense Hickey is telling the habitués of Harry Hope's to be genuine Americans.) One of the opening remarks in *Democracy in America* is to the effect that the tie between the generations was constantly being relaxed or broken. Indeed in America the woof of time itself was always being dissolved and the track of the generations wiped out. But the constant fluctuations of daily life had a tendency to obscure the future as well, for the present loomed so large that it tended to hide the future, "which becomes indistinct, and men seek only to think about tomorrow" (II, ii, 17).

The imagination and thoughts of each individual were

similarly split. On the one hand, his condition led him to untried thought, but, on the other, it prohibited thinking at all. His imagination expanded at the thought of the state, but it contracted at the thought of himself. Full of large, unsettled ideas he had only loose expressions in which to convey them. His curiosity was insatiable, but it was cheaply satisfied. He could get to know a lot quickly, but he knew few things well. He would engage in several serious occupations, but he would not give genuinely serious attention to any one of them. The great national defect was simple inattention.

He was "almost always a prey to doubt" (II, i, 16); but he could not turn to others, for "they hardly expect to learn anything from one another, . . . (II, iii, 2). If convinced of something, they had to be convinced individually, but they frequently entertained doubts "that no one, in their eyes, can remove" (II, iii, 21). For individualism has the final effect of throwing the individual "back forever on himself alone and threatens in the end to confine him entirely within the solitude of his own heart" (II, ii, 2).

This is the condition of the average citizen who participated in that mass opinion which, according to Tocqueville, ruled America with its massed might. The dissenter then was possessed by this kind of doubt, only multiplied. Far from having a sense of his own righteousness and the justness of his cause, he was plagued by uncertainties and consumed by a "sense of [his] loneliness and impotence" which drives him to "despair." The individual in such a position comes finally to "mistrust his own strength" and to doubt "of his own rights" (II, iii, 21). In short, it is a position like that of Dion Anthony in *The Great God Brown* or like Larry Slade in *The Iceman Cometh* where dissent is not a badge of merit but an index of guilt. In general, social rebels in O'Neill's world are neither happy nor convinced of their own virtue. Like Yank, they are consumed by the feeling that they do not "belong."

Collective American existence reflected these antinomies on a collective scale. Living between opposites Americans tended to fly in several different directions when they thought of the larger courses of human events and on the causes and reasons for force or happenstance in history. Thus they are simultaneously disposed to see the action

of human events as being under the aegis of several antithetical deities: Chance, Mutability, Determinism, and
Pantheism.

Mutability and chance are in a sense the opposite sides
of the same coin: the pessimistic side and the optimistic
side, respectively. "Cheerful" America worshipped chance
and valued it almost more than life itself. (And in "Self-
Reliance" Emerson warned his countrymen against this
national preoccupation.) Thus while in peacetime its
armies attracted only the most inferior of their citizenry, in
war it attracted the best. For the Americans, said Tocqueville, were passionately eager to acquire what they covet
and to enjoy it on easy conditions, and the conditions of
war open stellar vistas for ambitious men, especially when
they "worship chance and are much less afraid of death
than of difficulty" (II, iii, 24). But even in peacetime,
living in the midst of fluctuations, they have always
before their minds the image of chance and they ended
by preferring undertakings in which chance plays a part.
The westward move itself was part of the gigantic lottery
in which the Americans involved themselves: "Emigration
was at first necessary to them; and it soon becomes a sort of
game of chance, which they pursue for the emotions it
excites as much as for the game it procures" (I, 17).

But the national roulette wheel, like the legendary
Strumpet Fortune, bestowed her favors on all and her fidelity on none. Life seen as a game of chance is also life
seen as eternally mutable. Thus the Americans, said
Tocqueville, have a deep sense of the insubstantiality of
human affairs, so much so that the "prevailing notion"
is that nothing abides and men's minds are haunted by
the thought of "mutability" (II, iii, 6). Not the least
mutable thing is his own heart and mind: "what is most
unstable, in the midst of everything, is the heart of man"
(ibid.).

At the same time Americans tend to be determinists, as
their historians demonstrated. American historians, according to Tocqueville, had two correlated, although separate, habits of mind: first a desire to attribute hardly any
influence to the individual over his race or the history of
his race; and, second, an urge to assign all incidents, even
the most petty in a connected sequence to great general
causes. Thus a system is created for explaining history as if

its movements were involuntary and as if human societies were unconsciously obeying some superior force ruling over them. As a result, the "principle of human free-will is not made certain" (II, i, 20). This doctrine of necessity is elaborated under general plans by which the historians work their way back into the past, generation by generation, from necessity to necessity, forging an enormous chain which finally entangles in its grip the whole human race, for they are not only interested in showing how events occurred, "they wish to show that events could not have occurred otherwise" (*ibid.*). If this gigantic doctrine of necessity, said Tocqueville, should pass into the minds of the readers of these histories, it would be enough to paralyze the activity of modern society, for the individual as a factor in history would have been completely set aside and civilization could, so to speak, give up; progress would no longer be possible.

If American historians tended toward historical determinism, Americans in general inclined to another kind of determinism, namely, pantheism. Tocqueville pointed out that pantheism had made great advances in European thought in the early nineteenth century. But in a democracy, where the human mind would always be seeking to embrace a multitude of objects at once and to connect a variety of consequences with a single cause, pantheism, which Tocqueville regarded as being as insidious and pernicious as historical determinism, would be particularly irresistible. Even the primary divisions of creation and Creator would disappear, dissolved into one immense Being and destroying in the process the individuality of man, who would find his pride fostered and the indolence of his mind soothed by his immersion in the All. (And one is reminded of Irving Babbitt's description of Walt Whitman as a "cosmic loafer.") Thus it is that Melville closes "The Mast Head" (Chapter XXXV), that cosmic dream of immersion in the all, with the grim admonition:

> Over Descartian vortices you hover. And perhaps, at midday, in the fairest weather, with one half-throttled shriek you drop through that transparent air into the summer sea, no more to rise for ever. Heed it well, ye Pantheists!

In short, the American mind, or that part of it that did not believe in God, was suspended between two philosophical extremes: a belief in chance that on its optimistic side hoped for luck and on its pessimistic side feared mutability; and a belief in historical inexorability that on its optimistic side yearned for a pantheistic identification and on its pessimistic side feared the tyranny of events, both present and past, and felt a sense of individual helplessness.

Americans thus suffered from two general doubts: one subjective and concerned with the self; the other objective and concerned with the relationship between individuals and events. At least one American critic, Van Wyck Brooks, has observed, as did Tocqueville about American historians, that there tends to be in American literature a basic uncertainty about fate and free will (*The Confident Years*, p. 522). That this is true can be seen from the fact that even writers like Dreiser, whom we think of as the real determinists of American literature, are never quite so complete in their adherence to determinism as were, for example, European writers like Hardy or Zola. Frank Cowperwood's "sixth sense," for instance, is an individual power that rises above or penetrates the web of mysterious, overbearing circumstance. The classic expression of this uncertainty receives its classic metaphorical embodiment, of course, in *Moby Dick*, in the great metaphor of the mat-makers, Ishmael weaving, Queequeg striking the loom with his sword. The warp of the loom stands for necessity; Ishmael's woof, which is shuttled by Ishmael's hand through the strands of the warp, is free will; and Queequeg's sword, both impulsive and indifferent, hitting the woof slantingly or crookedly, strongly or weakly, is chance. Melville does say, however, that chance rules, by turns, the other two forces and gets in the last, featuring blow. O'Neill's most explicit version of these matters is put, dramatically, in *Anna Christie* where Anna speaks for determinism, Burke for free will, and old Chris, who has the last word, for fatality. (I should add that I am not trying to ascertain what O'Neill himself thought about these matters, but what the characters in his plays think.)

In O'Neill's plays as a whole there is no coherent, systematic dramatization of the relationship between fate and free will although each of Tocqueville's four goddesses: chance, mutability, determinism, and pantheism make their appearance. Considered philosophically, the world of the plays of the twenties and early thirties, from, say, *The Hairy Ape* through *Mourning Becomes Electra,* is an incoherent universe where mutability, determinism, and pantheism reign and do not reign, or contest in mutual confusion. It is a world such as Milton conjures up for the Pan-Anarchy through which Satan flies on his way from Hell to Earth (*Paradise Lost*, II, 890–97):

> . . . in sudden view appear
> The secrets of the hoary deep, a dark
> Illimitable Ocean without bound,
> Without dimension, where length, breadth, and heighth,
> And time and place are lost; where eldest Night
> And Chaos, Ancestors of Nature, hold
> Eternal Anarchy, amidst the noise
> Of endless wars, and by confusion stand.

Mutability, especially in what I have earlier called the elongated plays, is of the very essence of the fable of these plays: nothing is stable and nothing lasts. The two other, and mutually opposed, philosophical strains in all the plays are determinism and pantheism, which are the alpha and omega of this empire. Everyone fears, and rightly so, determinism, i.e., fears that the crush of history, the personal past, events, one's actions, one's own genes, constitute a vast chain that girds and binds individuals in an all-encompassing and iron necessity which leaves no one free. To combat or relieve this slavery the prophets and the seers, Lazarus, the Great Kaan, Cybel, Mrs. Fyfe, preach the nebulous doctrine of cosmic identification, the idea that there is a divine, unificatory stream or tendency flowing through the murk and confusion of history and the universe to which one attaches oneself and through its inflowing one can attain a state of grace or felicity. In Emerson's words: "Place yourself in the middle of the stream of power and wisdom which flows into you as life, place yourself in the full centre of that flood, then you are without effort impelled to truth, to right, and a perfect contentment" ("Spiritual Laws"). What this drive really represented, as Tocqueville observed, was a desire for the beatitude of simplicity. In the words of a sympathetic twentieth-century proponent of modern pantheism: "For surely when once the self has made the great surrender, and becomes content to be nothing, that in St. Paul's words, 'God may be all in all,' the whole problem of life is infinitely simplified, in the sense that no further degree of simplification is possible. Because all contradiction of pain and evil and sorrow are dissolved in that act of surrender." [20]

Chance does not loom large in O'Neill's dramatic world as a whole although it was beginning to come to the fore in the more comprehensive world of the late plays where gamblers, who are the spokesmen for and believers in the goddess of chance (Joe Mott or Erie Smith), begin to appear. O'Neill's only "luck" or "chance" play is *Hughie*. Its protagonist, Erie Smith, believes in and lives by luck, both good and bad. He has had in the past runs of good luck and at the time of the play is having a run of bad luck. But by the end of the play he believes that his fortunes have veered around once more and that he is in again for a run of good luck. (And who is to say he is mistaken in this hope?) Moreover, chance is the dominant external force in the play, for it is the random, and unlikely, chance of a sudden silence in the vast hum of the city, that impels the night clerk to turn to Erie, who was just on the verge of giving up in his attempt to become his old "lucky" self. It was chance then that turned the tide in the play.

Everything in O'Neill comes to rest finally in *Long Day's Journey Into Night*, to which I now return. It is a long line from *Democracy in America* to O'Neill's penultimate tragedy, but the lines are there and they are straight, for the four Tyrones believe, at least in part, in luck (James); mutability (Jamie); pantheism (Edmund); and determinism (Mary).

Now some qualifications must be made. Both the father and the mother believe in God although each in a different manner and, in a sense, in a different God. The father's God is purely conventional, a kind of eternal principle of sanity that helps those who help themselves. The mother's God is split between a Father God, who punishes wrongdoers, and the Blessed Virgin, who will always forgive repentant sinners. For the sons, of course, there is no God. But between God and the self (the parents) or nothingness and the self (the sons), there are always circumstances to which the human mind, theistic or atheistic, almost invariably ascribes a pattern of some kind. Thus each of the characters in *Long Day's Journey* looks out at human experience in a distinctive and characteristic manner.

The father believes the most in personal responsibility,

yet he also thinks that chance or luck always plays a crucial, even decisive, role in human affairs. His whole professional career had been dominated by his "good bad luck" of being a success in the lucrative *Count of Monte Cristo*. In his mind it is "damnable luck" that Edmund should be sick at the exact time that Mary Tyrone most needs serenity and to be free of worry. His whole business activity, speculation in land, is governed by the gambler's psychology, which, no matter how many failures it encounters, can never cease to believe in good luck; as his wife says to him, ironically, "I know. The famous one stroke of good luck" (I).

Jamie is a mutabilitist who believes that nothing good ever lasts, and once the good has disappeared, it will never return: "They never come back!" Accordingly, he is a cynic of the most uncompromising and corrosive kind. Edmund sees no pattern to anything, or, at best, he can see life only as a cosmic bad joke, but he had once experienced pantheistic ecstasy, at sea, and he regards this as the "white stone" moment of his life. His walk in the fog along the shore at night, described to his father in Act IV of the play, is an attempt to recapture this feeling in a more somber fashion. The determinist of the play is, of course, Mary Tyrone: "He [Jamie] can't help being what the past has made him. Any more than your father can. Or you. Or I" (II, 1).

In American literature, generally, neither chance nor determinism nor mutability is the dominant note, for each of these attitudes is too simple-minded. Rather the habitual mode of viewing the larger courses of human experience is analogous to that of Edmund Tyrone: no coherent pattern but two unconnected extremes. On the one side, the universe is seen as some kind of vast, bizarre puzzle at which one either shudders or laughs; on the other, the veil is occasionally rent in fitful, fleeting but real moments when subject and object come into harmony and a mystic moment of insight prevails, which, while it disappears as suddenly as it comes, leaves an indelible memory. Thus at its ultimate level the American systole-diastole moves between the cosmic shudder-laugh and the individual moment of transcendent insight.

The American cosmic shudder is well enough known; what I should like to call attention to here is the American cosmic laugh: the universe conceived of as an enormous joke, and God as, in the words of *The Great God Brown,* "that ancient Humorist."

This peculiar kind of humor runs throughout Melville as might be expected, beginning, at least with the "gallows humor" in the Cuticle episode of *White Jacket* when a grisly, bungled operation and a pathetic and quite unnecessary death are seen as an uproarious joke. So in *Moby Dick* the wilder speculations of Melville-Ishmael, or whoever is the real narrator, often spill over into a grotesquerie which must see all things in the world, the most horrible and the most sublime, as outrageously funny ("The Hyena," XLIX):

> There are certain queer times and occasions in this strange mixed affair we call life when a man takes this whole universe for a vast practical joke, though the wit thereof he but dimly discerns, and more than suspects that the joke is at nobody's expense but his own. However, nothing dispirits, and nothing seems worth while disputing. He bolts down all events, all creeds, and beliefs, and persuasions, all hard things visible and invisible, never mind how knobby; as an ostrich of potent digestion gobbles down bullets and gun flints. And as for small difficulties and worryings, prospects of sudden disaster, peril of life and limb; all these, and death itself, seem to him only sly, good-natured hits, and jolly punches in the side bestowed by the unseen and unaccountable old joker.

*The Confidence Man,* Melville's most ambitiously ambiguous and his darkest allegory, begins on April Fools' Day and is hardly ever, if ever, serious, for all the sad story it is telling of human folly, misery, duplicity, sorrow, and cruelty, and for all its metaphysical musings on the meaninglessness of it all. Even in Poe, the greatest adept of the American shudder, we hear the sound of laughter as well. In "The Assignation," Poe spells it out, this macabre link between the ultimate horror, death, and the human laugh: "Besides, some things are so completely ludicrous, that a man *must laugh,* or die. To die laughing must be the most glorious of all glorious deaths! Sir Thomas More—a very fine man was Sir Thomas More— Sir Thomas More died laughing, you remember." As in all things in American culture there is a "high-brow" and a "low-brow" manifestation of the same phenomenon. Thus the American laugh is heard both in folk and frontier humor and in the most serious writings of the most serious writers, who can hardly consider such things as death, time, and meaning without breaking into wild laughter. In no other literature are these matters quite so uproarious.

But the laughter is also a mystic: in D. H. Lawrence's words the "best" American writers are "mystics by instinct." Thus Edmund Tyrone in Act IV of *Long Day's Journey* was giving fumbling expression to what, so far, has been the climactic experience in American literature, what can only be called the American metaphysical ecstasy: man alone confronting a gigantic, looming feature of Nature, so huge or so all-encompassing that it seems to be some kind of Absolute endowed with all kinds of powerful but, once more, obscure meanings. Hester Prynne in the black forests around Salem, Ahab under the stars in the spacious watches of the night in the Pacific are souls gone wandering through the immeasurable eons of space and time and seem to be poised on great abysses. In Tocqueville's celebrated formulation: "Man springs out of nothing, crosses time, and disappears forever in the bosom of God; he is seen but for a moment, wandering on the verge of two abysses, and there he is lost" (II, i, 16). This is the most familiar description by Tocqueville. Equally to the point is his subsequent observation in the same chapter: "The destinies of mankind, man himself taken aloof from his country and his age and standing in the presence of Nature and God, with his passions, his doubts, his rare prosperities and inconceivable wretchedness, will become the chief, if not the sole, theme of poetry among these [democratic] nations." Dana's description of a solitary albatross on the immensity of the sea off Cape Horn is cited by D. H. Lawrence as an instance of this same American phenomenon: "He [Dana] sees the last light-loving incarnation of life exposed upon the eternal waters: a speck, solitary upon the verge of the two naked principles, aerial and watery. And his own soul is as the soul of the albatross." For American literature, said Lawrence, had, along with Russian literature,[21] come "to a real verge." The "outermost fringes" of French modernism or futurism had not reached the pitch of extreme consciousness that Poe, Melville, Hawthorne, Whitman (and O'Neill) had reached. For this experience is not always simply pantheism, in the traditional passive sense, but is often a kind of assertion of the human ego, or an attempt at an expansion of the human consciousness, or a desire to pass beyond the limits of traditional, conventional thought or experience, or an urge to feel or think or experience things that man has never felt or thought or experienced before. It is as if the voyage of the body that had been set off by the age of exploration were continued in America by a voyage of the mind out into space and time: man confronting the universe and freed of customary moral and intellectual restraints. As Hawthorne described the phenomenon in *The Scarlet Letter* "—she [Hester] cast away the fragments of a broken chain. The world's law was no law for her mind." Such speculations, he adds, were common enough in Europe. But there they were done in concert with others. In America they were done alone: "In her lonesome cottage, by the sea-shore, thoughts visited her, such as dared to enter no other dwelling in New England; shadowy guests, that would have been as perilous as demons to their entertainer, could they have been seen so much as knocking at her door (13).

It is true that in Poe it is often the terrors of such adventures of the mind that are stressed; but in Hawthorne and Melville, at least up through *Moby Dick*, it is their majesty and lonely grandeur. Hence Melville's restrospective description of what Ahab was like, before his monomania had seized control of him: "And when these things unite in a man of greatly superior natural force, with a globular brain and a ponderous heart; who has also by the stillness and seclusion of many long night-watches in the remotest waters, and beneath constellations never seen here in the north, been led to think untraditionally and independently; ..." (XVI). For a writer this impalpable but real urge means a sense of infinity, of limitlessness. In *The Middle Years* James has Dencombe, the protagonist-writer—when he is beckoned down by the siren's hand into the depths of fiction, where the strange objects float about by the great, glazed tank of art—rediscover or recapture his sense of infinity: "It was not true, what he tried for renunciation's sake to believe, that all the combinations were exhausted. They were not—they were infinite; the exhaustion was in the miserable artist."

About these matters, O'Neill was the least articulate of

men, but he was also one of the least exhaustible. In surveying his career as a whole, however, we get a glimpse of what James meant by this sense of artistic infinity: the continuous battering at the walls of his medium, the drama and the stage; the bursting of old modes and moulds, and the creation, with a splendid prodigality, of new ones; throwing up thousands upon thousands of teeming, restless words; aiming always at some ultimate break-through, never fully realized to his own satisfaction; attempting increasingly to say the unsayable; trying to expand dramatic consciousness until, like Lazarus' laugh, it rings the universe; bursting with a mighty, restless, creativity which managed in one way or another to give voice to almost all the voices of the vast cacophony of American culture.

## Introduction

1. See my "Eugene O'Neill," *Ramparts*, 2 (Spring 1964), 72–87.

## 1 – Cosmology and Geography

1. *Studies in Philosophy* (New York, 1949), p. 11.
2. *Reason and Nature* (Glencoe, Ill., 1953), p. 165.
3. Oscar Cargill, N. Bryllion Fagin, and William J. Fisher, *O'Neill and His Plays* (New York, 1961), pp. 454–58.
4. See Doris Falk, "The Way Out: The Many Endings of *Days Without End*," Cargill, pp. 415–23.

## 2 – History

1. Quoted in Arthur and Barbara Gelb, *O'Neill* (New York, 1962), p. 873.
2. Historically, these portraits—Pompeia excepted, of whose inner life we have no record although chances are decidedly against her having been in reality "gentle" and "girlish"—would seem to be fairly accurate. Tiberius was a strange, for us, combination of a tough and responsible soldier and administrator, who was also given to rather extravagant debauchery although probably not on the scale attributed to him by Suetonius. He also, and apparently with good reason, seems to have despised the human race. The most charitable thing that can be said about Caligula, who made his horse a consul, is that he was crazy, as O'Neill's characterization suggests.
3. George C. Warren, "*Lazarus Laughed*," a review of the play as performed by the Pasadena Community Playhouse and originally published in the *San Francisco Chronicle*, April 10, 1928; republished in Cargill et al., *O'Neill and His Plays* (New York, 1961), pp. 178–80.
4. O'Neill himself had written to Belasco asking him to produce *Marco Millions* (Gelbs, pp. 572–73).
5. Quoted by M. R. Werner in *Tammany Hall* (New

York, 1928), p. 123. A. Oakey Hall was a genuine pagan who loved money, power, alcohol, Latin quotations, literary allusions, and puns. When he was Mayor a newspaper said, "New York City is now governed by Oakey Hall, Tammany Hall and Alcohol." He was also a playwright, author of *Loyalina, Brigadier General Fortunio and His Seven Gifted Aides-de-Camp* (produced at the Olympic Theater when he was Mayor), *Humpty Dumpty, Fernande,* and *Let Me Kiss Him for His Mother.* He himself loved to appear on the stage and once gave a "Humorous Dramatic Reading" entitled *Dido versus Aeneas, an ancient breach of promise trial.* On one St. Patrick's Day he outdid every other official in dress with a green coat, green kid gloves, green cravat, and green bouquet. But he was also so solicitous of the large German vote that the newspapers dubbed him "Mayor Von O'Hall." When Tweed fell, Hall was tried for corruption. ("Who is going to sue?" he asked rhetorically.) Since he was a lawyer, he conducted his own defense and was acquitted. He served out his term as Mayor. Two years after his retirement from office he acted the hero in a play that he himself had written, called *The Crucible,* about an innocent man who is accused of stealing but is subsequently vindicated. The play was full of puns and ran for 22 performances. After this, Hall practiced law, both in New York and London, and was a newspaper editor. When Bryce's *The American Commonwealth* was published, Hall sued Bryce for libel because of Bryce's chapter on Tammany. Nothing came of this. Hall once revealed the secret of his many political successes in one of his inevitable puns: "Few persons have so many *tried* friends as I have, and tried friends are always magnanimous" (Werner, p. 118).

6. Henry Adams, *Letters, 1892–1918,* ed. Worthington Chauncey Ford (Boston and New York, 1938), p. 490. The letter to James is dated Feb. 11, 1908.

7. Cargill et al., p. 105. Originally in the *New York Tribune,* February 13, 1921.

8. Historically, of course, the Napoleonic era saw the last of the "romantic" wars, while the American Civil War was the first modern conflict.

9. *Eugene O'Neill and the American Critic* (London, 1962), pp. 130–31.

10. The present book was written before *More Stately Mansions* was published (New Haven and London, 1964). In his prefatory note to the play Donald Gallup, the editor, says that this MS was supposed to have been destroyed too, according to O'Neill's request, and was saved only by inadvertence. An acting script was subsequently fashioned by Karl

Ragnar Gierow, then director of the Swedish Royal Dramatic Theatre, and the play was performed in Stockholm on Nov. 9, 1962. The original is like *Strange Interlude* in size.

Mr. Gallup's edition is a "play" of great force, power, multiplicity of themes, and confusion; it is obviously an unfinished play. I have not discussed it because it is really an O'Neill MS, and I have purposely stayed within the list of published plays, all of which have O'Neill's imprimatur. Had I discussed it, it would have come into almost every chapter of the book, as do the other major plays.

11. For my information about American popular music I am relying on Sigmund Spaeth's invaluable *A History of Popular Music in America* (New York, 1948).

12. The literature on Tammany Hall is considerable and tends to verge into two extremes, whitewash and diatribe; the diatribe is preponderant and rightly so. As James Bryce said about Tammany: "The phenomena of municipal democracy in the United States are the most remarkable and least laudable which the modern world has witnessed; and they present some evils which no political philosopher, however unfriendly to popular government, appears to have foreseen, evils which have scarcely showed themselves in the cities of Europe, and unlike those which were thought characteristic of the rule of the masses in ancient times" (*The American Commonwealth* [New York, 1913], II, 379). The two most comprehensive histories, both in scope and documentation, of Tammany Hall are those of Gustavus Myers, *The History of Tammany Hall* (New York, 1901; revised, 1917); and M. R. Werner, *Tammany Hall* (New York, 1928). I am relying on these two books for my facts. The most interesting "inside" document is W. R. Riordon's *Plunkitt of Tammany Hall* (New York, 1948). George Washington Plunkitt was a district leader, like Sullivan, although not nearly so powerful, who in a series of conversations explained his "philosophy of government" to a newspaper reporter, William Riordon, who first published these conversations in 1905.

13. On October 31, 1909, "Big Tim" Sullivan made his only public speech, touching on experiences and sentiments which made up the apologia of James Tyrone in Act IV of *Long Day's Journey Into Night*. It was the end of a bitter political campaign, and Tammany and Sullivan had been subjected to many charges of corruption. Miner's Theatre, which Sullivan owned, was engaged for the occasion, and to a full house, with tears running down his pink cheeks, "Big Tim" made his justificatory speech for himself and for the Tammany-type politician. It was a masterpiece of melodrama and sentiment and not without a good deal of truth. Its key pas-

sage was just like the key passage of James Tyrone's account in *Long Day's Journey* about his childhood; in fact, the two situations were identical as to the number of children involved (six), the absence of a father, and the sweet, martyr-like mother: "I was born in poverty, one of six children, four boys and two girls. The boys used to sleep in a three-quarters bed, not big enough for two, and the girls in a shakedown on the floor. Some nights there was enough to eat and some nights there wasn't. And our old mother used to sing to us at night and maybe it would be the next day before we would think she had been singing but that she had gone to bed without anything to eat.

"That's the kind of people we come from, and that is the kind of mothers that bore us down here. If we can help some boy or some father to another chance we are going to give it to them" (Werner, p. 503). It would be tempting to think that Eugene O'Neill had heard, or heard of, this speech, but he had left New York for Honduras in early October 1909.

14. Richard J. Butler and Joseph Driscoll, *Dock Walloper* (New York, 1933): "I was one of those mourners when the crêpe-hanging reformers began getting the upper hand. The wide-open town was killed in 1912, when the Becker-Blumenthal scandal broke, ...." (p. 112).

15. Sullivan, Frank Farrell, the leading professional gambler of the day, and William S. Devery, Chief of Police of New York, ran the gambling syndicate (Werner, p. 416).

16. See Joseph Rountree and Arthur Sherwell, *The Taxation of the Liquor Trade* (London, 1906), pp. 352 ff.

17. *Hughie* seems unmistakably tied up with Jamie O'Neill who, like Erie Smith, was a Broadway "wise guy," a Lothario of Broadway "babes," a drinker, and often an habitué of broken-down hotels. The Gelbs ran down one anecdote of an encounter between Jamie and the night clerk of a "seedy West Side hotel," which is where *Hughie* takes place. The clerk had refused to give Jamie a room because of his drunkenness. Jamie told him, "I know why you're a night clerk, ... It's because you're too dumb to be a day clerk" (Gelbs, p. 415). There is a further link between Erie and Jamie provided by *A Moon for the Misbegotten*. In his more prosperous days Erie had followed the horses, south in the winter and north in the summer. This is a gambler's idea of paradise, every day at the race track. Similarly, Jamie Tyrone had once had this same dream; as he says to Josie in Act III: "From the time I was a kid, I loved race-horses. I thought they were the most beautiful things in the world. I liked to gamble, too. So the big dream was that some day I'd have enough

dough to play a cagey system of betting on favorites, and follow the horses south in the winter, and come back north with them in the spring, and be at the track every day."

18. Literature on Arnold Rothstein is not copious and what there is cannot be very reliable in any scholarly sense as it must deal with a man who was a notoriously close-mouthed and devious lone-wolf and who prided himself on carrying most of his "records" in his head, or, if written, in some kind of private code, and a good deal of his cash on his person. The best book-length treatment is Leo Katcher, *The Big Bankroll* (New York, 1958). Rothstein was born in 1882 on the lower East Side of Manhattan, and finally became the premier gambler on Broadway in the 1920's. He was also deeply involved in gambling houses, horse racing, floating crap games, politics, gangsters (he was the first sponsor of Legs Diamond), bucket shops, bootlegging, speak-easies, labor racketeering, dope, and, among other things, baseball. He was a middleman in the deal by which Charles Stoneham, an old bucket-shop man, bought the New York Giants. Rothstein's greatest exploit—which he himself disclaimed—was connected with baseball; he was the man who was supposed to have fixed the World Series of 1919. That allegation has never been proved. He appears as Meyer Wolfshiem in Fitzgerald's *The Great Gatsby*.

19. Connoisseurs of American popular music are well acquainted with the fact that the lyrics, even at their most sentimental, are often very suggestive of other matters in their implications. Part of the joy of composition on the part of the composers, evidently, lay in this game they were playing with a puritanical public opinion. It is as if Hollywood producers and directors, in the days of the Hays Office, played a game with the censors, which, I suppose they did, although not nearly so cleverly as did the song writers. One favorite device of the composers was to build up the listener's expectations and then reverse them with the last line. The classic example of this type of song, known as "the April fool" genre, is "Billy," by Joe Goodwin, James Kendis, and Herman Paley in 1911: the lyrics go:

> For when I walk I always walk with Billy
> 'Cause Billy knows just where to walk,
> And when I talk I always talk with Billy
> 'Cause Billy knows just how to talk,
> And when I dine I always dine with Billy,
> He takes me where I get my fill.

The first lines are repeated, and there is a new, and concluding line:

> And when I sleep, And when I sleep, I always
> dream of Bill.

Cole Porter is perhaps the most eminent modern practitioner of this art; while Lorenz Hart was the most subversive of the puritanism that had called in into being in the first place.

20. This had long been a national problem, along with the casualties from fireworks, and in suggesting plans for a sane celebration of July 4, Julia Ward Howe expressly proposed that there be no liquor served or sold during the entire day (*Independence Day*, ed. Robert Haven Schauffler [New York, 1912], p. 33).

21. Croswell Bowen, *The Curse of the Misbegotten* (New York, n.d.), p. 244.

22. "Eugene O'Neill," *Sewanee Review*, 68 (Summer, 1960), p. 499.

23. ". . . there is little in Tolstoy's writing that, in one way or another, is not [autobiographical]—" Isaiah Berlin, *The Hedgehog and the Fox* (New York, 1953), p. 36.

Or Joyce on Ibsen:

> Ibsen has persisted in writing what was essentially the same drama over and over again. I suspect that Ibsen met the four or five characters whom he uses throughout his plays before he was twenty-five.

Richard Ellman, *James Joyce* (N.Y., 1959), p. 276.

24. For examples of this kind of detective work see Gordon N. Ray, *The Buried Life* (on Thackeray) (Cambridge, Mass., 1952); and Gordon Haight, "George Eliot's Originals," *From Jane Austen to Joseph Conrad*, ed. Rathburn and Steinmann (Minneapolis, 1958), pp. 177–93.

25. *The Dickens World* (London, 1942), pp. 20–21.

26. "Eugene O'Neill" (cited in n. 22, above), p. 501.

27. The three big biographies so far are the Gelbs' *O'Neill*, Bowen's *The Curse of the Misbegotten*, and Doris Alexander, *The Tempering of Eugene O'Neill* (New York, 1962). As Miss Alexander's title implies, she deals only with the first part of O'Neill's life and career, up to the success of *Beyond the Horizon* and to the death of his father. Further volumes will follow. There are other biographies, in preparation, notably one by Lou Schaeffer. As for some discrepancies, there seem to be variant explanations for why and when Mrs. O'Neill became a morphine addict. Bowen and the Gelbs attribute it to the illness resulting from Eugene's birth. But Miss Alexander attributes it to the time when, at the age of twenty-nine, Mrs. O'Neill had a breast removed because of

cancer (1877). There are three different versions of the doctor or doctors consulted about Eugene's consumption. It does seem clear that none of them, in any version, was a quack.

28. See my review of *The Correspondence of Samuel Butler with His Sister May*, ed. Daniel F. Howard, and *The Family Letters of Samuel Butler*, ed. Arnold Silver, *Victorian Studies*, VI (June 1963), 375–76.

29. The present writer had a relative, now deceased, who knew James O'Neill and sputtered his indignation at the representation of him in the play. Doris Alexander is a defender of James O'Neill and claims that Eugene and Jamie O'Neill always made their father a scapegoat.

30. "O'Neill's *Long Day's Journey Into Night* and New England Irish-Catholicism" *Partisan Review*, XXVI (Fall, 1959), pp. 573–92. Reprinted in *O'Neill*, ed. John Gassner (New York, 1964).

## 3 – Mankind

1. See Rollo May, "Contributions of Existential Psychotherapy" in *Existence*, ed. Rollo May, Ernest Angel, and Henri F. Ellenberger (New York, 1958), pp. 37–91.

2. *English Drama, The Last Great Phase* (London, 1935), pp. 260–61.

3. I am using the word "myth" in this chapter in a very simple sense. By it I refer to a belief that makes an assertion or a series of assertions about the nature of a people, or a race, or a culture, however one wants to put it, which cannot be proved valid either scientifically or historically but which, nevertheless, generations of peoples have believed in and acted upon.

4. According to the Gelbs, John Dolan, the real New London pig farmer on whom Hogan is based, had a reputation for a biting Irish wit (p. 91).

5. Van Wyck Brooks, *The Confident Years* (New York, 1952), pp. 539–53.

6. I am indebted to the Gelbs for extensive background material on O'Neill and the Negro.

7. Jordan Y. Miller, *Eugene O'Neill and the American Critic* (London, 1960), p. 60.

8. About this aspect of the play, O'Neill said: "The play itself, as anyone who has read it with intelligence knows, is never a 'race problem' play. Its intention is confined to portraying the special lives of individual human beings. It is primarily a study of the two principal characters, and their

tragic struggle for happiness" (Gelbs, p. 550). Years later O'Neill was still embittered that the play was unappreciated. When he was interviewing the actress Mary Welch in 1946 for the role of Josie Hogan in *A Moon for the Misbegotten*, he brought up his earlier plays, especially the ones he had written about the Negro people. He had felt deeply about these plays but thought that the professional New York theater crowd did not really understand what he was writing; rather their reaction was, "Oh, look, the ape can talk!" (Mary Welch, "Softer Tones for Mr. O'Neill's Portrait," Oscar Cargill et al., *O'Neill and His Plays* (New York, 1961), pp. 85–91.

9. Cargill et al., pp. 168–69, 464–67.

10. "Eugene O'Neill," *Sewanee Review*, 68 (Summer 1960), 494–501.

11. "Incarnation in *Don Quixote*" in Angel Flores and M. J. Benardete, eds., *Cervantes Across the Centuries* (New York, 1947), p. 161.

12. "Blue eyes," alone almost type Parritt as unpleasant. What O'Neill had against blue eyes I do not know, but he invariably endows dubious characters with them. One can almost compile a list of undesirables in O'Neill's plays by the color of their eyes: Sweeney in *The Rope* has "*small, round, blue eyes*"; Mrs. Rowland in *Before Breakfast* has "*eyes of a nondescript blue*"; Mrs. Brennan in *The Straw* has "*little round blue eyes, hard and restless*"; Smithers in *The Emperor Jones* has "*little, washy-blue eyes*"; Hutchins Light in *Dynamo* has eyes "*small and gray-blue.*" In *A Moon for the Misbegotten*, Phil Hogan has them, which probably proves he is not to be trusted (this is true). Most importantly, Hickey has "*bright blue eyes,*" probably indicating that finally he too is not to be trusted either.

13. Helen Muchnic points out in an excellent essay on *The Iceman Cometh* and Gorki's *The Lower Depths* that one of the similarities between the two plays is that an "outsider" comes into the "depths" who supposedly has the truth. But, it turns out, he does not ("The Irrelevancy of Belief" in Cargill et al., pp. 431–42).

## 4 — The Form

1. Sigmund Freud, *Civilization and Its Discontents*, trans. Joan Riviere (New York, 1958), p. 37.

2. Stark Young, *Immortal Shadows* (New York, 1948), p. 128.

3. Despite the evidence of *A Touch of the Poet*, the cycle

plays would not all have been amenable to my generalizations. *More Stately Mansions*, for example, occupies some nine years, 1832–1841.

4. (New York, 1953), p. 325.

5. Doris Alexander, *The Tempering of Eugene O'Neill* (New York, 1962), p. 50.

6. In his review of *Dynamo* Benchley remarked that "the royal blood of *The Count of Monte Cristo*, which is always with Mr. O'Neill . . . gives him the power to throw a dramatic spot-light on all his works so that the lurid glow of the theatre lies over even his dullest passages. It is a question if this inheritance from his trouper father is not his most valuable quality as a dramatist (Oscar Cargill et al., *O'Neill and His Plays* [New York, 1961], p. 188). Bernard de Voto, among others, had made the same point, but for derogatory purposes.

7. A version of the "Fechter version" is reproduced in *America's Lost Plays* (Princeton, 1941), vol. XVI, ed. J. B. Russak. James O'Neill first played the role on February 12, 1883, and purchased the play in 1885 from John Stetson for $2,000.

8. *Modern Dramatic Structure*, University of Missouri Studies, 3 (October 1928), 125–58. This is the best and most detailed study of O'Neill's uses of repetitions and considers not only dialogue but sound, lighting, even silences.

9. *Between Past and Future* (Cleveland and New York, 1961), pp. 10–11.

10. "Eugene O'Neill" *Sewanee Review*, 68 (Summer, 1960), p. 496.

11. *The Rise of Scientific Philosophy* (Berkeley and Los Angeles, 1951), p. 144.

12. Lawrence Langner, *The Magic Curtain* (New York, 1951), p. 405.


## 5 – O'Neill as an American Writer

1. For twentieth-century writing this has already been done extensively in Edwin Engels' *The Haunted Heroes of Eugene O'Neill* (Cambridge, 1953).

2. *The Confident Years* (New York, 1952), pp. 551–52.

3. Oscar Cargill et al., *O'Neill and His Plays* (New York, 1961), pp. 271–82.

4. *Six Plays of Strindberg* (New York, 1955), p. 3.

5. Jordan Y. Miller, *Eugene O'Neill and the American Critic* (London, 1962), p. 81.

6. George Wilson Pierson, *Tocqueville and Beaumont in*

*America* (New York, 1938), p. 280. Subsequent page references to this work will be given in the text.

7. Harrison Hayford and Merton M. Sealts, Jr., eds., *Billy Budd, Sailor* (Chicago, 1962), p. 33.

8. According to the Gelbs, a set of Emerson was one of the mainstays in the library at the O'Neill home in New London, and Eugene O'Neill from adolescence was well acquainted with "the philosophy of Emerson" (p. 88).

9. John Lydenberg, "Emerson and the Dark Tradition," *Critical Quarterly*, 4 (Winter 1962), 352–58. Lydenberg concentrates mostly on Emerson's "Experience," his most thoroughly and explicitly pessimistic essay. My thesis is that the "Experience" point of view is spread throughout almost *all* the essays, as their most prominent and persistent counterpoint. See also Stephen Wicher, "Emerson's Tragic Sense," *American Scholar*, 22 (Summer 1953), pp. 285–92, Alexander Cowie, "Still a Good Light To Guide By," *The New York Times Book Review* (Sept. 7, 1963), pp. 1, 16, and Newton Arvin "The House of Pain," *The Hudson Review*, 12 (Spring, 1959), pp. 37–53.

10. Most notably and recently by Sherman Paul, *Emerson's Angle of Vision* (Cambridge, 1952), and Stephen Wicher, *Freedom and Fate* (Philadelphia, 1953). Wicher is much the less certain that Emerson can be synthesized, and he deals at length, and with great acuteness, on Emerson's skepticism and solipsism. Some of the difficulties in dealing with Emerson's thought can be gauged from one of Wicher's proposed schemata: "I propose, as a rude scaffolding for this analysis, the sufficiently difficult image of two crossed polarities." He continues, "Chiefly I would stress the analogy of a polar field. As with Whitman, Melville, and Henry Adams, we are dealing with a mind that makes any assertion of belief against the felt pull of its lurking opposite, . . ." (pp. 57–58). Again, "His is a baffling monistic dualism, or dualistic monism, 'of which any proposition may be affirmed or denied'" (p. 31).

11. George Santayana, "Emerson" in *Essays in Literary Criticism* (New York, 1956), pp. 224–33.

12. "His universe was a universe of levels and platforms, a progressive stairway leading to unity. Worldliness and otherworldliness, lower and higher, material and spiritual—he needed these polarities; they described the tensions he experienced and that as facts of consciousness his vision reconciled" (pp. 34–35).

13. Emerson's first book, *Nature*, is not generally relevant here. Most of the work of his middle life is. To avoid a tissue of quotations I give most of my reconstruction of the dark side of Emerson in direct discourse. Quotations are

ascribed in the text. All assertions, direct or indirect, are drawn from the following essays (I should stress that I have used only a small part of my evidence). First Series: "History," "Self-Reliance," "Compensation," "Spiritual Laws," "Love," "Friendship," "Prudence," "Heroism," "The Over-Soul," "Circles," "Intellect," "Art"; and Second Series: "The Poet," "Experience," "Character," "Manners," "Gifts," "Nature," "Politics," and "Nominalist and Realist." I have also used: "The Method of Nature," "Man the Reformer," "The Young American," "Montaigne" from *Representative Men,* "Society and Solitude" from *Society and Solitude,* "Perpetual Forces," "Considerations by the Way" from *The Conduct of Life,* and "Theodore Parker."

14. "Among the Avatars," *Prejudices, First Series* (New York, 1919), 240.

15. "Self-conscious America," *American Criticism,* ed. William A. Drake (New York, 1926), p. 139.

16. *Democracy in America,* ed. Phillips Bradley, 2 vols. (New York, 1954), II, i, 12.

17. *Journey to America,* ed. J. P. Mayer (New Haven and London, 1959), p. 183.

18. Throughout this book I have tried to resist the irresistible: to psychoanalyze O'Neill. But the fact that both *Desire Under the Elms* and *Ah, Wilderness!* should have both, alone of his plays, been dreamed in one night and then written very easily and quickly almost disarms this resolution. I shall, however, confine myself to a Jungian observation, with O'Neill's unconscious considered as a vessel for the American collective unconscious. For what can one say but that out of one dream came the sin, the greed, the crime, the brutality, the pain, the labor, the agony, the blood, and the guilt of American history (*Desire*) and that out of the other (*Ah, Wilderness!*) came its gentleness, decency, simplicity, and laughter? One of the few critics of O'Neill who took *Ah, Wilderness!* seriously, Richard Dana Skinner (who did not know that O'Neill dreamed both plays) explicitly linked the two: "The stern Ephraim Cabot turned out to be nothing more than lovable Nat Miller, the best father a boy could have" *"Eugene O'Neill: A Poet's Quest* (New York, 1939), p. 229.

And what of the culture that inspires both dreams? For one thing we can take as axiomatic Dr. Johnson's statement about the "delicious employment" of the poet: "To tell of disappointment and misery, to thicken the darkness of futurity and perplex the labyrinth of uncertainty...." As for official America in its never-failing optimism there is Charles Eliot Norton's infallible test for deciding if an anonymous article was written by an American: "Does it contain the phrase, 'After all, we need not despair?' If it does, it was written by an American." Bliss Perry, *The American Mind* (Boston and New York, 1912), p. 75.

More seriously to the point is Paul Elmer More's observation, in his essay on James Thomson in the *Shelburne Essays* (Fifth Series), that pessimism is never national—no nation, including the Hindus and Greeks, was "pessimistic"—but individual, and comes about when "self-consciousness, unbalanced by spiritual insight, is developed at the expense of irrational instinct."

19. Seymour Drescher, *Tocqueville and England* (Cambridge, 1964), p. 9, note 19.

20. J. Allanson Picton, *Pantheism* (London, 1905), p. 76.

21. The Russian "split," the gap between the "abysses," is precisely one of the ground themes of Dostoevsky. At the trial of Dimitri Karamazov the Public Prosecutor says:

> It usually happens in life that when faced with two extremes, one has to look for truth somewhere in the middle; in the present case this is not so. . . . Why? Because we possess broad, unrestrained natures, Karamazov natures—that is just what I'm leading up to—capable of accommodating all sorts of extremes and contemplating at one and the same time the two abysses—the abyss above us, the abyss of the highest ideals, and the abyss below us, the abyss of the lowest and most malodorous degradation.

Later in his speech the prosecutor remarks:

> Two abysses, gentlemen of the jury, two abysses at one and the same moment—without them we are unhappy and dissatisfied, without them our life is incomplete.

(Book 12, Chapter 6, Magarshack translation).

# INDEX